£15 —

The Cambridge Companion to Sa

Ferdinand de Saussure is widely considered to be the founder of both modern linguistics and structuralism. The first to establish the structural study of language, he identified the difference between the system of language (*langue*) and the speech of individuals (*parole*), and was first to distinguish between the 'synchronic' study of language (language at a given time), and the 'diachronic' (language as it changes through time). This companion brings together a team of leading scholars to offer a fresh new account of Saussure's work. As well as looking at his pioneering and renowned *Course in General Linguistics* of 1916, they consider his lesser-known early work, his more recently discovered manuscripts, and his influence on a range of other disciplines, such as cultural studies, philosophy, literature and semiotics. With contributions by leading specialists in each field, this comprehensive and accessible guide creates a unique picture of the lasting importance of Saussure's thought.

CAROL SANDERS is Professor of French at the University of Surrey, and has taught at universities across Australia, France, Italy, the West Indies and Britain. She has published many articles, books and translations in the fields of French language, linguistics and culture, including a monograph on Saussure (1979), and *French Today: Language in its Social Context* (Cambridge University Press, 1993).

The Cambridge Companion to Saussure

Edited by

Carol Sanders

PUBLISHED BY THE PRESS SYNDICATE OF THE UNIVERSITY OF CAMBRIDGE
The Pitt Building, Trumpington Street, Cambridge, United Kingdom

CAMBRIDGE UNIVERSITY PRESS
The Edinburgh Building, Cambridge, CB2 2RU, UK
40 West 20th Street, New York, NY 10011–4211, USA
477 Williamstown Road, Port Melbourne, VIC 3207, Australia
Ruiz de Alarcón 13, 28014 Madrid, Spain
Dock House, The Waterfront, Cape Town 8001, South Africa

http://www.cambridge.org

First published 2004

Printed in the United Kingdom at the University Press, Cambridge

Typeface Times 10/12 pt.   *System* LaTeX 2_ε [TB]

A catalogue record for this book is available from the British Library

Library of Congress Cataloguing in Publication data
The Cambridge companion to Saussure / edited by Carol Sanders.
p. cm.
Includes bibliographical references and index.
ISBN 0 521 80051 X – ISBN 0 521 80486 8 (pb.)
1. Saussure, Ferdinand de, 1857–1913. 2. Linguistics. I. Sanders, Carol.
P85.S18C33 2004
410′.92 – dc22 2004049741

ISBN 0 521 80051 X hardback
ISBN 0 521 80486 8 paperback

Contents

Notes on contributors

GEOFFREY BENNINGTON is Asa G. Candler Professor of Modern French Thought at Emory University. His most recent books are *Frontières kantiennes* (Paris: Galilée, 2000) and *Interrupting Derrida* (London: Routledge, 2000).

PAUL BOUISSAC is Professor Emeritus at the University of Toronto (Department of French Studies). He is the author of *La mesure des gestes: prolégomènes à la sémiotique gestuelle* (1973), and *Circus and Culture* (1976), and the editor of the Oxford University Press *Encyclopedia of Semiotics* (1998). His published articles bear upon issues in the epistemology and history of semiotics, the cultural anthropology of circus performances, the semiotic analysis of gestures and prehistoric rock art.

SIMON BOUQUET's interests are in linguistics and philosophy. He is a researcher at the University of Berne and lectures at the University of Paris 10 – Nanterre. He has devoted himself to making the manuscript texts of Saussure better known through critical editions (S. Bouquet and R. Engler's edition of the *Ecrits de linguistique générale* is frequently referred to in this volume). He is currently working on the consequences of Wittgenstein's thought for semantics. He is president of the Institut F. de Saussure in Switzerland.

RUDOLF ENGLER (1930–2003) taught for many years at the University of Berne. He wrote prolifically on Saussure, making frequent contributions to the *Cahiers Ferdinand de Saussure*, including bibliographical lists up to the 1980s. He is known in particular for his monumental comparative critical edition of the student notes for Saussure's lectures on general linguistics, for his chapter on 'European structuralism: Saussure' in *Current Trends in Linguistics* vol. XIII (ed. Sebeok, 1975), and for co-editing with Simon Bouquet the *Ecrits de linguistique générale*.

JULIA S. FALK is Professor Emeritus, Linguistics, Michigan State University, and a resident of La Jolla, California, where a courtesy appointment as visiting scholar, Linguistics, University of California, San Diego, facilitates her continuing research and writing on the history of linguistics in the United States. A member of NAAHoLS (North American Association for the History of the Language Sciences), she served as president in the year 2000.

W. TERRENCE GORDON'S works in the field of twentieth-century intellectual history include a critically acclaimed biography of Marshall McLuhan and *Saussure for Beginners*, which has been translated into Spanish and Japanese. Gordon recently relinquished the Alexander McLeod Chair in Modern Languages at Dalhousie University, Halifax, Canada, to assume the fulltime general editorship of an international publishing programme for issuing new editions of Marshall McLuhan's writings.

STEPHEN HUTCHINGS is Reader in Russian Studies at the University of Surrey. He is the author of *A Semiotic Analysis of the Short Stories of Leonid Andreev* (London: MHRA, 1990) and *Russian Modernism: the Transfiguration of the Everyday* (Cambridge University Press, 1997). He is currently completing two books for Routledge on the relationship between Russian literature and the camera media. Stephen's research interests include nineteenth- and twentieth-century Russian literature and culture, post-Soviet television culture, and Russian critical and cultural theory.

JOHN E. JOSEPH is Professor of Applied Linguistics at the University of Edinburgh, having previously held chairs at the University of Hong Kong and the University of Maryland at College Park. His books relating to the history of linguistics include *Limiting the Arbitrary: Linguistic Naturalism and its Opposites in Plato's Cratylus and Modern Theories of Language* (2000), *Landmarks in Linguistic Thought 2: The Western Tradition in the Twentieth Century* (with N. Love and T. J. Taylor, 2001) and *From Whitney to Chomsky: Essays in the History of American Linguistics* (2002).

ANNA MORPURGO DAVIES is Diebold Professor of Comparative Philology at Oxford University. She completed her doctorate for the University of Rome, but has spent most of her working life in Oxford with frequent periods in the United States. She has worked and published extensively on Indo-European (especially ancient Greek and the ancient Anatolian languages) and on the history of nineteenth-century linguistics. She is the author of *Nineteenth Century Linguistics* (London: Longman, 1998). Professor Morpurgo Davies is a Fellow of the British Academy and an Honorary Member of the Linguistic Society of America.

CLAUDINE NORMAND is Emeritus Professor at the University of Paris at Nanterre, where she taught for thirty years. Her research interests are in the history and epistemology of linguistics and semiotics, especially of the nineteenth and twentieth centuries. Her main publications include a monograph on Saussure (Normand, 2000), co-edited volumes (with M. Arrivé) on Saussure and on Benveniste, a chapter on 'La question de la linguistique générale (1880–1930)' in *Histoire des Idées linguistiques*, vol. III. (ed. S. Auroux, 2000).

CHRISTOPHER NORRIS is Distinguished Research Professor in Philosophy at the University of Cardiff, Wales. He has published more than twenty books to date on various aspects of philosophy, the history of ideas and critical theory. At present he is writing mainly about issues in philosophical semantics and philosophy of science, with particular reference to areas of shared concern between the so-called 'analytic' and 'continental' lines of descent. Among his most recent books are *Deconstruction and the Unfinished Project of Modernity* (2000), *Truth Matters: Realism, Anti-Realism and Response-Dependence* (2002) and *Philosophy of Language and the Challenge to Scientific Realism.*

MATTHEW PIRES lectures at the British Institute in Paris. His interests include syntax, stylistics and the discourse of popular culture. He is a co-translator, with Carol Sanders, of the *Ecrits de linguistique générale*.

CHRISTIAN PUECH lectures at the Centre de Linguistique Française at the Sorbonne Nouvelle (Paris III). He is a member of the CNRS research group for the History of Linguistic Theories, and since 1978 he has been publishing on the history of linguistic ideas in the nineteenth and twentieth centuries. His most recent publications include *Fondations de la linguistique: études d'histoire et d'épistémologie* (Louvain: Duculot, 1997), (with J. L. Chiss); *Le langage et ses disciplines: XIX°–XX° siècles* (Louvain: Duculot, 1999) (with J. L. Chiss); he is the editor of *Linguistique et partages disciplinaires à la fin du XIX° siècle début du XX° siècle: Victor Henry (1850–1907)*, Coll. Bibliothèque de l'Information Grammaticale 55 (Louvain and Paris: Peeters, 2003).

CAROL SANDERS is Professor of French at the University of Surrey. She has research interests in the history of linguistics, French linguistics, applications of linguistics and French-speaking culture. She is the author of, among other things, a commentary on the *Cours de linguistique de Ferdinand de Saussure* (Hachette, 1979), and *French Today: Language in its Social Context* (Cambridge University Press, 1993). She is the co-translator of Saussure's *Ecrits de linguistique générale* (published in French by Gallimard in 2003).

STEVEN UNGAR is Professor of French and Chair of the Department of Cinema and Comparative Literature at the University of Iowa, where he teaches on twentieth-century French fiction, poetry, film and critical thought. His book-length publications include *Roland Barthes: the Professor of Desire*

(1983), *Scandal and After Effect: Blanchot and France since 1930* (1995), and two co-edited volumes: *Signs in Culture: Roland Barthes Today* (1989) and *Identity Papers: Contested Nationhood in 20th-Century France* (1996). A study co-authored with Dudley Andrew, *Popular Front Paris: Between the Politics and Poetics of Culture*, is forthcoming. His current research involves urban spaces and everyday life.

PETER WUNDERLI is Emeritus Professor of Romance Philology at the Heinrich Heine University in Düsseldorf. His research interests are in the history of linguistics, syntax and morphosyntax, semantics, intonation and medieval philology. He is the author of numerous books and articles, among which are: *Ferdinand de Saussure und die Anagramme* (Tübingen, 1972); *Valéry saussurien* (Frankfurt am Main, 1977); *Saussure-Studien* (Tübingen, 1981); *L'intonation des séquences extraposées en français* (Tübingen, 1987); *Französische Lexikologie* (Tübingen, 1989); *Principes de diachronie* (Frankfurt am Main, 1990); *Studi esegetici su Ferdinand de Saussure* (Rome, 1993).

Acknowledgements

The initial preparation for this volume was done while I had the privilege of holding a Leverhulme Research Fellowship, and a subsequent small grant from the British Academy also facilitated the work. Matthew Pires, Peter Figueroa and I have translated, or where necessary edited, the chapters that were written in a language other than English. The first draft of the bibliography was very ably drawn up by Matthew Pires. In particular, I am very grateful for the important editorial assistance generously given by Peter Figueroa.

Abbreviations

The following abbreviations are used in the text to refer to works by Saussure; further information about the various editions of the *Cours de linguistique générale*, and also about translation and terminology, is given in the introduction, pp. 3–4.

CGL-B	*Course in General Linguistics*, trans. W. Baskin (Saussure, 1959, 1974)
CGL-H	*Course in General Linguistics*, trans. R. Harris (Saussure, 1983)
CLG	*Cours de linguistique générale* (Saussure, 1916)
CLG/D	*Cours de linguistique générale*, ed. T. de Mauro (Saussure, 1972)
CLG/E	*Cours de linguistique générale*, ed. R. Engler, 2 vols. (vol. 1, Saussure, 1968; vol. 2, Saussure, 1974)
ELG	*Ecrits de linguistique générale*, ed. S. Bouquet and R. Engler (Saussure, 2002)

Introduction: Saussure today

Carol Sanders

Why, still today, do we find the name of Ferdinand de Saussure featuring prominently in volumes published not only on linguistics, but on a multitude of topics, volumes with titles such as *Culture and Text: Discourse and Methodology in Social Research and Cultural Studies* (Lee and Poynton, 2000), or the intriguing *Plastic Glasses and Church Fathers* (Kronenfeld, 1996)? It is to this question that the present volume attempts to bring at least a partial answer, by looking afresh at the intellectual background to Saussure's work, the work itself, its impact on European structuralism in general and linguistics in particular, and its changed but continuing influence today.

The titles above, then, are enough to show that nearly a century and a half after his birth, the ideas of this Swiss linguist and thinker still excite interest. He is best known for his *Cours de linguistique générale*, edited after his premature death from the notes of students who had attended his lectures and first published in 1916. This 'Course in general linguistics' has gone through numerous editions in France, has been translated into numerous languages, and has had an influence far beyond the area of linguistics. This book, however, is far from being the sole reason for his importance as a thinker, the recognition of which has gone through various phases since his death. In his own lifetime, he was regarded – and regarded himself – primarily as a historical linguist who had made his mark with a brilliant and precocious study in Indo-European linguistics. At the turn of the nineteenth and twentieth centuries, general linguistics, as a discipline that examines how language works and how best to describe the current state of a living language (as opposed to tracing the history of past language states), was barely constituted; Saussure was one of the main thinkers who contributed to establishing the principles of the discipline as we know it today. However, although the *Cours*, on first being published, was received with praise by a few, and with a more muted mixture of praise and criticism by others, it was largely ignored in many quarters. In particular, in the English-speaking world references to it were almost non-existent (see Sanders, 2000a). It would only be in the mid-twentieth century that the significance of Saussure's thought came to be realised, initially in the context of the structuralist movement.

Structuralism was a school of thought (to some) or a method (to others) which for several decades of the second half of the twentieth century dominated some disciplines – linguistics, literary criticism, anthropology, film and media criticism, to mention but a few, and which had a strong impact on others, from psychology and philosophy to economics. The main text that inspired, and was constantly cited by, this movement was Saussure's *Cours de linguistique générale*, interpreted as a blueprint for describing how the structures of our social and cultural life are constituted, and the way in which once constituted they function as a system of signs. The concepts of the *Cours* thus inspired some of the most interesting and best-known thinkers of the period, in an astonishingly fertile period of ground-breaking work in what were often new disciplines, or radical departures within established disciplines, as well as work that crossed disciplinary borders. Such widespread acclaim for one book (which was not even by the thinker whose ideas it purported to represent) and such single-minded enthusiasm for one approach were bound to provoke a reaction, and towards the end of the last century, so-called Saussurean structuralism was accused, among other things, of ahistoricism, and of promoting a reductionist view of language as a code while ignoring real usage and language in context. These criticisms were to some extent countered by later studies based on manuscripts in which Saussure explores in great detail certain aspects of classical and medieval literature, in particular his claim to have discovered the widespread use of anagrams concealed in Latin poetry. So different was this facet of his work that commentators spoke of the 'two Saussures'. Even amidst the debates, studies continued to appear that testified to the relevance of the *Cours* in various domains (for example, Holdcroft, 1991, for the social sciences). Subsequently, it was partly with more balanced readings of the *Cours*, and partly with the further discovery in 1996 of notes in Saussure's own hand, that the pendulum began to swing back again. Interested readers began to construct a more nuanced view of the incomplete and suggestive work of this fascinating thinker, looking afresh at his original contribution to intellectual history, even to the extent in some cases of seeing in his reflections the embryonic beginnings of a theory of utterance and of speech acts.

There are also, of course, those Saussure scholars who, less swayed by changing intellectual fashions, have continued to work steadily to elucidate and make available his ideas. The purpose of the schematic account above is simply to give an initial overview which enables the reader to situate the subject of this book, and to understand the rationale for the topics that are covered. Specific names and works have not been cited so far, because these will emerge in the chapters that follow. Saussure himself was very aware of the history and epistemological status of linguistics, and an attempt has been made to reflect this. It is perhaps time to reexamine the place in Saussure's thought of the two centres of linguistics in which he spent his early years as a young scholar. In the first chapter, Saussure's work as an Indo-Europeanist, and its relation to nineteenth-century German scholarship as well as to the rest of his work, is examined. The second chapter focuses on Saussure's years of teaching in Paris, during which he was undoubtedly as much influenced by colleagues as he influenced them, although this mutual debt is not always as fully recognised as it might be. The four chapters of part II concern the *Cours* itself: the complex story of its compilation, and the interlocking sum of key concepts that explain its impact. Part III deals with the delayed 'aftermath' of the *Cours*, its reception and influence not only in European structuralism and post-structuralism, but also in other places and traditions, from Russia to North America. Finally, there is an opening out to the wider impact of Saussure's thought and the elements of it that are under discussion today or which are likely to continue to be of interest tomorrow, such as his contribution to theories of meaning, and to the discipline of semiotics which he foreshadowed in the *Cours*.

Rather than duplicating the numerous studies of Saussure that exist in French, the emphasis of this volume is on providing an up-to-date introduction to, and assessment of, Saussure's ideas to an English-speaking readership. There is thus a two-fold perspective. Firstly, the aim in some of the chapters is to shed a slightly different light on the Swiss linguist by setting his thought in the wider context of English-speaking approaches to linguistics and to contemporary intellectual history (as in the chapter by Norris). Inevitably, many major writers on Saussure publish in languages other than English, and in particular in French, so that a second aim is to try to make accessible to readers the work of certain scholars from other traditions. Chapters may be read individually; although certain key concepts inevitably recur, an attempt has been made to avoid undue overlap. However, because Saussure's ideas are looked at here in a variety of ways by the different authors, most will be gained from (preferably) reading the whole volume, or (at the very least) from following up the cross-references that are given from one chapter to others.

In the context of the above, a comment is called for about the various editions of the *Cours de linguistique générale*, which can be confusing, and also about translation and terminology. The *Cours*, first published in 1916, has been republished in a number of subsequent editions, which from the second edition on have kept the same page numbering. In 1972, an important scholarly edition with substantial notes by Tullio de Mauro (based on an Italian version published in 1967) appeared in French, still retaining the original page numbers for the text of the *Cours*. In this volume, page references to the *Cours* are simply given with the abbreviation *CLG*, and if a distinction needs to be made between the original publication and de Mauro's edition, the abbreviation *CLG*/D is used or the date is given. Manuscript sources of the *Cours* were first published by Godel (Godel, 1957), followed by a masterly juxtaposition of the various student notes available drawn up by Engler (*CLG*/E) in two volumes published in

1968 and 1974. Other works by Saussure are listed under his name and the date of publication in the first section of the final bibliography. The next section of the bibliography comprises a select list of major works on Saussure published in the last two decades, mainly in English, but with some references in other languages; it is hoped that this may prove a helpful reference tool for further reading and research. Finally, there is a consolidated list of references used by the authors of the chapters of this volume. (A small number if items appear twice: for example, Godel's compilation of the lecture notes taken by some students is commonly referred to as Godel, 1957, and it is listed as such in the references as well as among Saussure's works.)

Most of the quotations in the chapters are given in English, with occasional short quotations being provided in French also, in order to give the reader a taste of the original. There are two published English translations of the *Cours de linguistique générale*, and a number of critical volumes in which authors have provided their own versions. The first published translation into English, by Wade Baskin, appeared in the USA in 1959 (and then in Britain a year later). It was subsequently reissued with a useful introduction by Jonathan Culler in 1974, with the same page numbering. Baskin's translation is referred to as *CLG*-B. The second English translation is by Roy Harris and was first published in Britain in 1983 (*CLG*-H). Because each of these translations has its strengths and weaknesses, it was decided to allow authors the freedom to use either of them, or even to supply their own, as they thought fit. The translated quotations to be found in the chapters are not sufficiently different to lead to misunderstandings or inconsistencies; rather, they allow the reader to get the flavour of each, and perhaps eventually to select one or the other in order to read more of the *Cours*, as well, hopefully, as appreciating some of the difficulties involved in translating this text. There are bilingual French/English editions of some student notebooks (see Saussure, 1993, 1996 and 1997 in the bibliography). Some manuscript notes have been published over the years in French, for example in the *Cahiers Ferdinand de Saussure*; the major publication of manuscript notes, both those discovered in 1996 and some older ones, is the *Ecrits de linguistique générale (ELG)*, edited by Bouquet and Engler (Saussure, 2002), which will shortly appear in English published by Oxford University Press. Where no reference is made to an existing English version of a text, the translation is the work of the author (or overall translator) of the chapter.

A translation problem arises with certain of Saussure's terms. The first is the translation of the terms *langue* and *parole*, as used in the *Cours*. Over the years Saussure's own terminology varies, and it develops throughout the three lecture series on which the *Cours* is based. The solution which he adopted, and which has been consecrated by the *Cours* with occasional lapses, was to divide the overarching term for language, or the human language faculty, which he refers to as *langage*, into *langue* and *parole*. The former refers to the potential linguistic system which resides in the mind of all members of a speech community, and waits to be activated in *parole*, in individual utterances, or acts of speech. To complicate matters, *une langue, les langues*, etc. is used with its non-technical meaning of a language/languages, although this usage poses no translation problem. (See Gordon's chapter, and Sanders, 2000b.) The difficulty with the other three terms *langage/langue/parole* is that English only has two likely contenders: language and speech. Baskin uses 'human speech/language/speaking' for the triad, whereas Harris tends to use 'language' or 'language faculty' for *langage*, 'language structure' or 'linguistic system' (or less happily 'the *langue*') for *langue* and 'speech' for *parole*. There is no ideal solution, but of the English terms, 'language system' for *langue* and 'speech' for *parole* would seem the best in most contexts, as long as another phrase such as 'language faculty' is retained for *langage* where there is any possible confusion between it and *langue*. However, the French terms have now been used so frequently in English in any writing on Saussure or on structuralism in general that another solution is to borrow the French words. In these chapters, we have generally used either 'language system' or *langue* when talking about *langue*, and either 'speech' or *parole* for the latter. There are other Saussurean terms that have become 'naturalised', such as *état de langue* for the snapshot picture that we get of any language at a particular stage of its development. There is also another well-known pair of terms: the linguistic sign is made up of two inseparable parts, the 'signifier' and the 'signified', which are Baskin's translation of *signifiant* and *signifié*, while Harris uses 'signification' and 'signal'. (On the sign, see the chapter by Joseph.) We have used either Baskin's terms, or the French loan-words of *signifiant* and *signifié*.

The adoption of these terms, which will be found in English in a range of disciplinary fields, is just one more indication of the lasting impact made by Saussure's thought. These concepts were to be found embryonically present in other scholars of Saussure's time, but he it was who sharpened their focus and, above all, who wove them all into a coherent system which could be used as a model for us to understand and describe the workings not only of language, but also of other human sign systems. In our age of communication and information technologies, it is not surprising that there is once more interest in Saussure's thought, so that an 'Institut Ferdinand de Saussure' has been set up with the aim of exploring and promoting the relevance of Saussure to linguistics and beyond, for example in cognitive science, and in what the French are calling 'les sciences de la culture'. It is true that at one point, just at the time when it was fashionable to proclaim the death of the author, Saussure's elevation to almost cult-figure status may have owed something to the enigmatic nature of his work, unfinished, sometimes ambiguous and posthumously published by others. However, if since then it has shown that it will stand the test of time in its relevance to a range of disciplines, this is also in part due to the individual voice that comes through both the striking cadences of the *Cours de linguistique générale* and the more hesitant tones of the manuscript notes of the *Ecrits de linguistique générale*, despite the different circumstances of their publication. It is to be hoped that the reader of this volume will be motivated to go to the texts themselves to pursue the elusive, foresightful and fascinating thought of Ferdinand de Saussure.

Finally, a number of the distinguished commentators who have written about Saussure have contributed chapters to this Companion. There are inevitably other important names that are very much present, and feature in the bibliography, such as Harris, Koerner and Starobinski, to name but three. Among the 'giants' of Saussure scholarship, however, one name stands out. It is that of Rudolf Engler who, alongside his other works, compiled the indispensable comparative edition of student notes from Saussure's Geneva lectures (Saussure, 1968 and 1974). He prepared a chapter for this volume on the making of the *Cours de linguistique générale* shortly before his untimely death in August 2003. Hopefully, the entire volume would have met with his approval and pleasure.

Part I

Out of the nineteenth century

1 Saussure and Indo-European linguistics

Anna Morpurgo Davies

Saussure as seen by his contemporaries

In 1908 the Linguistic Society of Paris (Société Linguistique de Paris) dedicated a volume of *Mélanges* to Ferdinand de Saussure, then aged fifty and professor at the University of Geneva (Saussure, 1908). A very brief and unsigned preface stated that, since the few years that he had spent in Paris between 1881 and 1891 had been decisive for the development of French linguistics, the Society was happy to dedicate to him one of the first volumes of its new series. The Society also wished to thank the eminent Swiss linguists who had joined Saussure's earlier pupils in paying their respects to the author of the *Mémoire sur le système primitif des voyelles en indo-européen*. Two things are now striking even if they were not so at the time. First, no attempt was made in the preface or elsewhere to distinguish between the two main activities of Saussure: teaching and research in comparative and historical linguistics (*grammaire comparée*) and teaching and research in general or theoretical linguistics. Secondly the articles collected in the volume were all, with one exception, articles in Indo-European comparative linguistics. They include work by established scholars of considerable fame like Antoine Meillet in Paris or Jacob Wackernagel in Basle, but these were historical and comparative linguists rather than theoretical linguists. The one exception is a paper by one of Saussure's pupils and colleagues, indeed one of the editors of the *Cours*, Albert Sechehaye, who discusses the role of stylistics in the theory of language. Yet Saussure's current fame is tied to his views on theoretical linguistics.

Saussure as a comparativist

If Saussure's contemporaries had been asked, they would have simply called him a linguist since historical and comparative linguistics (often identified with Indo-European studies) was the prevailing form of linguistics at the time. Indeed all the work that Saussure published in his lifetime, and which was collected posthumously in a single volume (Saussure, 1922) concerned problems of Indo-European, and fitted in the tradition of historical and comparative work which had started at the beginning of the nineteenth century. Saussure, in common with most of his contemporaries, spoke of Franz Bopp's school and of the new science founded by Bopp (Saussure, 2002: 130ff.). The reference was to the German scholar who in 1816 had published a seminal book where he in effect demonstrated that a number of ancient languages (Greek, Latin, Sanskrit, Gothic) descended from a common prehistoric ancestor which had not survived; through comparison of the daughter languages it was possible to identify the common features which belonged to the parent language as well as the innovations which each of the descendants had introduced into the common inheritance. Bopp's more advanced work included a comparative grammar of Sanskrit, Avestan, Greek, Latin, Lithuanian, Gothic and German (1833–52) which in its second edition (1857–61) also discussed Old Slavic, Armenian and other Indo-European languages. In seeing himself in Bopp's tradition, Saussure was in line with most of his contemporaries; however, he went well beyond them in having doubts (which he did not express in his published work) about the exact nature of the 'new science' founded by Bopp and about the continuity between Bopp's work and the work of his contemporaries.[1]

Two Saussures?

A number of questions arise for the modern reader trained to think of Saussure as the founder of general linguistics or, more specifically, as the author of that posthumous *Cours de linguistique générale* (1916) which is often seen as marking the beginning of general or theoretical linguistics. If Saussure was in fact a professor of Sanskrit and Indo-European languages for most of his life, if practically all that he published of his own volition during his lifetime concerned historical and comparative linguistics, what is the link, if any, between these two sorts of activities? Is it true that there were two Saussures, as the title (though not the content) of a famous paper (Redard, 1978a) may suggest?

The *Cours* is well known, but in its published form it was not written by Saussure. We must focus on the work actually published. What was it about? How innovative was it? How important? How much of it, if any, survived? How necessary is it for the current practitioners of the subject to go back to the original publications? And above all, how did it fit with the contemporary beliefs? An answer is not easy because what in Saussure's time was the obvious subject matter of linguistics is currently the preserve of a small and highly specialised group of scholars. Some background is necessary.

Nineteenth-century linguistics

The very concept of linguistics as a university discipline is a novelty of the nineteenth century. In itself this is not surprising. The nineteenth century saw the beginning of the institutionalisation of academic disciplines as we now know them, as well as the identification and sometimes creation of a number of new disciplines. In most instances the German universities served as a model and trend-setters, not least because they had introduced the concept of a university dedicated to research as well as to teaching. Research involved specialisation. When Saussure started to study at the University of Leipzig in 1876 he either attended or could have attended seminars and lectures by a multitude of specialists: Georg Curtius (1820–85) was in effect teaching Indo-European and the historical grammar of the classical languages; August Leskien (1840–1916) was teaching Slavic and Indo-European; Karl Brugmann (1849–1919), who was to become one of the major Indo-Europeanists, was in Leipzig from 1873, as *Privatdozent* from 1877 and later (1887) returned as a full professor of Indo-European linguistics. The list could continue. Such a concentration of specialists, each one of whom at the time would have been called a *Sprachwissenschaftler* 'linguist' (and now would be labelled Indo-Europeanist), is remarkable and would have been unthinkable fifty years earlier (it is doubtful that at that stage as many 'professional' linguists existed in the whole of Germany). Even in the 1880s it was probably unthinkable outside Germany, though the new concept of research university was beginning to prevail in Europe and the USA. It may be useful to mention that in their specialised field all of these scholars produced work which is still known and used nowadays (see Morpurgo Davies, 1998; Auroux, 2000).

Textual and linguistic studies

The linguists of the time were not theoreticians but had to have erudition and scholarship. As well as linguists they could be medievalists like Braune and his contemporary Eduard Sievers (1850–1932), who were more than capable of editing Old English or Old High German or Old Norse texts, or they could be classicists like Georg Curtius, who also lectured on Greek and Latin literature. All of them knew Greek, Latin and sometimes Hebrew from their school days and most of them had studied Sanskrit at university as well as the ancient Germanic languages. All of them had to be competent textual and literary scholars because the data that they needed were found in ancient texts (inscriptions, papyri, manuscripts) which made sense only within certain cultural frameworks which the reader had to understand. The study and understanding of these texts could be, and often was, an end in itself, but Saussure's teachers or colleagues in Leipzig mainly wanted to use them as a source of linguistic data. The aim was to understand and explain the development of an ancient language from the period of the first evidence to the period in which it was best known. To explain, in this context, mostly meant to account for the irregularities in the later phases of the language through the reconstruction of sound changes and morphological innovations which had altered the earlier state of affairs. To take the simplest possible example: in classical Latin an accusative like *oratōr-em* 'orator' belonged with the nominative *orator*, but if so why did an accusative like *honōr-em* 'honour' correspond to a nominative *honōs*? This question was answered pointing out that *honōr-em* derived from an earlier unattested **honōs-em* which was the original accusative corresponding to the nominative *honōs*. But why had **honōs-em* been replaced by *honorem*? Here the answer was that in Latin at some stage (which could be documented) all intervocalic *s*-sounds had been replaced by [r] (the so called rhotacism).[2] In other words, the original forms *orator, oratōrem*; *honōs, *honōsem* had a degree of morphological regularity which their later descendants had lost, because of sound change. Somewhat later the regularity was reintroduced through the creation of a new nominative *honor*, formed in order to match the indirect cases and the regularity of the *orator: oratōrem* pattern. This assumption also allowed the linguist to link the newly formed *honor* with the adjective *honestus* (the original *-s-* of *honōs-* was preserved before a consonant) and in its turn the etymological link between 'honest' and 'honour', which was in this way not guessed at but demonstrated, could lead to a series of assumptions which were important for an understanding of Roman culture and its development. But for most linguists, and particularly for those of the earlier generations, the aim was mainly comparative: to compare the ancient phases reached through this sort of analysis with the earliest phases of related languages and try to define the position of the language in the family to which it belonged, while at the same time reconstructing, thanks to comparison, both its immediate antecedents and the more remote parent language.

The comparative method

In the last decades of the nineteenth century few linguists would have hesitated to say that the great discovery of their discipline was what we now call the comparative method. Through its application it was possible to demonstrate (rather than guess) that some languages belonged to the same linguistic family and to define their degree of kinship. The linguistic family tree was meant to indicate which languages belonged to the same family but also marked the type of relationship as defined by the different ways in which the tree's branches were drawn. In the third quarter of the century it had became possible to reconstruct – obviously with a high degree of approximation – some of the actual forms of the parent language, even if this belonged to a period earlier than the invention of writing. This is the stage at which we begin to find forms like **akvāsas* which was taken to be the closest possible approximation to the Indo-European for 'horses' (nominative plural) and the antecedent of Sanskrit *aśvās*, Gr. *hippoi*, Lat. *equī*. In the first part of the century it had been assumed that comparison permitted distinction in individual languages between innovations and preservations, and the emphasis had been on morphological analysis and segmentation but not on phonology. By the time the actual forms began to be reconstructed (eventually with an asterisk which indicated that they were not attested) it became imperative to make hypotheses about (a) the structure of the phonological system of the reconstructed parent language, (b) the phonological development which accounted for the differences between the reconstructed system and the attested systems. These may seem parochial problems – why should we worry whether Indo-European had a vocalic system which included five short vowels [a, e, o, i, u] like Latin or just three [a, i, u] like Sanskrit? Or given that nobody disputed that Latin *sequitur*, 'he follows' Greek *hepetai* and Sanskrit *sacate* all came from the same original root, was it worthwhile to discuss whether originally the second consonant was [k], [p] or a different consonant? In fact the problem was more substantial than it would appear at first sight and there were a number of points at stake. Suppose for instance that the verb 'to follow' was reconstructed with an internal [p] as in Greek. This would automatically speak against the older view that all these related languages were derived from Sanskrit since the <-c-> of Sanskrit would then reflect an innovation; the same could be said for Latin <-qu->. On the other hand, the initial [s] shared by Sanskrit and Latin was likely to be inherited and spoke against Greek [h] being original and in its turn against Greek being the parent language. Latin could then best represent the original form, if we accepted that a sound like [k^{w}] yielded [p] in Greek and <c>, i.e. [tʃ] in Sanskrit. But in other instances (e.g. Sanskrit *bhar-* 'to carry', Greek *pher-*, Latin *fer-*) there were very good reasons to assume that the original form of the first consonant was not like that of Latin and was more likely to be like that of Sanskrit.

This type of discussion, if conducted seriously, eventually provided a demonstration of what had been argued mainly on morphological evidence, namely that the parent language could not be identified with any of the attested languages. The historical consequences were important; if the parent language had to be identified with Sanskrit we would have had to assume movements of people from India to the West; if it was identified with Latin, from the West to India.

But the linguistic consequences of the correct reconstructions were important too. Through the reconstruction of Indo-European, their parent language, languages like Greek or the Indic languages or the Romance languages became languages with a history of more than 4,000 years. It was now becoming possible to dispel some of the old preconceptions: for instance, the view cherished by the Enlightenment that languages improved in rationality with time, but also the opposite view, supported by Romanticism, that the earliest phases of some languages had a level of perfection which was later followed by decay and that change (i.e. decay) did not belong to the early phases. In other words, a correct reconstruction of Indo-European, by now taken as pilot study for similar analyses of other language families, was not mere pastime or pedantry; it could add on the one hand to our knowledge of history, on the other to our understanding of the main features of language development. It also became possible to recognise patterns of development which could not have been identified before. One of the assumptions which was acquiring credibility in the 1870s concerned the regularity of sound change. As Saussure was to note at a later stage ([1903] 1960: 25), it was astonishing that if a sound [x] changed into [y] in a certain word and in a certain period, in the same period that sound [x] would also change into [y] in all other words where it occurred in the same environment. And yet it was becoming clear in the midst of violent academic disagreements that the whole of comparative and historical linguistics was founded on that assumption.[3]

The young Saussure

So much for the background. When the young Saussure arrived in Leipzig to pursue his doctoral studies in October 1876 he was not yet nineteen but he was not ignorant of linguistic work. In his very early teens he had been seduced by the 'paleontological' reconstructions of a neighbour and family friend, Adolphe Pictet, the author of two volumes of *Origines indo-européennes* (1859–63): 'The idea that with the help of one or two Sanskrit syllables – since that was the main idea of the book and of all contemporary linguistics – one could reconstruct the life of people who had disappeared, inflamed me with an enthusiasm unequalled in its naïveté' (Saussure, [1903] 1960: 16). At the age of fourteen and a half he had written and given to Pictet a lengthy essay (Saussure, [1872] 1978) in which he tried to demonstrate that it was possible to bring back all basic Greek, Latin and German roots to a pattern of the type Consonant + Vowel + Consonant where the consonants are defined as either labials, or dentals or gutturals. A striking character of the essay, in spite of the naïveté and, one may even say, absurdity of its assumptions and conclusions, is the immense clarity of argumentation and the professional style in which it is written. In 1874 Saussure started to teach himself Sanskrit using Bopp's Sanskrit grammar and began to read some technical literature (works by Bopp and Curtius); one year at the University of Geneva also gave him the experience of attending a course by someone who was de facto repeating what he had heard from Georg Curtius in Leipzig the previous year (Saussure, [1903] 1960: 20). Round that time he also joined the *Société de linguistique de Paris* (founded in 1866) and began to send in short articles. In other words, the Leipzig years were preceded by extensive self-teaching. Even before entering the Gymnasium in Geneva he had noticed that the contrast between forms like Greek *tetag-metha* 'we are arrayed' and Greek *tetakh-atai* 'they are arrayed', if compared to that between *lego-metha* 'we say' and *lego-ntai* 'they say', led to the conclusion that after a consonant *-ntai* had been replaced by *-atai* and to the assumption that in that position Greek *-a-* could be a replacement for the *-n-* of earlier Greek or Proto-Greek (Saussure, [1903] 1960: 18).

Saussure in Leipzig and the *Mémoire*

Saussure was in Leipzig for less than two years before moving for a short while to Berlin. During this period and in the previous year he wrote a number of things including four articles on Indo-European, Greek and Latin matters, all published in the *Mémoires de la Société de linguistique de Paris* (vol. 3, 1977), and a lengthy account of Pictet's work for the *Journal de Genève* 1878 (Saussure, 1922: 391–402). In December 1878 his masterpiece appeared, the 300-page monograph entitled *Mémoire sur le système primitif des voyelles dans les langues indo-européennes* (published by Teubner and dated Leipsick [sic] 1879).[4] One of the greatest French linguists, Antoine Meillet, later on called it the most beautiful book of comparative grammar ever written (Meillet, [1913–14] 1938: 183); the judgement is still valid. It remained the only full book that Saussure ever published. Louis Havet, professor of Latin in Paris, who had agreed to write a brief review, ended taking a full page of the *Tribune de Genève* and explained in a letter to the author that once he had read and understood the book he was bowled over by its novelty and its importance (cf. Redard, 1978a: 30). The review ended by stating that the book was likely to lead to a renewal of part of the discipline and that much could be expected of its author who was still only twenty-one years of age. (See Havet [25/2/1879] in Redard, 1978b.) The Indo-Europeanist who rereads the book today experiences a series of difficulties because of different terminology and different conventions, but finds the task much easier because most of the conclusions have become part of the acquired knowledge in the field; the first reaction is still stunned admiration.

Is this masterpiece the result of the training that Saussure had received in Leipzig? Saussure himself ([1903] 1960: 15f.) explained that, though everyone would normally assume that his work, written and published in Leipzig by a Leipzig student, was the product of the Leipzig school, in fact it was written in semi-isolation without help and without visible signs of influence by his teachers or contemporaries. This statement will have to be reconsidered, but first we must mention what Leipzig meant at the time for people in the subject.

Leipzig and the neogrammarians

The university was justly famous in a number of fields. In comparative linguistics it was in the forefront. Georg Curtius had more or less single-handedly persuaded the classicists that they had much to learn from serious historical studies of both Greek and Latin; a group of young scholars had congregated round him and his courses were attended by more than 200 students. In the mid 1870s, however, things were changing and there was excitement all round. The Slavist August Leskien, much younger than Curtius, had persuaded a number of advanced students, young assistants and *Privat-Dozenten* that a new methodology was needed; the title of *Junggrammatiker* given to this group (partly in jest) stuck as also did the mistranslation 'neogrammarians', which missed the point of the joke. They argued – vociferously – that the Indo-Europeanists had to learn from those working on more modern languages and that the study of language change took priority over that of language comparison. They adopted a dualistic approach to language change: phonetic change happened unconsciously, independently of the will of the speakers, and according to regular 'laws' which admitted of no exceptions; morphological change was heavily influenced by 'analogy': the speakers reintroduced regularity in the grammar, remodelling forms on each other. These two types of change applied to all periods and not, as previously supposed, only to the period of linguistic decay which followed the perfection of the reconstructed parent language. In other words the linguist had to adopt a uniformitarian approach and study the motivation of change on the basis of modern data in order to reconstruct what had happened in the past. All these assumptions and beliefs – uniformitarianism, exceptionless sound laws, importance of what had previously been called false analogy, priority of history over comparison, concern for recent phases of language, extensive methodological discussions – added as they were to extensive claims of novelty and criticism of the past, were bound to irritate. Curtius and most scholars of the previous generation did not react favourably. In Leipzig, some of the brightest young scholars – Brugmann, Osthoff, Hermann Paul (1846–1921) – became the leaders of the new movement. Their manifesto did not appear until 1878, when Osthoff and Brugmann, after a quarrel with Curtius, founded a new periodical which was prefaced with a lengthy methodological statement (Osthoff and Brugman, 1878),[5] but between 1875 and 1876 a number of books and articles appeared which, even when they were not by card-carrying neogrammarians, altered considerably some of the previously accepted reconstructions while at the same time contributing to define the new method (Verner, 1875; Hübschmann, 1875; Leskien, 1876; Brugman, 1876a, 1876b, etc.; cf. Hoenigswald 1978).

Saussure was too young to count as one of the neogrammarians, even if he had wished to, but in any case he kept himself separate from a set-up – 'le cénacle des docteurs' – which he did not find sympathetic. However, in spite of this latent hostility, it is likely that he would have approved of the substance of the intellectual shift, even if not of the form that it took. At the time when he wrote the *Mémoire* he was completely au fait with the concrete results reached by Leskien and his followers in their work about Indo-European and largely accepted their conclusions. If so, what is the originality of the *Mémoire*?

Scope and novelty of the *Mémoire*

The book concerns the vocalism of Indo-European; on the one hand this refers to the vowels that we can reconstruct for the parent language, on the other to the phenomena of vocalic alternation which mark grammatical contrasts, the so-called Ablaut or vocalic apophony (see below), its function and its origin. Anachronistically it could be stated that the book concerns the phonology and morphophonology of reconstructed Indo-European and the derived languages. Saussure states at the outset that his main concern is what is called the Indo-European *a*, but the discussion gradually makes clear that the whole vocalic system has been the focus of attention. In other words it is not one sound which is discussed but a whole phonological system, its contrasts, its hierarchies and its morphophonemic functioning.

The novelty is manifold. At that moment in time the whole subject was in a state of complete flux. Odd beliefs had been inherited from the beginning of the century and from the previous century and were occasionally fought against but in a desultory way. (On Ablaut and on the history of the reconstruction of Indo-European vocalism see Morpurgo Davies, 1998; Pedersen, 1962; Benware, 1974; Mayrhofer, 1981, 1983.) A few of these beliefs are now listed in no particular order, mixing technical and less technical assumptions:

(a) The 'perfect' or fundamental vowels, it was sometimes argued, were [a, i, u]; it seemed to follow that the parent language, which was taken to be more perfect than its descendants, could only have [a, i, u].

(b) The vocalic system of Sanskrit was based on [a, i, u]; consequently it was all too easy to assume that the parent language only had [a, i, u]. If so, the more complex system [a, e, o, i, u] of some European languages, including Greek and Latin, was due to an innovation, i.e. to a split of [a] into [a, e, o]. It was not clear how this innovation could have occurred; or what forms of conditioning had determined the split.

(c) It was often stated that the consonants changed according to recognisable patterns but the development of vowels was entirely arbitrary; consequently while languages derived from the same parent showed regular consonantal correspondences between related words (cf. Latin *tū* vs. English *thou*, Latin *trēs* vs. English *three*, etc.), the correspondences between vowels seemed to be unpredictable (cf. Latin *pēs* vs. E. *foot*, Latin *sē-men* vs. E. *seed*).

(d) The Indo-European languages showed traces of vocalic alternations used to indicate grammatical distinctions as in English *drive/drove* or in Greek *eleipon* 'I was leaving', *elipon* 'I left'. This so-called Ablaut (the technical term which Jacob Grimm made standard) was more prominent in the earlier phases of the Indo-European languages and was treated in the work of the early comparativists as a hallmark of perfection. Some scholars had even argued that it had a direct link with meaning: weakening of the vowel (as in Greek *-lip-* vs. *-leip-*) meant weakening of meaning.

(e) The Indian grammarians, followed by the European scholars, had understood the Sanskrit Ablaut as based on successive additions of an *-a-* vowel to the root (the root of the verb 'to make' could appear as *kr-*, *kar-*, *kār-*). If this was also the Indo-European pattern, alternations like those of Greek *lip-, leip-, loip-* for the verb meaning 'to leave' could not go back to the parent language. Moreover, even in Sanskrit there were other types of alternations. In forms like Sanskrit *punā-mi* 'I purify' / *pavi-tum* 'to purify' / *pū-ta-* 'purified' all sorts of vocalic alternations occurred. This was often ignored.

Each one of these assumptions, and there were numerous others, carried a heavy ideological baggage. Each could be tackled from a purely technical viewpoint provided that the linguist was not mesmerised by the earlier beliefs, but each also added to the general confusion. Which vowels could be attributed to Indo-European and how these vowels were exploited to indicate grammatical contrasts remained obscure. The question of the nature, role and origin of Ablaut was also controversial.

The mid 1870s saw some new developments. The assumption that Sanskrit [a] as contrasted with [e, o, a] of the European languages was original was no longer taken for granted but there was no agreement about the correct reconstruction. At the same time the range of reconstructed vowels increased. It was first suggested – by Hermann Osthoff – that Indo-European like Sanskrit had a vocalic [r] (cf. the first syllable of *Brno*) and possibly a vocalic [l] (cf. the final syllable of English *people*), even if most daughter languages had developed a supporting vowel next to it (Gr. *ar/ra*, Lat. *or/ur*, etc.). In a daring article published in 1876, which was the main cause of the quarrel with Curtius, Karl Brugmann (1876a), argued that Indo-European also had vocalic [n] and [m] (cf. the final syllables of German *leben*, etc.) which in most languages had developed supporting vowels and sometimes lost the nasal element (cf. the last syllable of Sanskrit *sapta* '7', Greek *hepta*, Latin *septem*, Gothic *sibun*). On his arrival in Leipzig the young Saussure was asked his views about Brugmann's discovery. He was forcefully reminded that he had made the same observation while still at school and found it difficult to accept Brugmann's priority, though he had no publication which supported his claim (Saussure, [1903] 1960).

The discovery of vocalic liquids and nasals [r, (l), m, n] was important not only because it added to the number of reconstructed phonemes but also because it accounted for some of the odd correspondences. If we found Latin [e] corresponding to Greek [e] in Lat. *ferō* 'I carry' vs. Gr. *pherō*, why did the ending *-em* of accusative singular in e.g. Latin *patr-em* 'father' correspond to Greek *-a*

in the accusative singular *pater-a*? Brugmann (and Saussure before him) reconstructed a vocalic nasal which turned into *-em* in Latin and into *-a* in Greek. The older view was that the development of vowels was unpredictable, but in this manner the way was open to establishing regular correspondences between vowels as well as between consonants. However, a number of problems were still not solved.

The striking character of the *Mémoire* is that the twenty-year-old Saussure tackles all these difficulties at once as well as a number of more substantial problems which had not yet emerged in the discussion. There is sureness of touch and both willingness and ability to integrate into a new system separate conclusions which had just been reached and were deemed to be tentative even by their authors. The articles quoted and on which part of the argument is built are often no more than one or two years old. Havet complained that the book was difficult to follow and required too much of its readers. But this is not because of lack of clarity (on the contrary); it is simply because the reader must be au fait with the state of the art, with what was known and what was being discussed. That is why modern Indo-Europeanists, once they have learned to recognise symbols and terminology which are now obsolete, find the argumentation so clear. They have a better knowledge of the starting point than Saussure's contemporaries could have had.

The results of the *Mémoire*

The conclusions of the *Mémoire* may be summarised briefly, once again at the cost of some anachronism. For Saussure the Indo-European parent language had an [e] and an [o] vowel (following Brugmann, he used the symbols a_1 and a_2) which merged in Sanskrit but were mostly preserved in Greek and Latin; in addition it had a number of *coefficients sonantiques*, i.e. resonants [i, u, r, (l), m, n] which functioned as vowels between consonants and elsewhere and as consonants between vowels and in other environments. A study of the basic form of each root established that this normally included an [e] vowel followed by a consonant or resonant; the [e] vowel regularly alternated with [o] in different grammatical forms and with no [e] or [o] vowel in other forms (cf. Greek *leip-*, *loip-*, *lip-* 'leave'). In contrast with earlier assumptions, Saussure accepts the view that the basic form of the root has [e] and that [e] is lost when the accent is deplaced. If so, Ablaut (i.e. loss of [e]) is the result of pure sound change and has no symbolic and semantic value. So far, Saussure is building on individual conclusions which had in one way or the other been stated or hinted at by other contemporary authors, though never in the context of a comprehensive study of roots, accentuation and Ablaut.

If Saussure had stopped here in 1878, his book would still have been an exceptional achievement, but there was more to come. One of the fundamental

steps is the observation that a Greek root of the type *Cei-*, *Ceu-*, *Cer-*, etc. (C = any consonant) alternates with *Ci-*, *Cu-*, *Cr-*, etc. in exactly the same circumstances in which a root of the type *Cā-* alternates with *Ca-* (Greek *phā-mi* 'I say', *pha-men* 'we say' vs. Greek *ei-mi* 'I (shall) go', *i-men* 'we (shall) go'). Through skilful use of Ablaut alternations and comparative evidence, Saussure shows that we have to reconstruct for Indo-European another *coefficient sonantique*, *A*, which was dropped after a preceding vowel lengthening it (and sometimes changing its quality), was lost before another vowel and in Greek, Italic and Germanic became [a] between consonants. In Sanskrit *A* was reduced to a sound which eventually emerged as [i]. Hence a root such as Indo-European **steA-* 'stand', appears in Sanskrit as *sthā-* and in both Greek and Italic as *stā-*, but the participle/verbal adjective is **stA-tós* which yields Greek *statós*, Latin *status*, Sanskrit *sthitá-*. On similar grounds, Saussure also identified another *coefficient sonantique*, *O̯*, which between consonants appeared as [o] in Greek and in Greek and Italic changed a preceding [e] or [o] into [ō]. The list of *coefficients sonantiques* now included *A* and *O̯* as well as [i, u, r, (l,) m, n]. The question of the phonetic value of *A* and *O̯* is still debated. Also, it is not clear whether Saussure thought of them as vowels (see Szemerényi, 1973) or resonants.

Some further developments should also be mentioned. First, Saussure could now explain Sanskrit alternations such as that of the infinitive *pavi-tum* 'to purify' vs. the verbal adjective *pū-ta-* as deriving from **peuA-* > *pavi-* vs. **puA-* > *pū-*, with the standard vocalic alternation between [e] and absence of [e]. He could go even further, assuming that the Sanskrit infinitive *pari-tum* 'to fill' derived from **perA-* and the verbal adjective *pūr-ta-* derived from **prA-* > *pr̥̄-* > *pūr*. In other words, *A* (and *O̯*) lengthened a preceding [e] and [o] but also a preceding vocalic [i, u, r, l, m, n] and a long resonant like **r̥̄* yielded *ūr* in Sanskrit.

Secondly, some of the apparently different formations of Sanskrit verbal presents could be brought back to the same basic type. The Indian grammarians distinguished a class of presents of the *yunakti* 'he joins' type (class VII) from a class of the *punāti* 'he purifies' type (class IX). The roots they quoted for these verbs were *yug-* 'join' and *pū-* 'purify'. Saussure showed that the formations had identical origins. An original root **yeug-* / **yug-* forms the present from a stem ** yu-ne-g-* (-> *yunak-ti*) with a nasal infix, an original root **peuA-/ *puA-* also forms a present with a *-ne-* infix, *pu-ne-A-* (-> *punā-ti*). Everything becomes clear; the short [u] of *punāti* vs. the long [ū] of *pū-* (< **puA-*), the long *a* of *punāti* (< **eA*) vs. the short *a* in *yunakti*. From the point of view of present formation, *-A-* and *-g-* fulfil parallel functions and instead of two different types of Ablaut and two different verbal classes we are dealing with a much simplified morphology. It is worth pointing out that Saussure's reconstructions were not based on any phonetic consideration and no attempt was made to define phonetically *A* and *Ǫ*.

Reception and impact of the *Mémoire*

The later history of Saussure's achievements is well known and has often been related. The conclusions had partial acceptance by the contemporaries who nevertheless thought that they were all too mathematical and too abstract to carry full conviction. There were some firm rejections, particularly by one of the leading neogrammarians, Hermann Osthoff, there was also here and there a conspiracy of silence and some tacit taking over of a number of conclusions sometimes without acknowledgement. The silence and the rejection have perhaps been exaggerated (see Redard, 1978a; Mayrhofer, 1981: 26 ff.; Gmür, 1986); however, the unpublished documents which became available over the years (letters, notes, etc.) made clear that Saussure felt that German scholarship had been hostile and his work had not been fully understood. The latter is indeed true. In 1898 Wilhelm Streitberg (1864–1925), a second-generation neogrammarian, wrote as much to Brugmann regretting that it had taken him so long to understand Saussure (Villani, 1990: 5). Of course there were flaws even in Saussure's argument and slowly these came to the fore. A list, and a correct list, is offered by Streitberg in the very sympathetic memoire of Saussure written after his death (Streitberg, 1915; cf. Szemerényi, 1973: 4f.), but solutions were available and were indeed found. The first real confirmation that Saussure was on the right track came in 1927, well after his death, when Jerzy Kuryłowicz recognised that the newly deciphered Hittite, the oldest attested IE language, had a consonantal phoneme (<h>) which was etymologically derived from Saussure's *A*. Conclusions reached largely on the basis of internal reconstruction were convalidated by newly found comparative data. At the same time a number of followers, Möller, Kuryłowicz, Benveniste and Cuny continued Saussure's work (Szemerényi, 1973; Mayrhofer, 1981). What is now called laryngeal theory has its foundations in the theories about vocalic alternations demonstrated in Saussure's *Mémoire*, but the theory's definitive form is not yet settled and it has not yet won total acceptance. Nevertheless, in the last twenty or thirty years few serious scholars have disputed its basic tenets. (On the reception of the *Mémoire* see Saussure, 1972; Szemerényi, 1973; Redard, 1978a; Mayrhofer, 1981; Gmür, 1986.)

Comparative method and internal reconstruction

The *Mémoire* is full of unbelievable riches – most of which, sometimes in an altered form, have become part of what we now find in our basic handbooks;

some are still to be rediscovered. Even now, or perhaps more now than before, the beauty of the way in which the argument develops is overpowering. There is a constant interplay between two different methods of linguistic comparison and reconstruction: on the one hand, the standard comparative method which was reaching at that stage its most advanced form and was based on the phonological comparison of semantically similar words in a number of related languages and the identification of regular sound correspondences; on the other hand, internal reconstruction, the method that did not really receive a name or was not formalised until after the Second World War (Morpurgo Davies, 1994). Apparent grammatical irregularities can be explained postulating earlier sound changes or the alteration of an earlier phonological system. Saussure as a schoolboy had naturally used that method when he had decided that the parallelism between Greek *lego-metha* and *lego-ntai*, on the one hand, and *tetag-metha* and *tetakh-atai*, on the other, spoke for a derivation of *-atai* from *-ntai* (see above). The identification of *A* and *O̯* as *coefficient sonantiques* is based on the parallelism between formations which end in a resonant [i, u, r, m, n] and formations which end in A or O. The term 'internal reconstruction' is much later than Saussure but the method had been used before, even if sporadically; nowhere else, however, are the two methods so explicitly and so clearly linked and to such good effect.

Before and after the *Mémoire*

Apart from unpublished papers, Saussure had published four articles and two short notes before the *Mémoire* as well as Pictet's review; they were all strictly technical articles about very specific problems of Indo-European comparison and historical linguistics. One of these (Saussure [1877] 1922: 379ff.) gives us a preview of the *Mémoire* and comes close to one of the great discoveries, made at the same time by a number of scholars, the so-called *Palatalgesetz*, i.e. the observation that the alternation between <*k*> and <*c*> in Sanskrit words like *ka-* 'who', *ca* 'and' and *cid* 'what' proved that Sanskrit [a] reflected two different original phonemes, one of which was capable of palatalising a preceding [*k*] (Mayrhofer, 1983: 137–42). After the *Mémoire,* Saussure concentrated on his doctoral dissertation on the use of the genitive absolute in Sanskrit which he submitted in 1880 and published in 1881; again Meillet notices the contrast between a narrow exercise on a limited subject and the broad views of the *Mémoire*, but de Mauro (Saussure, 1972: 330f.) stresses the importance of the work on syntax and of the synchronic and contrastive approach. The brief interlude in Berlin had allowed Saussure to learn more Sanskrit and to have a brief meeting with Whitney (Joseph, 1988), but it is doubtful that it had much influence on him. After Leipzig, the publication of the *Mémoire* and the doctorate, Saussure moved to Paris (see Sanders, this volume) where his classes in Germanic, in the comparative grammar of Greek and Latin, and in

Indo-European linguistics in general had an immense influence (see Meillet's testimonial in Saussure, 1972: 334ff.). Even when he returned to Geneva in 1891 his teaching activity mostly concerned Sanskrit and other Indo-European languages. It is only in 1906 that he was also entrusted with teaching general linguistics and began his three courses in the subject. If we look at the work published after the *Mémoire* and the doctoral dissertation, we find a very large number of short notes in the *Mémoires de la Société de linguistique de Paris*, mostly dedicated to individual etymologies (see Bouquet, 2003: 506ff). There are a few longer articles either in the same periodical or in volumes in honour of scholars to whom in some way Saussure felt indebted. Between 1894 and 1896 three long papers, one dedicated to Leskien, are concerned with Lithuanian declensions and accentuation and establish the law on accent shift which goes under the name of *lex Saussure* (Collinge, 1985:149 ff.). Some, indeed most, of this work has again the same lucidity, learning and originality of the *Mémoire*, but there is not the breathless excitement of discovery which the twenty-year-old had managed to convey. In the last fifteen years of his life, just when he was giving the general courses which provided the material for the *Cours*, Saussure published only three papers (for the last three *Festschriften* mentioned above). (See Saussure, 1972; Streitberg, 1915; Meillet, 1938; Gmür, 1990 and Vallini, 1978.)

The historiographical problems

Let us now reformulate and sharpen the questions that we were asking. How different was Saussure's historical and comparative work from that of his contemporaries? Did he really reach all his conclusions on his own without being influenced by his Leipzig teachers? More specifically, should he count as one of the neogrammarians? What continuity, if any, is there between the comparative-historical work and Saussure's theoretical work, once we allow for the fact that this was not published by the author? Less important in my view is a much (perhaps too much) debated question. Why did someone who, like Saussure, had published two books by the time he was twenty-four 'dry up' so significantly at a later stage? The question will be returned to at the end, not in the hope to settle it but because it is relevant to another and more important historiographical question.

Saussure, his teachers and contemporaries

Modern discussion about the *Cours de linguistique générale* has often turned to the question of the sources of its main tenets: the concept of sign, the contrast between synchrony and diachrony, *l'arbitraire du signe*, etc. An analysis of the comparative and historical work also raises the question of sources, though in a different context. Writing to Streitberg in 1903, Saussure ([1903] 1960) was eager to underline that most of the conclusions reached in the *Mémoire* were his own. In a letter to Streitberg of 28 November 1914 (Villani, 1990: 29f.), Karl Brugmann pointed out that to his knowledge Saussure had never openly acknowledged any dependence on his Leipzig teachers and noted that in the review by Havet, Saussure's teachers in Leipzig were not mentioned, as they would have been for any young German scholar. According to both Brugmann and Saussure [1903]1960: 22ff.), the latter had given up Bruckmann's classes in Leipzig because all too often he heard points which overlapped with what he wanted to say in his book and felt awkward in deciding what was his and what was Brugmann's.

However, when Saussure was making his point about the independence of his thought from the Leipzig scholars in general, and the *Junggrammatiker* in particular, he was in all instances speaking about some specific individual results (the role of *A*, the vocalic nasals, etc.) – he justifies his attitude saying that he did not want to be accused of plagiarism and relates an episode that shows that Brugmann had never seriously thought about the Ablaut alternation of the *-ā / ă* type, which was the linchpin of Saussure's own discoveries. For the rest, he is endlessly scrupulous in referring to German scholars; Villani (1990: 9) follows Vallini (1969) in counting in the *Mémoire* 67 references to Brugmann and 90 scholars quoted, out of whom 83 were German. This fact perhaps explains the misunderstanding. Brugmann was of course right in saying that Saussure had learned much from him and from the other Leipzig scholars; so much is more than acknowledged in the bibliographical references of the *Mémoire* and it emerges clearly from the contrast between the information (or lack of information) contained in the first papers published in the *Mémoires de la Société de linguistique* and the later ones. Yet whether Saussure had learned the new data and new techniques from written works or from word of mouth remains obscure. On the other hand, Saussure was obsessed by the idea of priority and by the fear of being accused of plagiarism, all the more so since he knew full well that most of his new views in the *Mémoire* were his own even when, as in the case of vocalic nasals, they had already been published by others. Brugmann in his turn was right in noting the difference between Saussure's silence and the standard system of acknowledgements to teachers and colleagues which appeared in all German dissertations. And indeed in a hierarchical set up such as that of German universities, this lack of conventional propriety must have looked arrogant and perhaps irritating. But the important point is that neither Saussure nor Brugmann are talking about theoretical or methodological divergences; Saussure and Osthoff violently disagreed about Ablaut, but as late as 1914 Brugmann clearly believed that in the great neogrammarians' controversy which saw Curtius and the older generation attacked by himself as well as Leskien, Osthoff and others, Saussure was on their side. The question is whether in fact he was.

Saussure as a neogrammarian?

A few principles which formed the main tenets of the neogrammarians have been listed above, and the list may perhaps be repeated with some additions, albeit in telegraphic style: uniformitarianism, i.e. the assumption that the same causes determined language change at all stages; antiorganicism, i.e. rejection of the views held by August Schleicher (1821–68), and partially shared by Georg Curtius, according to which language was an independent organism which developed according to laws of its own independently of the speakers; priority of linguistic history over comparison; the need to test the historical method on attested rather than reconstructed languages; the regularity of sound change; the importance of analogy. Paradoxically the 'mechanical' sound laws, strongly proposed by the neogrammarians in their fight against their predecessors answered to the same need as was served by Schleicher's organicism. Both the sound laws and Schleicher's organicism were meant to account for those regular forms of linguistic change which happened without the speakers being aware of them. (On the neogrammarians see e.g. Jankowsky, 1972, Einhauser, 1989 and Graffi, 1988.)

As has been seen, there is no reason to suppose that Saussure disagreed with any of these views; indeed Saussure ([1903] 1960: 15) praises Leipzig as a major centre of Indo-European linguistics. Later on in the same text Saussure stated that he did not consider analogy as a German methodological novelty, since it was something which he had always known about. For him 'le fait étonnant' was the phonetic fact, i.e. the regularity principle. 'One must approach linguistics, without the shadow of an observation or a thought to put on the same footing a phenomenon such as phonetic laws – which cannot be observed by individual experience – and the analogical action which everyone has experienced since childhood on his own behalf. *Montre moutonnièreté des Allemands*' (1960: 24f.). In spite of the outburst this is enough to confirm that Saussure accepted both phonetic laws and analogy. It also shows, incidentally, that Saussure, largely self-taught as he was, at that stage had not grasped the importance of the fight for analogy, which was in essence a uniformitarian and anti-organicistic fight by those who had been brought up to believe that 'false analogy' did not apply to the earliest stages of language or, more correctly, of Indo-European, and that all language change was unconscious and predetermined. The conclusion must be that Saussure shared most of the neogrammarians' assumptions but presumably, as in everything else, he had reached most of them on his own. There is one difference, however, which must be stressed. The *Junggrammatiker* seemed convinced that their set of principles amounted to a fully fledged linguistic theory, whereas Saussure did not delude himself that their set of principles provided anything even vaguely similar to a full theory of how language (*langage*) works.

Forms of continuity: Saussure as 'l'homme des fondements' and language as a system

We asked above whether there is a link between the historical comparative work of the *Mémoire* and related papers on the one hand and the theoretical work which is summarised in the *Cours* on the other. In other words, were there one or two Saussures?

Emile Benveniste, perhaps the only linguist who came nearer to Saussure in his ability to rethink everything afresh and to move between theory, history and reconstruction, called Saussure 'l'homme des fondements' who looked for the general characteristics underlying the diversity of empirical data (Benveniste, 1963: 8). It is indeed true that the *Mémoire* tackles the fundamental questions: what are the basic distinctive phonological elements? How do they function in the phonological and morphological system? Kuryłowicz (1978: 7f.), one of the greatest Indo-Europeanists of the following generation, saw in the *Mémoire* the first appearance of a new point of view, the hierarchy principle which eventually came to dominate modern structuralism; the elements of a language do not exist next to each other but thanks to each other. Watkins (1978: 60ff.) drew attention to the fact that Saussure in later years referred to his first book as to the *Système des voyelles*: there is little doubt that the historical comparative work by Saussure is dominated by the concepts of system, of distinctive characters, of contrast. This is indeed the *fondement* of which Benveniste speaks. It is of course also the leitmotiv of the *Cours* and of the theoretical work. Reichler-Béguelin (1990) has brilliantly highlighted the similarities between the glottological essay written by the fourteen-year-old and the *Mémoire*. In the first case, as she argues, Saussure aims at showing that the existing roots can all be linked to a much simpler underlying system; there is an apparent evolutionary assumption (the simple roots evolve into the attested ones), but in fact we are dealing with a sort of achronic classification where a strong level of abstraction (all labials treated as one sound, etc.) produces a 'satisfactory' account. For the *Mémoire* the position is different. In contrast with the standard view according to which the parent language had an [a] vowel which in the European languages split into two or three vowels, Saussure follows Brugmann and others in assuming that the two or three vowels had merged in Sanskrit. The result is a remarkable alteration of the morphology and morphophonology; if the theory of *coefficient sonantiques* is added, i.e. if we accept Saussure's conclusions, then the morphology and the morphophonology (the pattern of root alternations) become simple and crystal clear. The new version is both historically valid, i.e. assumptions are made about the earlier existence of surface forms such as those postulated, and in a sense synchronically valid in that it can provide a set of synchronically underlying forms; it 'explains' or 'accounts for' the functioning of the system. It is clear what the import of this is for the general question of the two Saussures. The discovery of *fondements* turns out to be a discovery of underlying structures and underlying systems. This is the characteristic of the earlier and later papers and of the *Mémoire*. But this is also the method that we recognise in the theoretical work. (Countering the accusations of atomism directed against Saussure's conception of diachrony see Saussure, 1972 and Reichler-Béguelin, 1980.)

Linguistic description and terminology

There is more. One of the most famous statements left unpublished by Saussure is found in a letter to Meillet (Benveniste, 1964: 95), probably written in 1894 when he was working on Lithuanian accentuation, and lamenting the fact that his 'historical pleasure' is constantly interrupted by the inadequacy of current terminology and the pressing need to reform it: 'Sans cesse l'ineptie absolue de la terminologie courante, la nécessité de la reforme, et de montrer pour cela quelle espèce d'objet est la langue en général, vient gâter mon plaisir historique, quoique je n'aie pas de plus cher voeu que de n'avoir pas à m'occuper de la langue en général.' This need for definition, for a terminology which is actually consistent and explicit, is typical of Saussure's *modus operandi* at all stages. In the essay written when he was fourteen, he had introduced two new terms; the same need for a 'correct' terminology emerges in the *Mémoire* and in all the historical-comparative papers. It is of course characteristic of the *Cours* too.

Saussure and abstract analysis

The systemic nature of Saussure's historical work, its emphasis on structure, has often been stressed and naturally this has been linked to the explicit contrast between synchrony and diachrony and the assumption that any systemic account of language requires a synchronic study. However, all too often the concealed agenda behind such observations is the desire to underline the contrast between Saussure and his contemporaries. On the one hand are the atomistic neogrammarians or their predecessors, strictly concerned with petty details of developments studied in isolation, on the other Saussure, the man with a global vision who exercises it equally in his historical and his theoretical work. At least for the early period this scenario is due to a misunderstanding. The distinction between synchronic and diachronic is well known (e.g. in Paul's work). Nor was there anything 'atomistic' in works like those of Verner or Brugmann which aimed at reconstructing an earlier phonological system and the way in which it operated. Similarly there is no form of atomism in theoretical accounts such as those by Hermann Paul, the author of the *Principien der Sprachgeschichte* (1880) which was considered the bible of the neogrammarians. On the contrary, the prevailing psychologism was in essence anti-atomistic. The real difference between Saussure and the neogrammarians is elsewhere. The neogrammarians were far more interested in questions of method and theory than their immediate predecessors; indeed they had noisily requested an explicit account of the principles which determined historical and comparative work. Their insistence on a strict adherence to the regularity principle was among other things a request for a consistent and explicit discovery procedure. However, they were far less aware than Saussure of how much they took for granted in linguistic analysis, and in most instances they were content with adopting the traditional analyses and descriptions without challenging them. They also differed from Saussure in their style of argumentation and in their attitude to abstraction. While in the *Mémoire* and elsewhere Saussure was prepared to produce an analysis of morphology and morphophonemics and then test it on the data – hence the mathematical and deductive style of his procedure – the neogrammarians much preferred an explicitly inductive approach; they started with long lists of data and tried to identify any patterns that emerged.[6] And while Saussure's analysis led, as we have seen, to the identification of underlying structures which in a sense provided that 'classification logique' of the linguistic facts which he was aiming at, the neogrammarians were not prepared to accept that level of abstraction either in linguistic description or in the study of linguistic development.

A final puzzle

The letter to Meillet quoted above reveals Saussure's dissatisfaction with the state of the subject; other remarks in the same letter and elsewhere reiterate the same sentiments. The dissatisfaction is both with the state of the subject and, one feels, with himself. He explains to Meillet that he will have to write, without enthusiasm or passion, a book where he will explain why there is not a single term used in linguistics which has any sense. Only after that will he be able to return to historical work. It is likely that we shall never know what exactly determined Saussure's 'thirty years of silence' (health problems may have played a part), but a further problem should be mentioned. To judge from the odd observations in letters or biographical accounts (such as the letter of 1903 meant for Streitberg), Saussure felt all his life that his work was not understood or not quoted or not appreciated. To be told by Hübschmann that Brugmann had discovered the vocalic nasals, when he knew that he had done so when still at school, clearly hurt even a quarter of a century after the event. To find that Gustav Mayer in his *Griechische Grammatik* (1880) used data and results published in the *Mémoire* without an explicit quotation was equally a reason for severe disappointment (Saussure, [1903] 1960: 23). The question which comes to mind concerns the link between the findings of the *Mémoire* and of the other historical-comparative papers and Saussure's general scepticism about linguistic work. Put more bluntly, Saussure's disappointment in the reception of his work, his need to establish his priority in order to avoid the accusation of plagiarism, implies complete faith in the validity of that work. How is this to be reconciled with the assumption that nothing is known about the nature or essence of language? In the letter to Meillet he explained that the only thing he still found interesting was the picturesque and ethnographic side of language (Benveniste, 1964: 95). This remark has rightly been adduced to explain some of the etymological work (Vallini, 1978: 114f.). However, the subject matter of the *Mémoire* and of most of the other papers belongs to the structural and not to the picturesque side of language. Should we resort to the simple explanation that nobody likes being slighted or plagiarised and Saussure was no exception, even if he had stopped believing in his work? Is this not too facile an account? Let us not forget Saussure's wish, also mentioned in the letter to Meillet, to be able to return to his work. The conclusion must be that Saussure was convinced that what he had done was quite simply novel and 'right'. For the historian of linguistics interested in Saussure's historical work the problem is crucial. But there is also an odd twist in the inquiry. One of the manuscript notes by Saussure recently discovered (and undated) returns to the question of the beginnings of linguistics (Saussure, 2002: 129–31). The school founded by Bopp, we are told, was interested in *la langue* or *l'idiome*, i.e. the set of manifestations of language (*langage)* at a certain time in a certain people; it did not consider language (*langage*) as a phenomenon or the application of a mental faculty. It is now accused of having misunderstood the essence of the object which it pretended to study. But in fact, Saussure continues, this is to attribute arbitrarily to that school a mission which it had no intention of undertaking and which many of its followers would no doubt have rejected. 'In fact it is the object that has changed and without realising it a different discipline has taken the place of the previous one. In doing so it has sought to condemn its predecessor, without having necessarily guaranteed its own legitimacy' (Saussure, 2002: 131). This is an important point and it opens new forms of historiographical inquiry. However, we miss a vital link. How did Saussure envisage his own historical work? Did it belong to the discipline founded by Bopp or to the new discipline which had replaced it? If the former, the puzzle with which we started would be solved.

2 The Paris years

Carol Sanders

> Saussure did not arrive in Paris from Leipzig and Berlin with the ideas that generated the *Cours de linguistique générale*, and he did not leave Paris without them. (Aarsleff, 1982: 393)

Underlying this chapter is the assumption that, in charting the history of ideas, it is important to situate them broadly in their contemporary intellectual context. In contrast to many commentators who sought the origin of some of the ideas contained in the *Cours* in the work of early German linguists, the intellectual historian Hans Aarsleff has insisted on the role of the 'Paris milieu' in shaping Saussure's ideas. This is not to deny the influence of the German comparative tradition, particularly on his dissertation or *mémoire.* While history and comparative linguistics remained an abiding interest for Saussure, it is nonetheless the theory of a systematic, synchronic linguistics as it appears in the *Cours de linguistique générale* which marks the beginning of European linguistics and which helped to launch structuralism in a wider arena. It is possible to argue that the young Saussure was already going beyond his German masters, with the ideas of language as a system, and of the phoneme as a concept if not a term, being embryonically present in the *mémoire*. Nevertheless, the ideas that would be published in the *Cours* were already shaped and articulated in his Paris lectures, according to Meillet. In order to understand developments in the study of language at the end of the nineteenth century, and the evolution of Saussure's own ideas and their subsequent impact, we shall look first at the discipline of linguistics as he found it on his arrival in Paris in the Autumn of 1880, and then at other disciplines, in line with Aarsleff's claim that 'The innovation begun by Bréal during the 1860s formed part of a broad movement in French intellectual life during the latter half of the nineteenth century' (1982: 310).

The linguistic context

Nineteenth-century German linguistics, in which Saussure had been trained in Leipzig and Berlin, was essentially historical (or 'diachronic'). In the case of the comparative grammarians, and their successors, the neogrammarians, this meant the study of the evolution of forms in related language families (see chapter 1). When Saussure arrived in Paris, it could be said that there were two schools – or at least strands – of linguistics, each of which was indebted in its own way to German comparative grammar. The adherents to what has been called 'la linguistique naturaliste' had their base at the Sorbonne and published in the *Revue de Linguistique et Philologie comparée*. They closely followed German linguists such as Schleicher in his Darwinist portrayal of languages as natural organisms, some of which are superior to others. Hovelacque in his *La linguistique* (1876: 9), sums up the organicist view: 'Les langues . . . naissent, croissent, dépérissent et meurent comme tous les êtres vivants' ('Languages . . . are born, grow, decay and die like all living beings'). Interestingly, in the same work (p. 33), Hovelacque refers to the faculty of language as being distinct from any individual's actual use of it, demonstrating that, out of the threefold terminology that would be developed by Saussure, the notion of *faculté du langage* was common currency, while that of *parole* was perhaps implicit but could not be logically and fully articulated without the Saussurean concept of *langue* (see chapters in this volume by Normand, Gordon and Bouquet). Although the main representative of the other strand, Michel Bréal, was even more familiar with the German comparativists, he nevertheless distanced himself from them and developed a more particularly French perspective. While there was some professional rivalry between members of the two schools, Bréal and Saussure maintained close and cordial relations with many of their colleagues at the Sorbonne. In an invited article written for the journal of the 'opposing camp' (*Revue de philologie*, 1 January 1878), Bréal attempts to minimise the differences between the 'philologists' and the 'linguists' (the latter used in this case to refer to the comparative grammarians, i.e. those who studied the bare phonological and morphological bones of language as opposed to those who studied language in its literary texts). There is no doubt about where Saussure's affiliation lay: as a graduate student in Leipzig, he had already come to give a paper at the *Société de linguistique de Paris*, frequented by Bréal and like-minded linguists, and the records show that once he was living in Paris, he attended meetings of the society regularly and assisted Bréal as *secrétaire adjoint*. Bréal is sometimes considered as the 'institutional' founder of linguistics in France, since he was responsible for setting up the subject at the Ecole Pratique des Hautes Etudes, and for establishing the first Phonetics Laboratory. Saussure was appointed to his post by Bréal and worked with him for the ten years he was in Paris. Bracketed together by Aarsleff (1982), they are also cited as the two founding fathers of French linguistics by Meillet (1916). Certainly, Bréal is not only an innovatory and interesting linguist in his own right, but also affords a valuable insight into the intellectual climate within which Saussure worked during his Paris years. We shall spend some time looking at his contribution, because this can help us to understand why it is the *CLG* and not the work of any other linguist such as Bréal that is taken to mark the beginnings of structuralism in Europe.

At a time when German universities were still considered to be the centre of language study, Bréal introduced into France the work of the German scholars in his translation of one of its seminal works, Bopp's volumes on comparative grammar. In his inaugural lecture to the Collège de France, Bréal outlines the importance of adopting Bopp's rigorous approach, but he distances himself from what he considers to be the latter's narrow view of language, with its sole emphasis on the evolution of forms, as well as from Bopp's predecessor, Schleicher, with his generalisations about the superiority of certain languages and his strong form of Darwinism, strangely allied to a sort of Romantic mysticism. We have seen that for much of the nineteenth century the prevailing metaphor, which came to be taken more and more literally, compared language to natural organisms with their cycles of growth and decay. Sound change was considered to follow blindly its own 'laws', claimed by the youngest group of German linguists, the 'neogrammarians', to be without exceptions. Thus, little attention was paid to function and meaning and in so far as the relationship between language and thought was broached at all, the implicit assumption was that language 'clothed' pre-existing thought.

For Bréal, whose view of language was in complete contrast to this, language exists for communication ('le but, en matière de langage, c'est d'être compris', Bréal, 1897: 7; 'The goal of Language is to be understood', Bréal, 1900: 7). Human intervention is apparent, even in the evolution of the phonology and morphology of a language, and the fact that language is first and foremost a social activity involving speaker and listener should always be borne in mind when analysing linguistic forms. Bréal's conception of language as firmly rooted in its social context is one which had long been present in the French intellectual tradition. For example, one view of language as a social institution, an idea which is present in the *CLG*, had been articulated in the eighteenth century by the philosopher Destutt de Tracy. The related concept of language as social interaction is not fully developed in Saussure, partly because of the incomplete nature of his work. Bréal, on the other hand, highlights language functions in a way that foreshadows pragmatics. Ever the practitioner, Bréal urges teachers to analyse authentic language. Bréal was also strongly committed to the application of the language sciences to education. As a school inspector, he recommended a sort of 'direct method' of language learning: associating vocabulary with pictures of the object, and learning structures by repetition and use rather than on the basis of rules. He concerns himself with spelling reform, a highly controversial subject in France at the end of the nineteenth century, to which he advocates a moderate approach. He strongly refutes Schleicher's idea that some languages are more 'primitive' than others. Advising teachers to draw on the children's knowledge of 'patois' to teach about language variation and even etymology, he defends the equality of languages: 'Even the humblest patois is subjected, all things being equal, to the same intellectual laws as is the French of Pascal or Descartes' (Bréal, 1991: 209).

The majority of French linguists (from both schools of thought to which we have referred) rejected the German quasi-mystical equation of language with race. This rejection is attributed by Bergounioux (1984) to the Jewish origin of many of these scholars (Bréal, Darmesteter, Halévy), who were writing at a time when they had begun to feel accepted as a full part of educated French society while retaining a Jewish cultural and religious heritage. In the article quoted above, Bréal derides the German conception, reminding us that one of the greatest Latin writers, Terence, was born a Berber. Bréal speaks out too against the extreme nationalism that promotes prejudice either side of a highly controlled border (no doubt at that time partly with Alsace in mind). The same lack of xenophobia characterises his article entitled 'Qu'appelle-t-on pureté de la langue?' (Bréal, 1881), in which he points out that languages have always been enriched by borrowings from other languages. A language is threatened less by loan-words, claims Bréal, than by pseudo-scientific terms and also by the devaluing of words by the overuse of superlative expressions. In an article published in 1879 and entitled 'La science du langage', Bréal demonstrates with some prescience that 'les annonces sont une des causes qui exercent une influence pernicieuse sur les mots' ('advertising affords an example of pernicious influence on words', Bréal, 1991: 134).

These are just some of the 'advanced' ideas that would have been enough to guarantee Bréal a place in the history of linguistics. However, it is chiefly as the founder of semantics that he is known today. His *Essai de sémantique*, published in 1897 but based on decades of work, is sometimes described as a book on general linguistics, and certainly challenges two of the basic tenets of mid-nineteenth-century German linguistics. Firstly, it consolidates Bréal's view that meaning is as important as form in language, and secondly, it attributes a role to 'human will' (*la volonté humaine*) as opposed to blind linguistic change, and thereby redresses the balance against those who saw the study of language as a natural rather than a predominantly human science: 'The Science of Language expresses man to himself... It must surely, then, amaze the thinking reader to be told that man counts for nothing, and that words – both in form and meaning – live a life peculiar to themselves' (Bréal, 1900: 2–3).

Despite Bréal's 'modern' views, including some references to the notion of *valeur*, he fails to take the next logical step, which would be to study meaning from a synchronic perspective. Although in his *Essai de sémantique*, Bréal discusses some of the main categories relevant to semantic description, he almost always exemplifies what he is saying with historical examples. In order to deal with the way in which meaning operates and evolves, he uses both existing categories and new ones. Among the former are, for example, metaphoric usage, *l'épaississement du sens* ('the concretion of meaning', Bréal, 1900: 134) and analogy. Analogy was a category much used by historical linguists, but Bréal marks his distance from his predecessors ('it is a mistake to represent Analogy as a cause. Analogy is nothing more than a means', Bréal, 1900: 60). Most interesting from our point of view is the term *polysémie* (one 'word' with multiple meanings), which was coined by Bréal and described in a chapter that brings together many strands of his approach to language. His explanation of the way in which the listener identifies the relevant meaning of a word involves both the concept of the listener as the mirror image of the speaker and as an active part of the 'circuit du langage' (as Saussure will call it, *CLG*: 27). It also draws on the cross-fertilisation that was taking place in the late nineteenth century between the two emergent disciplines of linguistics and psychology. Victor Egger's book *La parole intérieure* to which Bréal makes reference is of interest in that it uses the concept of *parole* to refer to the individual use of language in thought, taking it beyond the more common usage of 'spoken language'. Starting once more from the idea of polysemy, Bréal writes:

> It is not even necessary to suppress the other meanings of the word: these meanings do not impinge on us, they do not cross the threshold of our awareness . . . for the association of ideas is based on the sense of things not on their sound.
>
> What we say about speakers is no less true about listeners. These are in the same situation: their thought runs along with or precedes that of their interlocutor. They speak inwardly at the same time as we do: so they are no more likely than we are to be troubled by related meanings dormant in the depths of their minds. (Trans. of Bréal, 1897: 146)

Bréal seems to be working with an implicit and embryonic version of what would become the Saussurean concepts of *langue* and *parole*. Indeed, the metaphorical description of *langue* as a treasure (cf. *CLG*: 30) is present in Bréal's writings: 'Une langue bien faite . . . est un de ces trésors . . . que nous tenons de nos pères' ('A well-constructed language is . . . an invaluable gift . . . which we owe to our ancestors', Bréal, 1991: 151). Even more central to Bréal's semantics is the notion of *valeur*, which will be a key concept in the *CLG*. Ultimately, and despite their debt to German scholars, both Bréal and Saussure are marked by the French intellectual tradition. In the eighteenth-century French (and English) philosophers to whom Bréal pays homage, we find some of the concepts that resurface in late nineteenth-century French linguistics. Locke, Condillac and others referred to language as a system of signs, though not in as elaborated a way as Saussure (see Joseph in this volume). Bréal, too, distinguishes between the word and the sign. Of polysemy caused by the abbreviation of a word or compound, he writes: 'This is because the meaning of the two words having combined, they then form just a single sign: a sign may be broken, clipped, reduced by half; as long as it is recognisable, it still fulfils the same function' (trans. of Bréal, 1897: 152).

This idea of 'office' or function brings us to the distinction between meaning and value. The notion of *valeur* is present in Bréal in his exploration of *polysémie*: 'As a new meaning is given to a word, this word seems to multiply and to produce new versions, similar in form, but different in value' (Bréal, 1900: 139).

In *Essai de sémantique* it can be seen that Bréal is outlining and using certain concepts that will be central to semantics and indeed to linguistics in general; with his ideas of value, function and context, he seems to be close to seeing language as a synchronic system. Yet in the same writings we can see that he never takes the final step. Despite his aspirations to the contrary, he never fully shakes off a diachronic (historical) approach, and almost every example of meaning in context leads to a discussion of etymology. Polysemy caused by abbreviation, for example, is illustrated with several contemporary examples (everyone in France reading *le Cabinet*, for instance, knows that it means *le Cabinet des ministres*), immediately followed by the example of the etymology of *prince* (from *princeps senatus*), thus ensuring that the distinction between the evolution of the language and its current functioning remains blurred. Indeed, the quotation above is preceded by the comment: 'The new meaning, whatever it may be, does not put an end to the old. Both exist side by side' (trans. of Bréal, 1879: 143). While an acknowledgement of this continuity in the evolution of language and of the historical 'baggage' that accompanies every word is important (and it is what Bakhtine accuses Saussure of neglecting, cf. Hutchings in this volume), Bréal fails to see what Saussure so clearly explains in the *CLG*, that is, the methodological necessity of separating the synchronic and the diachronic. Put another way, while the history of a language is of course an important object of study (and it was Saussure's abiding interest), the way in which language actually functions, the way in which our utterances manage to mean something to the listener, needs to be studied independently of that history. As the competent speaker of a language, I am aware of the multiple meanings of a word, and I can appreciate a word's various connotations – archaic, poetic or other – without recourse to its etymology. It comes as no surprise, then, when Bréal, in complete contrast to Saussure, insists that language is *not* a system. Already in an article on spelling reform published in 1889 in the *Revue des deux mondes*, Bréal was both so close to, and so far from, the Saussurean idea of system:

> A language is not, as is too often assumed, a system. Nor is it, as is too often repeated nowadays, an organism. It is a collection of signs, of different ages and from different sources, which have accumulated over the centuries . . . A given language is a hereditary possession which each age cultivates, adapts and transforms according to its needs and its means: the true historical method would be to adhere to the latest linguistic state, so that we could understand its formation and could in turn use it to greatest advantage. (Bréal, 1991: 189–90)

While it has to be borne in mind that this was written in the context of the debate about spelling reform, where one of the main arguments for retaining existing spelling is that it creates a link with the history of the language, it is still hard to ignore the internal contradictions inherent in these comments. If language is not, according to the Schleicherian paradigm still being promoted by Hovelacque in late nineteenth-century Paris, a living – and dying – organism, and neither does it constitute a system at any one moment in time, then the reader feels entitled to ask: what in fact is it? More importantly, Bréal comes once more close to the idea of synchronic system, by speaking of language as a 'hereditary possession' and by implying that the true study of language is that of the latest *état de langue*. He fails to see, however, that this cannot be reconciled with his idea of language as nothing more that an unsystematic rag-bag of items thrown together from different ages.

Bréal's elegant writings, the result of many years of teaching and of thinking through some of the central problems of linguistics, are numerous and complete. In this respect, at least, the comparison with Saussure is apt. In terms of their view of language, the two have a good deal in common, and there are times when Saussure seems to echo Bréal – picking up, for example, Bréal's reference to those who portray language as a 'quatrième règne de la nature' ('fourth natural realm', Bréal, 1991: 51; *CLG*: 17; 'fourth natural kingdom', *CGL*-B: 4). Most thinkers, however innovatory, tend to be a blend of old and new, and this is true of both Bréal and Saussure to some degree. However, there is a significant difference between them: unlike Bréal, Saussure fully appreciated the implications of seeing language as a synchronic system, and his new conception of the linguistic sign marked an advance on that of previous philosophers and linguists.

It is worth signalling the existence of one other 'independent' linguist. Victor Henry, in whom critical interest has increased recently, also represents a sort of half-way house between nineteenth- and twentieth-century linguistics (see Puech, 2003b). He speaks of language as at once a social and psychic fact, as does Saussure, and the Kantian-sounding title to his book *Antinomies linguistiques* reflects the fact that he too explores some of the dichotomies and apparent logical contradictions with which the linguist is faced. While his rejection of the organicist model is spoken of approvingly by Bréal, Henry still regards sound change as mechanical in the neogrammarian fashion. Like many thinkers of his time, Henry wrestles with the need to ascertain the role of the unconscious in human behaviour. Stating that the ultimate *antimonie* is that 'le langage se confond absolument avec la pensée' ('language is absolutely indistinguishable from thought'), he reaches the compromise that: 'Le langage est le produit de l'activité inconsciente d'un subject conscient' ('Language is the product of the unconscious activity of a conscious subject', Henry, 1896: 65). In his lectures, he reportedly refined this further, distinguishing between unconscious sound change, semi-conscious grammatical and analogical change, and the conscious and deliberate creation of neologisms (Desmet, 1994). Towards the end of his career, Henry, like Saussure, became interested in the phenomenon of glossolalia (speaking in tongues). Observing the case of a woman speaking what he thought to be Martian, he declares that the ability of humans to engage in genuine language-like behaviour when in a state of dream or trance proves that language operations are themselves manipulated unconsciously (Henry, 1901). In a letter to Meillet, Saussure mentions that, although he did not know Henry well, he had some correspondence with him (*Cahiers F. de Saussure*, 21: 90–130, 1964).

The wider intellectual context

As a brilliant scholar appointed at a young age to a post at the Ecole Pratique des Hautes Etudes, Saussure was part of the expansion of French higher education. Between 1881 and 1900, the number of academics in higher education in France doubled (Charle, 1990: 38), and the student population of the recently formed faculties of Arts and of Sciences grew to about 6,000 in each between the 1880s and 1914 (Lough, 1978: 215). One of the beneficiaries was the newly emergent discipline of linguistics, with the appointment of young scholars contributing to breaking the traditional mould in which language and literary studies went hand in hand. The mood was buoyant: linguists such as Bréal and Gaston Paris were active members of a higher education society which called for the wholesale modernisation of higher education, in keeping with the belief of Renan (1871) that intellectual renewal was needed in the wake of France's defeat by Germany (cf. Bergounioux, 1984). Institutional changes have their part to play in intellectual history; the role played by 'intellectuals' in France was a growing one, as was the public role of the scientist (see Paul, 1987). Just as German comparative grammar had been able to flourish partly because its development coincided with that of the German university system (Amsterdamska, 1987), so too in the second half of the nineteenth century a combination of institutional and intellectual factors facilitated the burgeoning of a particular approach to the study of language in French-speaking universities. Among the intellectual factors were the decreasing influence of positivism that had held sway through the influence of Compte, Taine, Renan and others, and the revival of interest in certain aspects of eighteenth-century philosophy. Thinkers such as Taine were anxious to establish a 'scientific' basis for their disciplines. For linguists like Bréal and Saussure the reservations expressed about the analogy of language and a natural organism by no means implied a rejection of all scientific comparisons. Even more important, perhaps, in situating these linguists within contemporary currents is the emergence of the disciplines that would come to make up the 'social sciences'.

It is not possible to refer to all the French thinkers who contributed to the interdisciplinary richness of the second half of the nineteenth century, but Taine, described by Aarsleff (1982: 365) as the 'ruling intellectual influence', is of interest for a number of reasons. He sought to extend the method of the natural sciences to the social and moral sciences, speaking of systems and of structures as being made up of interrelated parts, after the example of the anatomist Cuvier. At the same time, he was one of those responsible for a renewed interest in the eighteenth-century rationalists, creating what in 1897 the sociologist Durkheim called 'l'empirisme rationaliste'. He made a major contribution to the study of history (*Essais de critique et d'histoire* 1858), as well to art and literature. He ranks as one of the founders of psychology in France, his writings linking experimental psychology to philosophy, and combining the empirical and the theoretical, in a way that would characterise much work in the French social sciences – to the incomprehension of many English-speaking thinkers. The only article of his that focuses specifically on language is on child language acquisition, and a translation of this in the English journal *Mind* inspired Darwin to write up his notes on the subject for a subsequent number of the same journal. However, Taine's more general but seminal *De l'intelligence* is of great interest to the linguist. This two-volume work, first published in 1870, begins with a chapter on signs, in which words are placed alongside other types of signs. However, it would be left to Saussure to make the all-important distinction between arbitrary and non-arbitrary sign systems, which would later prove central to semiology. The insight that the word stands for the *idea* that we have of something rather than the 'thing' itself (i.e. Saussure's *signifié*) is to be found in Taine, as well as in Humboldt, Locke, and others. What Taine is missing is the concept of *signifiant*, that is the mental image of the word. *De l'intelligence* is primarily an early work on psychology, and its main focus is concept formation and our knowledge of general ideas ('la connaissance des choses générales'). In his discussion of this, Taine refers to physical sensation and its counterpart in the central nervous system as 'un seul et même évènement à deux faces, l'une mentale, l'autre physique, l'une accessible à la conscience, l'autre accessible aux sens' (1870, vol.1: 329). This 'one and the same two-sided phenomenon, one side mental, the other physical, one accessible to the mind, the other to the senses' is compared by some with Saussure's description of the two sides of the sign (cf. *CLG:* 99). Even closer perhaps to Saussure's thinking is Taine's comment on the inseparability of language and thought (cf. *CLG*: 156): 'There is no thought without words, any more than there are words without thought. . . . If I may explain my view with a homely example, they resemble an orange and its rind' (1882: 386).

In his study of history, Taine distinguishes between the study of successive and simultaneous events in a way that is sometimes said to foreshadow Saussure's synchronic/diachronic distinction; moreover, he sees the human person as being constituted by a 'system', not a 'heap' of random scraps. Taine's definition of the great forces in history as the sum of individual actions is seen by Aarsleff as the precursor to Saussure's idea of *parole*, although the essential ingredient of *langue* seems to be missing in Taine's use of *valeur*. Taine draws on the idea of value in order to compare different periods in the history of art, and, in talking about language, to explain that the terms *Dieu, Gott, God* do not function as identical concepts in their respective languages. As with Bréal, it is as though Taine is attempting to use *valeur* as a concept without developing the notion of system, of which it has to be an integral part.

There is no direct evidence that Saussure read Taine, although similarities such as those mentioned above are felt by Aarsleff to be proof enough. Like Taine, Saussure has a propensity to use metaphors and similes from the natural sciences, but this is scarcely proof of knowledge of Taine's works. Even if we discount the popularity of the scientific turn of mind at the end of the nineteenth century, we have to remember that Saussure came from a family of scientists, and was initially obliged by his father to enrol as a student of natural sciences at the University of Geneva. Rather than arguing for an unproven influence, it may be more profitable simply to accept that Taine's ideas were so all-pervasive in nineteenth-century France and so well assimilated into various disciplines, that it is inevitable that some of the same concerns will crop up in Saussure. The concept of 'influence' being a contentious one anyway, what interests us here is to explore the extent to which Saussure was imbued with the ideas of his time and the manner in which he made something new of them.

Aarsleff also suggests (1982: 360) that Taine 'gave primary impulses to naturalism in literature and to impressionism in painting'. It is certainly true that between these major movements of the second half of the nineteenth century and developments in psychology, science, sociology and linguistics, there were considerable points of contact. Indeed, certain new departures in linguistics, such as approaches to language variation and to the relation between language and thought, or the relation between form and function, find a parallel in the literature and social sciences of the time, in ways to which we can only allude briefly here.

First of all, two major tenets of modern linguistics, that the main object of study is the synchronic language system, and, secondly, that all language varieties are worthy of study, have their origins in the late nineteenth century. It was then that serious dialectological research got underway. Gilliéron, a Swiss dialectologist whose *Atlas linguistique de la France* is cited in the *CLG* (276) as the model for linguistic cartography, taught at the Ecole Pratique des Hautes Etudes at the same time as Saussure. In terms of social variation, one of the first studies of colloquial working-class speech, conducted by Nisard, appeared in 1872. These developments find a counterpoint in literature, with the attempt to portray the life and language of the working classes in the 'naturalist' novels of Emile Zola. As Zola himself recognised, his 'crime' in the eyes of the bourgeoisie was that he used the language of the people. That old attitudes died hard is apparent from the fact that A. Darmesteter (whose memory has survived for his *La vie des mots, étudiés dans leur significations* 1886), was obliged, when defending his thesis on the formation of compound words at the Sorbonne in 1877, to withdraw certain colloquial examples, including that of the word 'soulographie' which is found in the novels of Zola.

It is true to say that when Saussure arrived in Paris in 1880, a reaction was setting in against the dominant positivist philosophy and its faith in rationalism and progress, and against realism–naturalism in literature and art. The realist novel would continue to be an important force, but would at the same time be challenged by writers seeking to escape from materialism, whether in the *fin-de-siècle* 'decadent' novel or in Catholic writing. However, it was particularly from poetry that the challenge came: Mallarmé, and then Valéry, stressed form and composition, and foregrounded the language of poetry. While their use of language and their thoughts on it are of course those of poets and not those of linguists, there are some striking parallels between the tenets of the *CLG* and the practice of writers from the Symbolists to the Surrealists, as if the radical shift in the study of language found an echo in the beginnings of literary Modernism. In the case of Mallarmé and Valéry, both writers subscribe to a belief in the inseparability of language and thought, and to the conviction that the form can create the content. Instead of considering that language clothes thought as did many in the nineteenth century (with Bréal's metaphor of language as a glass through which we see more or less clearly as a sort of half-way house), they believe with Saussure that language defines thought (*CLG*: 155). Valéry starts to write with a 'détail de langage' which suggests to him the subject of his poem (1945 CXXIX: 910). Moreover, both Mallarmé and Valéry invigorate language and seek to extend its powers of expression, Mallarmé by challenging conventional syntax and Valéry in numerous ways, including his use of metric form. Mallarmé, as a teacher of English (and author of *Les mots anglais*) has an obvious concern with language, although as a poet he is as much concerned with the mystery of words and their power to enchant. More than Mallarmé, it is Valéry, in his Notebooks (*Cahiers*), who reflects at length on language in ways that remind us of some of his linguist contemporaries. As well as his desire to systematise and to reach a mathematical denotation, he shows a modern interest in the pragmatic aspects of language. Valéry is both theorist and practitioner of language: among other things, he wrote a review of Bréal's *Essai de sémantique*. Although there is no proof of direct Saussurean influence, Wunderli, in his book *Valéry saussurien*, sketches the parallels and differences between the two. From a drawing in the *Cahiers* (9/417, 1923) it appears that Valéry worked with a model of human communication that is strikingly similar to the 'circuit de la parole' (*CLG*: 22). However, when Valéry refers to the sign, he favours not Saussure's 'two-sided' model, but a tripartite one favoured by many philosophers (see chapter by Joseph). Valéry refers to the potentiality of language, and to a distinction between *langage* and *parole*: Mallarmé and Flaubert, he writes, both tried to base 'l'art sur le langage . . . et non sur la parole, qui est le langage considéré sur les lèvres' ('art on language . . . and not on speech, which is language as observed on lips', *Cahiers* V: 203). When writing about Zola, Mallarmé had spoken of capturing the relationships between things: 'ce sont les fils de ces rapports qui forment les vers et les orchestres' ('it is of the networks of these relationships that poems and orchestras are made') – and it is the networks of relationships that create language also, he could have added. In his Notebooks, Valéry strives to gain what he calls a 'second consciousness' which can observe and understand the workings of his own mind. This interest in both the conscious and the unconscious is present in both of the newly emerging disciplines of psychology and linguistics in the late nineteenth century, and the recourse to introspection was an early manifestation of a trend that was to play a major part in twentieth-century linguistics.

This brings us to the final area that we wish to touch on in this attempt to give a flavour of the intellectual climate of late nineteenth-century France. This was the time of the founding as academic disciplines not just of linguistics, but also of psychology and sociology. In psychology, the burgeoning interest in the workings of the mind and in the nature of consciousness was of obvious relevance to linguists. Saussure cites the discovery by Broca in the 1860s of the location of language in the brain, and Wernicke in the 1870s. Bergson's *Essai sur les données immédiates de la conscience* was published in 1889. There was a growing body of information about dream, as well as about psychological conditions which might reveal the workings of the unconscious, such as hysteria. James (1995: 220) traces to the latter part of the nineteenth century the preoccupation with the notion of the 'divided personality', the 'dédoublement du moi', writing that the 'presupposition that the self is a unity had remained constant in nineteenth century thought until at least 1870'. The main batch of Saussure's manuscript notes discovered in 1996 is entitled *De l'essence double du language* (*ELG*: 15–88). According to Valéry, it is language which constitutes 'an other within you' ('Le langage constitue un autre en toi', *Cahiers* XVIII: 708). For Valéry, as for others after him, speech and the identity of the speaking subject go hand in hand, making the 'sujet parlant' much more than a mere mouthpiece: 'Le mot Moi n'a de sens que dans chaque cas où on l'emploie. Pas de moi sans parole – sin voce' ('The word "me" only has meaning in each instance of its use. There is no "me" without speech – sine voce', *Cahiers* XIX: 29).

It was the unconscious that was of greatest interest to the new discipline of psychology, at a time when the foundations of the three disciplines of linguistics, psychology and sociology were being laid. The Swiss psychologist,

Jung, developed the notion of the 'collective unconscious', and it is easy to see why this might appeal to the creator of the notion of *langue*, as opposed to Freud's interest in the unconscious of the individual. Jung it was who called upon Saussure after his return to Geneva to advise on a case of glossolalia, which was one of the psychic phenomena that aroused interest at that time. Two of the founding fathers of sociology are generally considered to be Weber and Durkheim, and attention has been drawn in each case to parallels with Saussure. At about the time when chairs in linguistics were being created (Saussure held the first such chair in Geneva) so too was the first chair of sociology in France created for Durkheim in Bordeaux in 1895. Durkheim's *fait social*, defined in his lectures, which were published in 1894 as *Les règles de la méthode sociologique*, has sometimes been held as the inspiration for Saussure's *fait de langue*. This, as well as Durkheim's unhistorical approach, and his formulations 'cast in terms of structure rather than of process' have been seen as showing similarities to the principles with which Saussure laid the basis for linguistics (Hughes, 1959: 286). Although Durkheim became increasingly less influenced by positivism towards the end of his career, it is sometimes claimed that the real reconciliation between empiricism and idealism, as well as the disciplinary separation between sociology and psychology, were effectively brought about by that other sociological giant of the end of the nineteenth century, Max Weber. Hughes points to a similarity in the lives of several of the founders of the social sciences, as if a *Zeitgeist* were at work. Weber laboured under the difficulties of creating the necessary viable concepts and terminology for a new discipline in the same way as did Saussure. On a very personal level, all die at the height of their careers. Durkheim, heart-broken by the death of his son in the First World War, died in 1917. Weber, rather like Saussure, had periods when he found it impossible to work and sought refuge in trips to Italy. Saussure, towards the end of his life, wrestles with the difficulty of writing about language although he does pursue interests in the German *Niebelungen* and in Latin anagrams (see chapter by Wunderli), and, after several periods of illness, dies in 1913 at the age of fifty-six. The more important parallels, however, are in their contribution to modern thought, as between them they were to a large degree responsible for laying the ground-rules and establishing the disciplinary frontiers which still characterise the social sciences today.

It is not easy to do justice to these thinkers and writers in the space available: what we have tried to do is to sketch out some elements of the intellectual climate at the time that Saussure was formulating the views that would later form the material of his Geneva lectures. We have moved from the changes in the study of language to its place in the wider world of philosophy, literature and the social sciences. Finally, if we widen our lens even further, we can try to imagine the everyday social and political life of Paris that provided the context for Saussure's decade of living and working there. In 1881, a brilliant young Swiss scholar arrived in a city that had known years of turbulence, but was poised to embark on a period of prosperity, and of great intellectual and artistic creativity. After half a century of unsettled government following the Revolution, see-sawing between republic and monarchy, and with military victory alternating with defeat, France in 1880 was beginning to emerge as a modern state. In 1875 France had once more become a republic and would remain so thereafter; in the early 1880s the aim of Jules Ferry as prime minister was to heal divisions between the political right and left, and to put an end to oppression, both economic and ideological. A common sense of nationhood was being forged again: the *Marseillaise* became the national anthem in 1879, the annual *fête de la Bastille* was instigated, and the abolition of the censorship led to the flourishing of journalistic and literary creativity. (This did not mean that there would be no more crises: an abiding interest in French politics is evidenced in the collection of French newspapers relating to the Dreyfus case which feature among the Saussure family papers held in a library in Geneva.) Nevertheless, the decade that Saussure spent in Paris was one in which intellectual and artistic ferment continued, but against a background of relative social stability. The mid-century rebuilding of Paris by Haussman had transformed the city into what we know today, and it is perhaps not too fanciful to imagine the excitement that the young Saussure, coming from the Protestant and more parochial towns of Leipzig and Geneva (letters containing his wry comments on the former are to be found in Bouquet, 2003) must have felt as he strolled down the thronging boulevards of what the Victorian writer Thackeray described as the 'wicked city'.

If all of this is a mere figment of the imagination, what is certain is that, after what some considered to be his attack on the approach of the German comparative grammarians and the not altogether warm reception accorded in Germany to his outstanding *mémoire*, he arrived in a city where linguists such as Bréal were forging a different path in the study of language and where the intellectual climate was new and challenging. In terms of the founding of modern linguistics in those last decades of the nineteenth century, we can see that the legacy of Bopp and the comparative grammarians was that of a rigorous methodological attention to formal detail, mainly at the levels of phonology and morphology – even though they did not use these terms as we do. As Bergounioux (1984) points out, their method involved treating language as an object, separate from its speaker, an issue which Bréal addresses but reference to which remains tantalisingly implicit in Saussure's writings, for example in his references to the *sujet parlant*. We have seen, however, that the biggest split from the German school came with the realisation that to understand the very nature of language, the way in which a sequence of sounds produces meaning and allows communication to take place, it was necessary to study language synchronically, as it operated at any given time, as opposed to documenting language change. Once the attention to formal detail was combined with a synchronic approach, the way was paved for the creation of the tools of descriptive linguistics, such as, initially, the International Phonetic Alphabet, which would be developed by Passy, a pupil of Saussure and Meillet. While language change alone had been seen by Bopp and others as regular and 'rule' governed, for the modern linguist it is language in its synchronic state that constitutes a system, or structure. For many linguists worldwide, and particularly in Europe, it was primarily from Saussure's ideas as they were represented in the *Cours de linguistique générale* that this realisation came.

Part II

The ‘Course in General Linguistics’

3 The making of the *Cours de linguistique générale*

Rudolf Engler

On the history of the *Cours*, the task which faced its 'author-editors' Bally and Sechehaye in 1913, and how they acquitted themselves, the reader can consult Godel (1957), Engler (1959, 1968b, 1987b), Vallini (1979) and Linda (2001).

Let us make a few points clear. The *Cours* (or *CLG*) does not contain Saussure's 'actual words' but a subsequent digest of three courses (based on lecture notes kept by a few conscientious students) and of certain handwritten observations which testify to a longstanding reflection on the 'essence' of linguistics. Saussure had always said that he would never publish any of these reflections. Without the bold and assiduous determination of Bally and Sechehaye, Saussure's thought would probably have never reached the reading public, any more than did that of his contemporary Marty. Without the *CLG*, the interest shown today in the discovery of any new Saussurean document would not exist.

Hence the existence of the *CLG* is in itself a fact of historical significance. The publication of the first 'authentic' texts associated with the linguist (Godel, 1957; Saussure, 1968 and 1974 (*CLG*/E, vols. 1 and 2)), is the second event of importance and it has allowed for a two-way evaluation. It led to new interpretations, valuable but provisional, as has been shown by the 1996 appearance of a Saussurean manuscript dating from 1891, and containing in essence the whole of Saussure's 'general and semiological linguistics', as well as totally unexpected thoughts on 'semantics' (Saussure, 2002 (*ELG*)). This would raise questions about the genesis of Saussure's theorems, while at the same time reaffirming their radical nature (Engler, 2000a, b). The *CLG*, as it was set out in 1916, and its historical impact, has however remained untouched, just as it was untouched by the existence of the supplementary notebooks for the 1907 lectures (notes on patois, discovered by Komatsu, see Saussure, 1993: 97) or the speculation surrounding the *n* (Avalle, 1973a; *CLG*/E 2: 75).

Nevertheless, let us put together a picture of the occurrences of references to 'general linguistics' in Saussure, including those in the evolving 'apocrypha' of the *CLG*. As early as Leipzig, in the context of the *Mémoire* (and thus of 'comparative' or 'Indo-European' – Germanic and Gothic – linguistics), we find theoretical reflections: *divination/induction* (*ELG*: 132), which suggests a move towards German idealism (Engler, 2001); *langage/langue/parole* (*ELG*: 129–31), where Saussure contrasts the linguistic *object* with the very different object defined by Bopp. Here, however, he takes care to defend Bopp against the charge of failing to understand the real object of linguistics, a charge which will later be implicit at the beginning of the Introduction to the *CLG*. In 1885–6 he set out, in his own words, 'some general remarks on linguistic method and an overview of language' (Saussure, 1964/65), which might well be what Meillet refers to after the publication of the *CLG*. In the *Cahiers lituaniens* of c. 1894 (*Documents*, 1996), he defines the *points of view* which define *accentuation* in contemporary Lithuanian as an object in its own right, with a historical *evolution* that is to be distinguished from its current *state* – see respectively the theorem in *Notes personnelles* (*CLG*/E 2) dated 1893 by Godel (1957) and its 1891 precursor. The latter (*De l'essence double du langage* in *ELG*) is the 'fortunate-unfortunate' work which Saussure summarises in his letter to Gaston Paris of 31 December (Décimo, 1994; Engler, 1997). Saussure here indicates that this arises directly out of his Inaugural lectures of November 1891 (*ELG*: 143–73), which is the only text on 'general linguistics' which – if not exactly 'published' – was at least *made public* by Saussure himself. Predictably, *De l'essence double du langage* remained unfinished, but it contains the seeds of the teaching of 1907–11, and in some cases, such as in the area of semantics, it goes much further. Furthermore, right from the text of 1891, Saussure never stopped improving, scattering reflections along similar lines throughout his papers, (personal) notes on linguistics, 'item' notes, aphorisms (see *ELG*: 91–123), legends, and anagrams. Lastly, traces of his thought found their way into print in Naville (1901), Odier (1905), Bally, and Sechehaye.

It is worth asking, therefore, whether it is conceivable that Saussure, who could not even make up his mind to finish and publish the 1891 text *Essence double*, even despite the advanced state of a text written in his own hand, would have allowed publication of students' lecture notes, jotted down in haste, which were inevitably approximate. In any event, the presentation of these notes (*CLG*/E, Saussure, 1993, 1997) shows that they would have needed almost as much editing as Bally and Sechehaye put in for the *CLG*; or as much 'falsifying', as their detractors put it.

Linda (1995) has analysed in detail the situation in which Bally and Sechehaye found themselves at Saussure's death (22 February 1913), and he sets out the 'events' which determined how they went about producing their text. Without hazarding any interpretation, I reproduce here a number of revelatory declarations by those principally concerned.

Bally, 1 March 1913:

Anyone present at his courses in general linguistics, enriched every year by new insights, has a lasting and dependable guide to research into language. These lectures were religiously recorded in his pupils' notes; any book made thereof would be a fine book. Will it never see the light? (Hellmann, 1988: 73; Linda, 1995: 28)

Meillet, 1913:
Of the reflection on general linguistics which took up a great part of [Saussure's] last years, nothing has been published. Saussure's greatest wish was to distinguish two ways of approaching linguistic facts: by studying language at a given moment, and by studying linguistic development in time. Only the students who followed Saussure's courses in Geneva have so far had the benefit of this thinking; only they know the exact formulations and the well-chosen images he used to throw light on a new subject. (Meillet, 1913: 174; Linda, 1995: 29)

Gautier, 13 August 1916:
What would Saussure's papers contain? That is what we wondered, quite justifiably, after his premature death. Exceptional figures give rise to much conjecture, so certain myths had gained currency in his lifetime: whole books ready to go to press, lacking only a conclusion – or even just the last page. It seemed obvious that his papers, and his personal notes, would contain treasures, which should of course be shared. Alas, not only were there no almost-finished works, but his notes were unclassified and impossible to follow. The whole magnificent scheme was in the author's mind alone. (See review of *CLG* in Linda, 1995: 34.)

Marie de Saussure to Meillet, 25 May 1913:
And now several of his students have asked me if there might not be, among his notes, something publishable . . . Perhaps by looking through the notes taken by various students in different years we might gain a relatively complete idea of one of his courses, but to do so we must not act in haste – Do you not agree? – One may by a too-hasty publication undo a body of work to which one might have done justice, given time . . . – I am, naturally, unversed in this area; I do however know that my husband never rushed into anything and that what he has left to his discipline was the fruit of much mature reflexion. (Benveniste, 1964: 124; Linda, 1995: 31)

Bally to Meillet, 29 May 1913:
As you were travelling, I have not been able to speak to you directly of a question I should have liked to bring up with you alone. As I think you are back, let me quickly inform you of what has happened, so that what I do creates no misunderstanding. I did not myself follow Saussure's course on general linguistics and know it only through the notes – admirably set out – by one of his students [Riedlinger] who had the fortune to follow it over two years. As soon as I learnt of Mr Regard's interesting project, I questioned some of Saussure's other students, particularly Léopold Gautier and A. Sechehaye. [On Paul Regard and his project and critique of *CLG* (1919) see de Mauro (Saussure, 1968, index: 484 – unfortunately absent from Saussure, 1972); Amacker, 1989: 102; and Linda, 1995: 35–40.] Without revealing the plan for an article, so as not to influence them, I asked their opinion on the nature of the lectures and the conditions most appropriate for a possible publication. Their views all concur on the following points: while the principles of his teaching did not vary, each yearly course (three in all) has its own character, an original aspect of its own, and many details from each one may profitably add to the other two without doing them a disservice. All are persuaded that the work is as valuable as a whole which presents an overall system as in its individual parts. All insist that whatever

the manner of publication to be adopted, the work must not be based on the notes of *one* student having followed *one* of the three courses. It is thought that before an article, the possibility of a book should be considered, at the risk of having to abandon it later if it is found to be unrealistic. – Madame de Saussure, whom I visited last week to inform her of developments, told me that Messrs Sechehaye and Léopold Gautier had already informed her of their ideas on the matter, and she is unwilling to make a decision before the inquiries mentioned above. Finally let me divulge to you a thing of some import that should, if you would be so kind, remain between us. I have it from a good source, one who has read Mr Regard's notes, that these notes, while conscientiously done, do not translate the spirit of Saussure's teaching, and even misrepresent it completely at times. I cannot verify this information, but it concurs with my own impression of Mr Regard's way of working in which he is more apt to grasp the detail rather than the question as a whole. – All that gives me some cause for concern; I hope, my dear colleague, that you will see in my way of doing things the simple wish to preserve a memory that we all respect; it might be better to delay starting the project so that it does not conceal any unpleasant surprises. If you allow me, I shall keep you abreast of anything that I undertake in this respect. At present I am busy collecting the students' notes, and I still hope that you will not deny us your precious advice. (Amacker, 1989: 102; Linda, 1995: 32)

Meillet to Bally, 31 May 1913:
I have indeed been back since last Monday . . . As I wrote to Madame de Saussure, the plan I had sketched out with young Mr Regard has been abandoned. It has always depended on your agreement, and as you had other ideas, it must no longer be entertained. – I find it difficult to evaluate the project of which you speak. In principle, I have great misgivings about posthumous publications, and that is in large measure why I showed Regard the project in question. I might have even more misgivings about the mixing the various courses. But you are in a better position than me to assess these things, and you have at your disposal information I have not. In any case, I would still be grateful if you could let me know what you have decided, when you have worked out a final project. (Amacker, 1989: 103; Linda, 1995: 36)

Bally to Meillet, 2 June 1913:
Thank you for your reply. I will keep you informed. Naturally, my idea does not constitute a project, merely a precautionary measure and an initial grounding for the material we possess. And if an overall publication is not possible, I shall be the first to come over to the idea proposed by yourself. Last year Saussure delivered a course on *Greek and Latin etymology* and I shall be able to consult the notes; if anything can be got out of them it will be in the form of separate extracts this time. I will come back to you about this. (Amacker, 1989: 104; Linda, 1995: 40)

Notes on the course in *Greek and Latin etymology* were taken by Louis Brütsch. The 'extracts' – no longer separate – that Bally inserted in the *CLG* are on page 265/259 (*CLG*/E: index 2834–42). The notes on *General linguistics* are those taken for the first course by Albert Riedlinger (co-editor of the *CLG*), for the second by Riedlinger, Bouchardy and Gautier, for the third by Dégallier, Joseph and (the future) Mrs Sechehaye. Riedlinger had apparently compared his notes with those of his fellow-students after the lectures, inserting any striking variants in the margins and between the lines of his notebooks, and he also (later?) inspected the shorthand notes made by Caille for the first course. Constantin (unknown to Bally and Sechehaye) continued collating the third course; his notebooks only came out in 1957, in the wake of Robert Godel's thesis (Godel, 1958/59). As for Caille's shorthand, in the 1960s Riedlinger, at my request, dug out the notebooks. He could not decipher the shorthand, and an appeal for help in the Geneva newspapers drew a blank; I therefore had to go through guides to French shorthand in the National Library in Berne before I managed to break the code.[1] So, Bally and Sechehaye used only Riedlinger and his annotations for the first course. However, for the subsequent ones they consulted others who were present, especially Gautier and Dégallier. Sechehaye produced a *Collation* of the three courses, which Bally subsequently annotated. This then provided a basis for the discussions between the editors and for the production of the *CLG* text. Linda (1995) gives a detailed analysis of the process.

Whether one looks at the *CLG* in detail or takes it as a whole, whether one pulls it apart or situates it in its overall context, there will always be different and often irreconcilable judgements of Bally/Sechehaye and of their *CLG*. In the final analysis, the Engler edition of the *CLG* makes no difference to this. Like Wells (1947), de Mauro (in Saussure, 1972 (*CLG*/D)), Amacker (1975), Stetter (1992) and Wunderli (1981), I am filled with awe at the task that Bally and Sechehaye undertook. I have outlined the view (1987b) that any errors on their part were less a case of infidelity than of excessive fidelity, an *a posteriori* reaction to some of Saussure's criticisms of their own work. I will now sum up my analysis (1987b) for those who cannot read it in the original German.

In 1913, Bally (1899–1913) and Sechehaye (1902, 1905, 1908a, 1908b) were by no means ignorant of general linguistics. Both would subsequently develop their own perspectives (Bally, 1932, 1944; Sechehaye, 1916, 1926, as well as an unpublished 'Morphologie'). Some have gone so far as to presume that it was not Saussure who influenced Sechehaye, but the other way around (Vallini, 1974; Wunderli, 1976b). There is no doubt that four of Sechehaye's (1908a) theses anticipate certain Saussurean theorems:

1. 'Conventional and discursive language [*langue*] manifests itself against the background of a natural language [*langage*] faculty'.
2. 'A symbol is not a sign chosen arbitrarily to correspond to an already-existing idea, but the linguistic precondition for a psychological operation, that is, the formation of a verbal idea' (p. 175 in French version).
3. 'Symbols, as elements of a sentence, must not be taken in isolation, but in synthetic, compound groups' (p. 178).
4. '*Langue*, a set of predispositions acquired by an individual, must not be confused with *langage*, which is *langue* put into practice in *parole* by someone possessing these predispositions' (p. 183).

However, given the close contact between the two, this in no way clears up the question of the 'authorship' of these ideas. While it is true that Saussure quotes Sechehaye's *Programme et méthodes de la linguistique théorique* (1908a) in the 1910/11 *Cours*, it is also obvious that this work of Sechehaye's (despite the debt that it acknowledges to his '*maître*' Saussure) actually owed more to Wundt, which was something that Saussure would reproach him for (*CLG*/E: index 3330; *ELG*: 258–61). In any event, in 1927 Sechehaye suggested that the relationship between those who inspired the *Ecole genevoise de linguistique générale* was complex:

If we dare make a comparison with Saussure, we should say that his disciple [Sechehaye] shares with him a taste – and only a *taste* – for large abstractions and for an intellectual vision which goes beyond and above the facts. However, Mr Sechehaye adds to this a desire to organise, to construct a system. This is what sets his *Programme et méthodes de la linguistique théorique* apart. (1927: 234)

Hence Sechehaye, although (presumably) understanding the reservations of Saussure, reaffirms his *structural* theses – including the notion of integrating linguistics within psychology (see below) – which is tantamount to asserting that he is responsible for the organisation of the 1916 *CLG*. And this counters Saussure's criticism that he had sacrificed the *grammatical* by incorporating it, in an elegant concession, into the '*langage–langue–parole*' theorem (which he had nevertheless adopted in 1908a and which explains why Saussure quotes him in 1910/11):

The system . . . , as laid out in Mr Sechehaye's book, is not completely convincing because it has not taken sufficient account of the Saussurean [!] distinction between *langue* and *parole*. As soon as we apply this new principle of classification – something which is unproblematic – we will be faced with a well-ordered system based on logical relationships which constitute the internal structure of any rigorously methodical linguistic thought. (1927: 235)

In other words, he is claiming that his book serves as a framework for the *CLG*. It is here – not in the production of the *CLG* itself – that I think we find a danger of misinterpreting Saussure, in the sense that Sechehaye attributes to him the idea of *integrating linguistics* (and in particular *langue*) into *social psychology* [sociology], which is itself integrated into *individual psychology*, while Saussure resolved the problem (this is again my own view) via the different *viewpoints* of various sciences, each one constituting facts of 'analogous' reality when viewed as a *real object* (Engler, 1987b: 142–9, 2002).

Bally is similarly both in competition with, and in awe of, the great linguist (Redard, 1982a, 1982b; Engler, 1987a). Once again the key text is from 1908:

Let me say clearly that it was in listening to you that the scientific basis of our discipline was revealed to me . . . One of your Geneva students, who reflects the excellence of your teaching, Mr Albert Sechehaye, dedicated to you the important book he has just published on theoretical linguistics and the psychology of language; his dedication contains the sentence 'My ambition, in writing every one of these pages, has been to win your approval.' How perfectly put. When, after a time under your wing, one seeks independence, the memory of your words emerges to confront one's own thoughts, and one wonders, 'Would he have approved of that? How would he have put it?' Yes, in you, sir, the teacher is inseparable from the scholar; but we know too that alongside the teacher is a devoted friend, giving unstintingly of his time and effort to illuminate the way for the hesitant student. (Speech at the presentation of the Festschrift *Mélanges linguistiques F. de Saussure*; Bally, 1908)

The second text is from 1913: the inaugural lecture by Bally, Saussure's successor to the chair of general and comparative linguistics. The tone is no longer celebratory, but one of serious confrontation of concepts and methods. While Sechehaye attempted to adapt and integrate, albeit in his own terms, in Bally we find opposition:

If you have retained Saussure's distinction between *langue* and *parole*, you will see easily that introspection is the cornerstone of this distinction. May I say that on this point, and by these methods, I have reached conclusions a little different from those of my illustrious teacher? As you may justifiably find this rather bold, allow me a word of explanation. Ferdinand de Saussure's fundamental approach was one of abstract intellectualising. His scientific temperament led him to seek, and helped him discover, what there is in any language, and in language in general, that which is regular, geometric, architectural . . . For him *langue* is the work of collective intelligence; it is an intellectual organism. I, for my part, happened to approach his thought from the other end of the field of observation. In the Seminar on Modern French . . . my aim was to study the expressive values of spontaneous, natural language, everyday spoken language without its literary cladding . . . The spoken language that we all use, every day and all day, did not seem to me a purely intellectual phenomenon, but on the contrary deeply emotional and subjective in its means of expression and action. As it is not intellectual, is this *langue* then mere *parole*? . . . A closer inspection brought me to this question: is this gulf situated at the very threshold of intellectual expression? Does a term created within speech have only two alternatives when it seeks to enter into the accepted language system, either to drown in the moat as it tries to gain admittance, or to be accepted into the language as it is, with its original value and meaning? . . . Intellectual, normal, organised *langue* caters to the communication and comprehension of ideas; *parole*, on the other hand, serves real life; it seeks to express feeling, will, action. This is why creations within *parole* are essentially emotional and subjective. The question now is whether these creations have any future and can become part of *langue*. Everything leads us to conclude that they can . . . Listen to anybody in real life: language is full to the brim with non-intellectual elements; but it is not, in each case, a spur-of-the-moment creation, or an improvisation; someone who speaks to express emotion, to pray or to command, hardly ever needs to invent to be expressive. Means of expression are readily found in the spoken language; indeed, these are the first to occur to anyone . . . It is, then, *langue* and not *parole*; and yet this *langue* gives each individual the illusion of speaking in a personal way . . . I would therefore situate affective language within the ambit of *langue* as a whole, in a peripheral zone which surrounds normal language; it contributes to its social character, since all individuals agree on the values it contains; this character distinguishes it clearly from *parole*, with which it has an undeniable affinity resulting from the way it adapts to the requirements of life . . . In sum, while still faithful to the distinction between *langue* and *parole*, I would add to *langue* an area which people find difficulty in attributing to it: that is, the emotional, subjective aspects of spoken language. These aspects require a discipline of their own, one that I would call stylistics. One of the objects of my teaching will be to show how stylistics may be integrated into general linguistics. (1913/1952: 157)

Ironically, after Saussure's death, a 'reply' to some of these points was to be found in papers eventually unearthed by Godel after the publication of his thesis (*CLG*/E: index 3347; *Rapport sur la création d'une chaire de stylistique*, *ELG*: 272):

The name *stylistics* is a name made necessary by the absence of any other. Style and stylistics create an unfortunate misunderstanding. A few corrections are needed if we are to see clearly what is meant, viz: 1. The word style evokes a person, an individual, an individual process. (Judge a man by his style, etc.) In fact stylistics, in the sense illustrated by Mr Bally's work, sets out to study the expressive processes of a language where these have been accepted into general usage, where they come under the heading of a social fact and are thus defined outside the scope of the individual. The presence in a language of 'I wasn't born yesterday!', or 'Damn it!' is clearly a stylistic fact, since their use is not individual, and because, crucially, although these expressions are perfectly banal, they still indicate a certain sensibility, and allow this to be studied. Style depends on the individual, and stylistics is initially situated above the individual in the linguistic or social sphere. – 2. The word *style* evokes the idea of literariness or at least of what is *written*. – Stylistics, while not unconcerned by what is written, has as its primary object the observation of what is spoken, in living forms of language, whether they be set out in a text or not. Style depends on the written word, and stylistics is better situated outside the written word, in the realm of the spoken word. – 3. Moreover, the *aim* of stylistics is not style, *although style may have its usefulness*. It is not a normative science, which lays down rules. It seeks and is right to seek to be a science of pure observation, setting down facts and classifying them. – Lastly, I hasten to add that it may do so for any language whatsoever. French turns of phrase and expressions do not exclusively constitute its material [for M. Bally]. Gentlemen, I have come to the real danger attached to a chair in *stylistics,* which is not related to concern over the ambiguities associated with the science of style, but rather it is to do with the objection 'Oh, so we're just getting linguistics under the name of stylistics'.

Saussure's assertion that *stylistics* was simply *linguistics* (and Saussure knew the views of Bally) can of course be interpreted as affirming the same *synchronic viewpoint* (encompassing the theorem *langage: langue-parole*). Anyone who still has doubts about this today need only consult the passages relating to *semantics* in *L'essence double du langage* (*ELG*: 72–81). The identification of *langue* with intellectual and *parole* with affective cannot be wholly justified. On one hand Saussure considers *langue* as passive, on the other his *parole* is a real activity involved with life itself. One has only to recall *CLG*/E index 3284.10 [1891] *décollecte/ je me décolte*: *ELG*: 162; – *CLG*/E 3342.5 [c. 1908/11] *vieillesse / sénescence*: *ELG*: 265; – the missionary wanting to 'instil in a primitive people the idea of *soul*': *ELG*: 78. Moreover, one should recall that Sechehaye (1927) had already tried to put the record straight: 'note that, in language as a subjective phenomenon, only elements of expression which are governed by a rule, or a collective habit, will be studied: stylistics covers only fixed values which langue makes available to all. As in the Saussurean distinction, it does not enter into the area of *parole*' (228).

With this he is going back on what he had noted down in 1908:

> What is represented by our words, or by any conventional element of our language (particles, prefixes, suffixes and syntactic combinations of these elements)? They justify themselves as linguistic substitutes for certain notions. As such their value is purely intellectual. We turn our emotional experiences into ideas, like the experiences which come to us via our senses. It is by assimilating the expression and the idea needing expression that we may call someone prodigious or a spendthrift [ ], just as we designate one animal by the word dog and another by the word cat. The only difference between the first two cases and the third is that in the first two we draw on the subjective impression that the thing leaves in our senses when we conceptualise the idea, while in the third it plays no role. (Sechehaye, 1908a: 167)

We can thus see that during Saussure's lifetime a prolonged debate took place between Saussure and his followers, in an attempt to go deeper into these questions, and that this continued after his death. It is moreover fascinating to see how each of his successors represented him. Meillet, famously, referred to Saussure as a 'poet', with 'blue eyes'; Sechehaye, as we saw, described him as 'going beyond the merely factual level'. Bally perhaps tended – precociously – to consider him as a 'hard-line' structuralist; after all, it was Bally who declared himself to Hjelmslev to be Saussure's true successor. After his death, his words and his ideas were captured through his students' notebooks; hence the continuing temptation for each to interpret the teaching of the *Cours de linguistique générale* according to his own ideas. The 'editors' are to be admired for the way in which they resisted this. There are of course some misinterpretations in the *CLG*; to restrict ourselves to one example, let us examine the treatment given in the *Cours* to the theorem *langage: langue-parole*, which should be considered in the light of Sechehaye's remark (1924: 234), that: 'It may be necessary to recall . . . that the ordering of subjects in the *Cours de linguistique générale* is not the work of Saussure. The three courses that he gave were structured in three different ways. The book's editors had to adopt a more or less systematic ordering, which they considered appropriate.' Observations by Engler (1959, 1968b), Vallini (1979) and the final conclusions (based on *Documents* 1996) of Engler (2002) all make the same point.

In 1916 people were well aware that the *CLG* had been put together from the lecture notes by Bally and Sechehaye. Then this was forgotten. In 1957 Godel reminded us of this again and laid the foundations for a new interpretation. My comparative edition, which appeared in 1967/68 and 1974, placed in parallel the text of the *Cours*, along with some of Saussure's handwritten notes. In 1962 I had produced an analysis of the arbitrary nature of the sign, which drew on an examination of the versions of the *CLG* in the light of chronologically arranged 'Saussurean notes' (manuscript and student notes), and in 1974 an analysis of linearity. It was only after this that the myth of the 'authentic' Saussure began to find currency. Some maintained that Saussure had been betrayed by Bally and Sechehaye and that *CLG*/E, which followed their use of the lectures, was necessarily inauthentic, and perpetuated the damage done by the *Cours*. Yet a system of cross-referencing allowed immediate reconstruction of the proper order of the courses and notes. Although I welcome any reflection on Saussure's linguistics, I do not feel that subsequent studies based on 'chronological' editions have improved things much, the new interpretations being too disparate In any event, how could Bally and Sechehaye have 'betrayed' Saussure? The only way might have been by substituting their own viewpoint for Saussure's. I can see no trace of this, such was their awareness of their responsibility, which is shown by the letters quoted above.

Let us return to our demonstration. Did Sechehaye knowingly falsify the '*langage: langue-parole*' theorem? He sets out his views in a 1908 article that I have not yet quoted:

> *Langue* resides in the brain alone. It is acquired by the assimilation of everything that one hears in one's environment, by learning to attribute to symbols and groups of symbols the same meanings that others attribute to them. As this operation is not carried out passively, and as each person adds something original to it, what is acquired varies from individual to individual, and each person has his *langue*, or grammatical state. A *langue*, in the normal sense, is an intermediate state, bringing together the common characteristics of many grammatical states which exist at a given time and place. *Langage* is *langue* in action; it resides in the individual speaker who voluntarily activates it to express by all available means the thought that he wishes to convey and the emotion that he feels. *Langage* is constantly original creation, the application of abstract and general processes to a specific end, that of the translation and interpretation of psychic states into gesture, words, organised sentences. (Sechehaye, 1908b: 184)

Does this conception of things, and that of Bally quoted above, come across in the *CLG*? Did Bally and Sechehaye draw on Riedlinger's *Cours I*, especially the passage confirmed by Caille, which should have suited them perfectly?[2]

> /R 2.23/ [*CLG*/E 2521] All <the> facts of *langage*, <especially facts about language change,> confront one on one hand with *parole*, and on the other with the whole repertory of forms thought of <or> known to thought.
>
> [2522] An <unconscious> act of comparison is necessary not only to create associations but to understand them. A given word may enunciate something intelligible only because

it is immediately compared with any that might signify something slightly different (*facias: faciam, facio*).

[= 2560] While it is true that the wealth of *langue* is always needed for speech, similarly >[b] any fact which enters *langue* was brought into being in *parole*, or to put it another way, everything which enters *langue* has already been tried out in *parole* a sufficient number of times to create a lasting impression; *langue* simply makes official what has previously been employed <in> *parole*.

<<The importance of the opposition between *langue* and *parole* <which> we have <here> is the way in which it illuminates the study of *langage*. One way of making this opposition particularly clear and <observable> is to set *langue* against *parole* within an individual (*langage* is social, to be sure, but for many facts it is easier to recognise it in the individual). Two almost tangibly distinct spheres could then be identified: *langue* and *parole*. Everything that reaches the lips as a result of the needs of discourse and by an individual operation is *parole*. Everything within an individual's brain, the stock of forms <heard> and produced and of their meaning, <[b] even when the individual is not speaking, represents what has been made official, <ie> *langue*.

Of these two spheres, the sphere of <*parole*> is the more social, the other is the more totally individual. *Langue* is the individual's repertory; everything that enters *langue*, *ie* in the head, is individual. [ ] <I can see that everyone at the lectures understood just as I did, even Caille who was taking it down in shorthand!> /[25]. <Everything in the head will have only got there by *parole* alone (cf. omnis compitio a sensu!) [b]>. Internally (the sphere of *langue*) there is never premeditation nor even meditation, nor consideration of forms, outside the act, <the opportunity> of *parole*, with the exception of one unconscious activity, which is almost passive, and in any case not creative, that of classifying. If everything new is necessarily produced in discourse, it follows that everything takes place on the social side of *langage*. Moreover, by putting together the sum-total of individual treasure-houses of *langue* one arrives at *la langue*.>> Everything that is taken to be in the individual's internal sphere [= *langue*!] must be social because nothing that <has not been> <made official by usage> of all speakers in the external sphere of *parole* [= social!] has ever entered that sphere>.

In fact, Bally and Sechehaye did not draw on Riedlinger's *Cours I*, since all the text within the double diamond-shaped brackets (<< >>) was deleted (despite Riedlinger's opposition), with *Cours III* (the latest to appear) apparently signalling a new direction. [Concerning this 'apparently' see Engler, 2002.] The same goes for *CLG*/E: 1828 (*CLG* 2 IV §1 pt 8):

The characteristic role of *langage* [ed. of *la langue*] with respect to thought, is not to be an acoustic, physical channel, but to create an intermediate environment in such a way that the coming together of thought and sound inevitably results in specific units.

[1829] Thought, by nature chaotic, is forced to define itself because it is taken apart, parcelled up *by langage* into units.

[1826: pt 3] But one should be wary of the commonplace that sees *le langage* [*la substance phonique*] as a mould: that would be to consider it as something fixed, rigid, whereas in fact acoustic matter is as inherently chaotic as thought.

All the sources have *langage* – note however that C[onstantin] had not yet enrolled in 1913/16. As the *Cours III* had in effect deprived this term of any substance, by portraying it as the simple sum of *parole* + *langue*, the editors must have wondered about giving it the role they themselves had accorded it in their own writings (see also on this subject Engler, 2002).

Finally, we come to the famous last sentence of the *CLG* (317): '*La linguistique a pour unique et veritable objet de la langue envisagée en elle-même et pour elle-même*' ('*the true and unique object of linguistics is language studied in and for itself*', *CGL*-B: 232) – which too is absolutely opposed to and incompatible with the frameworks of Bally and Sechehaye, and almost certainly a concession by Sechehaye to Saussure's criticism of his *Programme et méthodes de la linguistique théorique*:

> Mr Sechehaye, after rightly criticising Wundt for having neglected the problem of grammar, manages to underestimate it himself. This is because to give it its due would require one to state the grammatical fact in itself, and in its distinctness from any other psychological, or even logical act. The more the author endeavours to break down an unallowable barrier between framework of thought and thought, the more he seems to abandon his own stated aim, that of defining the field of expression, and establishing its laws, not in terms of properties they share with our psychic make-up in general, but in terms of their specific, and quite unique properties within the phenomenon of *langue*. (*CLG*/E: 3330.6)

(This chapter, including the quotations from *CLG*/E, was translated by Matthew Pires and Carol Sanders.)

4 The linguistic sign

John E. Joseph

Language as a system of signs

Although linguists remember him for a whole range of theoretical and methodological shifts he introduced, Saussure's more general fame stems almost entirely from his conception of a language as a socially shared, psychologically real system of signs, each consisting of the arbitrary conjunction of an abstract concept and acoustic image. He was by no means the first to conceive of language in terms of signs (some of the precedents will be discussed in the next section), but in the late nineteenth and early twentieth centuries it tended to be philosophers and psychologists rather than linguists and philologists who taught and wrote about language in these terms. Already in 1894 he had noted the need for a *sémiologie*, a science of signs (see Godel, 1957: 182).

In his first course of lectures on general linguistics in 1907, Saussure stated early on that 'A language is a system of signals: what makes the language is the relationship which the mind establishes among these signals' (Saussure, 1996: 23; Godel, 1957: 54). The first course was planned as an overview of Indo-European historical linguistics as practised since the last third of the nineteenth century, with some general considerations on the nature of language inserted along the way, and Saussure did not pursue the semiological perspective further.

But the second course (1908–9) would offer a much more personal vision of language in its synchronic dimension. This time the linguistic sign took centre stage almost from the start. After projecting the idea of semiology as a science that will teach us 'what signs consist of, what laws govern them' (*CLG*: 33), Saussure declared that 'For us . . . the linguistic problem is above all semiological, and all our developments derive their significance from this important fact' (34–5). However, the second course did not go on to analyse the internal workings of the linguistic sign, though it did note some of its characteristics and discussed in depth the related notion of linguistic 'value' (see below, pp. 65–7).

Detailed inquiry into the sign would finally be undertaken in Saussure's third and last course (1910–11), specifically in its second half. From here derives the bulk of the material on the sign in the posthumously published *Cours de linguistique générale* (1916). The *Cours* defines a language as a system of signs (32), and maintains that the signs of language have only one essential thing to them: the union of a concept (28–9, 98–9) and an acoustic image (28, 32, 98–9). Later the terms *signifiant* 'signifier' and *signifié* 'signified' are introduced for the acoustic image and concept respectively (99ff.). This pair of terms did not figure in Saussure's lectures until late in the third course.

In line with the third course, the *Cours* says that the linguistic sign operates on two principles. The first is that 'the linguistic sign is arbitrary', in the sense that there is no interior link between the concept and the acoustic image (101). Later passages will constrain this principle of arbitrariness in significant ways (see below, pp. 67–71). The second principle is that 'the signifier, being auditory in nature, unfolds itself in time only . . . and has a linear extension' (103). Although the linguistic sign is arbitrary, it is impossible for anyone to change it (104ff.). However, time can change the sign, specifically by bringing about a shift in the relationship between the signified and signifier (108–9). Saussure himself remarked on the apparent contradiction between these two statements, and it will be taken up further on pp. 72–4 below.

Had Saussure stopped here, he might still be remembered for having restored a venerable perspective on language that had been largely lost sight of in the heyday of nineteenth-century historical linguistics. But he contributed a further, highly original dimension to the linguistic sign with little if any precedent in earlier considerations of language, and very much in the modernist spirit of its time. As Saussure conceives it, each signifier and signified consists of nothing but *difference* from every other signifier and signified in the system.

This idea is already suggested in notes he wrote in the mid 1890s: 'The presentness of a form is in the forms which surround it from moment to moment and do not depend on it', 'every sign rests purely on a negative co-status' (Godel, 1957: 48, 49). It was raised late in the first course, in the context of a discussion of historical reconstruction (Godel, 1957: 65); acquired more significance in the second course, as part of its opening discussion of the linguistic sign; and became the climax of the third course, whence the following passage from the *Cours* is taken: 'in a language there are only differences *without positive terms*. Whether we take the signified or the signifier, the language contains neither ideas nor sounds that pre-exist the linguistic system, but only conceptual differences and phonic differences issuing from this system' (166).

However, when signifier and signified are joined together, they produce a sign which is of a positive order, and concrete rather than abstract. The third course also looks in detail at just how the oppositions within the system are structured. Every word or term or unit within the system is connected to an 'entourage' of other units, related to it either syntagmatically (the units that can come before or after it in an utterance) or associatively (the units with which it has something in common in form or meaning). The relationships of difference in these two domains generate the 'value' of the unit. Ultimately, then, no linguistic sign exists in isolation: 'it is a grand illusion . . . to think that we can start from the units and construct the system by adding them up, when on the contrary it is with the unified whole that we have to start, in order to obtain by analysis the elements it contains' (157).

The tradition of sign theory

To think about language in terms of 'signs' (rather than 'words') is to emphasise the signifying function – the mechanics of meaning and interpretation – and to draw an implicit analogy between language and other kinds of signs that people interpret and generate. This way of thinking about language dates back at least to Aristotle (see Baratin and Desbordes, 1981: 18–25, 93–103). It was further developed by the Stoics, who explicitly distinguished the *sēmainon*, the thing signifying, from the *sēmainomenon*, the thing signified (also called the *lekton*, the sayable), and made clear that the latter was incorporeal and not to be confused with the existing thing. Carried over into the Latin tradition, notably through St Augustine's *Dialectics* and *The Teacher* (see Baratin and Desbordes, 1981: 52–6, 211–46), the theory of signs flourished particularly at the end of the medieval period, with the development of 'speculative grammar' focusing on the *modi significandi*, modes of signifying. Sign theory did not fade into the background as Renaissance thinkers distanced themselves from Aristotelian scholasticism, but took on new forms, for instance in the writings of Locke and Leibniz, through which it came to occupy a prominent place in eighteenth-century Enlightenment thought.

But in the nineteenth century, the desire to create a 'science' of language brought about an emphasis on its unconscious dimensions, since only these were considered amenable to scientific study. Early in the century they were treated on the analogy of the mechanical, then increasingly as 'organic', culminating in the very powerful metaphor of languages as organisms with a life of their own detached from those of their speakers. Enlightenment linguistic thought was now eschewed on the grounds that it approached language as a series of rational, and thus implicitly wilful, operations. Sign theory, being associated with this form of rationalist inquiry, was considered old-fashioned and unscientific by linguists.

In time, a few linguists came to think that the organic metaphor had become so powerful (particularly in the wake of Darwin) that people were forgetting it was a metaphor at all. Resuscitating sign theory was a way to combat it. Saussure's mentor Bréal makes a statement precisely to this effect in his universally read *Essai de sémantique*, where, interestingly, the conception of words as signs is described as something folksy (*simple et honnête*): 'Our forefathers of the school of Condillac, those ideologists who for fifty years served as target to a certain school of criticism, were less far from the truth when they said, in simple and honest fashion, that words are signs. Where they went wrong was when they referred everything to a reasoning reason . . .' (Bréal, 1900: 249 [1897: 277]).

This suggests one route whereby the ancient semiotic heritage may have made its way to Saussure, but it was not the only one. Philosophers and psychologists had never distanced themselves from sign theory to the extent linguists had done, and in their discussions of language it continued to figure prominently. That Saussure read the psychological literature is evident for example in notes he made on types of aphasia (Godel, 1957: 40; *CLG*/E 1: 169). Possible philosophical sources have also been identified, but in truth it is probably because the idea of language consisting of signs was so widespread in both fields that Saussure himself saw no need to cite references.

One source does demand mention, however, because it was from within linguistics and we have Saussure's own testimony of its impact on his thinking. Whitney (1875) opens with two chapters in which consideration of language as a system of signs figures prominently. Notes Saussure made while rereading this book shortly after the American Sanskritist's death in 1894 show that in it he found the proof 'that language is nothing more than a particular case of the sign' (Godel, 1957: 44).

Overcoming 'nomenclaturism'

Part of the appeal of sign theory for Saussure is that it offered a solution to problems he saw with the ordinary conception of language as consisting of words and their meanings. Between the first and second course Saussure had reflected upon what he called the 'general public's' understanding of language as a collection of words. In Saussure's time as indeed today, a 'word' was generally thought of as a group of letters that together express a meaning, which is a thing or action or state of being, i.e. something in the world. The word *page* consists of the four letters shown and means the thing you are reading right now. The meaning of an abstract word like *beauty* derives from the actual instances of beautiful things, being the feature they have in common.

The first error here for Saussure (who was by no means the first to see it as such) was the failure to perceive that language really consists of sounds, not written letters, which are merely the secondary signs of sounds. Saussure goes further still, however, and argues that sounds are the physical realisation of a still deeper linguistic reality. With the word *beauty*, the actual sounds one produces or hears are not essential (and still less are the actual letters one writes or reads). Rather, there is a pattern in the mind that allows one to recognise a sequence of spoken sounds as the word *beauty*, even though these actual sounds vary from speaker to speaker, sometimes quite profoundly, as when across dialect boundaries. This same mental pattern, the 'acoustic image' or 'signifier', is the starting point for the production of sounds when one says the word.

In the same way, the meaning of the word varies from instance to instance. The statement above that the word *page* 'means the thing you are reading right now' is true, but incomplete, since obviously this is not *all* that *page* can mean. It can designate a whole class of things, of which the one you are reading is an example, and in this sense what it corresponds to is not a thing but a concept, a mental pattern that is in the mind of the person who says it or hears and understands it. Classes are concepts, even when the things they classify are concrete objects. Thus, for Saussure, there is no linguistic difference between a 'concrete' word like *page* and an 'abstract' one like *beauty*. In the mind of the speaker, both represent a conceptual mental pattern, a 'signified'.[1]

There arose too for Saussure a whole complex of problems emanating from our very way of talking about 'words and their meanings', or about words 'having meanings', as though the word is the sound part only and the meaning exists separately from it. What a word signifies, Saussure insists, is itself part of the word, indissociable from it. Whether words 'have' meanings or 'contain' them seems like a semantic quibble, but it is the very crux of Saussure's theory of the linguistic sign – and ultimately also of the great intellectual debates that have unfolded around structuralism and post-structuralism from the 1940s to the present (see Joseph, 2001).

This becomes less surprising when we consider its implications. In the traditional conception of the 'word', meanings already exist prior to language, which gives them names or encodes them. They are given in advance, by the world itself, as it were. They exist *in the world*, and it is through language that we discover them. Different languages discover them in different ways and encode them with different sound patterns. But ultimately languages and the speakers who use them are taken to be answerable to the reality outside language, in which are grounded the meanings of words, as well as logic and truth.

This whole mistaken conception of language as an inventory of names for things is what Saussure calls 'nomenclaturism' (*CLG*: 34), and opposes with his conception of the linguistic sign. Here meaning (as the 'signified') is not given in advance, but is created with the formation of the sign itself. This is not identical with the earlier point about all meanings being conceptual, for it could still be the case that signifieds emanate directly from the way the world is structured. To see why Saussure denies that this is so, consider the word/sign *cattle*. It has at various periods in the history of English meant all the property or wealth a person possessed, or just property in the form of livestock (including oxen, sheep, pigs, horses, etc.), or oxen only. All these species have existed since before the origins of human language, let alone of the English language, and in that sense are 'given in advance'. Yet the meaning of *cattle* is not so given, because which animals do or do not count as cattle is not determined by any criterion of nature. The usage of *cattle* has changed, perhaps to meet evolving social needs. But it is not any kind of change in the animals designated as 'cattle' that has caused the changes in the linguistic meaning. Rather the changes have been in how the social community that uses the word/sign conceives of the category 'cattle'.

It is the sign *cattle* that establishes the category 'cattle'. More precisely, the two of them are established simultaneously and inseparably by the linguistic community, through its usage. When what is included in the category 'cattle' changes, the entire sign changes. It becomes a new sign, even if the sound pattern (the signifier) remains the same. This again is a difference from our usual way of talking about a 'word' like *cattle* as having a continuous existence since Middle English, over the course of which it has possessed various meanings.

Abstractness of signifier and signified and concreteness of the sign

One of the most difficult aspects of the sign as the *Cours* presents it is that it is not an abstraction, but a real, concrete object. 'The signs of which a language is composed are not abstractions, but real objects . . .; they can be called the *concrete entities* of this science' (144). On the other hand, the signifier and the signified, considered separately from one another, are 'pure abstractions'. 'The linguistic entity exists only through the association of the signifier and the signified . . .; take only one of these elements, and the linguistic entity vanishes; instead of a concrete object, you no longer have before you anything but a pure abstraction' (144).

What makes this troubling is the repeated insistence elsewhere that a language is a form and not a substance (*CLG*: 157, 169), and that in a language there are only differences without positive terms. Might he mean that signs do not exist within a language, but are generated out of it? This would contradict many other statements (including the first one quoted in this section) which maintain that signs are precisely what a language consists of. How is it, then, that two pure abstractions combine to form a concrete entity, while the whole conglomeration of these concrete entities is devoid of substance?

The first thing to understand is that, for Saussure, 'real' and 'concrete' had a specific and somewhat idiosyncratic meaning. In an early unpublished note, probably dating from around 1894, he asked what can be called 'real' in morphology, and answered, 'what speakers are conscious of to any degree whatever' (Godel, 1957: 41). He adds the qualifying phrase 'to any degree whatever' to make clear that he does not mean that speakers are always directly aware of the concrete linguistic units they are using. Rather, their psychological reality is most often revealed unconsciously, for example in the formation of neologisms or the commission of errors by analogy, some of which lead to permanent linguistic change (see further Joseph, 2000a). In the second course, he would apply the same criterion to the definition of concreteness.

> A criterion for what is pure abstraction <and for what is concrete . . . This criterion is in the consciousness of each person. What is in *the feeling* of speakers, what is felt to some degree, is meaning and we can then say that the concrete, real, not at all so easy to get hold of in the language = what is felt, what in its turn = what is meaningful to some degree. (Saussure, 1997: 24; cf. Godel, 1957: 68)

Thus, when Saussure says that the linguistic sign is 'concrete', he does not mean that it has substance, only that it is something to which speakers of the language have conscious or unconscious mental access. Abstractions, on the other hand, are linguists' analytical inventions – and that includes the signifier and signified. In the third course, he takes up the question of the concreteness or abstractness of the component parts of the sign (see the extracts from the *Cours* in the first paragraph of this section), and specifically warns his students to avoid dissociating the two elements of the sign, lest they produce abstractions, units that appear to exist but are not actually part of the language. When he speaks of the inseparability of the signifier and the signified, comparing them to the front and back of a sheet of paper, this is a facet of their abstractness. The sheet is real, and it contains a front and a back. One can *think* of these two as having a separate existence from one another, but this existence is only a figure of thought, an abstraction.

In the *Cours*, what makes this complex discussion appear impossibly self-contradictory is the failure to make consistently clear that 'concrete' means 'psychologically real to ordinary speakers', and that the concrete–abstract dichotomy can be conflated with that between the linguistic and the non-linguistic. If something is part of a language, it is mentally accessible to the speaker, and therefore concrete. If not present to the speaker's consciousness, but merely a linguist's analytic convenience, it cannot be considered an actual part of the language, only an abstract non-linguistic 'idea'. The signifier and signified, taken separately, are *not* accessible to speakers of the language; they are accessible only in their conjunction. This ought to mean that the signifier and signified, conceived in isolation from one another, are not part of the language, indeed are nothing at all. However, the *Cours* obscures this with occasional statements (including three of them on p. 166 alone) that speak of the signifier and signified, taken separately, as being part of *langue*.

Value

In the second course, Saussure taught that a semiological system is a system of *valeurs* 'values'. In the case of the linguistic sign the values are especially complex because neither of its component parts is sufficient to define it, and because value can only exist through the collectivity of the community of speakers. Later references to currency exchange and the stock market make clear that Saussure is aware of the force of 'value' as a monetary metaphor. That this should have been prominent in his mind in 1908 is perhaps not unconnected to the fact that in that same year his younger brother René attracted widespread attention with a proposal for a supranational 'neutral monetary system – without coinage' (Guérard, 1922: 122n). This was a radically modernist proposal at a time when economists and politicians were struggling with the need to untie monetary systems from their traditional basis in precious metals.

The second course also introduces a comparison between a unit in a linguistic system and one in a game of chess (for an earlier language–chess analogy from his notes of the mid 1890s, see Godel, 1957: 47). This becomes the basis of the initial discussion of value in the *Cours*: 'Take the knight: is it, on its own, an element of the game? Assuredly not, since in its pure materiality, outside its square on the board and other conditions of the game, it represents nothing for the player and becomes a real and concrete element only once it has been invested with its value and has become one with that value' (153).

If a knight gets lost, not only can it be replaced by another knight, but 'even a piece devoid of any resemblance to one will be declared identical, so long as the same value is attributed to it' (154). He also makes clear that 'Value is not meaning' (Godel, 1957: 69; cf. Saussure, 1997: 29), and although he does not specify what the difference between them is, that question will become the point of departure for the discussion of value late in the third course. Here he introduces his famous point about the difference between the English word *sheep* and its French 'equivalent' *mouton*. The two words, he says, can have the same meaning, by which he apparently means that they can refer to the same animal. But they do not have the same value, because a Frenchman uses *mouton* when speaking of either the living animal or its meat, whereas an Englishman uses *sheep* only in the former case, and *mutton* in the latter.

This discussion has troubled many commentators (for a selection, see the long note 231 in the de Mauro edition of the *Cours* (Saussure, 1972 = *CLG*/D)) because when it comes to 'meaning' (*sens* or *signification*), Saussure reverts to the ordinary way of talking about words and things that he has dismissed as 'nomenclaturism' and that his whole concept of the *signe linguistique* aims to supersede. But as Burger (1961) concluded, the discussion makes sense if we graft the value/meaning distinction onto that between *langue*, the mental system, and *parole*, what people actually do with language. 'Meaning' is then to be understood in the ordinary way, as the use we make of spoken words to denote, things, actions, qualities and so on, whereas 'value' is what is intrinsic to mental signs that makes it possible for us to use spoken words in this way. The mistake of 'nomenclaturism' is to think that 'meaning' so conceived is how a language (*langue*) is structured, when in fact it has only to do with how it is put to use in *parole*.

What is dissatisfying in Saussure's discussion of value is that he is so insistent on its difference from meaning that he never gets to grips with their complex interrelationship. He points out that value is a part (and only a part) of meaning, but leaves us to infer what the rest of it is. He ignores the fact that, even in his own examples, the only way we know that the value of *mouton* is different from that of *sheep* is that the former has a broader range of meanings. While it appears to be implicit in his discussion that value emerges from meaning, he does not say so, let alone explain how it happens.

Arbitrariness and motivation

The idea that words are connected to their meanings merely in an arbitrary and conventional way is older even than sign theory itself, dating back to the Presocratics and the Sophists, with its *locus classicus* being the position taken by Hermogenes in Plato's *Cratylus*. Culler (1986: 29) summarises it thus: 'Since I speak English I may use the signifier represented by *dog* to talk about an animal of a particular species, but this sequence of sounds is no better suited to that purpose than another sequence. *Lod, tet*, or *bloop* would serve equally well if it were accepted by members of my speech community.' The ancient debates had been resumed by Whitney (1874), and Saussure's 1894 notes on Whitney include specific reactions to his view of language as a human 'institution'.

The arbitrariness of the sign makes scattered appearances from early in the second course, but only in the third course, where the relationship between signifier and signified becomes the centre of the linguistic universe, is it promoted to the status of 'first principle' of the linguistic sign. Saussure makes clear that 'arbitrary' does not mean that the signifier depends on the individual speaker's free choice, only that it is 'unmotivated' relative to the signified, with no natural attachment between them (101). But he does not discuss the principle in much depth, apparently considering it too obvious since it 'is not contested by anyone' (100), though its full ramifications are not appreciated. Perhaps his failure to analyse it further is connected to his admonition (mentioned on p. 65 above) against dissociating the two elements of the sign, to avoid wandering into the realm of abstract, unreal units.

The obvious objection to arbitrariness that Saussure takes up is onomatopoeia – words like 'bow-wow' that sound like what they mean – and exclamations that seem to represent direct bodily reactions. He dismisses them on the grounds that they are never organic elements of a linguistic system, are already arbitrary in some measure, being only approximate and half-conventional imitations of certain noises, and, once part of the language, undergo essentially the same evolutionary process as other words (101). Derrida (1974) has shown how the logic of this discussion turns against itself, to prove the uselessness of all the criteria Saussure summons to determine what is or is not an onomatopoeia, and in the absence of any such criteria, no element of any language can definitively be declared to be 'arbitrary' (see Joseph et al., 2001: 198–9).

But the intended effect is clearly to present the case for the arbitrariness of the sign in absolute terms. By placing absolute arbitrariness at the head of Part One of the *Cours*, the editors ensured that it would get the attention of everyone who opened the book. Considerably less attention has gone to the continuations of the discussion. The chapter on 'Linguistic value' (155ff.) includes an attempt to clarify the original presentation of arbitrariness. Saussure says that, before language, human thought was only an amorphous, indistinct, nebulous mass, a floating realm; and human sound was no different. Only with the appearance of language do thoughts, in conjunction with sounds, become distinct. He argues that:

> the choice which calls up a given acoustic slice for a given idea is perfectly arbitrary. If this were not so, the notion of value would lose something of its character, since it would contain an element imposed from without. But in fact the values remain entirely relative, and that is why the link between the idea and the sound is radically arbitrary. (*CLG*: 157)

De Mauro's edition of the *Cours* (*CLG*/D: 464, n. 228) points out that the last sentence turns the argument into a circular one, and shows that it is the result of a poor decision by the editors. Saussure did not try to *explain* the arbitrariness of the linguistic sign. By positing it as the first principle, he accepted it axiomatically as the primordial fact about language that need not and cannot be explained. Further on in the *Cours* the arbitrariness of the sign will be called an 'irrational principle' (182), and although this too is an interpolation by the editors of a word Saussure might have feared would lead to misunderstanding, it seems a fair interpretation.

Lurking unspoken in the background to this discussion is an ancient chicken-and-egg paradox concerning the relationship of language and thought. If they do not represent divine endowments, which came first? If our forebears created languages by establishing conventions, then how, before they had the language, could they have worked out what they wanted to say? The solution proposed by Epicurus would find many adherents from later antiquity through modern times, where it provided the basis of Romantic theories of language. It was that

> names . . . were not at first deliberately given to things, but men's natures according to their different nationalities had their own peculiar feelings and received their peculiar impressions, and so each in their own way emitted air formed into shape by each of these feelings and impressions, according to the differences made in the different nations by the places of their abode as well. (Epicurus, *Letter to Herodotus* 75–6, translation by Bailey, 1926)

An initial form of language, generated directly by the body, was enough to provide a first organisation of thought, after which deliberate, conventional refinements produced languages of the sort we know now. The existence of different languages is traced to bodily differences in the different *ethnoi*, races or ethnicities. By the mid nineteenth century, fed by misinterpretations of Darwin, this view had led to the development of theories of language and intelligence that formed an important part of 'scientific racism'. Although Saussure, following in the footsteps of Whitney, eschewed such views, they can be found fully blown in an 1899 book by his brother Léopold (see Joseph, 2000b).

It was partly in order to distance himself from the language–race link that Whitney characterised languages as human 'institutions'. But as Saussure wrote in his notes of 1894, Whitney's conception, although basically right, produced a further problem by seeming to suggest that languages are rational inventions, where again it is hard to avoid comparing their differences in terms of which is more logical than the other. Although Whitney believed that languages are *accidentally produced* institutions, his wording did not always make this clear, probably because the view he was contesting was the powerful racist one, not the almost forgotten Enlightenment notion of languages as deliberate logical creations.

For Saussure, however, rationally invented languages were in fact a very important feature in his intellectual and familial milieu. The years of his courses in general linguistics were also the ones in which his brother René was achieving much wider renown as the newly appointed leader of the Esperanto movement. It was believed that this language, in addition to its political advantages, would promote logical thought through its rationally structured principles of organisation. Esperanto was like a newly built modern city, French like a medieval one with alleys constructed for mule carts, through which automobiles could hardly be expected to pass. Ferdinand saw things the other way round: 'traditional' languages were in fact structured in an ultra-modernist way. It was the invented languages like Esperanto that were built on old-fashioned, wrong-headed notions.

It is certainly interesting, and maybe significant, that Saussure's theoretical path was cut between those of his two younger brothers, one caught up in a racist and the other a rationalist misunderstanding of language, and following the traces of Whitney, who however had strayed too close to the latter side. Saussure's correction was to make arbitrariness the starting point of the discussion, and to stress that although language is intimately bound up with thought, no reasoning is involved.

So, at least, readers of the *Cours* are led to believe until they get to the chapter headed *Mécanisme de la langue*, which looks at arbitrariness as a *problem* that the whole structure of a language is geared toward limiting. It states explicitly that 'everything having to do with language as a system demands . . . to be treated from the point of view . . . of limiting the arbitrary' (182). Although the earlier discussion of arbitrariness gave no hint that it admitted of degrees, Saussure says here that 'Only some signs are absolutely arbitrary; with others, a phenomenon intervenes which permits the recognition of degrees of arbitrariness without doing away with it: *the sign can be relatively motivated*' (180–1, italics in original). He then gives a series of examples, all from morphology:

> Thus *vingt* [twenty] is unmotivated, but *dix-neuf* [nineteen] is less so, since it evokes the terms which compose it and others associated with it, for instance *dix* [10], *neuf* [9], *vingt-neuf* [29], *dix-huit* [18] . . . Likewise for *poirier* [pear tree], which recalls the simple word *poire* [pear], and whose suffix *-ier* brings to mind *cerisier* [cherry tree], *pommier* [apple tree], etc. . . . The English plural *ships* recalls through its formation the whole series *flags, birds, books*, etc., whereas *men, sheep* recall nothing . . . (181)

When he says following these examples that 'the degree of motivation is always proportional to the ease of syntactic analysis' (181), one is reminded that the morphological units which he is presupposing here can only be part of *langue* if psychologically accessible to ordinary speakers (non-linguists), making them concrete realities (see p. 65 above).

Left without restriction, the result would be supreme complication. But 'the mind manages to introduce a principle of order and regularity into certain parts of the mass of signs, and therein lies the role of the relatively motivated'. More than anything, this approach is reminiscent of the neogrammarians by whom Saussure was trained in historical linguistics. According to them, languages evolve 'blindly' following laws of sound change that admit of no exceptions, but are occasionally contravened by 'analogy' – precisely the process of the mind finding and introducing order into what is, on the whole, an arbitrary procedure. Saussure believes that some languages, like Sanskrit, are highly grammatical in structure and therefore lean more to the side of motivation, whereas others, like Chinese, are more lexicological and therefore lean more to arbitrariness. However, 'within the interior of any given language, the whole movement of evolution can be marked by a continual passage from the motivated to the arbitrary and back again' (183).

By the end of this discussion, the arbitrariness of the sign appears to be a paradoxical principle indeed. It is the very basis of the linguistic system, yet the 'systematicity' of the system is all about limiting it. It is irrational, and relative motivation is introduced by the mind so as to create order, yet the sign is 'real' precisely because of its accessibility to the mind. As for the force that works against the rationalising action of the mind and ensures that the signs of a language remain essentially arbitrary, it is not identified, other than as the 'principle' of arbitrariness itself. This leaves a puzzle, for if languages are the products of human minds, this surely is no less true of their arbitrary than of their motivated parts. Saussure's view is that the most characteristic feature (the arbitrary signs) of language, which is itself the most characteristic attribute of the human mind, is founded on a principle diametrically opposed to that of the active workings of the mind. This ultimate mystery of language does at least offer a practical advantage that Saussure is known to have been concerned about. It means that linguistics could never be wholly subsumed into psychology, but must be constructed as an autonomous discipline.

Linearity

The second principle of the sign states that 'the signifier, being auditory in nature, unfolds itself in time only . . . and has a linear extension' (103). In his initial presentation of the two principles he had said, very confusingly, that 'the linguistic sign (image used as sign)' has a linear temporal extension (Saussure, 1993: 77). He rectified this in a subsequent lecture, making clear that the signifier is what is linear. Saussure was perhaps struggling to reconcile linearity with his strong conviction that the sign consists of the inseparable juncture of a signifier and a signified. This would seem to suggest that, if the signifier unfolds in time only and has a linear extension, so does the sign as a whole. But if the signified extended in time in the same way the signifier does, we would be obliged to say that the signified of *fourmi* 'ant' is twice as 'long' as the signified of *chat* 'cat', just because the signifiers have two syllables and one respectively. Obviously it makes no sense at all to speak of the 'length' of a signified in this way.

One of the challenges of interpreting Saussure is to work out why he thought linearity so fundamentally important. He emphasises that it makes the acoustic signs of language different from visual signs, for example, which 'can offer complications simultaneously in various dimensions' (*CLG*: 103). He proposes as a counterexample a stressed syllable, where 'it seems that I accumulate different meaningful elements on one same point. But this is an illusion. The syllable and its stress constitute a single phonetic act' (103). This view has been contested, notably by Roman Jakobson, who initially formulated his theory of distinctive features as a critique of it (see Joseph, 1989b).

Another point made by Saussure in his lecture on linearity was omitted from the *Cours*: 'If we can separate words, it is a consequence of this principle' (*CLG*/E 1: 157). This would seem to connect with the later passage on linguistic value (155ff., discussed in the previous section) which says that before language, human thought and sound were amorphous masses. The process of making thoughts (along with sounds) distinct by the creation of linguistic signs is, in effect, 'separating words'. What the principle of linearity maintains is that this process is driven by the nature of human sound production. If we were capable of producing and interpreting complexly meaningful single bursts of sound that could express holistic clouds of indistinct thought, there would have been no need for thought to become analytical.

This is very close to the account of the origin of human intelligence put forward in the eighteenth century by the Abbot of Condillac, in which the development of analytic thought began with the need to interpret sounds made by fellow early humans. These first impulses toward analysis then fed back, à la Epicurus, into the development of language. Saussure shows no inclination to be associated with phases in the history of linguistic thought earlier than Whitney, and perhaps this helps explain his failure to elaborate the importance of linearity for his theory of the linguistic sign. In any case, his view that the sound aspect of language is what has determined the development of human thought bolsters his belief that linguistics needs to be independent of psychology – indeed, it accords linguistics a certain historical priority.

Immutability and mutability

The final aspect of Saussure's discussion of the sign to be taken up here is an overtly paradoxical one which he developed at some length in the third course. It is that languages inevitably change, yet no one can change them. Both the mutability and the immutability of language, he argues, result from the arbitrariness of the sign. Were there some rational connection between signified and signifier, it would allow speakers of the language to intervene either to prevent inevitable change, or to initiate changes of their own. Saussure does not deny the validity of the usual explanation given in his day for immutability, namely the historical transmission of language. It excludes any possibility of sudden or general change, because generations always overlap, and because of the amount of imitative effort involved in mastering our mother tongue (*CLG*: 106). But Saussure insists that the *essential* explanation lies with the arbitrary nature of the sign, which protects the language from any attempt at modifying it, because the general populace would be unable to discuss the matter, even if they were more conscious of language than they are. For in order for something to be put into question, it must rest on a norm that is *raisonnable*, able to be reasoned about.

We saw above (p. 70) that in the systematic part of language arbitrariness is limited and 'a relative reason reigns', so here the populace (or at least specialists – grammarians, logicians, etc.) would be theoretically capable of changing things. Yet experience has shown that all attempts of the kind have failed. Here what he probably has in mind is the dispute between usage and logic, which dates back to the Stoics and Alexandrians and was memorably revived in seventeenth-century France. Despite all the attempts of grammarians to reform the 'illogicalities' of French grammar (which in truth usually meant cases where French differs from Latin), popular usage – or at least *le bon usage* of the upper classes – has always prevailed.

Immutability has a social dimension as well. The fact that the language is an integral part of everyone's life creates a collective resistance to change initiated by any individual. And it has a historical dimension: the language being situated in time, solidarity with the past checks the freedom to choose. 'It is because the sign is arbitrary that it knows no other law than that of tradition, and it is because it is founded on tradition that it can be arbitrary' (*CLG*: 108).

As for mutability, Saussure begins by stating that language change always results in 'a displacement of the relationship between the signified and the signifier' (*CLG*: 109). He cites the example of Latin *necare* 'to kill', which has become French *noyer* 'to drown', through a series of changes in both sound and meaning that it would be futile to try to separate. (Saussure has been criticised for speaking of language change here in exactly the terms of a Latin word 'becoming' a French word which he has explicitly rejected elsewhere; see above, p. 60.) Because the sign is historically continuous, it changes – inevitably, because language is not exempt from the general fact that time changes all things (*CLG*: 112).

This was not the usual explanation of language change at the time. Historical linguists assumed that movements of peoples, invasions and migrations were the main impetus for language change, followed by interchange with neighbouring peoples, and, to a lesser extent, the importation of new objects and ideas. Without these external impulses, it was expected that the forces of stasis would keep a language unchanged. Saussure argues instead that the source of change is to be found in the language itself, and in the very fact of its being situated in time. He says that this is true even of an artificial language like Esperanto – again raising the spectre of a dispute with his brother René, because one of the main arguments put forward in favour of artificial languages was that because of their rationally controlled origins they would not undergo change in the way that uncontrolled natural languages do (*CLG*: 111).

From these facts Saussure deduces that the reality of a language cannot be fully comprehended without taking account of both its social and its historical dimension, in conjunction with the arbitrariness of the linguistic sign. If we attended to the historical but left aside the social, 'imagining an isolated individual living for several centuries, we would perhaps note no alteration; time would not act on the language' (*CLG*: 113). And if we attended to the social without the historical, 'we would not see the effect of the social forces acting on the language' (113). But as soon as we put the two together, we find that 'the language is not free, because time will permit the social forces working upon it to develop their effects, and we arrive at the principle of continuity, which annuls freedom' (113).

Saussure's main targets in this chapter seem to be, on the one hand, the assumption by historical linguists that language change must be externally provoked, and on the other, the attempts to meddle in the natural evolution of languages through prescriptivism and the creation of artificial languages. These attempts are partly aimed at stopping languages from changing, in the belief that linguistic stability is necessary for the maintenance of logical thought. To stop a language from changing requires making changes in it – trying to enforce 'counter-natural' rules like the one against splitting infinitives in English, or in the extreme case, inventing a whole new language. Yet in spite of all these efforts languages continue to go their own way, the way of 'usage', what the general populace decides unthinkingly to accept. The combined arbitrariness and systematicity of the language give it an organic character that makes it essentially impervious to external forces.

Conclusion

Saussure could scarcely have imagined the subsequent history of his concept of the linguistic sign. The semiotics he envisaged would come into existence, partly through his influence and partly through that of the American pragmatist Peirce, who elaborated his own theory of signs under the rubric *semiotic* a few years prior to Saussure's *sémiologie*, though his writings on the subject remained unpublished until after Saussure's death. Moreover, a generalised 'structuralism', inspired directly by the Saussurean conception of signs as values defined by pure difference in a system where everything connects, would become the master paradigm in a vast range of fields of learning for decades, to be superseded by a 'post-structuralism' that originated largely with Derrida's wide-ranging critique of the linguistic sign as Saussure conceived it (see Joseph et al., 2001: ch. 13).

Interestingly, what has proved to be the most controversial aspect of the Saussurean sign is in fact one of the most venerable. The decoupling of the signified from things in the world goes all the way back to the Stoics and their conception of the *sēmainomenon* as incorporeal. Yet critics of post-structuralism regularly point to Saussure as the originator of this decoupling (which, by the way, is widely but mistakenly thought to be what Saussure meant by 'the arbitrariness of the linguistic sign') and blame it and him for the disintegration of meaning, order and civilisation itself in the modern world.

It is true that if meanings are not rooted in universal logic or in the world of common human sense experience, but are entirely at the whim of each particular linguistic community, then, when two communities construct different meanings, there is no objective basis for deciding which is right or better. All 'logic', all scientific knowledge, must be bound to the culture of a particular social group. These relativistic implications were not explicitly drawn by Saussure, but a manuscript note (reckoned by Godel (1957: 37) to date from the mid 1890s) shows that he realised his position had radical consequences for our understanding of the human mind: 'If ever anywhere an object could be the term on which the sign is fixed, linguistics would instantly cease to be what it is, from top to bottom; and along with it the human mind . . .' (*CLG*/E 1: 148).

But he did not specify what consequences he was thinking of, and his overall reticence has made it possible for all the implications discussed above to be read into his theory of the sign. Ogden and Richards were the first to have read him this way, and rejected his version of the linguistic sign on this account: 'Unfortunately this [Saussurean] theory of signs, by neglecting entirely the things for which signs stand, was from the beginning cut off from any contact with scientific methods of verification. De Saussure, however, does not appear to have pursued the matter far enough for this defect to become obvious' (Ogden and Richards, 1923: 8). They insisted that the linguistic sign must be triangular, with the concrete 'referent' as the third point, in order to anchor language in reality. (This was very different from Peirce's 'triadic' conception of the sign, where the third element, the 'interpretant', is another sign which causes the first sign to be interpreted in a particular way.) Otherwise, they believed, there would be no way to separate truth from fiction.

Ogden and Richards started a trend that continues down to those present-day opponents of post-structuralism mentioned earlier who, arguing from the anti-relativistic right, blame Saussure for the disintegration of meaning and civilisation. Actually, a very similar reading of Saussure's theory of the sign has given rise to a no less ferocious critique from the Marxist left, starting with Voloshinov (1929) and again continuing to the present day, where the notion of the 'free-floating signified' is condemned as intellectual collusion with the forces of hegemony and inequality to disengage language from the reality of class difference and class struggle.

None of these criticisms of Saussure is entirely fair. Far from floating free, the signified is bound to the social group's experience of the world. As far as Saussure is concerned, the linguistic sign is not an abstraction away from social reality, but a concrete social reality in its own right, and his criterion for this is what ordinary people think and feel. And as far as any individual is concerned, the linguistic sign is not relativistic at all, but so completely determined by society and history that it might as well be God-given. Still, such condemnation from both ends of the ideological spectrum is not only a tribute to Saussure's central importance in modern thought, but might in itself lead a reasonable person to suspect that with his conception of the linguistic sign – despite all the lacunas, ellipses and contradictions – he got something drastically right.

5 *Langue* and *parole*

W. Terrence Gordon

Preliminary remarks on terminology in Saussure and in his commentators

Throughout the *Cours de linguistique générale* (*inter alia* 24, 25, 56, 119, 121, 129) the reader finds the terms *opposition* and *dualité*. *Opposition* is used in its general sense in the passages cited above but occurs elsewhere (167ff.) in a specific sense which brings it within the compass of one of the paired terms[1] (*différence/opposition*) which shape the entire *Cours de linguistique générale* (henceforth *Cours, CLG*, or *CGL* in English), a sign's constituents, its form and its concept, being *different* from those of other signs for Saussure, but the sign as a whole being *in opposition* to other signs. In many commentaries on the *Cours*, the paired terms are themselves referred to as *oppositions* or *dualities*. While *opposition* is an apposite description of the relationship in which the terms in each pair stand to each other, i.e. a characterisation of the distinctiveness of the linguistic sign with respect to other linguistic signs, as defined in the text of the *Cours* (167), it is potentially misleading in its more general meaning, which can overshadow the Saussurean sense of distinctiveness by a suggestion of contrast or even of incompatibility. As for *duality*, though it does not entail the same problem, neither does it correspond to the sense in which Saussure uses *dualité* to denote a division inherent within the subject matter of linguistics itself (Hjelmslev's *objet étudié*), rather than in the analytical apparatus of the discipline. (See Gordon, 1996.)

Preferable to *opposition* and *duality* is the term *complementarity*, and while the cognate *complémentarité* is not in Engler's compendium of Saussurean terminology (1968a), it is very much in the spirit of passages from the *Cours* which reveal that, by its own sound-shape and derivation, Saussure's terminology deliberately and explicitly embodies the principle it describes and expresses through *différence/opposition*. Thus, while *s'opposant* and *opposition* appear in the following passages, where the *Cours* offers a commentary on its own terminology, they are linked in both instances to words and phrases (my italics added) that serve as reminders of the complementarity principle:

L'ambiguité disparaîtrait si l'on désignait les trois notions ici en présence [*signe, concept, image acoustique*] par des noms qui *s'appellent* les uns les autres *tout en s'opposant* [*signe/signifié/signifiant*]. (*CLG*: 99)
(The ambiguity (ed. 'sign' being used to mean both just the acoustic image *and* the acoustic image combined with the concept) would disappear if the three notions present here (sign, concept, acoustic image) were designated by three terms which mutually *imply* as well as *differentiate* each other.)

Mais pour mieux marquer *cette opposition et ce croisement* de deux ordres de phénomènes relatifs au même objet, nous préférons parler de linguistique *synchronique* et de linguistique *diachronique*. (*CLG*: 117)
(But to indicate more clearly *the opposition and crossing* of two orders of phenomena that relate to the same object, I prefer to speak of *synchronic* and *diachronic* linguistics. *CGL*-B: 81)

Such passages indicate that a reading of the *Cours* will reveal the coherence of Saussure's thought when it focuses on his terminological couplings as inseparable and interacting units, even in those cases where they are not marked by the characteristic echoes of *signifié/signifiant, synchronique/diachronique*. (See Gordon, 1997.)

The foundational complementarity of the *Cours de linguistique générale*

This is *langue/parole*. In comparison with the other complementarities which collectively structure the *Cours*, *langue/parole* has privileged status and unique status in itself. In the first place, none of the others can logically precede it. Secondly, as the *Cours* repeatedly reminds the reader, *langue* constitutes the sole autonomous element of linguistic analysis:

En effet, parmi tant de dualités, la langue seule paraît être susceptible d'une définition autonome et fournit un point d'appui satisfaisant pour l'esprit. (*CLG*: 25)
(Actually, among so many dualities, language alone seems to lend itself to independent definition and provide a fulcrum that satisfies the mind. *CGL*-B: 9)

[La langue] est un objet bien défini dans l'ensemble hétéroclite des faits de langage. (*CLG*: 31)
(Language is a well-defined object in the heterogeneous mass of speech facts. *CGL*-B: 14)

Thirdly, the inherent autonomy of *langue* as subject matter supplies an analytic framework that solves the problem of an arbitrary starting point and arbitrary organisation of linguistic data:

La langue . . . est un tout en soi et un principe de classification. Dès que nous lui donnons la première place parmi les faits de langage, nous introduisons un ordre naturel dans un ensemble qui ne se prête à une aucune autre classification. (*CLG*: 25)
(The linguistic system . . . constitutes a whole in itself as well as a principle of classification. As soon as we accord it the prime place among language phenomena, we introduce a natural order into a mass that does not lend itself to any other classification.)

Fourthly, *langue/parole*, defined in relation to each other and to the overarching term *langage*,[2] illustrate that the Saussurean complementarities are necessarily self-transcending. Taken separately, the terms *langue/parole* constitute the elements of a convenient analytical shorthand for the linguist; taken together, they constitute the interactive functioning of elements of language as a system in a virtual state and language as samples of the system in use for purposes of communication.

In a procedure which reflects the complementarity of *signification/valeur*, the *Cours* offers no single, unitary definition of *langue* but rather a montage from which the reader learns what *langue* is *not* and how it relates to both *parole* and *langage*. Thus:

(1) Mais qu'est-ce que la langue? Pour nous elle ne se confond pas avec le langage; elle n'en est qu'une partie déterminée, essentielle, il est vrai. C'est à la fois un produit social de la faculté du langage et un ensemble de conventions nécessaires, adoptées par le corps social pour permettre l'exercice de cette faculté chez les individus. (*CLG*: 25)
(But what is language (*langue*)? It is not to be confused with human speech (*langage*), of which it is only a definite part, though certainly an essential one. It is both a social product of the faculty of speech and a collection of necessary conventions that have been adopted by a social body to permit individuals to exercise that faculty. *CGL*-B: 9)

(2) . . . ce n'est pas le langage parlé qui est naturel à l'homme, mais la faculté de constituer une langue, c'est-à-dire un système de signes distincts correspondant à des idées distinctes. (*CLG*: 26)
(. . . it is not spoken language that is natural to the human person, but the faculty of creating a language, that is, a system of distinct signs corresponding to distinct ideas.)

(3) La langue n'est pas une fonction du sujet parlant, elle est le produit que l'individu enregistre passivement . . .

La parole est au contraire un acte individuel de volonté et d'intelligence, dans lequel il convient de distinguer: 1° les combinaisons par lesquelles le sujet parlant utilise le code de la langue en vue d'exprimer sa pensée personnelle; 2° le mécanisme psycho-physique qui lui permet d'extérioriser ces combinaisons. (*CLG*: 30–1)
(Language (*langue*) is not a function of the speaker; it is a product that is passively assimilated by the individual . . .

Speaking, on the contrary, is an individual act. It is wilful and intellectual. Within the act, we should distinguish between: (1) the combinations by which the speaker uses the language code for expressing his own thought; and (2) the psychophysical mechanism that allows him to exteriorise those combinations. *CGL*-B: 14)

(4) La langue n'est pas moins que la parole un objet de nature concrète . . . (*CLG*: 32) (Language is concrete, no less so than speaking . . . *CGL*-B: 15)

(5) . . . la langue est un système de pures valeurs que rien ne détermine en dehors de l'état momentané de ses termes. (*CLG*: 116)
(. . . language is a system of pure values which are determined by nothing except the momentary arrangement of its terms. *CGL*-B: 80)

(6) . . . la langue n'est pas un mécanisme créé et agencé en vue des concepts à exprimer. (*CLG*: 122)
(. . . language is not a mechanism created and arranged with a view to the concepts to be expressed. *CGL*-B: 85)

Interpreting Saussure's complementarities in relation to each other

Saussure's complementarities dictate a certain logic with respect to the connections among them. As a consequence, Saussure maintains a distinction between *signification*, reserved for meaning in *langue*, and *sens* designating meaning in *parole*. The distinction is not problematic in itself, but the use of *signification* in the text of the *Cours* can be in passages such as the following: 'un concept "juger" est uni à l'image acoustique *juger*; en un mot, il symbolise la signification . . . (*CLG*: 162) What precisely is to be understood by the notion of *symbolising signification*? The passage is typical of many in the *Cours* that are marked by overly succinct formulation and require some expansion before they yield their full meaning. In the present case, at least four paraphrases appear to be possible, revealing, among other things, the interpenetration of *langue* and *parole*, while shedding light on the somewhat obscure formulation of the original:

Le concept se symbolise par une image acoustique. (langue)
(The concept is symbolised in an acoustic image.)
Il se concrétise par une image acoustique. (langue)
(The concept is made concrete in an acoustic image.)
Il se concrétise par un acte de signification. (parole)
(The symbol is made concrete in an act of meaning.)
Il se concrétise par sa valeur relative aux autre concepts. (langue)
(The symbol is made concrete by its value relative to other concepts.)

Critical reception of Saussure's *langue/parole* complementarity

The literature reviewed below has been selected from the vast number of publications on the subject in an effort to show as much as possible of the diversity among the approaches that scholars have taken in their commentaries.

Ogden and Richards

In *The Meaning of Meaning* (1994 [1923]), C. K. Ogden and I. A. Richards reject the *langue/parole* complementarity as being chimerical and of no use to the linguist except as evidence of Saussure's mind being held in thrall by word magic and subjugated to the tyranny of hypostatisation. They infer this state of affairs from the occurrence of the word *objet* in the *Cours*, either conveniently ignoring or not recognising that it refers variously to a physical object (1994: 23, 32), to the subject matter of linguistics (1994: 16, 31), and to the objective of linguistics (1994: 13, 25). The same passages indicate that the complementarity principle discussed above in relation to Saussure's paired terms applies no less to the distinct meanings that can be detected in his exposition for single key terms such as *objet*.[3]

In reference to these same passages, Ogden and Richards misconstrue *objet* as being uniformly used in only one sense, that of a concrete object, a sense which the text of the *Cours* more frequently renders by *chose*, *entité*, etc. Moreover, in spite of the vigour with which Ogden and Richards pursue their make-an-example-of-him commentary on Saussure (it was one of the few passages in *The Meaning of Meaning* to be expanded after the first edition), they themselves distinguish between language as system and language in use when their analysis so requires, though without attaching any terminological distinctions thereto. The authors appear to be oblivious to their implicit acceptance of the *langue/parole* complementarity in such passages as 'A symbol becomes, when uttered, in virtue of being so caused, a sign to a hearer of an act of reference' (1994: 314).

While no direct counterpart to *langue/parole* is to be found in Ogden's and Richards' terminology, the facts of language that compelled Saussure to establish it as his foundational complementarity are precisely those that constitute the rationale of organising *The Meaning of Meaning* around a consistent distinction between *sign* and *symbol.* (See Gordon, 1994a, 1994b.) This primary complementarity for Ogden and Richards is a *de facto* equivalent of Saussure's *langue/parole*. The distinction for Saussure between the French terms which are cognates of Ogden's and Richards' *sign/symbol*, namely *signe/symbole*, is set out in a passage of the *Cours* where Saussure comments on the use of *symbole* to denote a *signifiant* partially motivated with respect to its *signifié* (*CLG*: 101). From his perspective, this is a marginal case of deviation from the dominant principle of the arbitrariness of the linguistic sign.

Whereas Ogden and Richards often concede valid points in discussing an author with whom they otherwise disagree, they maintain in their criticism of Saussure that he undermined all the potential of his study by positing an overdetermined entity (the term used by Strozier, 1988), *langue*. And while it is true that Ogden and Richards speak elsewhere of their affinity with Gardiner, who maintained a language/speech opposition, that affinity is only in respect of the fourth of their five symbol functions (the promotion of effects intended) and Gardiner's concept of volitional attitudes. Moreover, Gardiner's language/speech opposition is deliberately at odds with Saussure (see Gordon, 1989: 372).

J. R. Firth

An examination of J. R. Firth's writings, taken as a whole, reveals his ambivalence toward the tenets underlying Saussurean structuralism. But of the six major features in Saussure's work which Firth condemned, only one proves to be incompatible with Firth's position in his later works.[4]

Saussure's *langue/parole* opposition was anathema to Firth because of its inherent abstraction and positing of collectivity. His antipathy dates from 1935: 'There is no such thing as *une langue une* [sic] and there never has been' (1935: 68). There is even indirect reference to Firth's conviction about the irrelevance of *langue* as late as Firth (1968).

Firth's criticism of the concept of *langue* is consistent with his principles but not with his practice. It ignores the obvious fact that whereas speech activity may reveal systems, the systems are not the activity itself. If the linguist is to look for something 'in' speech, as Firth himself says, that is, something recurring in samples of speech, that something must be distinct from the speech activity and, therefore, it must be treated abstractly. The 'suitable language' (of analysis), which Firth began to develop in 1935, was *serial contextualisation*, which proved to be as much of an abstraction as Saussure's concept of *langue*. And though Firth could declare that science should not impose systems on language, he imposed a five-way split on meaning in his first paper on semantics (1935).

It is paradoxical, therefore, in the light of Firth's vigorous and sustained objection to the abstraction of *langue*, to find that he ultimately characterised a key concept in his work, that of *collocational meaning*, as an abstraction: 'Meaning by collocation is an abstraction at the syntagmatic level and is not directly concerned with the conceptual or idea approach to the meaning of words' (1951: 128).

In distinguishing *langue* from *parole*, Saussure characterises it variously as product, thing and object (*cf. supra*). Firth attacked this view. But in stating that he defined language as a thing, Saussure added that he was defining the thing itself, i.e. the phenomenon of language, and redefining it, rather than relying on existing definitions and existing terminology, which he viewed as ambiguous. There was, therefore, no intention on Saussure's part to reify language, even when he spoke of it as object or as product, for he added: '[La langue] est la partie sociale du langage, extérieure à l'individu, qui à lui seul ne peut ni la créer ni la modifier; elle n'existe qu'en vertu d'une sorte de contrat passé entre les membres d'une communauté' (*CLG*: 31) ('[Language] is the social side of speech, outside the individual who can never create nor modify it by himself; it exists only by virtue of a sort of contract signed by the members of a community', *CGL*-B: 14).

Rulon Wells

Wells is one of the few commentators to develop a critique of the *Cours* by juxtaposing passages from different sections. With respect to *langue*, he begins by citing from the introduction to the section of the *Cours* devoted to synchronic linguistics: 'D'ailleurs la délimitation dans le temps n'est pas la seule difficulté que nous rencontrons dans la définition d'un état de langue; le même problème se pose à propos de l'espace' (*CLG:* 43) (Wells, 1947: 28). From here, Wells moves to one of Saussure's lessons on geographical linguistics: 'That many dialects shade off into one another is set forth (275–80), but the most striking fact is not mentioned: there can be an area divided into a series of sub-areas such that people of any two adjacent sub-areas understand each other readily, but people from the two extreme sub-areas scarcely understand each other at all' (1947: 28–9). For Wells, this constitutes evidence that the concept of *langue* represents an ideal, and that as such it is at odds with Saussure's claim that *langue* is as concrete as *parole* (*CLG*: 32). Wells rhetorically asks how *langue* can be concrete without possessing fixed limits. He cites (Wells, 1947: 29) a passage in which Saussure apparently concedes that *langue* is essentially an idealised notion: 'a concept of a language-state can only be approximate. In static linguistics, as in most sciences, no course of reasoning is possible without the usual simplification of data' (*CGL*-B: 102).

Saussure's claim for the concreteness of *langue* is also undermined, according to Wells, by Saussure's paradoxical admission that *langue* is not complete in any single language speaker:

> C'est un trésor déposé par la pratique de la parole dans les sujets appartenant à une même communauté, un système grammatical existant virtuellement dans chaque cerveau, ou plus exactement dans les cerveaux d'un ensemble d'individus; *car la langue n'est complète dans aucun, elle n'existe parfaitement que dans la masse.* (*CLG*: 30, italics ours)

> (It is a storehouse filled by the members of a given community through their active use of speaking, a grammatical system that has a potential existence in each brain, or, more specifically, in the brains of a group of individuals. *For language is not complete in any speaker; it exists perfectly only within a collectivity. CGL-B*: 13–14, emphasis added)

More specifically: 'Among all the individuals that are linked together by speech, some sort of average will be set up: all will reproduce – not exactly of course, but approximately – the same signs united with the same concepts' (*CGL-B*: 13).

Wells adds a further dimension to his charge of inconsistency against Saussure, noting that his approval of Whitney's concept of language as a social institution is rendered spurious by the claim that language is *purely* conventional and traditional, and thus, unlike social mores, ethical or economic institutions, devoid of any rational norm to govern linguistic change. But Wells does concede that the lessons on analogical remodelling in the section of the *Cours* devoted to diachronic linguistics introduce something in the nature of a norm which motivates language change. While this concesssion on Wells's part may appear to absolve Sausure in part on the original charge of inconsistency, it merely opens onto a fresh problem with the foundation of the Saussurean edifice:

> So language is not so different from other institutions after all. And it may be asked whether de Saussure has not exaggerated the extent to which institutions other than sign systems are shaped by rational criticism, and subject to the deliberate volition of the community; and whether on the other hand, quite apart from analogy, he has not underplayed the element of natural symbolism, i.e. of onomatopy, in language. (Wells, 1947:31)

N. C. W. Spence

By 1957, published commentaries on Saussure's *langue/parole* were already so numerous as to inspire Spence's comparative evaluation of them. Taking his cues largely from Rogger at first, and later from Malmberg, Spence states that the notion of idiolect is implicit in Saussure's well-known 'equational' model for *langue*[5] (*CLG*: 38) and that Saussure's attempt 'to do justice to th[e] wider reality of *la langue* as a social institution' leads him to undermine both the basis of his *langue/parole* distinction (Spence, 1957: 6) and the possibility of practising linguistics as the study of *langue*, in that 'la somme des images verbales emmagasinées chez tous les individus' (*CLG*: 30) would logically include what Saussure describes as *faits de parole* (Spence, 1957: 7). This line of criticism ignores the subtler hints of terminological affinities and distinctions to be found within the very passage which Spence quotes, namely that of *image verbale* as a variant of *image acoustique* (hence an element of *langue*) and the force of *emmagasinées*, a term reserved by Saussure for describing elements of *langue*.

Spence agrees with Malmberg that the distinction between *Individualsprache* and *Kollektivsprache* is unsatisfactory, inasmuch as the former groups isolated linguistic phenomena in disregard of their specific social, lexical and phonological interconnections, but he adds that this does not sanction a 'return to the position represented by the Saussurean opposition between individual *parole* and communal *langue*' (Spence, 1957: 10). The impossibility of defining or delimiting precisely the collective system of *langue* is the point to which Spence repeatedly returns, apparently unwilling to allow that Saussure's assertion of the interdependence of *langue/parole* might be viewed as a concession to that impossibility which couples inseparable functional features of language (*langage*), while uncoupling them terminologically (*langue/parole*) for heuristic purposes. Saussure himself disappears in the central portion of Spence's essay, and it is not till the final section, where *langue/parole* as presented in the *Cours* is still condemned as 'largely artificial' (Spence, 1957: 21), that Spence introduces his own corrective: 'The *parole* of the individual is the exteriorisation of his individual linguistic system, his *langue individuelle* and the two are very closely linked' (1957: 22). Spence's conclusion is that neither the *langue/parole* dichotomy nor the notion of *parole* itself is essential as a basis for structural linguistics (1957: 26–7), and, being one of the 'practical men', identified at the beginning of his article, who study the near-infinite variety of speech without feeling any compulsion to either set it in a predetermined framework with theoretical implications or draw from it conclusions for determining such a framework, he offers no alternative.

John Hewson

Gustave Guillaume's work is not well known in the English-speaking world (see also Puech in this volume), but his legacy has been carried on by Canadian scholars such as Roch Valin, Walter Hirtle and John Hewson. While Roman Jakobson, for example, worked in close collaboration with other scholars whose names are associated with the structural linguistics identified as an outgrowth of Saussure's teachings, other European scholars took different paths – none more so than Gustave Guillaume. When Saussure's *Cours* appeared in print in 1916, Guillaume, it is said, was the first person to buy a copy in Paris. The book inspired him, offering a starting point from which to expand on Saussure's seminal ideas.

Just as Jakobson would replace *langue/parole* by *code/message*, Guillaume too would modify the primary Saussurean duality, speaking in his lectures of its shortcoming. The insight around which Guillaume developed his work was that *langue* is language in a potential state and that *parole* is language as actualised. The link between them, he asserted, provides an account of how speakers combine words into sentences. The essence of Guillaume's innovation lay in transforming what he viewed as the static Saussurean duality *langue/parole* into a dynamic model of the human capacity for using language. He achieved this by postulating a model for the operations that take place between *langue* and *parole*, operations that he viewed as the *act of language*. Guillaume's expansion of Saussure's complementarity consists in bringing in the element of time – the time required for a speaker to both think out the words of a message *and* to say them. Thus, whereas Saussure simply acknowledged the interdependence of *langue/parole*, Guillaume elaborated upon it.

Following Valin (1954: 48), Hewson illustrates the refinement of Guillaume's *act of language* into two components: the activity of *langue* and the activity of *discours* (Guillaume's substitute for Saussure's *parole*), constituting respectively 'the genesis of the word, and . . . the genesis of the sentence' (Hewson, 1976: 325). The elaborate detail in which Guillaume developed his operational model provided a framework for a unique approach to linguistics which may be legitimately viewed as foreshadowing much contemporary work in cognitive linguistics by more than half a century (Guillaume died in 1960). Hewson (1976) was one of the first publications to demonstrate clearly the bogus conflation of Chomskyan competence/performance with Saussurean *langue/parole* and to call for a sustainable integration of principles from the *CGL* with those of transformational generative grammar: 'In short, the Saussurean model, in order to treat *parole* as well as *langue*, needs to be made generative (but not in the artificial, positivist sense), and the transformational model requires to be reshaped to deal appropriately with morphology, so that the criticisms of the weaknesses of each can be reconciled' (Hewson, 1976: 329).

Recent commentaries in relation to earlier assessments

In contrast to a regrettable tendency among some of Saussure's commentators to either rigidify the paired terms of his terminology or to condemn them on the assumption that they admit no complementarity of interpretation and application, Béatrice Turpin (1993 [1994]) examines *langue–parole* as both the indispensable duo capturing the distinction between the objects and the objective of linguistic analysis *and* in relation to the over-arching sense of *langage*. Turpin (1995–6) extends this salutary counterbalance to the impoverished version of the Saussurean dialectic fashioned in the wake of the vulgate version of the *Cours*, directing attention to the development of the integrated terminological panoply of Saussure's lecture courses: *langue–parole–langage–discours*. The disappearance of the latter term from the third version of the course, in all but a very restricted sense, suggests, once again, that Saussure's linguistic reflections were constantly motivated by the indispensable requirement of refining terminology that would allow him to identify dualities without limiting himself thereto. Turpin's conclusion illuminates Saussure's alignment of logic and semantics with propositional structure and sentence construction respectively, showing Saussure's rationale in offering a course on the linguistics of *parole* to the auditors of his third course.

In contradistinction to both the perpetuated hypostatisation of *langue* and *parole*, such as found typically in Manczak (1969), and contextualised reassessments of the terms, such as Turpin's, is the extreme reductivism of the view typified by Chomsky (1980: 127), whose call for the elimination of *langue* is rejected by Antal (1990), on the grounds that it undermines the possibility of offering explanations of either language acquisition or linguistic change on an empirical basis. Antal's commentary focuses on Chomsky, while Joseph (1989a: 50) gives a larger picture, explicitly linking Bloomfield to Saussure:

> For him, Saussure's system consisted not of two units but of four. De Saussure's system is more complex [than the Ogden-Richards triangle of reference]: (1) actual object, (2) concept, (3) acoustic image, (4) speech utterance . . . [Bloomfield, 1927:] (177) . . . Bloomfield then clarifies that (4) is *la parole*, while the segment formed by the two purely mental terms (2) and (3) is *la langue*, the socially uniform pattern (177).

Between Bloomfield and Chomsky, an alternate four-term reconfiguration of Saussurean *langue–parole–langage* had been proposed by Andreev and Zinder (1964), who 'add' (the reason for the quotation marks will be indicated directly) the notion of *speech probability*. Reaction to their work came promptly from Gustav Herdan (1964), whose *magnum opus* (Herdan, 1956) had advanced the notion that Saussure's *langue* and *parole* corresponded respectively to statistical universe and sample. Herdan argues that no valid application of statistics to the field of language can be made unless Saussure's notion of *langue* is first modified in order to conform to the mathematical statistician's notion of *the universe*, concluding that for this reason Andreev and Zinder's 'addition' of speech probability to the existing terminological triad from Saussure simply fails to transform it into an integrated and coherent tetrad. The inattention to Herdan's work, which he lays to the charge of Andreev and Zinder, is perpetuated in the pages of the same journal where that charge is made (*Linguistics*), by Manczak (1969), who implicitly calls for correctives and modifications of Saussure's thought along precisely the same lines as those already developed by Herdan more than a decade earlier.

Chapter 2 of David Holdcroft's *Signs, Systems, and Arbitrariness* (see Gordon, 1992) introduces one of the author's main theses: that Saussure's *langue/parole* distinction does not derive from a fundamental semiological principle. While Holdcroft's concession on this point does not come until the final page of the book ('If distinctions such as that between *langue* and *parole* cannot be derived from first principles of an ambitious over-arching theory, they are none the worse for that', 1991: 160), he manages within the early chapter to undermine his own defence of Saussure. For he first states that 'the text makes it natural to assume that [Saussure] is trying to locate a place for *langue* in the [communication model] circuit, despite the fact that if he was it would be very difficult to make sense of the claim that *langue* is social' (26). Subsequently he quotes the passage of the *CLG* which categorically states that *langue* can be located in the speaking-circuit (34).

Thibault (1997) (see Gordon, 1999a) teases out three distinct and compatible meanings of *langue* in the *Cours* as pure value, lexicogrammatical forms, and typical patterns of language use in a community. This is in contrast to unitary readings of Saussure such as Jakobson's (Waugh, 1984), which merely serve to oversharpen the notion of *langue–parole* as oppositional rather than complementary. In Thibault's view, *parole* is not in opposition to *langue* but an instantiation of it. Thibault's subtitle, *The Dynamics of Signs in Social Life*, indicates an integrating perspective, useful in countering the popular notion that holds Saussure responsible for the tardy development of sociolinguistics. This view runs roughly as follows: (1) *langue/parole* is a dichotomy for Saussure; (2) the dichotomy privileged *langue*; (3) the study of the social and behavioural nature of language suffered neglect as a consequence. To be sure, not all commentators share this view (see *inter alia* Antal, 1990), but, in any case, Thibault's analysis absolves Saussure of responsibility in the matter by demonstrating that it stems from a narrow interpretation of his teachings. The so-called Saussurean paradox (Labov, 1972: 185–7) misconstrues lessons from the Geneva linguist as setting up a tension between the potential adequacy of an individual's *parole* to reveal *langue* and the necessity of an interactive *parole* to reveal *langue*. Such a view, a deconstructive initiative which reveals more of a paradox in its own disregard of the multiple meanings of *langue* than in Saussure's use of *langue/parole*, is disarmed by Thibault's reading of the *Cours*. The articulation of the 'Saussurean paradox' inadvertently reveals a failure to detect the multiple readings of *langue* outlined by Thibault and to grasp their compatibility with each other.

6 System, arbitrariness, value

Claudine Normand

Introduction

This chapter offers a historical and theoretical perspective. A comprehensive understanding of Saussure's ideas requires some idea of how other linguists at the time dealt with the same topics. Only in this way can the novelty of his theory become clear, a novelty of which contemporary linguists were not fully aware. The key notions that are addressed in this chapter – system, arbitrariness and value – are at the very heart of Saussure's objectives, and are abstract and theoretical, even more so than other concepts in the *CLG*.

Saussure's teachings were collected and reorganised, as is well known, from several sources, with the addition of unfinished personal papers and drafts. They are to be seen as the result of his previous efforts over many years concerning descriptive linguistics, and thus arise in fact from his own practice. The purpose of this new teaching (i.e. general linguistics) was not to put forward new data or discoveries about such and such a language, as Saussure did for instance when teaching Sanskrit or Gothic, but to confront the difficulties involved in making something worthwhile out of this mass of 'facts' from many languages, already fully described by linguists during the previous century. This, briefly speaking, was the goal of general linguistics among scholars at that time, although in Saussure's opinion it was far from being achieved, or indeed fully initiated.

Hence it is difficult to translate into empirical and tangible terms what was essentially an attempt by Saussure to forge an entirely new conceptual framework, with a few data being given just as examples. Nevertheless it would be wrong to consider the *CLG* as seeking to develop a philosophy of language, even though it does raise philosophical questions, and even though Saussure himself, on rare occasions, admitted that his research was to some extent philosophical. Rather, it is first and foremost an epistemological enterprise, i.e. an attempt to think through the conditions necessary for a wholly descriptive linguistics, or even better to provide a basis for the grammarian's task of describing languages. What Saussure constantly strove for was a way of proceeding to a correct description so as to be able to elaborate a genuine theory of language, that is a linguistic theory of language. He wrote in a letter to Meillet: 'The inadequacy of current terminology and the need to reform it and to show thereby what kind of object language is in general, constantly spoils my enjoyment of history . . .' (trans. of Godel, 1969a: 31).

But as abstract and in places obscure as the *CLG* can be – and it is even more so if we take into account manuscripts discovered later – it remains rewarding reading, even though linguistic trends nowadays seem far-removed from that kind of epistemological endeavour. The major problem which occupied Saussure's mind, as seen in his various papers throughout the ten years before his enterprise in general linguistics, was to clarify the nature of what he called *langue* as opposed to *langage* and *parole*. Whether this is a philosophical or speculative matter or a truly linguistic one remains an open question. His concern with the nature of *la langue* will be addressed here by considering his three notions of system, arbitrariness and value, to which we have already alluded.

Language (*langue*) as a system

La langue est un système

To start with there is the problem of translating 'la langue est un système' into English. 'Language is a system' sounds abstract; but 'language is systematic' seems trivial. More problematic in English, however, is the term 'language' itself since it does not differentiate, as Saussure did, between *le langage*, *une langue*, *la parole* and *la langue*. For Saussure *le langage* refers to the general human faculty of language. *Une langue* refers to any particular language, a language and *des langues* in the plural to 'languages'. *La parole* refers to a particular utterance, to an example of individual speech – a bit of language. *La langue*, however, is a new technical term developed by Saussure, and is the essential object of his investigations. In French this use of *langue* with the definite article, *la*, and no further modifier is very unusual, the definite article being normally used only with an adjective to name a specific language, for instance *la langue anglaise*, 'English'. With *la langue* Saussure is seeking to name an entity distinct from the general faculty, *le langage*. Clearly Saussure does not mean the same thing by these two general expressions.

In fact, nobody had previously felt it necessary to use two different terms to distinguish between language in the sense of a particular language in a given society and language as a general human ability, nor *a fortiori* to have a separate technical term to focus on language as a general entity incorporating all the features of any language, namely that every language comprises signs and is a system, etc. The American linguist W. D. Whitney, with whom Saussure is often compared since they were both critical of the terminology employed by linguists, used *language*, *speech* and even *tongue* interchangeably.

It is still, however, a matter of controversy, above all among sociolinguists, whether the general term *la langue*, refers to anything at all: it has been suggested that perhaps Saussure was ensnared by French lexical properties permitting an over-sophisticated differentiation. Nonetheless, while several scholars reject the entity termed *la langue* as speculative, it is essential to Saussure's conceptual frame as a whole. The distinction it introduces throws light on several points in the *Cours*, including the notion of 'language as a system'. Saussure sought to develop the notion of *la langue* as a scientific concept distinct from the philosophical notion of *le langage*, which he considered in his own words as 'hétéroclite ('a rag-bag'), that is obscure and ambiguous. *La langue* was for him the object of a new scientific approach, indeed of a new discipline.

The notion of 'system' suggests organisation, well-ordered relationships. When used in conjunction with 'language', it brings to mind the traditional practice of grammarians, that is, the classifying of words into morphological paradigms (conjugations, declensions, derivation), central to the description of Indo-European languages. Within this framework, grammar is that aspect of language which is strictly organised; while vocabulary (lexicon) is treated as quite separate and as a matter of speaker choice, to be investigated historically and etymologically. On the contrary, however, the notion of 'system' in Saussurean theory is not simply grounded in this tradition, even if it is partly influenced by it. Saussure sharply criticised the traditional distinction between lexicon and grammar, as if only grammatical features were organised – but without semantic content – while only lexicon was meaningful – but without organisation (see the old opposition between 'empty' and 'full' words). For him it is the case both that any item in a language has to be studied from the point of view of meaning (i.e. what it means for a speaker) and that every term is a part of some organisation, which is simply more visible in grammar than in lexicon, as we shall see.

Hence Saussure claims that language as a whole (*langue*) is to be taken as entirely grammatical, that is to say we have to describe it in its entirety, grammar and lexicon, as a system, a network of elements dependent on one another according to rules. This assumption, however, raises several problems. For instance, speakers have no awareness of the major part of these rules which are supposed to govern their speech. Also, languages are continually changing according to other kinds of rules (so-called 'laws') which demonstrate regularities that are not necessarily logical. This raises questions, for instance, about the appropriate way to approach the study of such a shifting system.

Such difficulties did not arise for Whitney's theory since he did not claim that language was a system, but only a 'social institution'. Saussure in fact also made this latter assumption, but applied it rather differently as shall be seen.

Antoine Meillet – a friend of Saussure's and his student in his Paris years – also adopted the formula of language as a system. It is not clear whether he got this idea from Saussure himself or whether this notion was already current among French linguists at the beginning of the century. In any case, when Meillet gave his first lecture at the Collège de France (1906), he argued that: 'Le langage est un système où tout se tient', that is all elements in language are interrelated (Meillet, 1965). But, as can be seen, Meillet did not distinguish between *langage* and *langue*. Furthermore he does not develop the idea of language as a system. Also, if he noted the Saussurean opposition – with which he was probably already familiar – between language as a system and language as historical change, he did not state any relation between these two aspects of linguistic enquiry.

On the contrary, although Saussure clearly differentiated between historical linguistics, ('diachronics') and the study of the system ('synchronics'), he considered that the two depended on each other. Moreover, unlike Meillet, Saussure never uses the term 'system' alone, but always conjointly with others: system of signs, system of relations, system of values, system of differences. All of these terms will be examined below.

The claim, however, that language is a system is not a simple one, and leaves much to be disentangled. Saussure's theory consists of a set of dovetailed concepts which have to be unfolded one after the other, though they are interdependent. First, some general points will be made, and then synchrony will be addressed.

Theoretical principles and rules of description

Before elaborating on Saussure's important theoretical notion of synchrony, it is helpful to clarify a general point which throws light on his approach to general linguistics. This is an epistemological orientation in his way of thinking. Unlike the approach of several other scholars at the time, Saussure's enterprise in general linguistics must be seen as a set of theoretical principles and their methodological consequences. If the general principles about the nature of language are right, the corresponding method of describing linguistic facts is also likely to be correct. Although it is not so clearly stated in the *CLG*, it seems reasonable to summarise Saussure's epistemological purpose in these terms. Besides, this view is supported by several passages in manuscripts where Saussure repeatedly states that his aim is to develop a new terminology, for that has theoretical implications.

The notion that language is a system is to be seen as a postulate or a guiding principle, for it is not possible directly to observe such a system, but the very fact of proposing this approach will enable us to give a better account of linguistic observations than hitherto. What then is the methodological consequence of this principle that language is a system? What this postulate does is to focus attention on the need to describe the varied and numerous relations that an ordinary speaker is involved in when he speaks to any member of his language community. That speakers do not consciously realise that their own speech conforms to certain rules does not prevent the linguist from seeking to identify these rules. This is similar to how grammarians had always proceeded in the past, although according to Saussure's proposal this can be done without the constraint of specific normative strictures. Thus, according to Saussure's view, the linguist has to describe what any speaker does, albeit unconsciously. In other words the description will be made according to the language behaviour of any speaker using a given language system at any given time. This was an entirely new idea at the time, as we shall see.

In Saussure's time research was still largely historical, in accordance with the accepted notion of linguistic change, although various explanations of the process were put forward. Thus, in the opinion of the neogrammarians, with whom Saussure became acquainted in Leipzig, everything in any language has to be seen from the standpoint of history, in other words, in terms of the laws according to which language has changed and is still changing, as the various dialects show. It was a common assumption that nothing serious could be said about language in any other way. Hence general linguistics was seen at the time as an endeavour to gather together all the results of so-called historical linguistics, with the prospect of finally attaining some synthesis revealing general (if not universal) features of language as a whole. This would be the true achievement of the science of language, according to Whitney.

According to that view the term 'general' (in general linguistics) implies an inductive approach leading to generalisation. By contrast, Saussure considered, as already indicated, that the principles of a general theory of language – which in his opinion needed to be entirely renewed – must be understood as a set of abstract features, starting from which a correct and accessible description becomes possible. Such general principles include 'language is a system' and other basic assumptions at the core of his research on the nature of language, such as: language *(langue)* is a social fact while speech is individual *(parole)*; signs are arbitrary and to be taken as values; and linguistics belongs to a more general science yet to be developed (*sémiologie*).

Here, Saussure refers to a kind of abstract generality, perhaps akin to the Cartesian method and thus influenced by the French intellectual tradition. Be that as it may, this is my understanding (which is one among many) of this epistemological undertaking of Saussure's. Indeed, at the time it would have been virtually impossible to display such an abstract position because of the dominant positivist and empiricist position taken by the emergent social sciences. In any case, whether the result of empiricist or rationalist reasoning, this assumption about a synchronic system as an aspect of linguistic investigation now needs to be addressed.

Diachrony / synchrony

By 'synchrony' Saussure was referring to a language *(une langue)* at a given time; by 'diachrony' he was referring to its various transformations throughout its history, reaching as far as back as possible. 'Everything that relates to the static side of our science is synchronic; everything that has to do with evolution is diachronic. Similarly, *synchrony* and *diachrony* designate respectively a language-state and an evolutionary phase' (*CGL*-B: 81).

As indicated, Saussure, by putting forward the synchronic point of view, intended to capture the language of any speaker in a given community at a given time, what we normally refer to as the language as practised by the 'native speaker'. In other words he was putting himself, as a linguist, in the place of this hypothetical native speaker, with the hope of elucidating his language use. In this way he departed from the common concern of most linguists who usually adopted a scholarly point of view. Language scholars at the time were very knowledgeable about the comparison and history of languages (as indeed was Saussure), while the so-called native speaker is only expected to be proficient in his own language, and not necessarily to be well educated. If his ability to speak is to be considered a real kind of knowledge, it is of a quite different order. Describing that layman's knowledge is the real object of what Saussure termed synchronic linguistics.

Saussure did not deny that language is continually changing (quite the contrary, as shall be seen), nor that every speaker displays some particularities in uttering sounds, constructing phrases or choosing words. Hence, the assumption that one can identify general common features which characterise something called *langue*, while setting aside changes over time or the differences of individual speakers, presents a challenge and raises many questions. Saussure's concept of *langue* needs to be seen as an idealisation which is needed in order to define the boundaries of a new scientific endeavour. Similarly, for him the opposition between synchrony and diachrony likewise represents a necessary scientific distinction.

A positivist method?

Saussure's proposal for carefully distinguishing between various facts, which initially appear quite entangled, can be linked to positivism, a trend in the philosophy of science, which was influential among French scholars at the time. In fact developing a typology, that is differentiating between different categories of data, so as to apply in each case an appropriate methodology, has often been considered as the first step in developing a new scientific field. As a result, many interesting data may be temporarily excluded from consideration. Such was the case for what Saussure called 'external linguistics' as opposed to 'internal linguistics', that is synchronic linguistics. Thus all language features relating to history and social agents in a given community are set apart as belonging to a so-called external study. Hence *langue* delimits what is to be included in the proper field of linguistic research, to be strictly differentiated from a different field of research about everything extrinsic to that field, which is often referred to as 'extra-linguistic' (cf. *CGL*-B: 20–3).

But why was it so important to be so strict about this distinction? A metaphor will throw some light on this:

> A game of chess is like an artificial realization of what language offers in a natural form . . .
>
> First, a state of the set of chessmen corresponds closely to a state of language. The respective value of the pieces depends on their position on the chessboard just as each linguistic term derives its value from its opposition to all the other terms.
> In the second place, the system is always momentary; it varies from one position to the next . . .
>
> Finally, to pass from one state of equilibrium to the next, or – according to our terminology – from one synchrony to the next, only one chess-piece has to be moved; there is no general rummage. Here we have the counterpart of the diachronic phenomenon . . . (*CGL*-B: 88)

What this famous comparison makes obvious is the real difference between two levels of fact. What is considered as a fact from an historical point of view (for instance French *mouton* becoming English *mutton)* is not at all a fact from a synchronic point of view. The latter is only concerned with relations between, for instance, *mutton* and *sheep* on the one hand, and *mutton* and *veal* on the other. These are specific relations within the English system, while there are quite different relations between the apparently corresponding terms in French. In what was a very radical departure, Saussure asserted in the clearest terms that declaring any particular data linguistic depends on the viewpoint adopted by the observer: 'Far from it being the object that antedates the viewpoint, it would seem that it is the viewpoint that creates the object; besides, nothing tells us in advance that one way of considering the fact in question takes precedence over the others or is in any way superior to them' (*CGL*-B: 8).

All this implies that in the case of diachrony and synchrony each of these points of view has to be dealt with separately from the other, as virtually belonging to two different disciplines. The same point is made by distinguishing between internal and external linguistics, and similarly by differentiating between research about language as *langue*, and research about speech, or *parole*. Specific data always require an appropriate method. It should be clearer now that, as stated earlier, theoretical concepts closely dovetail. This is what Saussure meant by saying that a theory has to be a system as closely interlinked as language itself: 'Language is a tightly interlocking system, and theory must be as tightly interlocking as language. This is the challenge, for it is easy to make assertions, to express views, one after the other, about language; the whole problem is to knit them together into a system' (trans. of Godel, 1969a: 29, Saussure's interview with A. Riedlinger, 19 January 1909). Because of these views many subsequent linguists (particularly in pragmatics) have in fact declared such a theory to be like a straitjacket, restricting the scope of valid linguistic research.

Besides highlighting the difference between diachrony and synchrony, the chess-game comparison will also help to clarify other important features of *la langue*, such as the arbitrary nature of signs and the notion that signs are values. But before developing these issues it will be useful to digress so as to consider the statement that 'language is a social fact'.

Language as a social fact

It might at first seem surprising that a consideration of the social character of language is regarded as a secondary digression. Many well-known commentators on the *CLG* rank the social character of language as being of primary importance. In doing so they link Saussure to Whitney for whom it was a major theme (if not the only one) of *Life and Growth of Language* (1875). Saussure in fact acknowledged that Whitney's contention that language was a social institution was an important development which definitively freed linguistics from the fanciful but strongly held belief that language was some sort of natural organism. Nevertheless Saussure never fully agreed with the American linguist that this 'axiom' was sufficient to provide the decisive insight necessary for the development of a true science of language. Saussure's feelings on the matter can now be seen from the tribute that he drafted in honour of Whitney. This was never dispatched nor indeed completed, for in fact Saussure was far from agreeing with Whitney's view, even though he considered it, as he wrote, more 'reasonable' than many others. One reason is probably that, although both Whitney and himself applied the same term, 'social', to language, they actually meant very different things by it.

For Whitney, and later on, for Meillet, who can be seen as the 'father' of French sociolinguistics, 'social' referred to how a given society, its history, its various institutions and different classes or ranks, affected the language. In this way they explained many formal and semantic changes. Saussure did not deny this, but saw it as part of the task of 'external linguistics'. What then did he mean by 'social' as applied to 'internal linguistics'? To understand this, it is necessary to refer to another major theoretical concept, that is, the arbitrariness of sign. How this relates to the social aspect, into which in fact it gives a sharper insight, will now be considered.

The arbitrary nature of the sign

Another chapter of this volume (Joseph) deals with the Saussurean theory of sign as a whole. The present purpose is only to make clear how the claim of arbitrariness implies the social nature of language. To explain the statement, 'le signe est arbitraire', 'arbitrary' is often replaced by 'conventional'. Thus Whitney argued that all linguistic signs are conventional. In other words, they could have been different, as it is plain when different languages are referred to. Whitney was adamant on this point in his long debate about the origin of language with some famous, but old-fashioned linguists, such as A. Schleicher and M. Müller, who adopted a naturalistic standpoint. In accordance with a long tradition, Whitney imagined a fictional contract, as though there were initially a common agreement to speak in such and such a way, thus making language the product of human activity and history. The same conceptual fiction could explain the origin of all social institutions and agencies governed by rules accepted generally, if not consciously, in any society. That was an important point Saussure clearly adopted, almost in Whitneyan terms:

> Whitney, to whom language is one of several institutions, thinks that we use the vocal apparatus as the instrument of language purely through luck, for the sake of convenience: men might just as well have chosen gestures and used visual symbols instead of acoustical symbols. Doubtless his thesis is too dogmatic . . . But on the essential point the American linguist is right: language is a convention, and the nature of the sign that is agreed upon does not matter. (*CGL*-B: 10)
>
> **. . . Principle I: The Arbitrary Nature of the Sign**
> The bond between the signifier and the signified is arbitrary . . .
>
> The idea of 'sister' is not linked by any inner relationship to the succession of sounds *s-ö-r* which serves as its signifier in French; that it could be represented equally by just any other sequence is proved by differences among languages and by the very existence of different languages . . . (*CGL*-B: 67–8)

However Saussure added that an even more important peculiarity of linguistic signs in relation to other kinds of conventional signs, such as specific customs for clothes, politeness, etc. was that a language is even more arbitrary than other social institutions, because its rules and various realisations depend on nothing other than itself and its own system. Neither natural nor rational, language (*langue*) is a unique object of investigation. More generally it is this kind of investigation of social signs that Saussure called semiology: 'Signs that are wholly arbitrary realise better than the others the ideal of the semiological process; that is why language, the most complex and universal of all systems of expression, is also the most characteristic; in this sense linguistics can become the master-pattern for all branches of semiology although language is only one particular semiological system' (*CGL*-B: 68).

At this point Saussure went far beyond received opinion about the origin of language as well as its ability to refer to things in the world and other traditional issues, and this can make it more difficult to accept his very abstract point of view. Let us try to understand what he meant.

First it must be stressed that Saussure's concern was not whether or how a language represents the world, nor how it is related to thinking. Such philosophical topics were not within his purpose. As a linguist, thinking about the nature of language (*langue)* and how best to portray it, his concern was to make apparent how a language works as an everyday mechanism, at anyone's disposal; in other words what is happening when one tries to think and speak in one's own language. Hence he distances himself from philosophical and psychological research into the genesis or acquisition of language. He even asserts that philosophers are generally wrong in this matter, as they look at language as if it were simply a matter of naming (like Adam giving names to the various animals). They are unaware, he says, of two important aspects: on the one hand that the most important function of language does not consist in designating things, but in relating and combining words in different ways; and on the other hand that language is continually moving and transforming itself.

On the first point the chess-game comparison will again be helpful:

> Finally, not every idea touched upon in this chapter differs basically from what we have elsewhere called *values*. A new comparison with the set of chessmen will bring out this point . . . Take a knight, for instance. By itself is it an element in the game? Certainly not, for by its material make-up – outside its square and the other conditions of the game – it means nothing to the player; it becomes a real, concrete element only when endowed with value and wedded to it . . . Not only another knight but even a figure shorn of any resemblance to a knight can be declared identical provided the same value is attributed to it. We see then that in semiological systems like language, where elements hold each other in equilibrium in accordance with fixed rules, the notion of identity blends with that of value and *vice versa*. (*CGL*-B: 110)

What this comparison makes strikingly clear is that the specific material that the pieces are made of does not matter at all, but only the fact that they consist of perceptible elements of any sort whatsoever and that these are linked with meaning in some indissoluble, albeit as yet unknown, way. More generally the comparison shows that no meaning can prevail without being linked to some concrete form, and also that none of the signifying pieces can be used as such without being related to the other pieces in the same system. Hence to identify any piece in such a system one has to look at its relations. Only in this way is it possible to know whether it is similar to or different from any other given piece. This is emphasised by another comparison in the same chapter:

For instance, we speak of the identity of two '8:25 p.m. Geneva-to-Paris' trains that leave at twenty-four-hour intervals. We feel that it is the same train each day, yet everything – the locomotive, coaches, personnel – is probably different . . . what makes the express is its hour of departure, its route, and in general every circumstance that sets it apart from other trains. Whenever the same conditions are fulfilled, the same entities are obtained. (*CGL*-B: 108–9)

However, there are other important features that these two comparisons cannot elucidate. Indeed, the comparison with the chess-game would be more appropriate for an artificial language, say a logical one. In such languages meanings and rules are strictly established by agreeing on certain conventions. If it seems necessary to change some aspect of these, one has first to agree and decide about it. Thus in scientific research scholars need to agree about an accepted language. However a living spoken language is continually shifting by being spoken, and the change happens without any specific agreement by the speakers, for it happens even without their being aware of it. A gradual transformation – although it may occur unawares and without anybody specifically willing it – results from the speakers' daily use: altering sounds, repeating words approximately, introducing new ones by applying some current frame (see the process of analogy). There are many ways in which a language slowly changes. This feature is linked to the fact that no language, whatsoever, can exist except by being constantly transmitted, and this depends very much on its social character:

Signs are governed by a principle of general semiology: continuity in time is coupled to change in time; . . .

. . . Contrary to all appearances, language never exists apart from the social fact, for it is a semiological phenomenon. Its social nature is one of its inner characteristics . . .

. . . But the thing which keeps language from being a simple convention that can be modified at the whim of interested parties is not its social nature; it is rather the action of time combined with the social force. If time is left out, the linguistic facts are incomplete and no conclusion is possible. (*CGL*-B: 76–8)

What then about synchrony? Does the above passage imply a return to historical linguistics? The methodological decision to describe a synchronic state must not ignore the fact that a language is, by its very nature, subjected to continual change. It is necessary on the one hand to describe the apparatus used at any given time by native speakers, which, as acknowledged earlier, is an abstract decision. On the other hand, taking into account the incessant and unwitting transformation of language enhances the assumption of arbitrariness, that specific feature which differentiates language *(langue)* from other fields of enquiry. In fact if the nature of a spoken language was rational or natural, if every sign was definitely linked to what it is supposed to represent, the incessant shifting in language would not be possible without perturbing its use by the speaker. Moreover it would also not be possible for a language to be unconsciously reorganised in accord with the patterns proper to it when items disappeared or did not exist to cover new things. In fact every change provokes some reorganisation so that the system remains constantly available for its users: 'Speech is continually engaged in decomposing its units, and this activity contains not only every possibility of effective talk, but every possibility of analogical formation . . . In short analogy, considered by itself, is only one side of the phenomenon of interpretation, one manifestation of the general activity that singles out units for subsequent use' (*CGL*-B: 166).

Another vivid extract from the manuscripts describes this incessant activity: 'It is wonderful to see how, in whatever way diachronical events may disrupt, the linguistic instinct manages to make the best of it . . . this brings to mind an ant-hill into which a stick is placed and the damage to which will be immediately repaired; in other words the tendency towards a system, towards order will never flag' (trans. of *CLG*/E 2: 49).

It must be clearer now that social does not mean the same for Saussure and Whitney or Meillet. For Saussure social and arbitrary are strictly dependent on each other. Speakers in a given society can go on using and thereby altering their language because it is arbitrary, and it is arbitrary because it is social, depending entirely on being transmitted without any debate:

> the arbitrary nature of the sign is really what protects language from any attempt to modify it. Even if people were more conscious of language than they are, they would still not know how to discuss it. The reason is simply that any subject in order to be discussed must have a reasonable basis . . . but language is a system of arbitrary signs and lacks the necessary basis, the solid ground for discussion. There is no reason for preferring *soeur* to *sister*, *Ochs* to *boeuf*, etc.
>
> . . . At every moment solidarity with the past checks freedom of choice. We say *man* and *dog* because our predecessors said *man* and *dog* . . . Because the sign is arbitrary, it follows no law other than that of tradition, and because it is based on tradition, it is arbitrary . . .
>
> Language is radically powerless to defend itself against the forces which from one moment to the next are shifting the relationship between the signified and the signifier. This is one of the consequences of the arbitrary nature of the sign. (*CGL*-B: 73–5)

An example of how difficult it is to change something in a language from above (by decree) can be found currently in France in the official requirement to mark grammatical gender in professional designations according to sex: for instance *écrivaine* instead of *écrivain* (writer), the latter of which was (and still is) used for both sexes. That 'politically correct' decision can lead to very ordinary names sounding quite ridiculous. This is what happens when 'reason' is imposed on language.

These two features together – the social and the arbitrary nature of language – can be summarised by saying that a language as a system of signs is better designated as a system of values.

Language as a system of values

When speaking of language what does this rather vague term 'value' mean? One way to understand this might be to use the metaphor of money: the value of something is the corresponding amount of money (or equivalent) that has to be paid for it. Would this be appropriate to the relationship between signifier and signified, where the signified would equate to the amount of money? Clearly this traditional equivalence between signifier and signified does not fit in with what has been said already about language. Saussure's text needs to be looked at more closely.

In the *Cours* the term, 'value', appears for the first time in the text quoted above which refers to the chess-game: 'The respective value of the pieces depends on their position on the chessboard just as each linguistic term derives its value from its opposition to all the other terms.' And, a little further on to distinguish 'a move' as an historical event from the resulting state of the system, Saussure writes: 'In each play only one chess-piece is moved; in the same way in language, changes affect only isolated elements . . . In spite of that, the move has a repercussion on the whole system; . . . Resulting changes of value will be, according to the circumstances, either nil, very serious, or of average importance . . .' (*CGL*-B: 88–9).

Nothing more is said at this point in the text about the conceptual use of value. But this term is used again more precisely later on in the comparison which throws light on both arbitrariness and value, as was seen above when defining arbitrary: 'Not only another knight but even a figure shorn of any resemblance to a knight can be declared identical provided the same value is attributed to it' (*CGL*-B: 110).

In fact, it is best not to overemphasise the apparent relation to money, as the manuscripts show that 'value' was decided on, not without some reservations:

> *Value* is at one and the same time synonymous with a term within a system of similar terms and entirely synonymous with that with which it may be exchanged . . . It is specific to value that it links these two things. It links them in a way which drives one to despair because of the impossibility of working out whether these two aspects differ in value or in some other way. (Trans. of *CLG*/E 1: 169)

In another fragment Saussure says he did not find a better term for the concept he wanted to elaborate: 'Value can no more be defined by the linguist than in other fields; we take it with all its clarity and all its obscurity' (trans. of *CLG*/E 1: 263).

Actually this metaphorical term is not explained any further. It seems to be taken as self-evident. In short, it implies system, as stated at the beginning of this chapter. The following quotation puts it well:

> Both factors are necessary for the existence of a value. To determine what a five-franc-piece is worth one must therefore know: (1) that it can be exchanged for a fixed quality of a different thing, e.g. bread; and (2) that it can be compared with a similar value of the same system, . . . or with coins of another system . . . In the same way a word can be exchanged for something dissimilar, an idea; besides, it can be compared with something of the same nature, another word . . . Its content is really fixed only by the concurrence of everything that exists outside it. Being part of a system, it is endowed not only with a signification but also and especially with a value, and this is something quite different. (*CGL-B*: 115)

It also implies arbitrariness and its social character:

> These views [i.e. 'Language as Organized Thought Coupled with Sound' as developed at p. 111] give a better understanding of what was said before (see pp. 67ff.) about the arbitrariness of signs. Not only are the two domains that are linked by the linguistic fact shapeless and confused, but the choice of a given slice of sound to name a given idea is completely arbitrary. If this were not true, the notion of value would be compromised, for it would include an externally imposed element. But actually values remain entirely relative, and that is why the bond between the sound and the idea is radically arbitrary. (*CGL*-B: 113)

Thus all the previously examined features of language *(langue)* are brought together and summed up in the term value linked to semiology: 'We see then that in semiological systems like language, where elements hold each other in equilibrium in accordance with fixed rules, the notion of identity blends with that of value and *vice versa*' (*CGL*-B: 110).

What are the methodological consequences of these abstract and quasi-axiomatic assumptions? First, that we have, as linguists, to describe a given system by looking for the relations each element entertains with others in the same system, and not by taking these elements one by one separately. Thus the appropriate method aims to chart what people do when they speak, that is when they choose words and combine them according to rules. This process will be represented along two axes called by Saussure respectively associative (the axis of choice) and syntagmatic (the axis of combinations). This method is similar to that used by comparative linguists in the identification of units from different languages. However, Saussure considered comparativists to be mistaken in so far as they confused such a description with a historical perspective on language. Thus every word in a language (and we can even say every phonemic or morphemic element, as Jakobson later stressed) operates at the same time on both axes, since a speaker cannot choose any lexical element without combining it with others according to grammatical rules.

So lexicon and grammar always work together according to equally arbitrary relations.

Relative arbitrariness

It was sometimes maintained that grammar was less arbitrary than lexicon. This interpretation was based on a noteworthy passage which seemed to place limitations on arbitrariness. Hence Saussure, reflecting on the term 'arbitrary', distinguished between absolute and relative arbitrariness:

> Some signs are absolutely arbitrary: in others we note, not its complete absence, but the presence of degrees of arbitrariness: *the sign may be relatively motivated.*
> For instance, both *vingt* 'twenty' and *dix-neuf* 'nineteen' are unmotivated in French, but not in the same degree, for *dix-neuf* suggests its own terms and other terms associated with it . . . The same is true of *poirier* 'pear-tree', which recalls the simple word *poire* 'pear' and, through its suffix, *cerisier* 'cherry-tree', *pommier* 'apple-tree', etc. (*CGL*-B: 131)

But it is easy to note that the so-called arbitrary link does not concern the same relationship in both cases: for in the case of *poire* (pear) the so-called arbitrary relation is that of the word with regard to the fruit, the concrete thing in the world or its representation, while in the case of *poirier* (pear-tree) the apparently less arbitrary relation is between two words of the same language, the second being derived from the first. Thus if *poirier* can be said to be relatively motivated, this is according to a specific rule of derivation – the same pattern apparently being applied in other cases as *pomme/pommier, cerise/cerisier*, etc. But this rule itself is as arbitrary as the sign *poire*, that is to say, it is neither based on a logical reason nor on a natural cause. If English apple-tree and German *Apfelbaum* seem to show a kind of rational order by joining the tree with its fruit, this apparent evidence is no more justified than in the case of *pomme* and *pommier* where, for a native speaker, the same result is obtained by a mere derivative morpheme. It can indeed be asserted that these cases of relative arbitrariness show a kind of order but that this order is a purely linguistic one:

> In fact, the whole system of language is based on the irrational principle of the arbitrariness of the sign, which would lead to the worst sort of complication if applied without restriction. But the mind contrives to introduce a principle of order and regularity into certain parts of the mass of signs, and this is the role of relative motivation. (*CGL*-B: 133)

The 'mind' refers to the constant activity of the speakers, who simultaneously alter the system and reorganise it according to existing patterns, so that language never ceases to function. The metaphor quoted above about the ant-hill disturbed by a stick comes to mind here: Saussure says that the ant-hill will be restored immediately and adds: 'Even if what was best about a language system was chopped off one day, the next day it would be seen that the remaining elements would have undergone a logical rearrangement of some sort, and that this rearrangement would be able to function in place of what had been lost' (trans. of *CLG*/E 1: 49).

Here what is at issue is the specific random logic of language, which Saussure liked to call semiology, and which is the principle that illuminates all the features of language: system, social use and change, arbitrariness, value. This idea was heralded at the very beginning of the *Cours*, but in a somewhat enigmatic way: 'We must call in a new type of facts in order to illuminate the special nature of language . . . if I have succeeded in assigning linguistics a place among the sciences, it is because I have related it to semiology' (*CGL*-B: 16).

A system of differences

We now reach the most abstract point of Saussure's theory, that is the statement of the equivalence between the system of values and the system of differences. This notion disturbed many scholars who nevertheless accepted prior assumptions. For instance, Saussure stated that:

> in French the concept 'to judge' is linked to the sound-image *juger*; in short, it symbolises signification. But it is quite clear that initially the concept is nothing, that is only a value determined by its relations with other similar values, and that without them the signification would not exist . . .
>
> The conceptual side of value is made up solely of relations and differences with respect to the other terms of language, and the same can be said of its material side. The important thing in the word is not the sound alone but the phonic differences that make it possible to distinguish this word from all others, for differences carry signification. (*CGL*-B: 117–18)

It may be difficult to imagine that our use of language is similar to a game of soap-bubbles, as suggested by Saussure in a note quoted by Fehr (2000): 'it is daily apparent to any student of language that the association – which we sometimes hold dear – is only a soap-bubble, is not even a soap-bubble . . .'. Here the philosopher will frown and take exception to such an irrational statement. However the chapter 'Linguistic value' (*CGL*-B: 111–22) seems to be the culmination of Saussure's argument, the point at which all previous features are gathered together and shown to be closely connected. Thus Saussure says here: '*Arbitrary* and *differential* are two correlative qualities' (*CGL*-B: 118).

To come back to the term 'value', the *Cours* again uses the comparison between *mouton* and sheep to specify what is meant by 'difference'. Even if both words refer to the same part of the 'real' world, what is generally referred to as the meaning of a word by philosophers, this does not mean that they are simply interchangeable in translation. In English, as noted above, sheep is distinguished from mutton while in French *mouton* is used in both cases: 'The difference in value between *sheep* and *mouton* is due to the fact that *sheep* has beside it a second term while the French word does not' (*CGL*-B: 116). Other examples, well known to translators and grammarians, are invoked to make clear that it is the different relations which particular values have in each system that make them different from each other. Hence, in the case of both the signifier and the signified, units do not signify by their own concrete form and content but by their relation to other units: '*Their most precise characteristic is in being what the others are not*' (*CGL*-B: 117 – emphasis added). This may sound somewhat strange but it fits absolutely with all the other statements.

To conclude, it can be seen that this array of Saussurean concepts has a common aim: to separate the linguistic point of view from any direct relationship with the 'real' world. For logicians it is this relationship to the 'real' world which is the very matter of semantics. Saussure's steadfastly repeated position sets him apart among scholars who are fascinated by language – if not in a realm entirely on his own.

(This chapter was edited by Peter Figueroa and Carol Sanders.)

Part III

After the *Cours*

7 Saussure and American linguistics

Julia S. Falk

When William Dwight Whitney died in 1894, the American Philological Association, of which he had been co-founder and first president, asked scholars in America and Europe to contribute appraisals of his work for a memorial meeting. Professor of Sanskrit and comparative philology at Yale College, Whitney had a long and distinguished career, and his work on Sanskrit and on general linguistics reached students, scholars and even a lay readership. Absent from the many prominent linguists sending public tributes to Whitney's work was Ferdinand de Saussure. It was not that Saussure disapproved of Whitney's work. To the contrary, he was a strong proponent who 'never ceased to feel indebted to the American scholar [Whitney] and . . . when he offered courses in general linguistics at the University of Geneva, he did not fail to mention Whitney's name with praise and to discuss his ideas' (Godel, 1966: 480).

The American Philological Association had invited Saussure to contribute to the Whitney memorial, and he began a notebook for drafts and comments of what he planned to write, but he never completed the letter. The notebook, however, survived and fragments were eventually published (Godel, 1957; Engler, 1968–74; Jakobson, 1971b). From these it is clear that what Saussure most admired in Whitney was his attempt to move forward from the details of nineteenth-century comparative grammar, especially German comparative grammar, and toward generalisations about the nature of language. The new linguistic science that Whitney envisioned 'makes the laws and general principles of speech its main subject, and uses particular facts rather as illustrations' (Whitney, 1867: 315).

In the 1894 notebook Saussure wrote: 'Whitney a dit: le langage est une *Institution* humaine. Cela a changé l'axe de la linguistique' ('Whitney said: language is a human institution. That changed the axis of linguistics', quoted by Jakobson, 1971b: xxxiv). Concepts that attracted Saussure and for which he may well have been indebted to Whitney are readily apparent in an examination of Whitney's two major books on the nature of language, *Language and the Study of Language: Twelve Lectures on the Principles of Linguistic Science* (1867) and *The Life and Growth of Language: An Outline of Linguistic Science* (1875).

Whitney wrote:

> Speech is not a personal possession, but a social; it belongs, not to the individual, but to the member of society. No item of existing language is the work of an individual; for what we may severally choose to say is not language until it be accepted and employed by our fellows. The whole development of speech, though initiated by the acts of individuals, is wrought out by the community. (Whitney, 1867: 404)

He also wrote: 'We regard every language . . . as an institution' (1875: 280). Closely connected to this central concept of language as a social institution was Whitney's view on the 'arbitrary and conventional' nature of human language 'in all its parts' (Whitney, 1875: 282). His position was so like that later attributed to Saussure that it is worth quoting in greater length:

> every word handed down in every human language is an arbitrary and conventional sign: arbitrary, because any one of the thousand other words current among men, or of the tens of thousands which might be fabricated, could have been equally well learned and applied to this particular purpose; conventional, because the reason for the use of this rather than another lies solely in the fact that it is already used in the community to which the speaker belongs. (Whitney, 1875: 19)

Saussure noted that 'Whitney, whom I revere, never said a single word on the same subjects [concerning 'a theoretical view of language'] which was not right; but like all the others, he does not dream that language needs systematics' (Jakobson's translation, 1971b: xxxvii), and later scholars seem generally agreed that a major element missing from Whitney's theorising about language was indeed the notion of systematic and interconnected linguistic structure (e.g. Silverstein, 1971: xv). Whitney was certainly not a structuralist in any sense, modern or not, but it must be kept in mind at this point that the term 'structuralism', now so closely associated with Saussure's legacy, would not arise in any significant way within American linguistics until nearly half the twentieth century had passed.

When the young American Leonard Bloomfield published his first textbook in 1914, the title, *An Introduction to the Study of Language*, recalled Whitney's books, which Bloomfield acknowledged in his Preface and to which he directed readers for further information (Bloomfield, 1914: v, 315). He saw his book as an updated report on the 'great progress of our science in the last half-century' since Whitney 1867. Like Whitney, Bloomfield wrote of the 'social character of language' and noted that a speech utterance 'depends for its form entirely on the habits of the speaker, which he shares with his speech-community. These habits are in a sense arbitrary, differing for the different communities . . .' (Bloomfield, 1914: 17, 81–2). It should come as no surprise, then, that when Bloomfield reviewed the second edition of Saussure's *Cours de linguistique générale* in 1924, he was to say: 'Most of what the author says has long been "in the air" and has been here and there fragmentarily expressed' (Bloomfield, 1924: 318).

This review is an important document in the history of American linguistics, first because Bloomfield was a principal figure, and second because it seems to be the only review of the *Cours* published in any American journal until new editions were prepared in the second half of the twentieth century. For these reasons, Bloomfield's review has been the subject of several analyses (Joseph, 1989a; Koerner, 1989; Falk, 1995) and has acquired a prominence that it did not have when it was published.

The review of the *Cours* was not Bloomfield's first public discussion of Saussure's contributions to linguistics. Two years earlier, in a review of Edward Sapir's now-classic book *Language* (1921), Bloomfield pointed to Saussure's *Cours* as a book 'which gives a theoretic foundation to the newer trend of linguistic study' in which one 'critical point' was that linguists were 'coming to believe that restriction to historical work is unreasonable and, in the long run, methodically impossible' (Bloomfield, 1970 [1922]: 92). Here Bloomfield referred to Saussure's distinction of 'synchronic' and 'diachronic', using the Saussurean terms when pointing out that Sapir, too, dealt with 'synchronic matters . . . before he deals with diachronic . . . [giving] to the former as much space as to the latter' (*ibid.*).

The synchronic/diachronic distinction was one of the Saussurean concepts highlighted in Bloomfield's review of the *Cours* and it appeared again in the article 'On Recent Work in General Linguistics' (1927). But Bloomfield dated what he called the 'theoretical justification' for the precedence of descriptive linguistics over historical studies not primarily to Saussure, but rather 'especially' to the earlier work of Franz Nikolaus Finck (Bloomfield, 1970 [1927]: 179). A similar passage, but with an expanded list of predecessors, appeared in Bloomfield's only reference to Saussure within the text of his book *Language* (1933), the most influential work in American linguistics in the first half of the twentieth century.

> some students saw more and more clearly the natural relation between descriptive and historical studies. Otto Böhtlingk (1815–1904) . . . applied the descriptive technique to . . . Yakut of Asiatic Russia (1851). Friedrich Müller (1834–1898) published an outline of linguistic science (1876–1888) which contained brief sketches of the languages of the world, regardless of whether a historical treatment was possible. Franz Nikolaus Finck (1867–1910), both in a theoretical essay (1905) and in a little volume (1910) in which he analyzed descriptively eight unrelated languages, insisted upon descriptive study as a basis for both historical research and philosophical generalization. Ferdinand de Saussure (1857–1913) had for years expounded this matter in his university lectures; after his death, they were published in book form (1915) [sic]. (Bloomfield, 1933: 18–19)

Bloomfield did not use the Saussurean terms. Instead, he discussed 'two streams of study, the historical-comparative and the philosophical-descriptive' (Bloomfield, 1933: 19; see also Hockett, 1989: 1–3).

'Descriptive' and 'historical' became the standard terminology of American linguistics, with the distinction recognised as existing in the linguistic literature long before Saussure's *Cours*, not only in the European works Bloomfield cited, but in American work as well:

The fact of the matter is that Sapir, who had completed his Takelma grammar . . . some time before February 20, 1911 . . . had no need of a 1916 publication to stimulate him to the synchronic, analytic study of languages . . . By 1916, Sapir, indeed, had laid the basis for our knowledge of the structure of six languages (Takelma, Wishram, Yana, Southern Paiute, Nootka, and Chasta Costa). (Hymes and Fought, 1981: 15–16)

Despite occasional claims to the contrary by commentators on the history of linguistics who provide no documentation, there is no evidence that Sapir was directly influenced by the *Cours*; he certainly never cited it in his work (Levin, 1965: 84; Hymes and Fought, 1981: 15; Anderson, 1985: 228).

Sapir's Takelma grammar was part of a project designed by Franz Boas, often credited as the founder of modern American anthropology. Boas's *Handbook of American Indian Languages* (1911) predated the appearance of the *Cours*, and Boas's framework for the grammars to be included in the *Handbook* owed nothing to Saussure:

the method of treatment has been throughout an analytical one. No attempt has been made to compare the forms of the Indian grammars with the grammars of English, Latin, or even among themselves . . . Although . . . an analytical grammar can not lay any claim to present a history of the development of grammatical categories, it is valuable as a presentation of the present state of grammatical development in each linguistic group. (Boas, 1911: 77–8)

Bloomfield, too, had prepared what he termed 'the first scientific analysis of the structure of the [Philippine] language' Tagalog, refraining from 'any and all historical surmises beyond the indication of unassimilated loan-words', based on work with a native speaker he conducted in 1915 and 1916, before he had had any opportunity to read Saussure's teachings on synchronic linguistics (Bloomfield, 1917: 10).

There is, then, ample evidence that the notion of linguistic description of the current state of a language, as contrasted to traditional studies of historical change, was well entrenched in American linguistics before the *Cours* appeared. Bloomfield and his contemporaries viewed Saussure's synchronic/diachronic distinction as little more than a terminological innovation, which most Americans did not adopt until the 1940s or later.

In his review of the *Cours*, Bloomfield introduced the famous *langue/parole* distinction as follows:

This rigid system, the subject-matter of 'descriptive linguistics', as we should say, is *la langue*, the language. But *le langage*, human speech, includes something more, for the individuals who make up the community do not succeed in following the system with perfect uniformity. Actual speech-utterance, *la parole*, varies not only as to matters not fixed by the system . . . but also as to the system itself . . . (Bloomfield, 1924: 318–19)

Bloomfield took up the distinction again in 1927 where he reduced Saussure's system of signs to the physically observable elements of actual object and speech utterance, casting aside what he considered 'the purely mental terms' of 'concept' and 'acoustic image' (Bloomfield, 1970 [1927]: 177). The resulting reconceptualisation of *langue* and *parole* was tantamount to a rejection of the Saussurean distinction, and indeed after 1927 Bloomfield made no use of these terms. It can be argued, however, that in both his theoretical work and his descriptive analyses, Bloomfield actually took the speech-utterances of *parole* as 'the subject-matter of linguistics' with the abstraction by analysis from the speech utterances yielding 'a description of *langue*' (Levin, 1965: 87). Of course, the same might be argued for any linguist who works from samples of the language to a generalised description that goes beyond the corpus.

Bloomfield did credit Saussure with the concept of what would later be called the phonemic system, but he did not view Saussure's contribution here as unique: 'developed by the school of [Henry] Sweet, [Paul] Passy, and Daniel Jones . . . [t]he same concept was developed (independently, I think) by Franz Boas (Handbook of American Indian Languages, 16) and by de Saussure (Cours de Linguistique Générale [Paris, 1916])' (Bloomfield, 1970 [1922]: 92). Charles Hockett wrote that 'the synchronic phonemic principle . . . Bloomfield got mainly, it would seem, from Henry Sweet' (1989: 4).

There were few specific contributions in the *Cours* that were compelling to Bloomfield, but he praised the book for more general qualities: 'its clear and rigorous demonstration of fundamental principles' mapping out 'the world in which historical Indo-European grammar (the great achievement of the past century) is merely a single province; [Saussure] has given us the theoretical basis for a science of human speech' (Bloomfield, 1924: 318–19).

After 1933, in his published works Bloomfield never mentioned Saussure again. The review had been reserved (hardly the 'eulogy' that Roy Harris (1987: xiii) claimed), and it was a minor piece, appearing in a relatively new journal devoted mostly to high school and college language-teaching materials and methods, not one of the prestigious linguistics journals of its time. Further, the review of the *Cours* was but one of fifteen reviews Bloomfield wrote during the 1920s, and his references to Saussure in other articles during the 1920s and early 1930s were often little more than inclusion in listings of earlier works. For example, in 'On Recent Work in General Linguistics', the *Cours* is twenty-first in a list of twenty-eight linguistics texts published between 1876 and 1926 (Bloomfield, 1970 [1927]: 173–4). Bloomfield admired Saussure and on several occasions referred his readers to the *Cours*, but he did not adopt Saussurean terms. He viewed most basic Saussurean concepts as ideas that had been set forth by other, earlier scholars.

Arguably excepting only his contemporary Edward Sapir, Bloomfield stands tallest as the major figure in American linguistics in the first half of the twentieth century. Nearly the entire generation of linguists who followed him was trained on his *Language*, his major articles, and his teaching, so much so that this generation of American linguists is often called the 'Bloomfieldian', 'post-Bloomfieldian', or 'neo-Bloomfieldian' school. They themselves referred to the work they did as descriptive linguistics, and they dominated American linguistics until the mid 1950s when the work of Noam Chomsky began its ascendancy. The most prominent members were Bernard Bloch, Robert A. Hall, Jr, Zellig S. Harris, Archibald A. Hill, Charles F. Hockett, Martin Joos, Floyd G. Lounsbury, George Trager and Rulon S. Wells. In addition, in the mid 1930s, Yuen-Ren Chao and W. Freeman Twaddell contributed to American phonological theory and practice as it was being developed by Bloomfield and his followers.

As in Bloomfield's own work after 1933, they rarely, if ever, referred to Saussure or the *Cours*. Take, for example, the six articles chosen by Martin Joos to represent the American development, after Bloomfield's *Language*, of the phonemic principle and descriptive phonology. In his collection *Readings in Linguistics: The Development of Descriptive Linguistics in America since 1925* (Joos 1958), we have: Morris Swadesh, 'The phonemic principle' (1934), Yuen-Ren Chao, 'The non-uniqueness of phonemic solutions of phonetic systems' (1934), W. Freeman Twaddell, 'On defining the phoneme' (1935), Morris Swadesh and Charles F. Voegelin, 'A problem in phonological alternation' (1939), Bernard Bloch, 'Phonemic overlapping' (1941), and Charles F. Hockett, 'A system of descriptive phonology' (1942).

Only Twaddell made any mention of Saussure. Following extended discussion of phonological principles in the work of N. S. Trubetzkoy, Daniel Jones, Harold E. Palmer, Sapir and Bloomfield, Twaddell stated:

> It cannot be too strongly emphasized that the phoneme, so defined [as a unit Twaddell termed the macrophoneme], is meaningless as applied to any particular linguistic element: it is a negative, relational, differential abstraction; it is a unit of that sort of relation which de Saussure describes: 'Dans la langue il n'y a que des différences sans termes positifs' (Cours de Linguistique Générale [1922] 166) [in language there are only differences without positive terms]. (Twaddell, 1958 [1935]: 74)

Not one of the other five articles made any mention of Saussure or the *Cours*, and even Twaddell's brief excursion into Saussurean territory did not attract his contemporaries; the 'macrophoneme' was not adopted.

The Americans' failure to even acknowledge Saussure and the *Cours* in the decade following Bloomfield's *Language* cannot be attributed to ignorance of European linguistic work in general, or to American political and academic isolationism during the interwar period, or to some 'sense of discontinuity from the past', or to the valorising of 'a distinctive American version of linguistics', points raised about the period by Andresen (1990: 210, 208) and Hockett (1982), among others, although these may have been contributing factors. But these articles contained ample citations of Daniel Jones, Harold E. Palmer, Otto Jespersen, and Nikolaj Trubetzkoy, Roman Jakobson and other members of the Linguistic Circle of Prague. The fact is that, as Stephen Anderson said of Saussure, 'there is very little in his work which is specific enough to serve directly as the foundation for concrete descriptions of phonological structure' (Anderson, 1985: 55). And it was precisely the establishment of principles and procedures for concrete descriptions of phonological structure in which the Americans of this period were most fully engaged.

While phonology was the focus of the 1930s, the 1940s in American linguistics have been referred to as 'the Decade of the Morpheme' (Hockett, 1987: 153). Examination of five articles on morphology from Joos, 1958 (Harris, 1942, 1946; Hockett 1947; Nida 1948; Lounsbury 1953) reveals no references at all to Saussure. Indeed, the descriptivists now were citing virtually no one other than their fellow American descriptivists (see Murray, 1994: 157–60 for a chart and discussion of their citation patterns). As these same linguists moved into the 1950s, several began to write on the history of descriptive linguistics in America (Hall, 1951–2; Hill, 1955). Again there was no discussion of influence from Saussure and the *Cours*, although in a final footnote Hall mentioned an article by Rulon Wells (1947) titled 'De Saussure's system of linguistics', to which we return below.

It should be noted here that Joos's selections for his volume were not uncontroversial. Hymes and Fought mentioned its 'partisan character' and noted that omission of work by Roman Jakobson and Kenneth Pike 'makes the volume seriously unreliable as a representation of the period it treats' (1981: 40). However, it had not been Joos's intention to represent the period but rather, as his subtitle showed, to reflect 'the development of descriptive linguistics in America' (Joos, 1958: iii). Jakobson was never an American descriptivist, but Pike's work certainly should have been included, especially Pike, 1943 and 1947, papers of insight and lasting importance that challenged some of the precepts of orthodox descriptivism while upholding others. The challenges were surely the reason for Joos's exclusion. Despite the sometimes idiosyncratic nature of Joos's choices, however, an examination of the major articles by a good number of the most important descriptivists represented in his anthology does provide a valid view of how they viewed Saussure and the *Cours* in the two decades following Bloomfield's *Language*.

American linguistics has never been a homogeneous discipline. Descriptivism clearly was the dominating approach of the 1930s, 1940s and the beginning of the 1950s, but it was not the only form of linguistics in America. With the start of the Second World War in Europe, European linguists began moving to the United States. Foremost among these was the Russian-born Roman Jakobson, co-founding member of the Linguistic Circle of Prague, who arrived in New York in 1941.

Unlike Bloomfield, whose overt attention to Saussurean concepts was brief, lasting just a decade, Jakobson's engagement was virtually lifelong, beginning in his years in Europe and extending throughout the four decades of his life in the United States. The major Saussurean themes that occurred repeatedly in Jakobson's writings during the Prague years were presented in seminal form in a single paper read to the Prague Linguistic Circle on 13 January 1927, a paper that Jakobson himself later selected as the lead item for the first published volume of his *Selected Writings* in 1962 (Jakobson, 1962 [1928]: 1–2). Here Jakobson maintained that 'Saussure and his school broke a new trail in static linguistics, but as to the field of language history they remained in the neogrammarian rut' and he went on to challenge 'Saussure's teaching that sound changes are destructive forces, fortuitous and blind' (*ibid.*). In the same paper, Jakobson rejected Saussure's 'antinomy between synchronic and diachronic linguistic studies' and called for 'a transformation of historical phonetics into the history of the phonemic system' and 'a comparison of phonemic systems', both synchronic and diachronic, that 'enables us to lay down certain universally valid sound laws' (*ibid.*). He also argued for 'the relevance of acoustical analysis' (*ibid.*). These lifelong Jakobsonian themes of dynamic synchronism, phonological universals and the relevance of acoustic analysis were – for Jakobson – the antitheses of Saussurean concepts.

Saussure repeatedly served as a foil to Jakobson, who would set forth the positions of the Genevan linguist only to argue against them. A reflection of Jakobson's beliefs about the nature of scientific inquiry, this was not just a rhetorical strategy. Jakobson saw the practice of linguistics as a continual rectification of inaccurate theories and the positing of new theories, useful and important even if incomplete. Further, Jakobson was committed to recognising the contributions of his central and eastern European intellectual ancestors, and he often did so in relation to concepts widely credited to Saussure. For example, in 'Phoneme and phonology' (1932) he introduced the concept of the phoneme 'first outlined in the works of Baudouin de Courtenay and F. de Saussure' (Jakobson, 1962 [1932]: 231) and he attributed 'the first foundations of phonology to 'Baudouin de Courtenay, F. de Saussure, and their disciples' (1962 [1932]: 232). In other papers he credited Tomás G. Masaryk with the synchronic/diachronic distinction (Jakobson, 1971a [1933]: 542) and Filipp F. Fortunatov with the notion of negative form (1971a [1939]: 211n.1).

Within a year of his arrival in New York, Jakobson had become vice-president of the Ecole Libre des Hautes Etudes, a French-language institution founded by exile scholars in New York, which provided a place to teach and study for those who had not found regular university positions in the United States. Here, in 1942, Jakobson gave two lecture series which together provided a focus on Saussurean concepts that was unprecedented in American linguistics. One series was devoted entirely to Saussure's linguistic theory ('La théorie saussurienne en rétrospection') while the other treated Saussurean concepts in phonology ('Six leçons sur le son et le sens') (Falk, 1995; Joseph, 1989b; Waugh, 1984).

Based closely on a lecture series he had presented in Copenhagen in 1939, Jakobson used his six lectures on sound and meaning to challenge Saussurean linearity, which he considered incompatible with his own theory of phonological distinctive features, and to oppose Saussure's claims on the arbitrariness of the linguistic sign, at variance with his 'means-ends model of language' (Jakobson, 1963) and with his interest in sound symbolism (Reichard, Jakobson and Werth, 1949). He did, however, acknowledge that in Saussure's work was to be found an 'idea crucial for the functional study of sounds, the idea of the relations between the phonemes, i.e., the idea of the *phonological system*' (Jakobson, 1978: 42 [emphasis in original]). Jakobson's thinking on phonology was to have a major impact on American linguistics, especially his theory of distinctive features (see Anderson, 1985: 116–29 for an account and critique). His view of phonological structure 'was taken over in largely intact form by (at least early work in) generative phonology' (1985: 117).

Also in 1942, Jakobson gave a second course at the Ecole Libre on Saussurean theory, this time focusing on the *langue/parole* distinction (portions reproduced from lecture notes and translated into English in Jakobson, 1990: 80–109; see also Waugh, 1984), with additional discussion of other topics including what he termed dynamic synchrony, a precursor to later sociolinguistic approaches to the study of language. Soon he was also to write about Saussure in his first American publication dealing with general linguistic theory, an obituary article on Franz Boas (Jakobson, 1944).

This article and the lectures on Saussure, even when critical, brought greater awareness of the latter's views than had occurred previously in American linguistics, and as Jakobson's prominence increased among American linguists, so did further attention to Saussure. When he and the other linguists of the Ecole Libre joined forces with New York area linguists to found the Linguistic Circle of New York/Cercle Linguistique de New York in 1943, an organisation was formed that presented and promoted European ideas in America. The New York Circle soon created the journal *Word* which provided a publishing outlet for papers dealing with European-based linguistic concepts, as well as for American studies that did not fit well with the dominant descriptivist approach favoured by *Language*, journal of the Linguistic Society of America (LSA). In *Word*, for example, two articles on Saussurean linguistics appeared in the third volume: 'De Saussure's system of linguistics', Rulon S. Wells (1947); 'La linguistique saussurienne à Genève depuis 1939', Henri Frei (1947). It was no accident that the descriptivist Wells placed his analysis of Saussure in *Word*.

Here there was a readership knowledgeable about Saussure and interested in connections between American and European linguistics. (See Costello, 1994, for personal opinions and recollections, but not documented historiography, about the early years of the Linguistic Circle of New York and of *Word*.)

With all of this activity going on in New York, Bloomfield in January 1945 wrote from Yale to his friend J Milton Cowan, then secretary-treasurer of the Linguistic Society of America: 'There is a statement going round that De Saussure is not mentioned in my *Language* text book (which reflects his *Cours* on every page)' (Cowan, 1987: 29). The parenthetical remark was an exaggeration, as was the previous sentence in which Bloomfield, the most well-established living figure in American linguistics of the time, said: 'Denunciations are coming thick & fast; I expect to be completely discredited by the end' (*ibid.*). The reintroduction of Saussure that led to these remarks was centred in the Linguistic Circle of New York. Although the actual source of the 'statement' has not been firmly ascertained, those who have been suggested were within the Circle's membership (Koerner, 1989: 440; Hall, 1990: 78–9). In any case, what matters here is the evidence the letter provided for the attention Saussure was then receiving in America.

Bloomfield and Sapir had written about structure, e.g. 'grammatical *structure*' (Bloomfield, 1933: 264 [emphasis in original], 'linguistic structure' (Sapir, 1921: 127–56), but the terms 'structural linguistics' and 'structuralism' in the 1940s were largely confined to European approaches to linguistics. In two articles in *Word*, the anthropologist Claude Lévi-Strauss attributed 'structuralisme' to Trubetzkoy (Lévi-Strauss, 1945: 35) and the historian Ernst Cassirer wrote of 'the program of structuralism developed by [Viggo] Bröndal' in the 1930s (Cassirer, 1945: 117). Only in the later 1940s did the terms 'structuralism' and 'structural linguistics' begin to appear in the writings of American linguists working in the descriptivist tradition.

An important impetus came in two reviews by Zellig Harris in the early 1940s. A review of *Foundations of Language* by Indo-Europeanist Louis Gray (Gray, 1939) was for Harris an opportunity to distinguish traditional historical linguistics from the newer American 'method of structural analysis, i.e. of organized synchronic description' (Harris, 1940: 216). Harris was not yet using the terms 'structuralism' or 'structural linguistics', but the review was saturated with the words 'structure' and 'structural', e.g. 'Failure to organize data by their place in the structure often leads to unsatisfactory classifications' (1940: 218). 'Neglect of structural analysis of each language leads to disregard of the differences between language structures' (1940: 219). 'Since one cannot do entirely without structural interpretations, the linguist who does not explicitly work out the structure of other languages is in danger of interpreting them in his own terms' (1940: 220–1). And so forth on nearly every page to the conclusion.

Nowhere in this review did Harris associate 'structure' with Saussure. Where he did mention Saussure by name it was to reject 'the langue-parole dichotomy of Saussure' and the 'science sémiologique' (1940: 228). The latter involved 'a relation of "signifying" . . . which requires something like teleology for its understanding' (*ibid.*); 'it cannot be studied objectively' (*ibid.*). '"Parole"', Harris argued, 'is merely the physical events which we count as language, while "langue" is the scientist's analysis and arrangements of them' (*ibid.*). The following year Harris returned to this point in a review (Harris, 1941) of Trubetzkoy's *Grundzüge der Phonologie* (1939). He wrote that Prague Circle terminology 'gives the impression that there are two objects of possible investigation, the Sprechakt (speech) and the Sprachgebilde (language structure), whereas the latter is merely the scientific arrangement of the former' (Harris, 1941: 345).

Archibald A. Hill, writing on the history of the LSA summer Linguistic Institutes, recalled that it was during the 1947 Institute that people began using the phrase 'structural analysis' where previously most would have said 'descriptive analysis' (Hill, 1964: 8, quoted in Hymes and Fought, 1981: 9). By the following year, European structuralism and American descriptivism were referred to jointly as 'structural linguistics' in a number of American articles (Preston, 1948: 132; Hockett, 1958 [1948]: 279; Voegelin, 1948: 115), and the new label began to take hold.

Interestingly, this development occurred, in part, in the context of a debate over the issue Harris had raised in his review of Trubetzkoy's work, that is, whether linguistic structure resides in the language or is the result of linguistic analysis (Preston, 1948; Hockett, 1948; Householder, 1952). Concerning 'descriptive or structural linguistics', Hockett wrote: 'The task of the structural linguist, as a scientist, is, as Preston [1948] implies, essentially one of classification', but Hockett went on to conclude that '[f]or the scientist . . . "linguistic structure" refers to something existing quite independently of the activities of the analyst: a language is what it is, it has the structure it has, whether studied and analyzed by a linguist or not' (Hockett, 1958 [1948]: 279–80). The label 'structural linguistics' was then used by Harris as the title to his influential book *Methods in Structural Linguistics* (Harris, 1951). The manuscript had previously circulated with the title 'Methods in Descriptive Linguistics' (LSA *Bulletin*, July–September 1948: 15, October–December 1949: 13), but in the preface, dated January 1947, Harris already had written: 'the logic of distributional relations . . . constitutes the basic method of *structural linguistics*' (Harris, 1951: v, emphasis added).

Not all American descriptivists immediately adopted 'structuralism' as the label for their work. Even in 1957, Joos continued to use 'descriptive linguistics' in his book title (Joos, 1958), as did H. A. Gleason for his widely used textbook *An Introduction to Descriptive Linguistics* (1st edition 1955, revised edition

1961), and Hockett, who was one of the earliest to use the term for American linguistics, later wrote: 'I have never been sure just what structuralism is supposed to be (Hymes and Fought [*American Structuralism*, 1981] . . . assiduously avoid telling us) – unless it is just a fancy way of referring to the twentieth-century emphasis (promoted especially, though not exclusively, by Saussure) on system and pattern in contrast to the somewhat atomistic nineteenth-century approach' (1987: 133). But gradually, American descriptive linguistics, particularly for the period of Bloomfield and the post-Bloomfieldians, came to be referred to as American structural linguistics, especially so in histories of the discipline (e.g. Hymes and Fought, 1981; Murray, 1994; Newmeyer, 1980).

As the discussion here attempts to show, so-called American structuralism was not built directly on a Saussurean foundation. Indeed, Gadet has argued that there is 'no direct line of descent leading from Saussure to linguistic structuralism; it was constituted through the creation of a number of linguistic schools', including 'the Prague Circle, glossematics (the Copenhagen Circle), the Geneva School' (Gadet, 1989: 119). Structuralism in its broader sense, 'generalized structuralism' (Gadet, 1989: 112), became an important part of literary and cultural theory in the late 1950s and the 1960s with the work of Roland Barthes, Jacques Derrida and Jacques Lacan, among others. The rather loose connections between any type of structural linguistics and such expanded structuralism is touched on by Gadet. But as structuralism in this broader sense permeated the general intellectual climate, some American linguists, too, began to view the origin of their own structuralism as resting with Saussure, and it became increasingly common to nod in his direction and to cite from the *Cours* what often amounted to little more than slogans when early twentieth-century American linguistics was discussed.

This new practice was supported during the 1950s and early 1960s by increased American openness to European linguistics, including the publication of the first English translation of the *Cours* (1959), and a growing interest in semiotics and semantics.

First, as some of the wartime refugee linguists became established in the United States and communication restrictions prevalent during the war disappeared, Americans' interest in reestablishing connections with European linguistics extended beyond the efforts of the Linguistic Circle of New York. In 1950 Einar Haugen, in his LSA presidential address, began by pointing out that 'Linguistic science is today in every sense of the word an international science', lamenting that '[r]arely does one see a reference in American writings on linguistic theory to the works of de Saussure, Trubetzkoy, or other European writers', and arguing for greater attention to European work (Haugen, 1951: 211). And that began to happen with increasing frequency as the decade went on, enhancing the earlier discussions of structuralism.

In the *Modern Language Journal* John Waterman introduced Saussure to the modern language teachers of America with the statement that 'much of the theoretical foundation of modern structuralism stems from Ferdinand de Saussure's formulations of linguistic principles' (Waterman, 1956: 307). Martin Joos, organising the papers for his 1958 anthology, pulled Wells's 'De Saussure's system of linguistics' (1947) out of the chronological ordering of the rest of the volume and placed it in lead position, implying a foundational role in American linguistics that Saussure's work did not have. He also claimed, without evidence, that 'half of these authors [in Joos, 1958] had read the Cours. The others got it second-hand' (Joos, 1958: 18). As Hymes and Fought noted, Joos 'marvelously confuses' Saussure's effective role and his symbolic role (1981: 16). It is generally best to treat Joos's remarks on Saussure's place in American linguistics as after-the-fact myth-making, but it is worth noting the importance that he was now attributing to Saussure and the *Cours*.

The publication of an English version of the *Cours* in 1959 was another sign of the new American receptiveness to Saussure's work. More than forty years after the original and well after translations had appeared in other languages, e.g. Japanese 1928, German 1931, Russian 1933, Spanish 1945 (see Koerner, 1972: 62–3), the English *Course in General Linguistics* may have been prompted and aided by the French linguist André Martinet, a member of the Linguistic Circle of New York and the Columbia University faculty during the late 1940s and early 1950s (Martinet, 1993: 360).

The International Congress of Linguists was held in the United States for the first time, in Cambridge, Massachusetts, in 1962. Papers in the congress proceedings (Lunt, 1964) show several American contributors making determined efforts to comment on past and current European work, including early remarks on Saussure by Noam Chomsky (Chomsky, 1964b; see Joseph, 1990, for information on the several publishings and revisions of this important paper).

Chomsky discussed Saussure in a number of articles published around the time of his paper at the International Congress of Linguists and occasionally in later work. His concerns and interpretations shifted over the years (see Joseph, 1990, for discussion and analysis), but it was Saussure's *langue* and its relationship to Chomsky's concept of linguistic competence that received the most attention. One point of agreement was that *langue*, or competence, was theoretically prior to *parole*, or actual performance (Chomsky, 1964a: 52). However, Chomsky did not fully accept *langue*, seeing it 'as essentially a storehouse of signs (e.g. words, fixed phrases), their grammatical properties, and, perhaps, certain "phrase types"' (1963: 328), not the 'generative process based on recursive rules' of Chomsky's generative grammar (*ibid.*). Further, Chomsky did not accept what he believed was Saussure's relegation of sentence formation to 'a matter of *parole* rather than *langue* . . . (or perhaps, in some obscure way, as on the border between *langue* and *parole*)' (1964a: 59–60). It is important to note that Chomsky's discussions of Saussure were never as consistently positive as his references to two other European linguists, Wilhelm von Humboldt and Otto Jespersen (see, e.g., Chomsky, 1963 and 1966, on Humboldt, Chomsky, 1975 and 1986, on Jespersen).

Linguists who proposed non-generative approaches in the 1950s and 1960s also made reference to European work. Kenneth Pike, founder of the approach known as tagmemics, for the most part did not accept Saussurean notions: 'we reject the theory of signs of de Saussure' (1954: 24); 'we abandon the distinction between *la langue* and *la parole* proposed by de Saussure' (1960: 52); he found the work of J. R. Firth much more compatible (e.g. Pike, 1954: 6, 42, 74). Sydney Lamb, whose stratificational grammar (Lamb, 1966) attracted some attention in the 1960s, acknowledged Saussure as one of the 'renowned scholars who have provided precedent' for 'the assertion that linguistic structure is stratified' (Lamb, 1965: 38), but much of Lamb's work at the time was more connected to the glossematics of Louis Hjelmslev (1953) than to Saussure.

By the mid 1970s the subject of the European background of non-historical American linguistics was so well established that it served as the topic of a symposium celebrating the fiftieth anniversary of the founding of the LSA (Hoenigswald, 1979). Here, quotations from the *Cours* and references to Saussure appeared frequently (e.g. pp. 89–90, 123–6, 147–8, 165–7). Saussure's place in American linguistics was now retroactively but well established.

During these years, a shift had been occurring in the place of semantics within American linguistics. Many of the descriptivists had avoided the study of meaning, and even as late as 1949 Wells had written of semantics and linguistics as two distinct fields:

> there will be a branch of science that describes the vehicles, the forms, the signifiants used by various languages, and another branch that describes the meanings of these forms . . . both of these [and] other sciences . . . will be included in the still more comprehensive science of semiotic . . . On the whole the decision that seems most advisable is to restrict the term 'linguistics' to the study of linguistic forms, i.e. to the conjunction of phonemics, morphology, syntax, and some other fields. Linguistics will make use of certain statements about meaning which are, to it, postulates, but which are inductively established by its coordinate science, semantics. (Wells, 1949: 322)

Although many American linguists still view semiotics as a separate field of inquiry, there is some overlap, as in the work of Thomas A. Sebeok, 1975 LSA president, who early on became an internationally known specialist in semiotics (see Sebeok et al., 1964, and then Sebeok, 1976, 1979, 1991, 1994), 'unifying Saussurean "semiology" (practiced mostly by European linguists) and [Charles Sanders] Peircean "semiotics" (practiced mostly by American philosophers) into a single paradigm' (Joseph, 1995: 236).

There was in the 1950s a developing line of work in semantics associated with descriptive linguistics, but its still tenuous status at the time was reflected by Joos's decision to include no articles on meaning in the 1958 anthology. For the most part American semantics was constructed not on a Saussurean model, but from a British and American background, especially C. K. Ogden and I. A. Richards's *The Meaning of Meaning* (1927) and Charles W. Morris's theory of signs (Morris, 1938, 1946). Ogden and Richards dismissed Saussure: 'this theory of signs, by neglecting entirely the things for which signs stand, was from the beginning cut off from any contact with scientific methods of verification' (1927: 6). And Morris, who drew on Bloomfield's linguistic behaviourism, followed Peirce's semiotics: to determine the meaning of any sign 'we have . . . simply to determine what habits it produces' (1946: v).

When the American linguist Floyd Lounsbury turned to semantic analysis of kinship systems, he brought together ideas from Ogden and Richards (1927) with Morris's theory of signs and the distributional analysis of descriptive linguistics (Lounsbury, 1956, 1964). He made no reference to Saussure, but other descriptivists nodded at least in passing. Thus, William Wonderly began an article on 'Semantic components in Kechua person morphemes' by relating Bloomfield's term 'sememe' ('the meaning of a morpheme') to Saussure's *signifié*: 'we have the morpheme as the minimal unit of meaning speech form (Saussure's signifiant) and the sememe as the minimal unit of discretely classified reality (Saussure's signifié) corresponding to it' (Wonderly, 1952: 366). Wonderly's and Lounsbury's semantics and that of other descriptivists was largely morpheme and word based.

In the 1960s, generative linguists sought a place within their framework for the semantic interpretation of sentences. In a foundational book on this subject, *An Integrated Theory of Linguistic Descriptions*, Jerrold Katz and Paul Postal began their Preface with a reference to Saussure, most likely because of the discussion of *langue* and *parole* appearing at this time in Chomsky's work.

> In any linguistic study, it is necessary to distinguish sharply between *language* and *speech*. Although this distinction has been classic in linguistics at least since the time of F. de Saussure, modern linguistics . . . has often confused the two. Because of this confusion, the importance of this classic distinction must be re-emphasized. (Katz and Postal, 1964: ix)

The aim of their book was 'to provide an adequate means of incorporating the grammatical and the semantic descriptions of a language into one integrated description' (1964: x). This goal has proved difficult to achieve, but ever since, semantics has remained an integral part of American linguistics.

The 1970s brought yet another development that enhanced American knowledge, appreciation and further investigation of Saussure – the rapid growth and expansion of studies in the history of linguistics. Especially consequential was the work of E. F. K. Koerner, whose doctoral dissertation on Saussure was published in 1973, preceded the year before by his *Bibliographia Saussureana 1870–1970* (Koerner, 1972). Koerner and other historians of American linguistics have examined the interpretations of Saussure by Bloomfield, Chomsky, Jakobson and Wells (e.g. Andresen, 1990; Falk, 1995; Joseph, 1990; Koerner, 1995; Levin, 1965), and this focus has sometimes led to the impression that Saussure was the most important European predecessor to American work. Only additional studies of other European linguists and their relation to American linguistics (e.g. Falk, 1992) can demonstrate whether this is indeed the case.

Meanwhile, American linguists in the 1980s and 1990s widely ignored Saussure and the *Cours*. The four-volume *Linguistics: The Cambridge Survey* (Newmeyer, 1988), 'a comprehensive introduction to research results and current work in all branches of the field' (vol. I, p. vii), was largely American in orientation. The editor and seven of the nine members of the Editorial Board held appointments at United States universities, and 49 of the 63 contributors were affiliated with institutions in the United States and Canada. Of these North American authors, only five mentioned Saussure in their texts, all either as brief historical comments, e.g. 'de Saussure himself apparently held that the domain of the sign relation . . . was the word or complex form' (Anderson, 1988: 152), or as source for a standpoint to be corrected by more recent linguistics:

> Following Saussure, the synchronic and diachronic perspectives have been considered diametrically opposed . . . In order to heal the Saussurean division of our discipline and construct a dynamic or organic theory of language accommodating both structure and change, we must address issues of social class and sociolinguistic variation. (Guy, 1988: 56)

The latter position is reminiscent of Jakobson's 1928 rejection of the 'antinomy between synchronic and diachronic linguistic studies' in Saussure's work and his own theme of dynamic synchronism (Jakobson, 1962 [1928]: 1–2).

In the final decade of the twentieth century, many overviews of contemporary American linguistics made no mention of Saussure at all (e.g. Napoli 1996, Yule 1996). Works that did so usually had nothing more than a brief acknowledgement of general influence: 'Ferdinand de Saussure . . . turned his attention . . . to the structural principles of language rather than to the ways in which languages change and develop, and in so doing, became a major influence on twentieth-century linguistics' (Fromkin, 2000: 5); 'de Saussure (1959) investigates the relationship between linguistic "signs" and what they represent, developing what has come to be known as semiotic theory' (Weisler and Milekic, 2000: 230).

Concerning Saussure and American linguistics, the conclusions of Dell H. Hymes, 1982 LSA president, remain relevant in the twenty-first century:

> Just as the comparative-historical approach has its mythical founder in Sir William Jones, so the structural approach has had its mythical founder in Ferdinand de Saussure. The great respect one must have for both men does not bar inquiry into the actual part they played; in both cases, it was, most dramatically, in the symbolic use made posthumously of each. (Hymes, 1983: 375)

8 Saussure and structuralist linguistics in Europe

Christian Puech

It is difficult to depict – even with broad strokes – the fortune of Ferdinand de Saussure's work in the French context. This context is characterised by a whole series of historical paradoxes which arise out of some of the deeply rooted characteristics of French linguistic culture: the power of academic grammar in the social context of universal schooling from the 1880s; the status of normative grammar; the status accorded to the 'genius' of the French language; the very late setting up of linguistic studies (compared with Germany). But from the perspective which interests us here, these negative reasons also have a positive counterpart, which is no less paradoxical: in French culture from the 1960s/1970s on (in fact since the Second World War, although less noticeably so) Saussure, or at least the *Cours* edited by Bally and Sechehaye, has been present in every branch of the social and human sciences and philosophy.

France did not have a 'linguistic circle' like those of Prague, Copenhagen, Geneva and New York, and the organisational dynamics required to bring in new forms of knowledge very often came up against institutional inertia. Since the end, or last third, of the nineteenth century most innovations came from outside France. Initially they came from Germany, then subsequently from the USA came the converging strands from the eastern and northern European developments of the 1920s, 1930s and 1940s. The French school of semiotics which developed in the 1970s had its origins in Greimas's reading of Hjelmslev and Brøndal. Its repercussions and its success in French structuralism (see chapter by Ungar, this volume) are largely due to foreign contributions, which owe their favourable acceptance to a few scholars (such as Benveniste) working in prestigious but marginal institutions.

In these circumstances Saussure's teachings have experienced an astonishing trajectory. Between the wars academic linguistics was dominated by the scholarly work of Antoine Meillet (1866–1936), which was at once open and authoritarian. One only has to read *Linguistique historique et linguistique générale* to realise that in France Saussure's general linguistics was largely subordinated to historical and comparative linguistics. The theme of 'linguistic change' has remained the touchstone of theoretical research, and the Saussurian notion of synchrony has not really been taken on board, even though the notion of system appears frequently in Meillet's work. From early interest in the *Cours*, it can be seen – in the work of Meillet, as also of Vendryès – that the thesis of 'the social character of linguistic phenomena' has continued to be understood in terms of change from outside, without an appreciation of the importance, novelty and implications of Saussure's ideas about the intrinsic character of the social dimension in linguistic phenomena. There was, then, a good deal of ambiguity about the way in which Saussurean themes stemming from the *Cours de linguistique générale* were widely diffused after the Second World War, through the very varying strands that went under the name of 'structuralism'.

This chapter aims to outline the milestones of the French reception of the *Cours* in a European context, and to underline some of the distinctive characteristics of this feverish and chequered adoption of the ideas of the *Cours*. To this end we shall try in the first section to identify different phases in the reception of the *CLG*. Then in the second section we will attempt to convey the low-profile presence of Saussure in the period between the two world wars in which there were a range of positive and negative reactions to Saussure's ideas, which gave rise to some original work. Finally in the third section, we discern in the period between 1950 and 1980 a new phase in references to Saussure. In this phase Benveniste tries to take Saussure's ideas further by using the concepts of *énonciation* (utterance theory) and the speaking subject (*le sujet parlant*), while Culioli – without feeling any need to stick very closely to Saussures views – arrives at his own proposal for an independent linguistics that would recognise the diversity of languages but still meet the need to develop a general linguistics of *language*.

France and how the *Cours* was received

The problem here arises because our 'immediate' understanding of the period is largely retrospective and coloured by the end result. In many histories of linguistics of the 1960s, Saussure is represented as the beginning and end of all linguistic theorising, with little awareness of the way in which our perception of his theory is mediated through the responses and interpretations of those who came in between. If we do our best to avoid this end-point-orientated history, the reception of the *CLG* in France can be described in four main phases, all closely interrelated.

The initial reception of the *CLG* goes back to the time of its publication. In 1916 this text was not always considered of prime importance within the linguistic community (Normand, 1978b). There was a tendency to see the speculative Saussure of the *CLG* as a distortion of the 'real' Saussure of the *Mémoire sur le système des voyelles en indo-européen*, or else as an overly abstract speculation which failed to take account of the empirical, social approaches of Meillet and Vendryès, and of sociolinguistic variation. Significantly, it is undoubtedly Sechehaye, one of the editors of the *Cours*, who provides the best gauge of Saussure's novelty. First and foremost a psychologist, he published a thirty-page review in 1917 in the *Revue philosophique*. This was not a simple glossary of Saussurian concepts, but an attempt to bring out the underlying conceptual organisation of the *Cours*. In particular he was the first to highlight the importance of a set of ideas often ignored by reviews at the time: *value – difference – opposition – the relatively arbitrary*. He concluded more incisively than all his contemporaries: 'the science of language (*langue*) will be a science of values'. Sechehaye deserves all the more credit because it took many years for the importance of the semiological status of *langue* to become apparent to the readers of the *Cours*, although after the Second World War Saussure would appear essentially as the originator of what Barthes called 'the adventure of semiology'.

The second phase in the reception of the *CLG* developed from the 1920s on, notably on the occasion of the first international congress of linguists at La Haye in 1928, where the *CLG* was indeed seen as the main starting point for innovation in linguistics. This was confirmed at later congresses of Slavic linguists, and the *CLG* then became, along with the manifestos of the Prague Circle, a strategic text for those at the periphery to win over the mainstream. At this stage in France, Saussure's ideas were transmitted by a few isolated individuals. Martinet, for example, acted as a link between Prague and Paris before leaving for the United States. He created the chair of Phonology at the Ecole Pratique des Hautes Etudes (1938) but it is indicative that it was only in 1955 that he was appointed to the chair of General Linguistics at the Sorbonne. Scholars like Gougenheim (1900–72), Guillaume (1883–1960) and Wagner showed that they were familiar with the *CLG*, although generally only indirectly via Prague and within the specific parameters of French linguistics between the wars, many of whose practitioners (Brunot, Damourette and Pichon) were mainly obsessed with the question of the relation between thought and language.

In the third phase the *CLG* became the common property of linguists, sociologists, anthropologists and philosophers. It is without doubt the philosopher Merleau-Ponty who played the main role here, in particular as mediator between Lévi-Strauss, Jakobson and Lacan. (See his inaugural lecture at the Collège de France as well as his course on the psychology of the child at the Sorbonne.) After the articles by Greimas (in particular 'Saussure aujourd'hui' in *Le français moderne*, 1956), a more rigid definition of Saussurean dichotomies is adopted. Notions such as synchrony/diachrony and language system/speech (*langue/parole*) become the focus of general debates about the shape and status of semiology, and even of a debate between Sartre and Lévi-Strauss on the philosophy of history. A part of Barthes's work arose from this intense but relatively brief period when Saussure's ideas reigned supreme in structuralism and beyond. What is undoubtedly not sufficiently underlined about this third phase, given the prestige of 'French structuralism' of the 1960s/1970s outside France, is the extent to which this return to Saussure was both belated and indirect, in that it was mediated by the reinterpretations of Jakobson and Hjelmslev. When one realises that the affiliation of structuralist linguists to Saussurean ideas dates back to 1929, and that the first general usage of the term 'structuralism' was in a 1945 article by Cassirer in the journal *Word*, one can gauge the degree of inertia on the French scene. It also becomes possible to appreciate why so many misunderstandings surrounded the 'rediscovery' of the *Cours*.

Finally, in the fourth phase of reception there is Godel's work on the manuscript sources of the *CLG* (1957) and Engler's critical edition of the *CLG* (1968–1974), as well as de Mauro's critical edition of the *Cours*. A period of philological research began which was to spearhead what was taken to be a return to Saussure's 'true thought'. The study of the manuscripts, for example on the German legends or the anagrams in Latin poetry, was felt to be particularly revealing, and, more recently, the recently published manuscript material (Saussure, 2002) has provided an impetus for a reassessment of the 'real' Saussure. There is no doubt that this return to the manuscript sources has made for a more moderate interpretation of the Saussurean dichotomies (see in particular Fehr, 2000, but also Bouquet, 1997). However, this does not alter the fact that the *CLG* has continued to have an impact from the time of its first appearance, and has been an inspiration for various fields of knowledge, for linguistics and in France has served as a way of bringing students into linguistics.

This rough sketch of the four phases is simply meant to underline the complexity of the reception given to Saussure in France. Despite almost ten years of Saussure being taught in Paris, despite the very strong influence that he exerted on the audience at the Ecole Pratique des Hautes Etudes (1882–9), the ideas of the *Cours* were for a long time marginalised, and then only attracted interest belatedly and mediated by 'general structuralism'. Finally, only relatively recently has there been research into Saussure's 'true thought' on the basis of various available manuscripts. This research is on-going at present, so one can wonder what the outcome will be. According to some, who perhaps set too much store by this discovery, Saussure was responsible for pre-programming whole chunks of modern linguistics, unbeknown to those sociolinguists, speech act theorists and discourse analysts who mistakenly thought that they had gone against Saussure's teaching to develop these areas themselves! Yet others attribute to Saussure the development of an original linguistics, a linguistics of languages which requires us to rethink the accepted view of Saussure as 'formalist' and 'abstract objectivist', in the words of Bakhtin. This requires the rebuilding of the Saussurean edifice on a different foundation, that of the semiological status of languages (Fehr, 2000). In any case, the stakes entrusted to historians of linguistics are high, as Saussure remains the prism through which an attempt can or must be made to understand a large part of the development and history of contemporary sciences of language.

Another way of presenting Saussure's legacy in France would no doubt be to distinguish between two ways of 'receiving' the *Cours*. The first would be the adoption of a conceptual framework constructed either actively or reactively on the basis of the *Cours*, on the model of Prague phonology or Danish glossematics. The second would just be a 'heritage' consisting of the belated recognition of a source, and post-hoc imitation, borrowings and recourse to numerous intermediaries. A case in point would be the vaguely French structuralist thinker who owes more to Jakobson and Hjelmslev than Saussure, and who is concerned with something 'beyond' language or languages, such as approaches to the text, narratology, philosophy of culture and even the 'deconstruction of Western thought'. (On the distinction between the reception given to Saussure and his legacy and on the complexities of the ways in which modern linguists refer back to Saussure see Chiss and Puech, 1999, and Puech, 2000.)

The additional advantage of the second way of proceeding is that it avoids the sharp distinction often made in relation to Saussure and the linguistics of his time, between a view stressing continuity (such as that which manages to see in eighteenth-century debates about synonymy a 'foreshadowing' of Saussure's theory of value, Auroux, 1985) and a view emphasising radical discontinuity which tends to credit Saussure with founding structuralism single-handed and from scratch. In fact, the historiography of linguistics is only just beginning to gain a better understanding of both the way in which Saussure's conceptual framework was rooted in his times and his originality within this context (see Auroux, 2000). The need for a general science of the phenomena of language became evident in the last third of the nineteenth century in different ways, in particular with various undertakings in 'semantics' (in France, Darmesteter, 1886 and Bréal, 1897). But it happened above all in reaction to the narrow selectiveness of the 'phonetic laws' of historical and comparative linguistics, the mechanical and/or biologist interpretations of phonetic changes, and the minimising of the role of the group and of the speaking subject. Without making Victor Henry (1850–1907) a 'precursor' of Saussure, and precisely because he is a less wide-ranging linguist, his *Antinomies linguistiques* (1896) offers a perceptive analysis of the epistemological problems facing linguistics at the time. He addressed the lack of an agreed meta-language, had a lively interest in an empirically based psychology of language (language acquisition, internal language, glossolalias, speech pathologies), and above all saw the need to define boundaries in order to put on an empirical footing a formulation of what is 'specific' to linguistics. Henry synthesised in a few pages the questions that linguistics had left to one side, the gaps that called for a new general way of seeing, without himself providing satisfactory answers to these general questions (see Puech, 2003 and 2004). However, by putting these questions he has made possible a better understanding of both Saussure's questions and the originality of his answers.

In any event, it is clear that linguistics in France in the mid twentieth century between the wars is not the same thing as the reception given to the *Cours* nor the beginnings of a structuralism which often had little to do with linguistics (see 'Le structuralisme introuvable' in Chiss and Puech, 1997). Saussure was not unknown, but his influence followed a vague and diffuse path which we will try to follow, while remaining aware of all the obstacles to its reception.

Geographical dimensions of Saussure's legacy

One might think that in the French-speaking world the fate of Saussure's thought would be played out in the two towns where he taught: Paris and Geneva. Yet it is not altogether clear that a Geneva school of linguistics exists (Amsterdamska, 1987), and its own position with regard to a structural linguistics going back to Saussure is qualified. It is known that his immediate followers, Bally whose *Linguistique générale et linguistique française* was published in 1932 and Sechehaye whose *Programme et méthode de la linguistique théorique* appeared in 1908, produced work which although it dialogued or chimed with Saussure's propositions, nevertheless had its own orientation. Bally in fact developed a linguistics of expression which some see as foreshadowing today's theories of enunciation and of pragmatics, while Sechehaye was interested, from a distinctly psychological perspective, in speech acts and what he termed a 'pre-grammatical' science. Paradoxically it seems to be a post-Saussurean and a post-structuralist parentage that is heralded by the two editors of the *Cours de linguistique générale*!

In later generations Prieto (born 1926) developed a theory of meaning based on the principle of relevance (*Messages et signaux*, 1966; *Pertinence et pratique: essai de sémiologie*, 1975). His publications appeared during a short-lived discussion about communicative as against expressive semiology (cf. Barthes). *La grammaire des fautes* by Frei (holder of the chair of General Linguistics in Geneva from 1945) seems today like an illustration of the functioning of language systems along the two axes proposed by Saussure: the syntagmatic and the paradigmatic. His influence was weak and his recognition came late.

Even the existence of French structuralism is problematical. Although the seminal work by Martinet (born 1908) embodies the unmistakable continuation of the linguistics of the Prague Circle, especially in the area of phonology, he rejected the epithet 'structuralist' in favour of 'functionalist'. His *Eléments de la linguistique générale* (1960) nevertheless represented an important stage in the diffusing of structuralist ideas, while *Economie des changements phonétiques* 1955) – an analysis of linguistic shifts within a synchronic framework – had less of an impact. Martinet's work in the field of diachronic phonetics made a major contribution to the structuralist notions of language systems with respect to the interpretation of the Saussurean distinction between synchrony and diachrony. If, as Martinet believes, the requirements of communication for a maximum number of phonetic differences are set against 'the tendency to least effort', then synchrony exists in a state of unstable equilibrium tending towards an ever increasing efficiency in the means available to speakers in the community. The diachronic effect of this economy is to be found in the fact that a relatively infrequent opposition will disappear more easily than a more greatly used opposition. Hence the diachronic and synchronic perspectives are no longer mutually opposed here, but rather are complementary. In any language at any given moment there are weak points in the equilibrium which can be analysed as tendencies to change.

Meillet's student, Benveniste (1902–76), contributed substantially to a reinvigoration of the comparativist tradition, as well as to work on general linguistics, in which he develops further some of Saussure's propositions, for example on the arbitrary nature of the sign. In some respects his theoretical focus on the place of 'the human being in language' marked the beginning of structuralism being overtaken by enunciation theory and pragmatics. It is in France that one can best get a measure of the misunderstandings over the relationship between Saussure's teachings and the development of structuralism. In addition to the linguists that we have already mentioned, another important figure was Guillaume (1883–1960). Guillaume was a persistent reader of Saussure who elaborated a theory of language (called a 'psycho-systématique' or 'psycho-mécanique du langage') which drew less on Saussure's definition of the language system than on the dynamics of the language–thought relationship. With this he laid the basis for a very lively Guillaumian school of linguistics, which has certain reservations about calling itself structuralist and which has tended to develop on the basis of its own principles.

To understand this situation it is no doubt necessary to go back to Meillet's influence. He dominated linguistics in France for nearly fifty years (*Linguistique historique et linguistique générale*, vol. II, 1921–36). Although he attended Saussure's classes at the Ecole Pratique des Hautes Etudes, even replacing him 1889–90, his name – even beyond linguistic circles – depends on the promotion of a 'general linguistics' which, despite his assertions, owes little to Saussure. Instead, along with Vendryès (*Le Langage*, 1921), he represented a dominant tendency in French linguistics which is most often described as the 'sociological school'.

Saussure's influence on Meillet and Meillet's influence on Saussure is a very widely debated question. Indeed, reference can be made to Meillet himself on this matter: 'For my part, I've hardly published a single page without some qualms about claiming all of the credit for myself: Saussure's thought is so rich that it has permeated my thinking' (Meillet, 1936: 179). But, beyond the assertion that 'language (*la langue*) is a system', the authorship of which continues to be debated among historians (see Koerner, 1993), it is difficult to see in the extensive work of the professor at the Collège de France anything other than a parallel development to Saussure's propositions. Historically the interest of this work lies in the differing assessments that can be made of the various proposals for a 'general linguistics' developed in France at the turn of the twentieth century (see articles by Normand in Auroux, 2000, and Chiss and Puech, 1999). However, from this point of view, it must be observed that Meillet's initiative owed little to Saussure. Meillet was in fact seeking to define: 'general laws which are not valid only at a single point in the development of a language, but are instead valid for all times; which are not limited to a single language, but apply instead equally to all languages' (Meillet, 1921: 11).

For Meillet, then, these laws are necessarily laws of historical development, and his general linguistics is in essence inevitably a typology of linguistic change. Carrying on the German comparative and historical grammar of the nineteenth century, Meillet really only modified it in one respect, by bringing out absolutely binding *general* phonetic and semantic laws which went beyond the 'atomistic' point of view of the neogrammarians. In this approach the notion of *system* does indeed take on a major importance, but this really only concerns the rules of correspondence which take account of the passage from one language state (or *état de langue*) to another. In brief, this *system* does not take account of the way language *functions* as does Saussure's, but rather of its historical development. Similarly Saussure's assertion of the social character of linguistic phenomena was taken up by Meillet; but, whereas Saussure was referring here to a founding principle of the semiological status of *langue* (the internal principle of 'the arbitrary appropriateness' of signifier and signified), Meillet (who collaborated with the sociologist Durkheim in the journal *L'année sociologique*) was interested in the correlation between linguistic and social factors in his attempts to account for linguistic change by means of an *external* causality. In other words, a particular state of society corresponds to a given *état de langue*, and thus the coherence of the system is due in the last analysis to a causality exterior to the actual language system. Likewise, whereas Saussure's general linguistics took its place in a 'general science of signs within social life', within a semiology which takes linguistics as its model, Meillet's general linguistics set out the contours of an interdisciplinary anthropology which aimed to classify tendencies in language behaviour (Meillet, 1921: 53).

Meillet's use of the term 'system', denoting a theoretical construct relying on empirical facts, is quite far removed from Saussure's own usage. System here does not refer to the order intrinsic to language, but to a post hoc assembling of 'tendencies', of findings which do not heed Saussure's warning about the impossible utopianism of trying to adopt a point of view covering all periods of time. While in linguistic structuralism after Saussure there was indeed, within the perspective of a dynamic structuralism, a questioning of the distinction synchrony/diachrony (especially in Prague and by Martinet in France), it seems that Meillet's own thinking fell short of the structuralist debates and had a dubious similarity to some of Saussure's distinctions. Could this diluted approximation to Saussure's ideas be one of the reasons for the fate of his teaching in France?

The other reason would definitely be the strength in the French context of what might be called a 'psychological' grammar. For phonology, that drove forward the development in Europe of a structuralism inspired by Saussure, only became established late in France, where all the discussions seemed instead to be dedicated to the development of a science of grammar, in an unbroken debate stemming from the seventeenth century and continuing during the nineteenth century in school grammar (see Chervel, 1977). Brunot, Damourette and Pichon, as well as Guillaume, all sought to continue the seventeenth-century Port Royal tradition; they were aware of, but resisted, Saussure's ideas.

Brunot attempted to develop an onomasiological approach which would go from thought to language, claiming that this choice was a result of the a-logical and poorly structured nature of language. Brunot substitutes the analysis of conceptual units, or 'thought phenomena', for the analysis of the function and meaning of linguistic units, using for example the categories of *animate*, *inanimate*, *concrete* and *abstract* as a basis on which to deal with 'gender', 'number', 'determinacy' and so on. 'The forms available to language, as numerous as they are, are always far fewer in number than the forms available to thought. Hence each of the former is used for various purposes' (Brunot 1922, xvi).

Damourette's and Pichon's monumental work, which was subtitled *Essai de grammaire de la langue française*, was published over the years 1911 to 1927. The telling title *Des mots à la pensée* in fact encapsulates their reaction to Brunot's onomasiological approach. However, their principal targets are Meillet and Saussure. In Saussure's case it was above all the very notion of 'the arbitrariness of the sign' (see their para. 74) that was called into question, and through it the entire Saussurean concept of the sign and of language as a system. This is revealing of the pattern of discussion and opposition surrounding the *Cours de linguistique générale*, which was triggered by an article by Pichon in 1937 in the *Journal de psychologie* ('La linguistique en France, problèmes et méthodes'), followed up in *Acta linguistica* in 1940 in reply to the subsequently famous article by Benveniste ('La nature du signe linguistique'), feeding a discussion in which Bally, Sechehaye and Frei took part in the *Cahiers F. de Saussure* and *Acta Linguistica*. This discussion, which was to have other repercussions, led the *Société genevoise de linguistique* to publish a manifesto, 'Pour l'arbitraire du signe' (For the arbitrary nature of the sign).

This would merit extensive analysis because it sums up the whole situation of French linguistics within Europe in relation to the new ideas of Saussure. The rejection by Damourette and Pichon of the arbitrariness of the sign is rooted in a long-standing view of language that is particular to French culture in which 'the development of a people and of their language are simply two aspects of the same phenomenon' (para. 6). Hence it seems that the analysis of any language needs to be undertaken by someone 'whose thought has been moulded on the model of the grammar with which he thinks' (para. 6). Consequently it seemed justified to ascribe to Saussure's bilingualism the error of 'reasoning' which led him to the thesis of the arbitrariness of the sign!

Polemics aside, this debate about the arbitrariness of the sign provided one of the main ways in which Saussure's theses became known in France. Despite Sechehaye, the reception of the *Cours* in France seems to have focused essentially on 'the nature of the linguistic sign', either to reject its validity, or on the contrary to see it as Saussure's main innovation. From the 1930s to the structuralism of the 1960s and 1970s, a disproportionate amount of importance was attached to this issue, with unfortunate results. It led to a neglect of the various past discussions of this issue that can be traced back to Aristotle's *Peri hermeneias*, to downplaying the theory of value, relative motivation and the degree of interconnectedness of the syntagmatic and paradigmatic axes, all of which are key issues in defining the semiological status of languages in the *Cours* (see Normand, 1970).

Guillaume represents yet another response to the *Cours* at around the same time. As early as 1919, his 'psycho-system' (*Le problème de l'article et sa solution dans la langue française*) claims Saussure as its source of inspiration more than Meillet, Guillaume's mentor. The *Cours* in fact remains a major point of reference throughout the linguist's entire career. In 1945, Guillaume presented himself as a follower of the teaching of the 'much admired and little followed' *Cours* (1945 : 221), and in 1952 as an 'experimental' Saussurean to whom it fell to provide proof for Saussure's ideas. In the illuminating words of Wilmet:

> Let us say that *Le cours de linguistique générale* will have allowed the young Guillaume to sort out his intuitions which up to that point were still tentative. Subsequently he would have wanted to take advantage of the success that Saussure's work enjoyed, while retaining in his heart of hearts (as many pages of the *Leçons de linguistique* show) a strong awareness of the corrections or improvements that he had brought to Saussure's thought. (Wilmet, 1991: 205)

Chez Guillaume, Saussure is invoked as supporting evidence, often retrospectively. The theory of the sign is taken up by Guillaume . . . and profoundly transformed. In replacing *parole* with *discours*, Guillaume made *langage/langue/parole* the three pillars of his edifice. *Psychomechanics* is the analysis of the *effective time* of a language act which effects the passage from what goes before (*langue*) to what comes after (*discours*). *Psychosystematics* studies more particularly the *permanent* system of *langue*, taken as *a system of representing the world* developed generation after generation, as distinct from the contingent oppositions of discourse. Finally, psychosemiology is assigned the remit of studying the close relationship of potential meaning (*langue*) to the appropriate lexical means of conveying it. There is nothing in this framework to prevent a complete reinterpretation of the fundamental principles of the *Cours*, which was constantly to hand during Guillaume's theoretical analyses. Is it appropriate to speak of influence here? Perhaps it is more that Guillaume was the first to call on Saussure in a way which was destined to become commonplace. To a period at a turning point in the history of linguistics, the *Cours* offered a projector screen, a disciplinary matrix for diverse and often original projects which were thus able to find a place and a justification for themselves.

'*Enonciation*': a most unsaussurean return to Saussure

Another way of evaluating the impact of Ferdinand de Saussure on linguistics in France may consist in looking at the most recent period, the mid 1970s, in which the so-called hegemony of Saussure's ideas in linguistics started to be challenged. In fact the identification of structuralism with Saussure was so strong after the Second World War that the move against structuralism was very frequently presented as the need to find an alternative to Saussure in the shape of sociolinguistics, discourse analysis, enunciation theory or pragmatics. The emergence of the field of enunciation in France and its complex relations with Saussure's ideas will be considered here.

As Delesalle (1986) has shown in the introduction to the proceedings of the symposium on 'L'histoire des théories de l'énonciation', there already existed some scattered elements of enunciation theory before the modern period (the turn of the twentieth century). Recent definitions of enunciation theory seem to have in common a negative element: the rejection, or the drastic revision, of Saussure's distinction between *langue* and *parole*. This allows Delesalle to state that 'We have gone from a plural notion which has different labels to a single label designating a notion which is still plural (Delesalle, 1986).

More generally, at the turn of the century the quantity of work on interaction, speech acts and conversation brings into question the hallowed myth that authentic acts of language had to be sacrificed for the greater good of an autonomous linguistics. (On this two-fold reduction of Saussure's system to structure and of the speaking subject to the individual, perpetuated by the very people who take on the task of 'rehabilitating' the subject in opposition to structures, see Meschonnic, 1995: 4.) In fact, an interest in authentic utterances was already present at the very genesis of structuralism. For two key figures, Jakobson and Benveniste, it is the case that the concern with theories of enunciation emerged in very close relation to the structuralist paradigm as it developed. A comparison, even brief, of these two authors should make it possible to highlight both this common origin and the divergence of viewpoints that it gives rise to. This can be seen not only in the very notion of the *champ énonciatif* (the 'field of enunciation') but also in the notions of linguistics and in the approaches which stem from Saussure.

For instance, it is clearly to Benveniste's article on the nature of pronouns (1956) that Jakobson refers in 1957 (republished in Jakobson 1963) with regard to the first-person pronoun and its semantic functioning as an 'index'. But this reference is mainly used in carrying out a commentary on the famous schema of communication, which it develops, tests and finally confirms. To this extent shifters introduce for Jakobson a sort of hierarchy into language functions. Just as proper names have the distinctive feature of referring the code back to the code, so shifters refer the message back to the message. Proper names and shifters thus operate like second-level functions in communication alongside first-level functions (expressive, conative, referential). Hence it is essentially the notions of function and communication that Jakobson is concerned with when he speaks of the indexicality of pronouns. It needs to be borne in mind here that the analysis of their distinctive semantic features was part of an approach whose prime goal was a comprehensive and universal taxonomy of all 'generic verbal categories'. To this extent the borrowing from Benveniste seems rather selective for it excludes what might be considered the network of utterance phenomena that Benveniste, in contrast, will continue to work on and to systematise up to his 1970 statement ('L'appareil formel de l'énonciation'). Neither the status of 'il' 'non-personne' ('he' 'non-person') nor that of deixis, nor the distinction between history and discourse, although it relates to distribution of verbal forms, is mentioned. It could be said that it is the entire dimension of 'discourse' peculiar to Benveniste, the dimension of meaning linked to semantic analysis as distinct from semiotic analysis that is omitted. In fact shifters, although he himself hardly uses this metaphorical term, are for Benveniste less signs with noteworthy features than traces of a linguistic activity which cannot be reduced to the notion of sign. It is thus a question 'of going beyond Saussure's notion of the sign as the sole postulate on which both the structure and functioning of the language system would depend' (Benveniste, 1970: 66).

Hence, for Benveniste it is less a matter of accounting for the functioning of a code and for the trace of a subject that might be prior to it than of bringing to the fore the processes of positioning the subject (Benveniste, 1966: 174). This can be seen in the following powerful statement on this topic by the author of *Problèmes*:

The 'subjectivity' that we are concerned with here is the ability of the speaker to see himself or herself as a 'subject'. It is defined, not by the feeling that everyone has of being himself or herself . . . but as the psychic individuality which transcends the totality of lived experiences that it brings together and which ensures the continuity of consciousness. (1966: 259–60)

Where Jakobson sees the need to modify the *langue/parole* distinction, so as to divide up differently the dyad social/individual, and to include an enunciative point of view while leaving intact the semiotic framework (in Benveniste's sense) of Saussure's functionalist and communicative analysis (as read by Jakobson), it is in fact much more a *re-founding* that Benveniste aspires to. The homonym 'communication', used by the two linguists, must not mislead. The notion of double meaning implies that a radical change of perspective is required in going from the smallest units to the whole, which for Benveniste is the sentence: 'With sentences the domain of *langue* as a system of signs is left behind and a different universe is entered, that of *langue* as an instrument of communication, realised as discourse' (1966: 129–30).

This is why the status of discourse linguistics which Benveniste wishes for could not be realised within a vision in which linguistics would merely have to understand its relationship with neighbouring disciplines in some integrated approach such as Jakobson's. Thus while the closed world of semiotics (Saussure's signs) may be opposed to the open world of discourse, nevertheless the semantic and the semiotic concern one and the same reality, the system of language (*langue*). This predicament is attributed by the critics of Benveniste to a number of causes: to confusion (Culioli, 1983), to contradiction (Tamba-Mecz, 1983), to being faithful to but surpassing Saussure (Normand, 1989), or finally to the mutually inclusive relationship of semantics and semiotics, since a language system is like a Moebius ring (Vogüé, 1997). It is the 'empty signs' of the language system which exemplify the subject of enunciation by 'appropriating it'. But by the same token, no exemplification would be possible without the structuring which alone makes possible the system of signs. As Vogüé (1997: 156) has written, Benveniste's language 'in every respect turns back on itself to integrate its exterior'.

This last thesis has the advantage from our point of view of pointing up the main problem with the visibility, the diffusion and the transmission of enunciation theories. In Benveniste these theories portray a situation that is not easily assignable because the language system is involved on the edges of linguistics, semiology and pragmatics, being both non-negotiable and open to the outside. From this point of view the well-known text of the *Problèmes de linguistique générale* II, where Benveniste describes the relationship between a language system and society, thus perhaps rediscovering the profound meaning of Saussure's saying that 'the social nature of a language system is one of its intrinsic characteristics', has in fact a symbolic value while at the same time perhaps constituting the final metamorphosis of the way in which linguists have since the end of the nineteenth century made use of the inherent dichotomies of linguistics:

If the situation in respect of *langue* and society is delved into . . . , the sociologist will note that a language system functions within society which encompasses it . . . But semiological examination inverts this relationship, for only language systems make society possible . . . Hence it could be said that it is the language system which encompasses society. Thus the interpretative relationship, which is semiological, goes in the opposite direction to the relationship of embedding the one in the other, which is sociological. (Benveniste, 1970: 62)

This is why one looks in vain in Benveniste for a reassuring, all-encompassing overview of the science of signs, as is often found in Jakobson. In his report for UNESCO on 'Les relations entre la science du langage et des autres sciences', the notion of 'communication' is used to divide the human sciences generally into three concentric circles: 'Three integrated sciences encompass each other and present three gradually increasing degrees of generality: (1) Study in communication of verbal messages = linguistics; (2) study in communication of any messages = semiotics (communication of verbal messages implied); (3) study in communication = social anthropology jointly with economics (communication of messages implied)' (Jakobson, 1971a: 666).

'Integrate' here for Jakobson means locating what is known about the language system in the encyclopaedic compass of a circle, in a cumulative interlocking hierarchy, in an order of knowledge of successive and increasing generalisation. For Benveniste on the contrary the relation of linguistics to the other sciences seems rather to replicate the structure of chiasm integral to the analysis of language systems. The status of linguistics is left somewhat indeterminate, with projected aims giving their meaning to present projects. The emphasis is on laying the foundations, for example for the study of meaning in the cultural sciences as a whole and not just in linguistics, and on accommodating a variety of perspectives.

Taking account of 'enunciation' in post-Saussurean linguistic theories involves a wide range of disciplinary profiles, which differ substantially from each other even in related areas. This has meant the delineation of scientific schemes that are not very homogenous even where these are closely related. In these circumstances 'enunciation', pragmatics and discourse theory sometimes seem complementary, and at other times seem to offer an alternative to structural linguistics. It is in this context that the discovery and rediscovery of Saussure's manuscripts only now gain their full importance. It remains to be seen whether this newly acquired importance is merely retrospective, with a growing realisation that being anti-Saussure is only another form of being 'true' to the Saussure who was masked by 'structuralist' interpretations, or whether on the contrary it looks forward in the assumption that the 'true' Saussure has opened up new paths to be explored. This question is currently being asked in France, as the European country which was most affected in the 1960s and 1970s by an almost militant following of Saussure, but which was at the same time the least well prepared by its traditions and by the inertia of its institutions to receive with an open mind the *Cours de linguistique générale*. The history of Saussure and structuralism in France is one in which the Saussure of the *Cours* is very much present, but often indirectly, as a thinker to be argued against, taken further or put forward on new foundations.

(This chapter was translated by Peter Figueroa and Carol Sanders.)

9 The Russian critique of Saussure

Stephen C. Hutchings

> Saussure's *Course* . . . is a bold attempt to revise and overcome the legacy of the investigator's . . . own past . . . It is therefore not a definitive doctrine but rather a working hypothesis. (Jakobson, 1990: 84)

> The role of the icon is . . . not conservative but dynamically creative. The icon is . . . one of the means by which it is possible . . . to achieve the task set before mankind, to achieve likeness to the prototype, to embody in life what was manifested and transmitted by God-man. (Ouspensky, 1982: 43–4)[1]

Introduction

When Saussure's linguistic revolution first came to light it met with an enthusiastic reception in Russia. Like the rest of Europe, Russia had experienced a wave of reaction against nineteenth-century positivism. Rather than treat the world as so much empirical data to be recorded and typologised, thinkers like Marx and Freud had begun to seek the non-observable structures and processes underlying those data. Nietzsche, meanwhile, questioned the very foundations of reason through his rediscovery of the pagan elements of human existence. The end of the nineteenth century coincided with Russia's coming to maturity as a nation state and the corresponding need to assert a distinctive identity. By rejecting western tradition, the anti-empiricist trends provided Russian intellectuals with weaponry in their struggle to differentiate themselves from the societies to which they were indebted. It is no coincidence that the avant-garde art which catapulted Russia to the forefront of world culture combined the influences of those anti-empiricist trends with a revival of interest in Russian icon-painting, nor that the Bolshevik revolution which confirmed Russia's international presence drew inspiration from Marx. (The stylised canvases of Natalia Goncharova and the suprematist abstractions of Kasimir Malevich, for example, betray a strong iconic influence.) It is in this context that Roman Jakobson, himself associated with the revolutionary poet, Maiakovskii, seized upon the *Cours de linguistique générale* as the means to spearhead the anti-positivist revolution he instituted in Russian linguistics.

Saussure's influence on Jakobson and, more recently, on the semiotics of Iurii Lotman, is undeniable. Also profoundly affected by the ideas of Saussure was Russian literary formalism, to which Jakobson was a prime contributor and which, along with Saussure, anticipated continental structuralism. Saussure's call for the disentangling of linguistics from philology and the establishment of a separate science of language was echoed in the formalists' insistence on approaching literature as a field of study with its own rules, rather than as what Viktor Shklovskii called a 'handmaiden' to other disciplines. Jakobson and Iurii Tynianov learned from Saussure's interest in system, and in the sign. As formalism and Jakobsonian linguistics matured, weaknesses in Saussurean thinking began to be perceived, precipitating the emergence of divergent currents in literary structuralism whose full consequences have yet to be appreciated. It is the purpose of this chapter to establish the parallels and trace the divergences.

The reasons for the divergences, which will emerge during the course of my argument, can be summarised as follows: (1) the Marxist context in which Russian critical theory developed through most of the twentieth century; (2) the emergence of Russian formalism from the artistic avant-garde, rather than from academic disciplines; (3) the unique status accorded to literature as a tool of social and moral critique in Russian society since the nineteenth century (all the theorists treated below began as literary critics); (4) Russian intellectual culture's enduring attachment to Humboldt's romantic conception of language as *energeiia* (creative dynamism) rather than *ergon* (static product); (5) the heritage of Byzantine theology with its emphasis on the embodied Christ which bequeathed to Orthodox culture a distinct, non-Augustinian epistemology. I will suggest in my conclusion that the consequences of these divergences are considerable and that they have implications for the impasse that much post-Saussurean cultural theory has reached. The sequence in which I proceed is roughly chronological: from Tynianov's modifications to Saussurean synchrony proposed in the mid 1920s, through Jakobson's later corrections of the *langue/parole* distinction, followed by Bakhtin's dialogistic critique of Saussure.

Saussure and Tynianov: closed and open systems

Iurii Tynianov was one of the second generation of formalists who expressed dissatisfaction with the obsessive interest of early theorists like Viktor Shklovskii in identifying literary 'devices' – those techniques which mark a text as 'poetic' and enable it to be distinguished from everyday 'prosaic' language. (See Shklovskii, 1965, the classic text illustrating this approach.) For Tynianov, the search for factual devices seemed to mirror the very empiricism which formalism had attacked in nineteenth-century criticism's superficial hierarchies placing a text's philosophical core over its stylistic shell. Boris Eikhenbaum

(1978: 12), one of the leading proponents of Formalism, argues that: 'the Formalists . . . freed themselves from the traditional correlation of "form-content" and from the conception of form as an outer vessel into which a liquid (the content) is poured'. Whilst still committed to the formalist project of defining literary specificity, Tynianov recognised that literary qualities are not immutable, or even restricted to fiction, but vary from text to text, period to period, and as with metaphors, are capable of migrating to non-fictional texts, just as non-fictional features like photographic precision can migrate to fiction to become marked as 'literary'.

When dealing with literary specificity, Tynianov was openly accused by purists like Viktor Vinogradov of 'retelling Saussure in literary-historical terms' (quoted in Steiner, 1984: 108). Facing the problem of defining linguistic units and their values, Saussure distinguished linguistics from sciences like astronomy in which the units (stars) are 'perceptibles de prime abord' (*CLG*: 149) ('perceptible at the outset', *CGL*-B: 107). Language, by contrast, creates its units through convention. According to Saussure, linguists must proceed by examining not the inherent traits of phonological phenomena, but the interrelations between similar and opposing terms as established by common accord. Like chess, Saussure argues, language is 'un système dont tous les termes sont solidaires et où la valeur de l'un ne résulte que de la présence simultanée des autres' (*CLG*: 159) ('a system of interdependent terms in which the value of each term results solely from the simultaneous presence of the others' *CGL*-B: 114).

Tynianov utilises the Saussurean relational system when, in answer to his own question: 'Is the . . . immanent study of a literary work possible without comparing it with the literary system?', he answers: 'The very existence of a fact *as literary* depends on its differential quality . . . on its function. What in one epoch would be a literary fact would in another be a matter of social communication, and vice versa, depending on the whole literary system in which the given fact appears' (Tynianov, 1978: 68–9). Like a linguistic unit, a literary fact is determined not by its immanent properties, but by its function within a textual system, within the larger systems of genre and of literature itself, and in the interrelationship between literature and other systems. Tynianov relied, like Saussure, on identifying sets of similarities and oppositions to analyse how values are attributed within such sytems. This Saussurean insight proved useful for approaching the question of the status of biographical data relating to a writer's life. For example, a published letter from a writer to a friend might be treated as an extra-literary fact in one era, yet part of the author's artistic oeuvre in another, depending on rules deciding when letters are to be conceived as distinct from 'untrue' fictional narrative and aligned with the 'factual' document, and when they might be assimilated with the personalised register of art and differentiated from documentary prose. Equally, within one era, such a letter might be considered a literary fact when included within a larger autobiographical narrative, but an extra-literary fact if published in a separate collection.

It would be misleading to assume that Tynianov merely transposes Saussurean *langue* from linguistics into literature. Under the influence of Hegelian–Marxist dialectics, Tynianov changed Saussure's emphasis on *langue* as a relatively stable structure of evenly weighted components to one of system as a constantly shifting interrelationship of elements struggling for dominance: 'Since a system is not an equal interaction of all elements but places a group of elements in the foreground – the "dominant" – and thus involves the deformation of the remaining elements, a work enters into literature and takes on its literary function through this dominant' (Tynianov, 1978: 72–3). And since, at some periods, rhyme might be the dominant component in poetry, at others, metre, or the use of metaphoric language, definitions of what constitutes poetic discourse will change accordingly.

Tynianov's concept of 'the dominant' does not amount to a deliberate rejection of Saussure. Indeed, he makes it clear that it is precisely this concept which differentiates literature from other systems, including language. For it is tension resulting from shifts in the hierarchy relating the dominant to subordinate elements which accords literature its unique dynamism. However, the theoretical import of Tynianov's notion of system as a dynamic hierarchy reaches well beyond literature and has implications for language too. It produces an understanding of evolution at odds with that proposed by Saussure for whom language is 'avant tout . . . un facteur de conservation' ('above all a conservative force', *CLG*: 108). This view results from Saussure's emphasis on the lack of a natural relationship between the signifying component of a linguistic unit and its signified meaning. Such arbitrariness means that the signifier/signified bond depends on agreement by tradition. This is not to deny that language changes. Indeed, because 'l'arbitraire de ses signes entraine théoriquement la liberté d'établir n'importe quel rapport entre la matière phonique et les idées' ('the arbitrariness of its signs theoretically entails the freedom of establishing just any relationship between phonetic substance and ideas' *CLG*: 110), there remains potential for almost unlimited change. It means instead that such changes result from forces outside the systemic relations constituting *langue* to which it must respond passively as new conventions replace old: 'Une langue est radicalement impuissante à se défendre contre les facteurs qui déplacent d'instant en instant le rapport du signifié et du signifiant. C'est une des conséquences de l'arbitraire du signe'(*CLG*: 110) ('Language is radically powerless to defend itself against the forces which from one moment to the next are shifting the relationship between the signified and the signifier. This is one of the consequences of the arbitrary nature of the sign', *CGL*-B: 75). It is why Saussure insists on separating linguistics into synchronic analysis which will be 'concerned with the logical and psychological relations that bind together coexisting terms and form a system in the collective mind of speakers', and diachronic analysis which will study 'relations that bind together successive terms not perceived by the collective mind but substituted for each other without forming a system' (*CGL*-B: 99–100). Synchronic linguistics – on which Saussure's reputation rests – requires the linguist who is describing the state of a language at a particular time to 'discard all knowledge of everything that produced it and ignore diachrony', since 'the intervention of history can only falsify his judgment' (*CGL*-B: 81).

By contrast, evolution for Tynianov comes about not from external forces acting on forms and their meanings, but from shifts in the disposition of that system's components, from 'change in the interrelationships between the elements of the system – between functions and formal elements' (Tynianov, 1978: 76). Tynianov places stress on the *function*, rather than the formal *properties* of the signifying elements. Thus, the parameters differentiating literary prose as a system from poetry shift according to shifts in poetry's 'verse function' – those features which function to define a text as verse rather than prose. The shift may be from metre, to rhythm, or use of a particular lexicon or syntax, opening up the possibility of metrical prose or prose poems.

Because it is the changing function of textual and linguistic properties which determine what is considered to be a 'literary fact', Tynianov links the definition of literary specificity inextricably to diachronic evolution, suggesting that literary change arises from the tension between our identification of 'speech constructions' and our sense that such constructions have become 'automatised' (or 'worn out'): 'Evolution is caused by the need for a ceaseless dynamics. Every dynamic system inevitably becomes automatised and an opposite constructive principle dialectically arises' (Tynianov, 1929: 9). Later, in an article written with Jakobson, Tynianov presented his theories as an open critique of Saussure. The two Russian scholars acknowledge that 'the sharp opposition of synchronic and diachronic cross sections has become a fruitful working hypothesis, both for linguistics and for the history of literature' (Tynianov and Jakobson, 1978: 79). But, turning Saussure against himself, and using the example of the way archaisms function actively in modern language, they argue that the insights which this sharp division of labour produced have now altered our understanding of the relationship between past and present:

> The idea of the mechanical agglomeration of material, having been replaced by the concept of system or structure in the realm of synchronic study, underwent a corresponding replacement in the realm of diachronic study as well. The history of system is in turn a system. Pure synchrony now proves to be an illusion: every synchronic system has its past and its future as inseparable structural elements of the system. (Tynianov and Jakobson, 1978: 79–80)

In a summary of their position, Tynianov and Jakobson suggest that Saussure's synchrony/diachrony distinction is rendered defunct when 'we recognise that every system necessarily exists as an evolution, whereas, on the other hand, evolution is inescapably of a systemic nature' (Tynianov and Jakobson, 1978: 80).

Tynianov deserves credit for questioning another Saussurean axiom – the notion of *langue* as an immanent system to be studied 'en elle-meme et pour elle-meme' (*CGL*: 317) ('in and for itself', *CGL*-B: 232). He does so indirectly, by modifying early formalism's commitment to literary specificity. In 'On literary evolution' Tynianov strove to maintain the autonomy of the individual literary text while linking it with other literary works by dividing his notion of function into a 'syn-function' and an 'auto-function':

> The interrelationship of each element with every other in a literary work and with the whole literary system may be called the constructional *function* of the given element. On close examination such a function proves to be a complex concept. An element is on one hand interrelated with similar elements in other works in other systems, and on the other hand it is interrelated with different elements within the same work. The former may be termed the *auto-function* and the latter, *the syn-function*. (Tynianov, 1978: 68)

It was a logical step from here to posit the relationship between literature in its entirety and extraliterary spheres as one between different systems, a move which facilitated a resolution to the problem of how particular elements and not others assume then cede the position of 'dominant' within literary systems:

> The question of . . . the dominant, can be solved only by means of an analysis of the correlation between the literary series and other historical series. This correlation (a system of systems) has its own structural laws, which must be submitted to investigation. It would be methodologically fatal to consider the correlation of systems without taking into account the immanent laws of each system. (Tynianov and Jakobson, 1978: 80–1)

The other historical series referred to would presumably include language, politics, religion etc., while the 'system of systems' echoes Saussure's call for a general science of signs, or 'sémiologie', of which linguistics was only one component. He wrote: '*A science that studies the life of signs within society* is conceivable; it would be part of social psychology and consequently of general psychology; I shall call it *semiology*' (*CGL*-B: 16, *CLG*: 33; the italics are Saussure's).

From Saussure's autonomous system of language we progress to literature as one system in a nexus of mutually interacting systems whose meta-description would amount to a theory of Culture writ large. In the case of Marxist precursors of modern cultural studies like the early Barthes, Saussure's *langue* is used as a model for culture as a single system in which arbitrary links between signifier and signified are 'naturalised' in the name of a ruling ideology (see Barthes,

1972a). It is ironic that Tynianov's pluralistic model was developed within a society in which Marx's ideas were put into practice.

Saussure and Jakobson: from sign to icon, *langue* to *parole*

Tynianov's pluralist emphasis was consolidated by Jakobson who, nonetheless, never deviated from his view of Saussure's *Cours de linguistique générale* as 'the work of a genius' in which 'even its errors and contradictions are suggestive' and which serves as 'a point of departure for . . . discussion of . . . all the essential problems of modern linguistic thought' (Jakobson, 1990: 84–5). Of the original formalists it was Jakobson who moved furthest from the original precepts of the movement. Indeed, he was the only leading formalist to make the switch from literary studies into linguistics proper without, however, abandoning certain formalist preoccupations which accounts for many of his disagreements with Saussure.

Russian formalism was itself born out of an interest in language. The Society for the Study of Poetic Language (Opoiaz) which marked formalism's birth in 1916, and which Jakobson was central in instigating, believed that practical language 'in which language resources . . . are merely a means of communication' is opposed by 'language systems in which the practical aim retreats to the background . . . and language resources acquire autonomous value' (Eikhenbaum, 1978: 9). Opoiaz scholars collaborated closely with futurist poets like Khlebnikov and Maiakovskii who were themselves experimenting with autonomous sound and form in an attempt to rediscover a prelapsarian Transrational Language (*zaumnyi iazyk*, or *zaum*) in which, as in the glossolalia of certain religious sects, sound, form and meaning were united. Opoiaz developed the notion that utilitarian language in which form and sound are subordinated to meaning is merely transrational language in its automatised form. Through 'enstrangement' (*ostranenie*), artists can restore automatised language to its original condition in which we perceive the form of words as autonomous values which transcend everyday meaning. In Shklovskii's words, 'artistic perception is perception that entails awareness of form' (quoted in Eikhenbaum, 1978: 12).

Influenced by Romanticism's hostility to the everyday, and by the belief of the nineteenth-century Ukrainian linguist Potebnia that poetry replaces linguistic articulations of abstract concepts with independent 'thinking in images', Opoiaz placed itself at odds with Saussure for whom arbitrariness is the natural state of the linguistic sign and for whom 'our thought – apart from its expression in words – is only a shapeless and indistinct mass' (*CGL*-B: 111).[2] Jakobson never abandoned his commitment to linguistic iconicity, arguing for an 'intimate link of solidarity and interdependence between . . . the phonemic and the grammatical' (Jakobson, 1990: 406), and tracing the false idea of an absolute breach between the sensuous and the intellectual aspects of language to

St Augustine whose dualistic denigration of bodily matter helped shape western linguistic science.

Roman Jakobson's attempt to attenuate Saussurean arbitariness relies not on a return to the utopian belief in a hidden Edenic substratum of language, but on demonstrating a form of secondary iconicity. Accepting the basic precept of the contingent nature of the link between signifier and signified, he invokes Charles Peirce's claim that the difference between the three categories of signs – iconic (signs based on similarity with their object), indexical (signs based on contiguity with their object) and symbolic (signs in which the link with the object is abitrary) – is not total but 'merely a difference in relative hierarchy' (Jakobson, 1990: 411). (For a critique of Peirce's typology of signs, see Eco, 1985.) Jakobson himself introduced the notion of indexical signs into language through his work on shifters: words, like personal pronouns, whose object shifts because they are tied indexically to the communicative context in which they are used (Jakobson, 1990: 386–92). And in a late essay he enumerates linguistic phenomena which temper primary-level arbitrariness with secondary-level iconicity. Citing Caesar's *veni, vidi, vici*, Jakobson points out that 'the temporal order of speech events tends to mirror the order of narrated events in time or in rank' (Jakobson, 1990: 412). He compares such iconicity with Peirce's definition of the 'diagram' in which the likeness between *signans* and *signatum* exists 'only in respect to the relations of their parts'. He also cites morphological examples of signs displaying an equivalent relation between their *signantia* and *signata*: such as positive, comparative and superlative degrees of adjectives showing a gradual increase in the number of phonemes – *high-higher-highest, altus-altior-altissimus* (1990: 414); plurals 'echo[ing] the meaning of a numeral increment by an increased length of the form', and constellations of phonemically similar words with similar meanings (bash, mash, smash, etc.).

Well beyond the Opoiaz period, Jakobson reserved in his linguistic theory a key role for literary concepts, as in his pioneering work on aphasia. Jakobson takes as his starting point Saussure's division of language operations into paradigmatic selection (e.g. parts of a verb are selected from a list present *in absentia* – the verb's full conjugation), and syntagmatic combination (verbs are combined *in praesentia* with adjectives, nouns, etc.). He reprimands Saussure for succumbing 'to the traditional belief in the linear character of language' which, for Saussure, 'excludes the possibility of pronouncing two elements at the same time', denying concurrence as a form of combination (Jakobson, 1990: 119). Jakobson demonstrates that aphasic speech behaviour may take the form of a selection disorder in which patients cannot choose appropriate terms from a paradigm and who may, for example, say 'knife' when they mean 'fork' (effectively, and in defiance of Saussure, pronouncing two terms concurrently). The other group of aphasics suffer from combination (contiguity) disorder which prevents them from analysing sentences into their combinatory parts, causing them to reduce them to 'word heaps' combined on the basis of similarity alone ('knife – sword – saw').

Jakobson developed his explanation of aphasia into a theory of the bipolarity of language itself, adopting the literary terms 'metaphor' and 'metonymy' to describe the two poles. He claims, for example, that in discourse 'one topic may lead to another through their similarity or through their contiguity. The metaphoric way would be the most appropriate term for the first case and the metonymic way for the second' (Jakobson, 1990: 129). (For the best explication of Jakobson's theory and some excellent examples of how it might be applied in practical literary analysis, see Lodge, 1977.) The principle of iconicity is thus integrated into language in a way unthinkable for Saussure. Indeed, poetry is portrayed as the supreme case of interpolar interference in which 'the principle of equivalence is projected 'from the axis of selection onto the axis of combination' (Jakobson, 1990: 77), enabling the phonetically equivalent words 'cat-sat-mat' to be combined as 'the cat sat on the mat'.

Despite Jakobson's interest in linguistic essences and poles, his theory of language can barely be accused of lacking dynamism. Having worked closely within Tynianov, he developed the latter's notion of single linguistic units changing function according to context into the hallmark of the Prague structuralist movement he inaugurated in the 1940s. (For a comprehensive treatment of the Prague school, and of Jakobson's role within it, see Steiner, 1984.) Rather than atomistically breaking it into discrete objects of study (a trait he associates with Saussure), linguists, argues Jakobson, should approach language as they would the study of a bus, considering its basic elements (material constitution, historical significance, shape, etc.) in relation to the requirements of its cardinal function, whether transportation or communication. Acknowledging Saussure's achievement in highlighting the social nature of language and the relational nature of its units (one unit of form or meaning is identifiable through its relationship with units to which it stands in contrast), Jakobson turns the famous Saussurean metaphor of language as a card game against itself by insisting on the need to consider the goals of linguistic units in particular communicative contexts: 'it would be wrong to analyse [language] without taking into account the multiplicity of possible tasks without which the system does not exist. Just as we have no rules for a universal card game of rummy, poker, and card-house building, linguistic rules can be determined only for a system defined by its goal' (quoted in Steiner, 1984: 211).

Eventually, this led to Jakobson's theory of the six key functions of language: emotive, referential, poetic, phatic, metalingual and conative. According to this theory, certain linguistic phenomena are naturally oriented towards one particular pragmatic function. For example, the conative function (where the addressee is the main focus) finds its purest grammatical expression in the vocative and imperative (Jakobson, 1990: 74) and the phatic function (oriented towards establishing contact between speakers) is best represented by expressions such as 'Well!'. In other cases, words shift between functions. A word normally fulfilling a referential (or denotative) function, such as 'horrible', can assume a poetic function (where the palpability of the sign itself is emphasised) when combined with a proper name in the paranomasic utterance 'horrible Harry', whose referential function could equally have been filled by 'dreadful Harry' or 'terrible Harry' (1990: 76). This example, drawn from everyday speech, confirms that no single discourse is tied to any one function; a poem simultaneously refers, makes contact, expresses and underscores the palpability of its signs.

It is, for Jakobson, numerous goal-oriented communicative functions rather than the rules of a single abstract *langue* which constitute the linguistic object of study. This explains his substitution of 'code' for *langue*; a code is established by particular groups in particular situations, rather than universally agreed for all speakers. Indeed, a single language contains multiple hierarchically organised codes or dialects, each with its own *langue* (Steiner, 1984: 212). This leads to a fundamental modification of the *langue/parole* relationship. While accepting Saussure's assertion that *langue* is a norm, Jakobson questions whether such norms are predominantly collective: 'Each of us has, in addition to general linguistic and cultural practices imposed on us by the community, a number of personal habits . . . Certain words have in personal usage a meaning that is constantly at variance with the collective norm . . . the linguistic values approved by collective assent still need the personal consent of the speaker' (Jakobson, 1990: 90).

Saussure implicitly recognises this phenomenon when he indicates that *langue* 'is not complete in any speaker', and that therefore unique individual selections from amongst a multiplicity of collective values are always involved (*CLG*: 30; *CGL*-B: 14). But by not making this specific, Saussure ensures that the individual becomes identified with the peripheral and the temporary, 'forgetting that the individual, like the community, is a structure . . . a body of customs . . . that reflect . . . the unity . . . of individual identity' (Jakobson, 1990: 91).

Jakobson effectively deconstructs the *langue/parole* distinction by showing that, if *langue* has an individual aspect to it, then *parole* possesses a collective element. He decries Saussure's nineteenth-century 'atomistic' tendency to isolate the individual from the community and disregard the role of the listener. Such a failure to take into account the act of receiving – as indispensable to *parole* as the act of sending – is to posit utterances addressed to no one which Jakobon dismisses as 'pathological' (Jakobson, 1990: 92). *Parole* is, then, 'an intersubjective phenomenon, and, consequently, a social one' (1990: 93). Rather than Saussure's dualistic model according to which a homogeneous, collective norm is realised in discrete, individual utterances, Jakobson presents us with a picture in which the social and the individual are in all aspects intertwined, since it is in linguistic exchanges between individuals that the reality of language is to be situated. Accompanying Jakobson's interest in dialect as a reflection of the multiplicity of norms at work within human communication, is a corresponding emphasis on dialogue as the mode in which language is best realised – something which links him closely to Bakhtin.

Jakobson's recognition of the individual element in *langue* leads him to take issue with Saussure on the role of time and change in language. In the *Cours*, Saussure repeatedly insists that change occurs at the level of individual utterances which, over time, become subject to chance deviations and innovations eventually coded as *langue*. However, when discussing analogy, he concedes that isolated innovations are preceded by 'une comparaison inconsciente des matériaux déposés dans le trésor de la langue ou les formes génératrices sont rangés selon leurs rapports syntagmatiques et associatifs' (*CLG*: 227) ('an unconscious comparison of the materials deposited in the storehouse of language, where productive forms are arranged according to their syntagmatic and associative relations', *CGL*-B: 165). This amounts to an admission that improvisation and change already exist potentially within *langue*, enabling Jakobson to assert that 'Saussure . . . unwittingly refutes his own affirmation that the source of all changes is to be found in parole' (1990: 105). He accommodates this point within his reconceived notion of the interpersonal nature of utterance and norm, claiming that 'even if the new form is at first . . . adopted only by the individual, it is already a phenomenon of the *langue* of the individual' (1990: 105). As far as genuinely normative changes are concerned, Jakobson distinguishes between arguing, like Saussure, that the evolution of language is brought about *by* individual utterances, and believing along with Jakobson himself that it is manifested *in* them (1990: 106). In these pronouncements, Jakobson provides considerable scope for individual creativity, which shifts from the marginal position of arbitrary deviations from a stable norm, to that of the driving force of *langue* – a further reflection of the aesthetic (and ultimately iconic) bent to his thinking. Indeed, Jakobson specifically calls for linguistics to correct the bias against the deliberate creativity exhibited by literary language manifested in Saussure's emphasis on the unconscious spontaneity of spoken language (1990: 107).

Finally, the revisions of Saussurean views on linguistic change also evidence Jakobson's dynamic approach to time. A natural corollary of his deconstruction of the *langue/parole* distinction is a dismantling of the synchrony/diachrony opposition. Jakobson applies to language the argument he and Tynianov had earlier made with respect to literature, namely that, just as system is not restricted to synchrony and modification is not the sole prerogative of diachrony, so in language 'coexistence and succession are . . . intertwined' (Jakobson, 1990: 171). Like the literary system, language cannot be abstracted away from time, since at every moment it contains its own future and past. Jakobson suggests that Saussure erred in equating synchrony (a theoretical abstraction) with stasis (a physical state), just as he had incorrectly associated diachrony with dynamism. To illustrate the correct position, he deploys a cinematic metaphor. If a spectator describes what he sees on the screen at any given moment 'he will inevitably give a synchronic answer, but not a static one, for at that moment he sees horses running, a clown turning somersaults . . . these two effective oppositions, synchrony-diachrony and static-dynamic do not coincide in reality' (Jakobson, 1990: 165). Elsewhere, Jakobson reinvokes von Humboldt by restoring the Romantic unity of *ergon* and *energeia*: 'The identification of *ergon* with *langue* and of *energeia* with *parole* has penetrated . . . various linguistic doctrines and is one of the most dangerous errors. All *langue* as well as all *parole* is at one and the same time *ergon* and *energeia* . . . solidarity with the past . . . and infidelity to this past' (Jakobson, 1990: 108). One might add that the formula of 'solidarity with, yet infidelity to the past' encapsulates precisely Jakobson's own transformation of Saussure.

The incarnate word: iconic critiques of Saussure in Voloshinov/Bakhtin

The mature Jakobson's emphasis on context and dialogue reflected the influence of Bakhtinian post-formalism. Himself inspired by a synthesis of Marxist theory, German philosophy and Orthodox theology, Bakhtin mounted an assault on the philosophical foundations of Saussurean linguistics. In a seminal work written under the name of Bakhtin's junior colleague, Voloshinov, Saussure is named as an archetypal representative of a trend in linguistic philosophy termed 'abstract objectivism' which stands in opposition to 'individualist subjectivism'.[3] If the latter considers 'the basis of language . . . to be the . . . creative act of the individual psyche' and the laws of language to be 'the laws of individual psychology', treating grammar as 'the hardened lava of individual creativity' (Voloshinov, 1973: 48), abstract objectivism does the opposite. A product of the Enlightenment, it regards language as 'a stable, immutable system of normatively identical forms which the individual consciousness finds ready made and which is incontestable for that consciousness' whose laws are those of connections 'between linguistic signs within a . . . closed linguistic system' and are 'objective to any . . . consciousness' (Voloshinov, 1973: 57).

Voloshinov identifies Leibniz's Universal Grammar as abstract objectivisim in its purely rationalist phase, pointing out that the idea of linguistic arbitrariness is a typical one for rationalism (1973: 57). He pinpoints Saussure as 'the most striking expression' of the trend in its present phase, to which he also consigns formalism's obsession with the immutable laws of Poetic Language. He stresses that Saussure is interested 'only in the inner logic of the system of signs . . . taken . . . independently of the ideological meanings that give the signs their content' and divorced from 'the subject expressing his own inner life' (1973: 58). Acts of individual speaking are for Saussure secondary to 'the normatively identical forms of language present in it', to which 'everything else is 'accessory and random' (1973: 60), including history which Saussure regards as 'an irrational force distorting the logical purity of the system' (1973: 61).

Defenders of Saussure might object that Voloshinov fails to distinguish between claiming that language's ontological status is that of a set of arbitrary norms, and positing language as a set of such norms for the purposes of scientific analysis. Voloshinov, however, is aware of the distinction and concedes that Saussure is not 'inclined to assert the unmediated reality of language as a system . . . of norms' but maintains that he ultimately 'provides no clear-cut solution' to the contradiction (1973: 67). Voloshinov calls instead for a return to the position of the individual speaker from whose position what matters about a linguistic utterance is 'not that it is a stable and always self-equivalent signal, but that it is an always changeable and adaptable sign' (1973: 68), a stance mirrored in the attitude of the person listening to that utterance. Laying the foundations for the Bakhtin School's dialogistic approach, Voloshinov argues that: 'the task of understanding does not amount to . . . recognising the form used, but rather to understanding it in a particular concrete context . . . to understanding its novelty and not to recognising its identity' (1973: 68). Underlying the argument is a conception of the sign which, while framed in Marxist terms, differs both from the Saussurean sign as an impersonal contract agreed at the level of the linguistic collective, and from conventional Marxist accounts of how the grand master-narrative of 'class struggle' subordinates individual human interaction to itself. Distinctions between the individual user of a sign and the collective arena in which the sign is established are replaced with an emphasis on the sign as an ideological gesture grounded in the *inter*individual: '[Ideology]'s real place in existence is in the special, social material of signs created by man. Its specificity consists precisely in its being located between organized individuals, in its being the medium of their communication. Signs can only arise on interindividual territory' (Voloshinov, 1973: 12). Under this definition, 'the content of the 'individual' psyche is by its very nature just as social as is ideology', but equally 'ideological phenomena are just as individual (in the ideological meaning of the word) as are psychological phenomena. Every ideological product bears the imprint of the individuality of its creator' (Voloshinov, 1973: 34).

Voloshinov's semiotic theory subverts the idea that linguistic meaning is based on 'un système dont tous les termes sont solidaires et où la valeur de l'un ne résulte que de la présence simultanée des autres' (*CLG*: 159) ('a system of interdependent terms in which the value of each term results solely from the simultaneous presence of the others', *CGL*-B: 115), and that words signify solely through their similarities to and differences from other words. For Voloshinov, we never encounter words in a reified form divorced from the living context of the ideological moment in which they are exchanged. By rejecting the monologistic word of dead linguistic form embraced by abstract objectivism, Voloshinov, like Jakobson and Tynianov, rejects Saussure's sharp differentiation between language's synchronic and diachronic aspects. Invoking the dialectical method, he also revalidates the creativity of the individual speaker which remains so diminished in both mainstream Marxist and Saussurean thinking: 'Abstract objectivism . . . is incapable of tying together the existence of language in its abstract, synchronic dimension with the evolution of language . . . This excludes any possibility for the speaker's consciousness to be actively in touch with the process of historical evolution. The dialectical coupling of freedom with necessity is . . . utterly impossible on these grounds' (Voloshinov, 1973: 81). This Hegelian turn enables Voloshinov finally to transcend both abstract objectivism and subjective individualism and inaugurate the dialogistic tradition of locating linguistic reality at the level of concrete verbal interaction: 'The actual reality of language-speech is not the abstract system of linguistic forms, not the isolated monologic utterance . . . but the social event of verbal interaction implemented in an utterance' (1973: 94). The fact that each individual speech act is infected by the speech acts of others impacts upon the unity of Saussurean *langue* since 'the utterances . . . of others, acknowledged and delineated as such, import into . . . the speech act something irrational from the point of view of language as a system' (Voloshinov, 1973: 287). Even inner consciousness is permanently oriented towards the anticipated response of others, unerringly constituted by words shot through with the history of their prior usage, saturated with previous speakers' values whose very appropriation is itself a dialogic act.

Voloshinov's critique of Saussure owes as much to Orthodox trinitarian theology as to Karl Marx. The Eastern Church never accepted the *filioque* formula so influential on European metaphysics and according to which the Spirit is realised equivalently in the Father *and* in the Son. It continued instead to cite early Patristic interpretations holding that the Spirit proceeds from the Father *through* the Son (Lossky, 1985: 93). This facilitated a more dynamic conception of the Trinity in which the Spirit cannot be abstracted away from two equivalent terms and in which, ultimately, the act of embodiment of One in Another through a Third becomes more than simple instantiation (of universal Spirit in infinite individual bodies, or of universal *langue* in infinite individual *paroles*); the stress on the embodied context of God's realisation in Man requires each individual to attain Christhood via his/her own path (Ouspensky, 1982: 34). Similarly, Byzantium's defence of icons in the iconoclastic dispute by which early Christianity was riven rested on the notion of Christ as the first living icon of God – the incarnate Word – and a repudiation of God as an unrepresentable essence (Meyendorff, 1983: 48). There is an unbroken line connecting Orthodox trinitarianism to Bakhtin/Voloshinov's insistence on words iconically incarnating their meaning rather than mechanically instantiating it. In this context, we are to understand linguistic iconicity not as slavish likeness to an external object, but as individual verbal acts of creation embodying universal meanings through a dialectical unity of unique and general, inner word and outer world, in which both terms remain undiminished. This, then, is the sense of our second epigraph.

Bakhtin developed the dialogism articulated by Voloshinov into a radical reconception of the grounding of all the human sciences. Like Jakobson, however, he drew unceasingly on literary models. The dialogism characterising all discourse, for example, reaches its apotheosis, argues Bakhtin, in the polyphony of the Dostoevskian novel. The literary influence is also to be discerned in a significant intervention into linguistics – the replacement of the sentence as the basic unit of analysis with the speech utterance. Bakhtin contends that the analysis of speech in terms of the structure of individual sentences ignores the embodied context in which utterances are articulated and speakers respond, and that the shape of utterances is determined not by abstract grammatical constructs (sentences), but by one speaker's interruption of, or response to the speech flow of another. The borders of speech acts reflect specific speakers' intentions not the laws of sentence structure (Bakhtin, 1986: 263). It is therefore not possible to establish a universal rule about the size or structure of any speech unit. In dialogic situations (to which all speech acts belong): 'It is not sentences, or words and combinations of words (in the strict linguistic sense) that are exchanged, but utterances constructed with the help of linguistic units: words, word combinations, sentences. Moreover, an utterance can be constituted by one sentence, or by a single word' (Bakhtin, 1986: 267).

It might seem, to conclude this section, that Bakhtin and Saussure simply do not engage upon the same territory. Saussure clearly does not deny the reality of units of speech larger or indeed (as his work on the phoneme confirms) smaller than the sentence, any more than Bakhtin denies the validity of units of analysis such as the sentence, to which he accords 'strict linguistic sense'. Influenced by the different philosophical traditions from which they emerged, they merely choose to locate language's essence at different levels of abstraction. Bakhtin acknowledges as much when recognising that 'the neutral dictionary meanings of words guarantee . . . the possibility of mutual comprehension', and that 'any word exists in three aspects: as a neutral word belonging to no one, as another's word full of the echoes of other peoples' utterances and as my own word' (Bakhtin, 1986: 282–3). It is only in the latter two aspects that the word acquires the living expressivity so crucial to his concerns. But linguistics is not exhausted by the study of expressivity. Saussure would presumably have countered that Bakhtin is missing the point of language as he understood it.

However, the force of Bakhtin's assaults on specific Saussurean tenets cannot be neutralised completely. For example, while stressing the precedence of concrete dialogic situations over artificial linguistic abstractions, Bakhtin does not entirely individualise the utterance. Rather he introduces the intermediary notion of speech genres – those typical and relatively stable forms of utterance which exist in micro-dialects and into whose moulds we pour our own speech outputs and organise those of others – standardised modes of greeting, cursing, instructing, etc.:

> Despite all its individuality and creative character, the single utterance can never be considered an absolutely free combination of forms, as is supposed by Saussure . . . who opposes the utterance as a purely individual act to the system of language as a purely social and regulatory act . . . Saussure ignores the fact that apart from the forms of language there exist also the forms by which these forms are combined, i.e. he ignores speech genres. (Bakhtin, 1986: 274)

These speech genres are, as Bakhtin points out, more flexible than grammatical forms, and can be reaccented by individual speakers so as to be inflected with meaning specific to particular contexts (an official greeting can be transferred into a familiar sphere to be given a parodic inflection, for example), whilst remaining in the social arena. Through the notion of speech genre, Bakhtin further subverts Saussure's rigid opposition of collective to individual. Saussure defines *parole* (speaking) as 'un acte individuel de volonté et d'intelligence' ('an individual act . . . wilful and intellectual'), arguing that, within this act, 'we should distinguish between (1) the combinations by which the speaker uses the language code for expressing his own thought; and (2) the psychophysical mechanism that allows him to exteriorise those combinations' (*CLG*: 30–1; *CGL*-B: 14). But, far from recognising the significance of individual creativity, the contrast between the fixed abstraction of *langue* and *parole* as the 'wilful' (and unanalysable) act of free will exteriorised by a mysterious 'psychophysical mechanism' relegates it to a realm outside of scientific analysis. If, however, account is taken of the socially 'given' nature of the fluid micro-genres within which utterances are expressed, the social and the individual moments in language can be accommodated equally within linguistic analysis. Ultimately the Bakhtin–Saussure controversy amounts to rather more than a meta-level disagreement about the object of linguistic analysis.

Conclusion: wider implications of the disagreements

The post-formalist critique of Saussurean *langue* grew out of Tynianov's belief in the inherent openness and dynamism of language, and of cultural forms (such as literature) modelled upon it. It gained momentum via Jakobson's success in reestablishing a role for secondary-level iconicity in language and shifting emphasis away from Saussure's unitary system onto the contexts in which linguistic forms are actualised – a development taken to its conclusion in the Bakhtin school's rejection of the philosophical foundation of Saussure's theory of linguistic signs. The word as a sign communicated from individual to individual according to rules established by a homogeneous collective is reconceived as an act of iconic embodiment where 'collective' meaning is inseparable from the dialogised speech acts in which it is incarnated, just as the meanings of utterances cannot be understood outside the interindividual contexts in which they are expressed. It should certainly be pointed out that such criticisms are inevitably based on a selective reading of the *Cours*. The Swiss linguist is by no means inattentive to iconicity, dialogue, the relationship between synchrony and diachrony, or, indeed, to linguistic units above the level of the sentence. He chose to emphasise synchronicity and arbitrariness because the moment in the history of linguistics which he occupied demanded it. Equally, the Saussure we find in Bakhtin is a Saussure objectified for Bakhtin's ideological purposes, a Saussure, to turn Bakhtin against himself, inflected with Bakhtin's intentions and coloured by the anticipated response of his opponents.[4] Nor, when setting the balance straight, should we forget Jakobson's acknowledgement, expressed in our first epigraph, that Saussure is 'right' even when he was 'wrong', since he never intended the *Cours* to do anything other than lay the ground for future linguists to come up with the unassailable axioms, and since his ability to pose correctly questions which had never before been posed far outweighed the demerits of his own answers to those questions. It is in this spirit that, by passing Bakhtin and Saussure through the crucible of information theory, Iurii Lotman, founder of the Moscow–Tartu school of semiotics, discovers a productive way of blending the two into a single, coherent brand of semiotic analysis retaining both Saussure's insights into the relational nature of meaning, and Bakhtin's insistance on openness, multiplicity and dialogue (see Lotman, 1990).

However, it is the irresolvable differences between Saussure and, in particular, Bakhtin, which have most significance for a present in which key post-structuralist advances on Saussurean semiology have undoubtedly paved the way for new insights whose ramifications stretch well beyond the sphere of linguistics. But many of these insights are beset by the same constraints affecting Saussure's theory of language. Even the subversive Derridean gesture by which signifiers, rather than being anchored to their signifieds, are propelled into an abyss of infinite deferrals (words referring not to concepts but to other words which in turn refer to yet more words and so on) merely develops Saussure's premise that meaning is relational to its conclusion. Jonathan Culler implicitly makes this point when he links Saussure with Derrida via Peirce's concept of the 'development' of a sign through its 'interpretants' – the other signs by which it is replaced in the process of attaining its meaning (Culler, 1975: 19–20). And cultural studies enthusiasts at pains to reestablish the centrality of politics to all meaning by exposing the ideological artifices behind 'neutral' concepts like sexuality and gender likewise take for granted the arbitrariness of the sign permitting such manipulation. Culler makes the Saussurean case for the arbitrary sign in cultural studies as follows:

> In the case of non-linguistic signs there is always the danger that their meanings will seem natural; one must view them with a certain detachment to see that their meanings are . . . the products of a culture, the result of shared assumptions and conventions . . . by taking linguistics as a model one may avoid the familiar mistake that signs which appear natural . . . have an intrinsic meaning. (Culler, 1975: 5)

Such diehard 'constructivists' have recently met opposition from reborn 'essentialists' eager to reinvigorate nature's cause without reinvoking conservative mantras, creating a situation little short of an impasse. (For an 'insider's account' of the paradoxes with which this impasse forces feminist theory to work, see Grosz, 1990.) Thus, contemporary feminism remains fundamentally split between proponents of the notion that all femininities are at root masculine constructions, and defenders of the idea that women must recapture an irreducible feminine essence in order to assert a truly non-masculine identity.

Could the stalemate be broken, one might ask, if femininity were to be reconceived as neither constructed through masculine manipulations of arbitrary signifiers, nor inherent within feminine essences, but rather as the effect of the iconic embodiment of one discourse, itself internally split between masculine and feminine, in another? Since it is fully contextualised, such iconicity remains sensitive to ideological considerations, such as the loaded nature of gender relations. But because it relies on irreducible differences between entities in dialogue with one another, it avoids being abstracted away into some unchanging male-dominated *langue*. Mikhail Epstein, who has been influenced by both Bakhtin and Jakobson, arrives at a similar conclusion with respect to contemporary discourses on ethnicity. For multicultural theories, argues Epstein, reject assimilation (the absorption of ethnic minorities by the dominant culture) only by skirting the corresponding danger of separatism (the fragmentation of multicultural society into competing tribes). To multiculturalism Epstein contrasts something called 'transculture':

> Multiculturalism proceeds from the assumption that every ethnic, sexual or class culture is important and perfect in itself, while transculture proceeds from the assumption that every particular culture is incomplete and requires interaction with other cultures . . . No sooner does the process of differentiation penetrate the intimate self of an individual, than it turns into a process of integration with the other. (Epstein, 1995: 303, 306)

It is perhaps by revisiting Saussure in the light of other such insights derived from post-formalist positions that we might finally move beyond him without, however, trampling his still fruitful legacy underfoot.

10 Saussure, Barthes and structuralism

Steven Ungar

The emergence of semiology in post-war France coincided with renewed interest in the work of Ferdinand de Saussure and his 1916 *Course in General Linguistics* (henceforth *Course*). This interest extended beyond linguists, to include anthropologists, philosophers, literary critics and others associated with the rise of structuralism in France between the late 1940s and the mid 1960s. Received knowledge of Saussure as the founding father of modern linguistics drew largely on the *Course* that Charles Bally and Albert Sechehaye edited, following Saussure's death in 1913, on the basis of notes taken by students in courses he offered at the University of Geneva between 1907 and 1911. Questions concerning the accuracy of the *Course* as an account of Saussure's teaching extended debate within and outside France, even after critical editions appeared in 1967 and 1973. Yet such debate accounted only in part for the ongoing importance of the *Course* with reference to the origins, development and aftermath of Parisian structuralism that dominated French intellectual life during much of the latter half of the twentieth century. My aim in what follows is to trace and comment on the evolving role of Saussure's *Course* in the writings of Claude Lévi-Strauss, Roland Barthes and Jacques Lacan. In so doing, I mean to describe how and why references to the *Course* became standard in texts associated with the first wave of Parisian structuralism of the 1950s and 1960s (Dosse, 1997: 33).[1]

Lévi-Strauss, Merleau-Ponty and the post-war inception of structuralism

The emergence of Saussure and the *Course* in post-war France was of the order of a return to origins, akin to similar returns in the writings of Jacques Lacan and Louis Althusser to Sigmund Freud and Karl Marx. The critical nature of all three of these returns linked them to broad changes in the conception and practice of scholarly disciplines across the humanities and liberal arts. These changes were partly generational among those moving toward what Simone de Beauvoir termed in her memoirs of the period as the force of circumstances and prime of life. These changes in the mode and content of critical thought during the two decades following the 1940–4 German occupation was enhanced by calls for institutional reform. Structuralism, which grew from this drive for change, was less of a shift or transition than a self-styled break with the recent past, cast as a critical rethinking of object of inquiry, method of study and ambition or goal. A key reference for the advent of structuralism in early post-war France was a 1945 overview, 'Structural analysis in linguistics and in anthropology', in which the anthropologist Claude Lévi-Strauss argued for the potential gain in knowledge that a sustained and systematic collaboration between the linguist and the anthropologist might provide. Lévi-Strauss took care to specify the nature of this collaboration by linking it to questions of method he encountered in conjunction with his ongoing study of kinship. Accordingly, he asked whether the anthropologist, using a method analogous *in form* (if not in content) to the method used in structural linguistics, could not achieve the same kind of progress in his own science as that which has taken place in linguistics. Lévi-Strauss answered this question later in the same piece when he asserted that a literal adherence to linguistic method disclosed aspects of kinship systems that he deemed essential. Adherence as he understood it thus went beyond the loose or figurative analogy that extension might otherwise have implied:

> Kinship terms not only have a sociological existence; they are also elements of speech. In our haste to apply the methods of linguistic analysis, we must not forget that, as a part of vocabulary, kinship terms must be treated with linguistics methods in direct and not analogous fashion. Linguistics teaches us precisely that structural analysis cannot be applied [to] words directly, but only to words previously broken down into phonemes. *There are no necessary relationships at the vocabulary level.* (Lévi-Strauss, 1963: 36)[2]

Several remarks are in order. First, the structural linguistics to which Lévi-Strauss referred in the 1945 article cited above drew less on Saussure and the *Course* than on Nicolas Trubetzkoy and, especially, on the work of Roman Jakobson. This is the extent to which it is fair to hold that Lévi-Strauss read Saussure, in large part, through Jakobson. Second, the fact that Lévi-Strauss identified the phoneme rather than the word as the minimal unit of signification was motivated by his desire to overcome earlier obstacles to a structural analysis of kinship terminology founded on linguistics understood as phonetic, psychological and historical analysis. This break with a linguistics founded on historical contingency was also one asserted in the *Course* with reference to language as system (*langue*), unified along the synchronic axis. Finally, the assertions that kinship systems were something more than vocabulary or terminology and that there were no necessary relationships at the level of vocabulary followed an emphasis on function, structure and general system designated in the *Course* in terms of language, in opposition to individual utterance (*parole*). Lévi-Strauss reiterated these assertions, as follows: 'In the study of kinship problems (and, no doubt, the study of other problems as well), the anthropologist finds himself in a situation which formally resembles that of the structural linguist. Like phonemes, kinship terms are elements of meaning; like phonemes, they acquire meaning only if they are integrated into systems' (Lévi-Strauss, 1963: 34).

As early as 1945, Lévi-Strauss foresaw a major problem of method for the projected practice of structural analysis across the disciplines of anthropology and linguistics he advocated. The problem was that of how to account for the specific nature of kinship phenomena without losing the progress in understanding that critiques of observable linguistic phenonema by Trubetzkoy and Jakobson had made possible. The problem derived from a lack of clarity concerning the linguistic model and what was at stake in its application:

> The problem can therefore be formulated as follows: Although they belong to *another order of reality*, kinship phenomena are *of the same type* as linguistic phenomena. Can the anthropologist, using a method analogous *in form* (if not in content) to the method used in structural linguistics, achieve the same kind of progress in his own science as that which has taken place in linguistics? (Lévi-Strauss, 1963: 34)

Lévi-Strauss addressed this problem in terms of scholarly discipline, which allowed him to posit the elision of disciplinary distinctions to which structural analysts of the 1950s and 1960s would often return. In addition, the invocation of general and implicit laws parallel to the shift among structural linguistics from historical contingency to systematic concerns echoed the emphasis in the *Course* on language system over utterance. Lévi-Strauss did not refer explicitly to Saussure. Yet the implied relay to the *Course* via Jakobson in the 1945 article was permanent enough for him to pay homage to Saussure in his 1961 inaugural lecture at the Collège de France. Twelve years later, he again invoked Saussure, 'to whom we owe the establishment of the systematic character of language apparent from its synchronic structure' (Lévi-Strauss, 1985: 153).

Lévi-Strauss's remarks of 1945, 1961 and 1973 cast linguistics as the most highly developed among the social sciences, and one to which anthropologists and others might aspire in order to renovate the social sciences much in the way that nuclear physics had renovated the physical ('exact') sciences. What Lévi-Strauss characterised in 1945 as the 'phonological revolution' represented by the work of Jakobson and Trubetzkoy drew on what Jonathan Culler has aptly termed a Saussurean legacy marked by a shift in focus from objects to relations (Culler, 1977: 126). This shift, cast by Lévi-Strauss in the form of a challenge to rethink and renovate existing methods of inquiry among various disciplines of the social sciences, came to spawn the wider phenomenon of Parisian structuralism.

The impact of this shift in method went beyond the social sciences, understood in a narrow sense. For the philosopher Maurice Merleau-Ponty, engagement with Saussure and the *Course* was twofold. First, Merleau-Ponty's sense of the unity of language as one of coexistence, 'like that of the sections of an arch which shoulder one another', recalled passages in the *Course* that posited language as a system whose unity was based on difference rather than on positive entities (Merleau-Ponty, 1964: 39). It was as though Merleau-Ponty grasped by intuition the philosophical relevance of the *Course* for his ongoing interest in the writings of Edmund Husserl on first ('foundational') philosophy and the origin of language.

Second, Merleau-Ponty's concerns with structure were already evident in his first books, *The Structure of Behavior* (1963 [1937]) and *The Phenomenology of Perception* (1945). Where the former drew on Gestalt psychology and the work of Wolfgang Köhler, the second disclosed the influence of Edmund Husserl. These concerns were inflected after the Second World War through acquaintance with the work of Lévi-Strauss, providing broader expression to questions of language Merleau-Ponty was raising in his own way. A passage from a later essay on Lévi-Strauss disclosed the convergence of Merleau-Ponty's interest in language with structural anthropology and, by extension, the renovation of critical approaches to the study of language marked by the *Course*:

> The notion of structure, whose present good fortune in all domains responds to an intellectual need, establishes a whole system of thought. For the philosopher, the presence of structure outside us in natural and social systems and within us as symbolic function points to a way beyond the subject–object correlation which has dominated philosophy from Descartes to Hegel. By showing us that man is eccentric to himself and that the social finds its center only in man, structure particularly enables us to understand how we are in a sort of circuit with the socio-historical world. But this is too much philosophizing, whose weight anthropology does not have to bear. What interests the philosopher in anthropology is that it takes man as he is, in his actual situation of life and understanding. The philosopher it interests is not the one who wants to explain or construct the world, but the one who seeks to deepen our insertion in being. Thus his recommendation could not possibly endanger anthropology, since it is based upon what is most concrete in anthropological method. (Merleau-Ponty, 1964: 123)

The passage is close to a programmatic statement of faith on the part of a philosopher for whom the notion of structure, as found in the writings of anthropology (Lévi-Strauss) and linguistics (Saussure), provided a means of overcoming the impasse represented by the subject–object correlation. (The impasse is, in fact, one to which the philosopher Jacques Derrida would return a decade later, with explicit reference to Husserl and Saussure.) Moreover, the desire to study mankind in specific historical and cultural circumstances represented less a rejection of traditional philosophy than an attempt to look to social sciences in order to deepen philosophy's insertion in being and the historical present. Merleau-Ponty openly acknowledged 'what we [philosophers] have learned from Saussure' (Merleau-Ponty, 1964: 39). The lesson that he had in mind was one of a receptiveness to a critical rapprochement with other disciplines by means of which philosophy might renovate itself, much as

Lévi-Strauss and Saussure had sought each in his own way to renovate anthropology and linguistics.

More than any philosopher of his generation – more than Paul Ricoeur and certainly more than Jean-Paul Sartre – Merleau-Ponty wanted to make post-war phenomenology a bridge linking disciplines in the humanities and social sciences within a broad rethinking of method and object for which Saussure's *Course* was crucial. Like Lévi-Strauss, Merleau-Ponty advocated the central role of the *Course* in asserting the primacy of linguistics for the renovation of anthropology and philosophy they sought to promote. Yet some linguists saw such advocacy instead as disclosing the limitations of non-specialists who tended to read the *Course* in the light of an emergent structuralism whose equation of system with structure they questioned. Early use of the term 'structuralism' at the First International Congress of Linguists at The Hague in 1928 was recorded in statements by Russian and Swiss participants making common reference to Saussure in descriptions of language as system. Jakobson first used the term in 1928; Saussure had written instead of 'system', a term which was repeated 138 times in the three hundred pages of the *Course* (Dosse, 1997: 44–5). Algirdas-Julien Greimas, from whom Barthes first heard about Saussure, cast a dissenting opinion when he noted in 1956 that while Saussure's name was invoked – by Merleau-Ponty in philosophy, by Lévi-Strauss in anthropology, by Barthes in literature, by Lacan in psychoanalysis – nothing similar was happening within linguistics. Questioning the appropriation of Saussure and the *Course* among non-linguists, he asserted that was it was 'high time that Ferdinand de Saussure be put in his right place' (cited in Dosse, 1997: 45).

Roland Barthes: one, two or three semiologies?

The incidence and frequency of references to Saussure shown in figure 10.1 provide an initial measure of Barthes's apprenticeship in linguistics and its impact on what he described in 1975 as the two semiologies (see Barthes, 1977). I take incidence to mark when and where Saussure's name appears in Barthes's writings. Frequency designates pages containing at least one explicit reference, rather than the raw total of mentions, which may be more than one per page. Impact is understood first in terms of explicit references during a given year; and second, as an arc or pattern extending over a designated duration. Indices in the three volumes of Barthes's complete works (1993a, 1993b and 1995) list a total of eighty-two references to Saussure in published texts, interviews and related materials between 1956 to 1980. References over the same period to the *Course* total fifteen, with two additional references to Saussure's work on anagrams. Sixteen references to Saussure and four to the *Course* appeared in the 1964 *Eléments de sémiologie* (I have dated this text as 1964, when it was published in issue 4 of *Communications*. Volume 1 of Barthes's complete works (1993a)

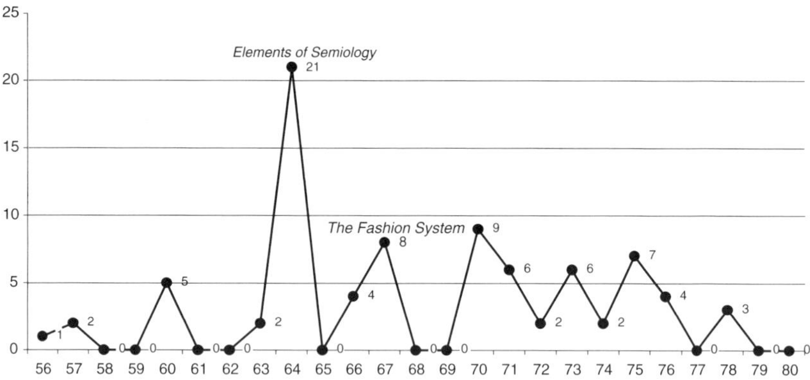

Figure 10.1 References to Saussure in Barthes's writings, 1956–80

lists it in 1965, when it was republished in book form. Whenever relevant, my chart identifies the year of initial publication for texts later republished in book form.)

The breakdown for frequency of reference by decade is three for the 1950s, forty for the 1960s and thirty-nine for the 1970s. Spikes of higher frequency (between four and twenty-one references each) occur in 1964, 1967, 1970, 1973 and 1975. The first two spikes correspond to Barthes's efforts to apply concepts of language and code adapted from his readings of Saussure and other linguists to analyses of complex ('secondary') systems such as literature, fashion and visual media such as photographs, advertisements and film. These efforts culminated in the 1967 *Fashion System*. The period from 1970 to 1976 constitutes a phase during which Barthes formulated and defended revised concepts such as author, text and literature. Two early intervals without explicit references to Saussure occur in the 1960s. The first, during 1962 and 1963, corresponds to the period Barthes devoted in large part to *On Racine* (1983a, first published 1963). The second, during 1968 and 1969, corresponds to the seminar at the Ecole Pratique des Hautes Etudes that produced *S/Z* as an initial exploration of the revised ('second') semiology from 1970 onward. Except for the four references in *Roland Barthes by Roland Barthes* (see Barthes, 1977), Saussure's name appears in Barthes's writings between 1970 and 1978 exclusively in articles and interviews. The last reference to Saussure occurs in an October 1978 interview with Teri Wehn Damisch, filmed for the television station, Antenne 2. (A transcription of this interview was published after Barthes's death in *Critique*, no. 425, 1982.) The remarks that follow focus on Barthes's writings of the 1956–67 period, coincidental with the first wave of structuralism in France.

Barthes first heard of Saussure in 1949–50 during conversations with A.-J. Greimas in Egypt, where Barthes spent a year as a visiting lecturer at the University of Alexandria. According to Louis-Jean Calvet (1995), Greimas suggested that Saussure might be useful for a work in progress on the nineteenth-century historian, Jules Michelet, that Barthes was hoping to submit as a thesis for an advanced degree. (He published the project as a book by the Editions du Seuil in 1954 under the title *Michelet par lui-même* – see Barthes, 1987a. He never submitted it as a thesis.) When Barthes asked who Saussure was, Greimas answered that he was essential reading (Calvet, 1995:194). Calvet conveyed this sentence more forcefully in French as 'Mais on ne peut pas pas connaître Saussure', literally 'But one cannot not know Saussure'. Barthes started to read on and around linguistics, in what soon became a long-term apprenticeship whose tutors in text and in person over the following two decades ranged from Greimas, Lévi-Strauss, Jakobson and Louis Hjelmslev to Emile Benveniste and Vladimir Propp.

Barthes's reading of Saussure was first evident in 'Myth today', an essay added to the 1957 reprint in book form of the fifty-three 'little mythologies' he wrote mainly for *Lettres Nouvelles* between 1954 and 1956 (see Barthes, 1972a). (See Ungar, 1983 and 1997, on aspects of *Mythologies*. The present essay focuses on Barthes's references to Saussure and the notions of semiology they postulate, either openly or by implication.) In this concluding text of *Mythologies*, Barthes (1972a) asserted that myth belonged to the province of a vast science of signs, coextensive with linguistics, that Saussure had postulated some forty years earlier under the name of *semiology*, and whose objective was to study significations apart from their content. In an oft-cited passage, Barthes (1972a) related the open nature of this semiology 'not yet come into being' to ongoing research on meaning (*signification*). Meaning as *signification* was understood as distinct from *sens*, the fixed meaning of words to be found in dictionaries. It referred instead to the variable meanings produced by words, gestures and other forms of meaning as they occurred in specific circumstances. Barthes asserted such inquiry into signification was a common concern of psychoanalysis, structuralism, eidetic psychology and some new types of literary criticism. Perhaps too quickly, he held that to postulate a signification was to have recourse to semiology. It was an assertion that he qualified almost immediately: 'I do not mean that semiology could account equally well for all these kinds of research: they have different contents. But they have a common status: they are all sciences dealing with values. They are not content with meeting the fact in itself; they define and explore it as a token [*valant-pour*] for something else' (Barthes, 1972a: 111). (I have slightly altered Annette Lavers's translation.)

Several pages later, Barthes reinvoked Saussure when he wrote that 'signification is the myth itself, just as the Saussurean sign is the word (or more accurately the concrete unit)' (Barthes, 1972a: 121). Both passages disclosed the extent to which Barthes tempered his references to Saussure and semiology with a critical concern to disclose the foundational values of a post-war French bourgeoisie whose signs he analysed in various forms and media of mass culture, from magazines and advertisements to photographs and feature films. Twenty years after the fact, Barthes recalled in his 1977 inaugural lecture at the Collège de France that around 1954, he held hope that 'the science of signs might stimulate social criticism, and that Sartre, Brecht, and Saussure could concur in this project' (Barthes, 1982: 271).

Barthes's statements of 1977 recast the statements on method in 'Myth today' as a synthesis that one might qualify as hybrid or eclectic. Simply stated, Barthes admitted after the fact having used terms encountered in the *Course* to recast myth as a gesture or utterance (*parole*) within a system for which neither Sartrean, Brechtian, nor even Marxist theory proved sufficient (Calvet, 1995: 157). This mixing of sources and ambitions on Barthes's part derived from the zeal with which he sought to mobilise semiology in the name of a critical project arguably at a remove from relevant passages in the *Course*. The transition from mythologist to semiologist in 'Myth today' was a first instance of a looseness with regard to linguistics that would set Barthes at odds with more traditional figures in the field such as André Martinet and, especially, Georges Mounin (see below). Yet the transgressive nature of this looseness would also inspire many other readers to champion Barthes's openness to linguistics and other forms of French new criticism against the practices of university scholars still modelled on Gustave Lanson's 1894 *History of French Literature*.

Another kind of looseness in 'Myth today' is visible in Barthes's remarks on the two-tiered diagram in which myth operated as a second-order system, or metalanguage, by which the semiologist spoke about a primary language-object (see figure 10.2). Signification at the levels of language and myth derived, in turn, from interaction between signifier and signified, as per the *Course*. But as is the case with references to significance at the very start of Barthes's *Writing Degree Zero* (1968a, original published 1953), these terms were not used in any specifically technical, theoretical or linguistic sense (Calvet, 1995: 82). Instead, their specificity was elided within Barthes's overriding concern to posit a two-tiered model of signification, one of which was staggered in relation to the other (Barthes, 1972a: 115). To his credit, Barthes acknowledged that the spatialisation that this two-tiered model implied was best understood as a metaphor. The grounding of signification in a two-tiered model of language and myth also heralded references from *Mythologies* onward to the interaction between denotation and connotation that the Danish linguist Louis Hjelmslev studied in his 1943 *Prologomena to a Theory of Language* (see Hjelmslev, 1963). L.-J. Calvet has argued that Barthes could not have read the *Prologomena* before it was translated from Danish into French in 1968. Accordingly, he concluded that the distinctions between *signifier* and *signaler* in *Writing Degree Zero* derived from an almost intuitive distinction between denotation and connotation that

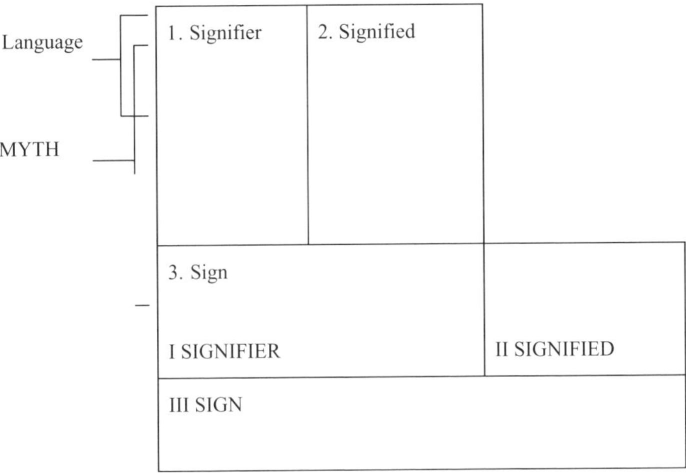

Figure 10.2 Language and myth, from *Mythologies* (Barthes, 1972: 115)

Barthes adapted to his own ends, 'just as one borrows someone else's clothes' (Calvet, 1995: 82). Barthes did not cite Hjelmslev by name until 1960 and not in any extended way until the *Elements of Semiology* four years later (see Barthes, 1968b).

Mythologies combined hybridity and intuition in a first phase of what Barthes would later call the semiological adventure in which Saussure's *Course* would remain central. But was it theory? And if so, was it something linguists might consider seriously? Probably not. Did Barthes intend it as such? Possibly; but if he did, it was only with qualification. A decade after the fact, Barthes began his preface to the 1970 re-edition of *Mythologies* with the following statement:

> This book has a double theoretical framework: on the one hand, an ideological critique bearing on the language of so-called mass culture; on the other, a first attempt to analyse semiologically the mechanics of this language. I had just read Saussure and as a result acquired the conviction that by treating 'collective representations' as sign-systems, one might hope to go further than the pious show of unmasking them and account *in detail* for the mystification which transforms petit-bourgeois culture into a universal nature. (Barthes, 1972a: 9)

In his preface to the 1957 edition of *Mythologies*, Barthes had written that his reflections on French daily life were guided by his own interests at the time. By which one can understand him to have made no claim to theory beyond a cultivated openness to new ideas. L.-J. Calvet provided an alternative take on this openness when he maintained that Barthes did not really like theoretical systems and that he preferred intuitions, immediate reactions and moods he would later turn into theories by using whatever concepts he came across (Calvet, 1995: 140). This take sheds light on the idiosyncratic nature of Barthes's evolving statements concerning semiology. It also helps to account for the range of responses to Barthes's invocations of Saussure among readers relatively uninformed about the history of linguistics and others who might well question the viability of Barthes's adaptive readings of Saussure and his remarks on linguistics, in general. Finally, what Barthes referred to in 'Myth today' as a myth of the mythologist may well have been his way of disclosing – without apologies – the synthetic nature of the analyses in *Mythologies* as a series of innovative readings founded on disparate sources. In such terms, 'Myth today' would best be taken less as a theory of mythology founded on passages in the *Course* than a preliminary formulation of method adapting concepts in the *Course* to a project of social criticism.

The subject and structure of *Elements of Semiology* disclosed a systematic attempt to define and apply concepts adapted from linguistics, ethnology and sociology. Those cited in the 1965 book version included V. Brøndal, R. Godel, Z. S. Harris, Hjelmslev, Jakobson, Martinet, C. W. Morris, C. S. Peirce and Trubetskoy. Subject and structure combined with these references to make *Elements* a measure of what Barthes wanted semiology to become at the apex of structuralism's Parisian ascendancy. It is then all the more important to recall that the *Elements of Semiology* was an attempt by Barthes to rethink and formalise assumption related to method and objective in *Mythologies*. Alongside the 1966 'Introduction to the structural analysis of narratives' and the 1967 *Fashion System*, the *Elements* culminated a period during which Barthes sought to found a programme for the fledging discipline of semiology by applying linguistic concepts to study other signifying phenomena (Culler, 1983: 72). This was also the period during which Barthes contributed work-in-progress to journals such as *Communications*, where research across disciplines promoted the institutional rise of structuralism in the social sciences and humanities. After the fact, the texts in and around the *Elements* can be seen as marking the limits and limitations of Barthes's commitment to semiology, as it evolved between 1957 and 1967. By 1970, Barthes had come to equate semiology with a semioclastics – literally, 'a breaking of signs' inspired by the subtitle of Nietzsche's 1888 *Twilight of the Idols*, as *'How to Philosophize with a Hammer'*. The same year, *S/Z* and *The Empire of Signs* illustrated the extent to which Barthes no longer adhered in a sustained way to the semiology he had sought to ground on Saussure's *Course*.

How, then, did Saussure and the *Course* appear in the *Elements* and what role did they have in the model and application of semiology that it set forth? The major engagement with Saussure and the *Course* occurred in conjunction with preliminary statements concerning semiology and a trans-linguistics whose materials Barthes listed as myth, narrative, journalism, or 'other objects of our civilisation'. The object of this trans-linguistics was distinct from language studied by the linguist. Barthes described it as more of a second-order language whose minimal units were no longer monemes or phonemes, but larger fragments of discourse related to meaning that underlay language without existing independently of it:

> In fact, we must now face the possibility of inverting Saussure's declaration: linguistics is not a part of the general science of signs, even as a privileged part, it is semiology which is a part of linguistics; to be precise, it is that part covering the *great signifying unities* of discourse. By this inversion we may expect to bring to light the unity of research at present being done in anthropology, sociology, psycho-analysis, and stylistics round the concept of signification. (Barthes, 1968b: 11)

This departure from the model of semiology set forth in the *Course* derived from what Barthes stated as a need for semiology to test its limits ('explore its possibilities and impossibilities', Barthes, 1968b) in the form of an investigation that was diffident and rash. The choice of adjectives conveyed the polemic that motivated Barthes to postulate a revised semiology as a privileged application of structural analysis within a more general trans-linguistics. Accordingly, the research Barthes sought to undertake on the basis of the *Elements* was diffident in the sense that 'semiological knowledge at present can be only a copy of linguistic knowledge; rash because this knowledge must be applied forthwith, at least as a project, to non-linguistic objects' (Barthes, 1968b: 11). A second departure from the *Course* was visible in a schema/usage dichotomy inspired, at least in part, by Hjelmslev, that seemingly replaced the Saussurean *language/speech* dichotomy. The assertion of usage over speech extended Barthes's ongoing concern with ideology, stemming from *Mythologies* and going as far back as the definition of writing as the morality of form at the start of *Writing Degree Zero*. It was also in line with Barthes's statement that language was always socialised, even at the individual level (Barthes, 1968b: 21). Finally, this assertion foreshadowed the inflection toward word (*parole*) rather than language in Barthes's revised semiology of the 1970s.

In more practical terms, the linking of semiology and trans-linguistics in the *Elements* derived from Barthes's ongoing efforts to complete and defend a dissertation that would qualify him for a permanent position in the French university system. His 1954 book on Michelet started as a first attempt at such a dissertation. A second attempt produced the extended semiological analysis of clothing in *The Fashion System* (1983b, originally published 1967). But as with the *Michelet* a decade earlier, Barthes never submitted *The Fashion System* as a dissertation. Analyses in the *Elements* suffered from the emphasis Barthes placed on language used in conjunction with clothing and/or food. Barthes had long excelled at rhetorical and discursive analysis. But his attempts to recast them in terms of semiology were often less than convincing because what he meant by language did not coincide with what most linguists tended to take as their object of study. Culler has rightly argued with reference to the *Elements* that even if language were the only evidence semiologists had, this would not make semiology a part of linguistics any more than the reliance of historians on written documents makes history a part of linguistics (Culler, 1983: 73–4). In addition, evidence in the *Elements* of Barthes's growing preference for systems or mechanisms of signification over what was signified emerged from and was substantiated by a systematic perspective that he later denigrated (Culler, 1983: 76). This contradiction, in turn, accounted for the subsequent shortcomings of *The Fashion System* as a large-scale application of the semiology formulated in the *Elements*.

In retrospect, the break between semiology and semioclastics visible in Barthes's writings between 1967 and 1970 was arguably less of an evolution than a mutation. Barthes stated in a 1971 interview that semiology as he had come to live it was no longer the semiology he had seen, imagined and practised at the start. Four years later, he returned to this break in *Roland Barthes* and a revised understanding of science for which Saussure was central:

> He suspected Science, reproaching it for what Nietzsche called adiaphoria, its indifference, erected into a Law by the scientists who constituted themselves its procurators. Yet his condemnation dissolved each time it was possible to *dramatise* Science (to restore to it a power of difference, a textual effect); he liked scientists in whom he could discern a disturbance, a vacillation, a mania, an inflection; he had learned a great deal from Saussure's *Course*, but Saussure had come to mean infinitely more to him since he had discovered the man's desperate pursuit of the Anagrams. (Barthes, 1977: 160–1)

A third and final formulation of semiology 'in the Greek' paradigm was that of semiotropy – literally a 'turning of signs' – that Barthes first invoked in his 1977 inaugural lecture at the Collège de France. It recast his evolved sense of semiology by attributing to its inception a strictly emotional impulse to found a science of signs in which Sartre, Brecht and Saussure might concur. Notable was the tempering of ambitions linked to semiology as science in Saussure's *Course* with his more personalised and 'desperate' inquiry into anagrams embedded in Latin poetry. It was as though Barthes had found in the new or 'other' Saussure of the anagrams the internal contradiction with which he could identify his own withdrawal from a semiology founded on the *Course*. In its place, Barthes reverted to a model of social critique whose roots in Sartre and Brecht he inflected toward Michel Foucault's archaeologies of the institutional links between power and knowledge. By 1977, Barthes could assert that 'semiology (my semiology, at least) is generated by an intolerance of this mixture of bad faith and good conscience which characterises the general morality, and which Brecht, in his attack upon it, called the Great Habit. *Language worked on by power*: that was the object of this first semiology' (Barthes, 1982: 471).

Barthes set the critical concerns of semiotropy alongside the rhetorical trope of apophasis when he held that this revised semiology denied the possibility of attributing to the sign traits that were 'positive, fixed, ahistoric, acorporeal, in short: scientific' (Barthes, 1982: 473). But if this denial of positive identity recalled the diacritical nature of the sign in the *Course*, the links to Saussure were mediated significantly by a sense of paradox more in line with deconstruction. This mediation was evident when Barthes wrote that semiology could not (no longer) be a metalanguage because it could not function *outside* language, treating it as a target, and *within* language, treating it as a weapon. (An alternative formulation in a more deconstructive mode might hold that semiology could not claim to function outside language *except from* within language.) From which Barthes concluded that semiology's relation to science was ancillary, in that it could provide an operational protocol starting from which each science could specify the difference of its corpus.

Jacques Lacan: from structure to the floating signifier

Jacques Lacan (1901–81) was a medical doctor, clinician and psychoanalyst whose self-styled mission of 'a return to Freud' set him repeatedly at odds with colleagues in the fields of medicine and psychology. His maverick stance with regard to the practices and institutions of psychoanalysis also earned him a cult following, especially among literary scholars and feminists within and outside France. Lacan's turn to Saussure centred on a 1953 report given at the University of Rome, published the same year under the title of 'The function and field of speech and language in psychoanalysis' and a 1957 essay, 'The agency of the letter in the unconscious, or reason since Freud'. Both disclosed a new emphasis on language in the form of the words uttered during the psychoanalytic session. This emphasis was evident in the 1953 'Rome report', in which Lacan asserted that the words of the analysand constituted the prime medium of psychoanalysis, and that 'the self-evidence of this assertion, was 'no excuse for our neglecting it' (Lacan, 1977: 40). The tone of the latter remark conveyed the polemical force with which Lacan meant to challenge the mix of dynamic psychology and psychiatry that had displaced the systematic study of the unconscious he sought to revive via close readings of Freud.

The 1953 'Rome report' drew on the notions of imaginary and symbolic orders Lacan had first set forth in a 1936 address published in 1949 as 'The mirror stage as formative of the function of the I as revealed in psychoanalytic experience'. Lacan did not invoke Saussure and the *Course* outright until the 1957 'Agency of the letter in the unconscious'. Indeed, the sense of the symbolic function in 'The Rome report' drew as much on tropes of classical rhetoric as on Freud. Moreover, the specific concern with the analysand's word or speech (*parole*) was at odds with clear emphasis in the *Course* on language (*langue*) as

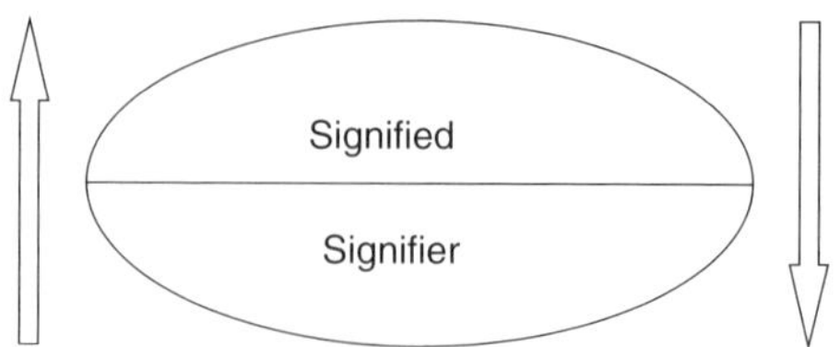

Figure 10.3 The sign in Saussure's *Course*

system. Yet there was little doubt that 'The Rome report' disclosed the extent to which Lacan looked increasingly to recent work in linguistics as a guide to which he and other psychoanalysts could not remain indifferent.

Four years after 'The Rome report', Saussure and the *Course* had become central to the systematic study of language by means of which Lacan sought to reform and revitalise psychoanalysis. The effects of this direct reading in 'The agency of the letter in the unconscious, or reason since Freud' were explicit and sustained. But much like Barthes several years later, Lacan modified and adapted aspects of the *Course* to his own ends, as if Saussure provided Lacan with a new vocabulary in support of his own hypotheses (Dosse, 1997: 105). And again like Barthes (as well as Lévi-Strauss), Lacan's reading of Saussure was mediated by Jakobson's writings on metaphor and metonymy. Nowhere was the tendency to modify and adapt more apparent than in an algorithm (see figure 10.4, below) that Lacan attributed to Saussure and, by extension, what he took (mistook?) to be the founding of modern linguistics. Jane Gallop has argued that what seemed a 'straight' formula representing the relation of signifier to signified differed in several ways from relevant passages in the *Course* (Gallop, 1985: 120). Along similar lines, Elisabeth Roudinesco noted that the Saussure whom Lacan read for 'The Rome report', with Lévi-Strauss on one side and Heidegger on the other, was not the same Saussure he read afterwards (Roudinesco, 1990: 297). For Gallop as for Roudinesco, Lacan created readings of Saussure that he revised in the light of his evolving ideas about language, signification and the unconscious.

The *Course* featured a diagram (figure 10.3) of the sign as an entity constituted by the two-way interaction of concept (*signifié*) and sound-image (*signifiant*). It conveyed this interaction by the ellipsis surrounding them and by the upward and downward directions of the arrows to its left and right. Concept and sound-image functioned exclusively as components of the sign. Their implication was inherently reciprocal and as mutually interdependent as two sides of a sheet of paper. Accordingly, the horizontal line between them inside the ellipsis represented their union.

Lacan modified the diagram in the *Course* in the light of what he described as the topography of the unconscious, whose effects he divided into two

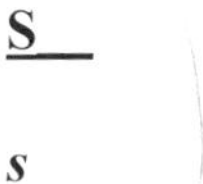

Figure 10.4 Lacan's Saussurean algorithm (S for signifier and *s* for signified)

fundamental structures called metonymy and metaphor. An algorithm (figure 10.4), which Lacan attributed to Saussure but which was more his own creation, differed from the diagram in the *Course* in important ways. First, it placed the signifier (which Lacan capitalised) over the signified (in lower-case italics) in what amounted to an inversion of the diagram in the *Course*. Second, it deleted the ellipsis and the arrows in order to make the signifier capital and pre-eminent in its authority over the signified (Gallop, 1985: 120–1). Third, the deletion of the ellipsis and arrows destabilised the structure of the sign that the diagram in the *Course* had conveyed in terms of interdependence and reciprocity. This destabilisation was enhanced by the fact that Lacan took the line or bar between signifer and signified to represent a break constituting a resistance to meaning (Lacan, 1977: 164). This break, in turn, recast the stability of the sign in the *Course* in conjunction with Lacan's hypothesis that signification was an unstable phenomenon observable as a slippage along a chain of signifiers.

Lacan's insistence on the signifier as the basic unit of language destroyed the integrity of the sign set forth in the *Course*. As a result, his references to Saussurean concepts and models were challenged and even dismissed outright among those who did not consider the study of psychosis and the unconscious as central to the ambitions or ends of linguistics. Such challenges were predictable in the light of the relative disinterest on the part of many linguists to address language and psychosis in systems of multiple symbols where, in the words of A. Lemaire, a single signifier could designate any number of defined concepts (cited in Dosse, 1997: 110). Yet Lacan's concern with the structured linguistic underpinnings of analysis, resumed in the oft-cited phrase that the unconscious was structured like a language, drew him to the *Course*, as to the writings of Jakobson and Lévi-Strauss. In the end, the clinical context and Lacan's self-styled mission to reform psychoanalysis drove his readings of the *Course* away from the model of a general science of signs toward a narrower concern with 'the floating signifer' (Mehlman, 1972). Or as Lacan put it in a typically oracular formulation, meaning 'insisted' in the chain of the signifer, even though none of its elements 'consisted' in the signification of which it was capable at any particular moment (Lacan, 1977: 153). Which is to say that meaning occurred as a phenomenon of displacement through reference to previous signifiers and in the absence of an actual signified. The implication that signifers constituted an autonomous order of meaning removed from the signified once again set Lacan's use of Saussurean terms at a distinct remove from the model of the sign in the *Course*. (See also the references to Saussure in Jacqueline Rose's astute linking of psychic identity in Freud and Lacan to the problem of the sign – Rose, 1986: 228–9.)

Georges Mounin: a dissenting voice

I have described how Barthes's references to Saussure in *Mythologies* and *Elements of Semiology* were instrumental in making the *Course* a compulsory point of reference for post-war French structuralism. These references also spawned a number of disclaimers among those linguists for whom his understanding of Saussurean concepts was founded on a misreading. Georges Mounin wrote that the analyses in *Mythologies* were 'founded on a series of confusions of all the basic concepts of current linguistics' (Mounin, 1970: 190). He illustrated his critique with reference to the essay entitled 'The world of wrestling' (Barthes, 1972a), in which he noted Barthes's failure to question the equation of wrestling and communications system on which he based his analysis. Other confusions noted by Mounin included those between a system and a medium of communications as well as those between concepts of sign, symbol and index and symptom.

At the source of these confusions Mounin identified Barthes's metaphoric extension of terms taken from linguistics in order to recast social facts as indices or symptoms. While claiming not to judge the validity of what Barthes wanted to state about wrestling as a fact of social psychology, Mounin held that the extension of linguistic concepts to a general semiology of the bourgeois world reduced semiology to its medical usage in conjunction with the study of symptoms. Mounin found nothing illegitimate about this symptomology. But he contended that what Barthes studied were never signs in the Saussurean sense of the term, but more often symbols and indices. Such remarks were the professional equivalent of a territorial response on the part of a linguist warning against a manipulation of technical terms and concepts by a non-specialist whose understanding was arguable. A veneer of politeness barely concealed the hostility with which Mounin cast his misgivings, as when he wrote that Barthes clearly knew what he wanted to say, but that the way he stated it in linguistic terms was frankly inadequate and almost always incorrect (Mounin, 1970: 196).

Questioning whether Barthes had failed to understand the Saussurean theory of the sign, as Mounin asserted, is less relevant than examining what he contended concerning the two-tiered model of meaning in 'Myth today' on the basis of which Barthes grounded his subsequent semiological adventure. Mounin correctly noted that the diagram was a graphic treatment of Hjelmslev's hypothesis concerning denotation and connotation, but without direct reference to Hjelmslev and in a vocabulary seemingly derived from the *Course*. Hjelmslev's connotation became Barthes's metalanguage; the former's denotation became the latter's language object. Clearly, Barthes's diagram was a synthesis or hybrid. Mounin described it in less generous terms as an example of terminological contamination that departed from Hjelmslev's sense of the term *connotation*. In addition, he characterised Barthes's usage of the term *metalanguage* as a misuse of the prefix *meta* as he cited it in the Aristotelian notion of *meta-physics*, to designate something latent beyond the manifest content of a language (Mounin, 1970: 193).

Conclusion: the Saussure effect and the structuralist moment

Barthes's writings between 1956 and 1967 invoked and adapted the concepts of sign and semiology set forth in Saussure's *Course in General Linguistics* toward the programme of a projected science of literature that Barthes later linked to *his* semiological adventure. The ambitions of this projected science coincided with a first wave of structuralism in France that, in turn, brought unprecedented attention to the structure of language among literary scholars within and outside France. *Mythologies*, *Elements of Semiology* and *The Fashion System* thus lent a visibility to Saussurean concepts and to a general science of signs whose viability among social scientists remains a topic of ongoing debate. On one side of debate are those for whom Barthes's references to the *Course* constituted a serious misreading with regard to a Saussurean orthodoxy grounded in the methods and ambitions of linguistics as a social science. On the other are those for whom the alleged liberties taken by Barthes with regard to these concepts drew out implications of a programme that the *Course* only began to sketch. Barthes's writings of the period between 1956 and 1967 thus disclosed the ambitions and liabilities of a first wave of structural analysis seemingly inspired by the assertion in the *Course* that since semiology did not yet exist, no one could say what it would be (*CGL*-B: 16).

11 Saussure's anagrams and the analysis of literary texts

Peter Wunderli

For a long time Ferdinand de Saussure has been considered the source of the *Cours de linguistique générale*, and to better-informed scholars he was also the author of important Indo-European studies, among which the *Mémoire sur le système primitif des voyelles dans les langues indo-européennes* holds a particularly high rank. Only about fifty years after his death, another field of research was discovered, one that has – at the first glimpse – hardly anything in common with the other two. In the search for the sources of the vulgate version of the *Cours*, eight cardboard boxes of notebooks and sketches were found, which dealt with the anagrammatical components of Indo-European (and particularly Latin) poetry. Starting with the phenomenon of the anagram and some other similar phenomena, Saussure tried to develop a general theory of poetry. This almost obsessive interest also influenced his correspondence with Antoine Meillet, Léopold Gautier and Giovanni Pascoli (Wunderli, 1972b: 36, n.5). As in the case of the *CLG*, he never published anything on this topic during his lifetime. This is not necessarily a cause for regret because – from a contemporary point of view – the theory of anagrams as developed in Saussure's notes is not adequate. This, however, does not mean that we can simply consider the matter closed. As soon as this work became known, avant-garde French literary theorists of the late 1960s and the early 1970s received it enthusiastically and integrated it in their own approaches. These were basically the authors around the journal *Tel Quel*: Julia Kristéva (1969a and 1969b), Philippe Sollers (Ponge/Sollers, 1970), Jacques Derrida, Jean Ricardou and others (Wunderli, 1972a: 37). Although Saussure's anagram theory proved to be inadequate for its original object, Indo-European poetry, it became almost indispensable for modern literature and literary theory. So Saussure even achieved fame posthumously in the field of literary studies!

The starting point for Saussure's reflections on the theory of poetry and the anagrams is his preoccupation with Saturnian verse, which he probably started to study in May 1906 and which first aroused his interest because of the distribution of stresses and quantities (Wunderli, 1972a: 7; 1972b: 37). Subsequently he then noticed that he was able to discover certain phonetic repetitions in both anonymous and named authors who wrote Saturnian verse; the phonetic repetitions became more frequent the more Saussure focused his attention on them. Somewhat bewildered, he extended his investigation to authors of the classical epoch such as Vergil, Catullus, Tibullus, Ovid, Horace – with the same result. Even in the prose of Pliny, Cicero, Caesar and Valerius Maximus he had discovered similar repetition phenomena. He extended the limits of his investigation once again and finally came to the conclusion that he had discovered a long tradition, reaching from Sanskrit to Homer, from the authors of pre-classic and classic Latinity to middle and new Latin poetry. This impressive panorama led him to the speculation that he had discovered the decisive principle underlying old Indo-European literature (Wunderli, 1972b: 37).

The most detailed formulation of this hypothesis is to be found in a letter to Antoine Meillet, dated 23 September 1907 (Benveniste, 1964: 109ff.). It consists essentially of three components or rather conditions that are closely connected with each other and all have to be fulfilled equally in the poetry[1].

The first condition requires that within a verse all sounds (or better still, all phonemes) have to appear in pairs. This rule, however, cannot be maintained in such a rigid form because there are verses with an odd number of syllables in which at least one vowel *has to* remain without an equivalent. In these cases, Saussure found a compensating 'orphan' in the preceding or following verse. Soon, however, he had to recognise that there are orphaned consonants or groups of consonants, and finally he found himself obliged to accept not only neighbouring verses as part of the mechanism of compensation, but blocks of texts of six to eight verses as well (Starobinski, 1969: 9ff.). Having been forced to relax his originally very strict rule, he eventually declared himself satisfied when the formation of a pair was realised for two-thirds of the phonemes within one verse (Starobinski, 1964: 248). This concession, however, makes it less likely that formations of phonemes as pairs are constructs intended by the author. It is just as likely that it is only an accidental collocation, a problem of which Saussure himself was also aware (Benveniste, 1964: 11ff.).

The second condition does not apply to isolated phonemes, but to clusters of phonemes, so-called *diphones* and *polyphones*. It is said that a compensation phenomenon for groups of phonemes also exists in Indo-European poetry, but that it cannot be formulated as precisely as that of the isolated phonemes. Saussure did not succeed in defining the space in which the group of phonemes had to recur. Finally, the text as a whole seems to constitute a field of compensation for the cluster. Moreover, it seems impossible to decompose a text into *polyphones* without some remainders, which are not compensated, and without taking certain phonemes in different *polyphones* into account (Starobinski, 1964: 249; Benveniste, 1964: 110ff.). Here too, the question arises as to whether the apparent regularities are not merely accidental collocations. Saussure himself asked this question as well and talked about the rules only once in his letter to Meillet dated 23 September 1907. Later on, this point seems to have been worked out in his anagram theory, which is based on *diphones* and *polyphones*.

The third component of Saussure's hypothetical rules is his anagram theory proper: besides the term *anagram*, Saussure also used terms such as *paragram, hypogram, syllabogram* and *cryptogram* in his search for a better way of classifying and designating the phenomenon. Saussure's use of 'anagram' differs from more general usage (Typus *Voltaire* < *Arouet l[e] j[eune]*)[2] in several respects: it is not based on letters, but on phonemes. It is not about isolated units, but about clusters of at least two components (*diphones*, *polyphones*). These components do not form a block, but are dispersed over a longer segment of text and are separated by groups of phonemes, which do not belong to the anagram. In the following example of Giovanni Pascoli's *Catullocalvos* we see an anagram for the Falerner, probably for the Falerner's wines, too (Nava, 1968: 80):

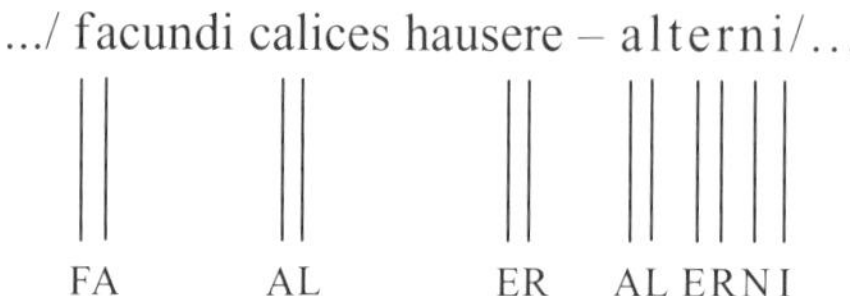

This example shows a special case insofar as the *diphones*, which constitute the anagram, appear in the same order as in the underlying key word. This, however, is not obligatory: usually this order is not respected, and the sequence of the elements forming the anagram is optional.

This example, moreover, focuses on two essential characteristics of Saussure's anagram: on the one hand, it shows that a phoneme can be part of two different *diphones* and, therefore, appears twice in the anagram (FA-AL > FAL). On the other hand, it is permissible for the *diphones* to be repeated, which can thus be realised several times within the text (twice AL-ER). The restriction of the anagram to only one verse is the most frequent case occurring in Saussure's analysis, but this phenomenon was never proclaimed as a law or condition. There are many examples in which the complete anagram is only achieved across various verses (Starobinski, 1969: 21). Saussure recognised this as well (Starobinski, 1964: 259).

According to Saussure's view, this kind of anagram is the basis of Indo-European poetry, regardless of the validity of the rules for the appearance of the phonemes in pairs and the repetition of the *polyphones*:

> Ce qu'on peut très heureusement aborder sans résoudre ni le point *a* ni le point *b* concernant le décompte des monophones ou des polyphones, c'est le fait *indépendant* – ou pouvant être *considéré d'une manière indépendante*, car je ne voudrais pas aller plus loin –, que les polyphones reproduisent visiblement, dès que l'occasion en est donnée, les syllabes d'un mot ou d'un nom important pour le texte, et deviennent alors des polyphones anagrammatiques. (Benveniste, 1964: 111)

(What one can quite happily broach even without resolving point *a* or *b* concerning the breakdown of the monophones or of the polyphones, is the *independent* fact (or so at least it can be *considered*) that as soon as the occasion arises, the polyphones clearly reproduce the syllables of a word or name that is significant in the text, thereby forming a polyphonic anagram.)

The question, however, arises of how we know which elements are liable to be anagrammatised. Saussure's answer was that it would normally be a name or a word of central importance for the text (Benveniste, 1964: 109). Since the anagram technique appears to have its origins in religious literature, the most likely candidate is the name of god invoked by the poet, and strenuous efforts are made accordingly to discover his 'presence' in the text (Starobinski, 1964: 250f.). Allegedly, trivial poetry adopted the anagram technique later on. As a 'motto', the name of a patron or of another addressee, of a celebrated or dead person would have been chosen, as for example SCIPIO in the following epigraphic verse (*Carmina epigraphica*; Starobinski, 1964: 245):

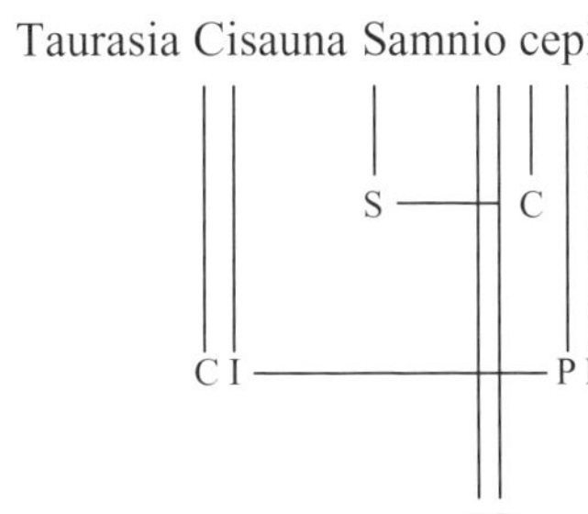

Later on, also the name, profession or some characteristic of a protagonist were anagrammatised, such as for example the term PICTOR in Polizian's epitaph, which was dedicated to Filippo Lippi (Rossi, 1968: 119):

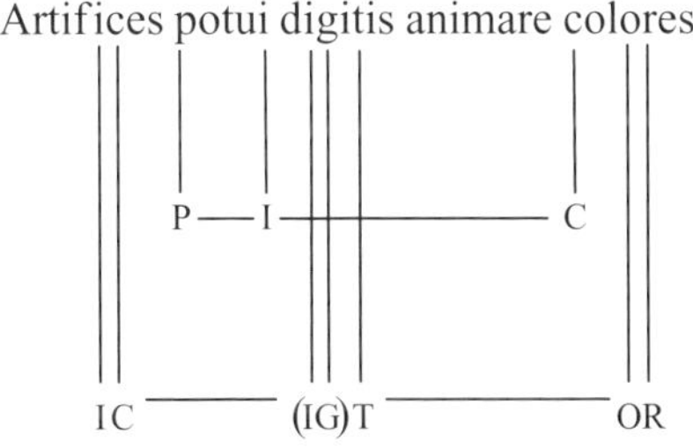

Finally, any word playing a decisive role in the text might have been chosen as a basis for an anagram, such as e.g. CAVE, a word which Saussure found several times in one of Caesar's letters to Cicero (Starobinski, 1969: 26), among others:

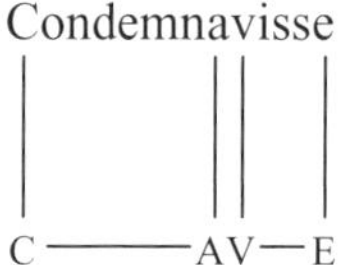

Saussure's investigations, however, were by no means unproblematic, above all because he did not consider the diphonic basis of the anagrams in a consistent way, and far too often included isolated phonemes. He did try to restrict the invasion of isolated phonemes by permitting them only if they formed a kind of supplement to a *diphone* and belonged to the same word (cf. for example C and E in CAVE within the scope of *condemnavisse*); his efforts in this respect, however, were not crowned with much success. The examples taken from *Carmina epigraphica* and Polizian demonstrate that Saussure continuously violated his own rules. Moreover, he claimed that the elements of a *diphone* had to appear in the same order as in the key word, and that a metathesis was not acceptable. In the anagram *Leonora* in Polizian's verse quoted above (Rossi, 1968: 125f.),

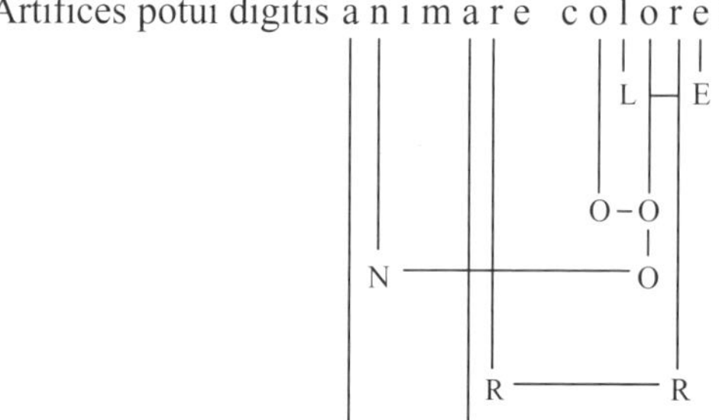

he found himself compelled to add the following comment: 'ar + ar = RA', i.e. to sanction the metathesis (Rossi, 1968: 119). All these concessions open the door to coincidence and finally turn the anagram into a phenomenon of probability. In the end one is left wondering whether it is not possible to extract any word out of any text of a certain length.

Saussure was himself troubled by serious doubts. If one disregards the technical problems already mentioned, it is mostly the frequency of the anagrams that worried him and he asked himself 'si l'on ne trouverait pas tous les anagrammes du monde dans trois lignes d'un auteur quelconque' ('whether one couldn't find any anagram one wished in a few lines by absolutely any author', Benveniste, 1964: 112). His doubts regarding this were absolutely justified as the following slip-up shows: in Polizian's epitaph for Filippo Lippi, Saussure believed that he had found the anagrammatised name of the painter's lover in several verses: *Leonora* – unfortunately his muse was called *Lucrezia*, and the latter name is to be 'found' as easily as the other in the little text (Rossi, 1968: 121f.)! A further problem is the fact that an entire anagram is often only realised across several lines (Starobinski, 1964: 259). One wonders whether an anagram, which emerges over seven or eight verses, is proof of anything at all. In order to get out of this impasse, Saussure analysed an even vaster amount of texts, but the increased quantity did not lead anywhere. Therefore, he began to search for metapoetic statements of the technique of the anagram exploring authors and theorists of the (classical) Latin literature – again, without success. In 1909, he finally decided to turn to a living author writing in Latin and interview him: Giovanni Pascoli. Saussure's letters were found in Pascoli's correspondence (Nava, 1968). To this day, we don't know if Pascoli ever gave an answer. Only one thing seems to be certain: Saussure gave up his research on the anagram at the end of April 1909.

One can, of course, ask whether discontinuing his research on anagrams was related to the fact that his anagram theory seemed to be contradictory in a number of ways to the views put forward in the 1907–11 lectures (and subsequently published in the *CLG*). A first apparent inconsistency concerns the linearity of the linguistic sign. One of the determining characteristics of Saussure's *signifiant* is that it consists of a series of phonemes (Wunderli, 1981: 93ff.). He wrote about this in his notes on the anagram as well as in the *Cours*, in which he defined the principle in the following way: 'The signifier, being auditory, is unfolded solely in time from which it gets the following characteristics: (a) it represents a span, and (b) the span is measurable in a single dimension; it is a line' (*CGL*-B: 70).

In the special case of anagrams, however, things are different. Here, the principle of linearity is abolished from the outset with regard to the sequence of *diphones* or *polyphones* because Saussure's anagram is not compact; his elements are rather scattered throughout the basic text. This affects the principle of linearity in so far as the *diphones/polyphones* are separated from each other by elements which do not belong to the anagram. Usually, however, other disruptive factors are added, such as the recursiveness of singular *diphones* or of phonemes, which are included in the *diphones*. For example, in the anagram of FALERNI the *diphones* AL and ER are included twice and in SCIPIO the I is represented in two *diphones* (PI – IO). In addition, the order of *diphones* often does not correspond with the one in the key word. It is this latter phenomenon which represents the most obvious violation of the principles of linearity. Even if one even allows metatheses between the phonemes constituting the *diphone* (as Saussure did very often), next to nothing remains of the 'normal' linear order of phonemes. Nevertheless, thus far these phenomena are not neccessarily in such contradiction to the statements made in the *Cours* that they would cause or even force Saussure to give up his research. The deviation from the principle of linearity in the anagrams should rather be considered as poetic licence, which in no way casts doubt on the rules of the everyday language. On the contrary, poetic licence is a kind of epiphenomenon of everyday language, for without a basic text which is subject to the principle of linearity, the superimposed anagram could not be realised at all. This shows that a special status exists for poetic language alongside the (communicative) rules of 'normal' language. Saussure made this quite plain when he said the following about the anagrams: 'Dans un domaine infiniment spécial comme celui que nous avons à traiter, c'est toujours en vertu de la loi fondamentale du mot humain en général que peut se poser une question comme celle de la consécutivité ou non consécutivité . . .' ('In a highly specialised area such as the one with which we are dealing here, it is always in accordance with the basic rules of human speech that the issue of the consecutive or non-consecutive nature of language can be raised', Starobinski, 1964: 254).

Apart from the principle of linearity, there is also an unusual relation between *signifié* and *signifiant* when we are dealing with anagrams. According to the explanations in the *Cours*, the two psychological components defining the linguistic sign are inseparably linked with each other. The link between them is essential to the existence of the sign: 'The linguistic entity exists only through the associating of the signifier with the signified . . . Whenever only one element is retained, the entity vanishes; instead of a concrete object we are faced with a mere abstraction. We constantly risk grasping only a part of the entity and thinking that we are embracing it in its totality . . .' (*CGL*-B: 102–3).

If I loosen the link between the *signifié* and *signifiant*, I destroy the linguistic sign; the object of my research is no longer part of the area of linguistics, but of psychology or phonology (see Godel, 1957: 190). Yet it happens within the scope of Saussure's anagram theory that the link between both sides of the sign[3] is at least temporarily loosened or neutralised. If I analyse a *signifiant* in *diphones/polyphones* or even in phonemes, I leave the field of the sign and, therefore I leave, strictly speaking, the linguistic field (according to Saussure): the results of decomposing the *signifiants* of a *monem* into smaller units are not signs with a meaning anymore, but only fragments of *signifiants* (figures), which have nothing but a distinctive function. The fact that this is possible and that the link between *signifiant* and *signifié* within the scope of an anagrammatical reading can be restored by the recipient is due to the arbitrary and at the same time conventional character of the (normal) sign. Otherwise the mechanism required by Saussure would not work at all. There is no contradiction here either. As in the case of linearity, the laws of the standard language remain untouched as regards the basic text. Since the anagram is superimposed only *qua* epiphenomenon, loosening the link between *signifié* and *signifiant* turns out to be a law specific to poetic language, which leaves the regularities of standard language untouched.

Things are similar regarding a third aspect of the phenomenon, the question of the formal or substantial character of the sign. We should begin with one of the most famous passages in the *Cours*, where Saussure emphasises that language is not substance but form: 'But language [*langue*] being what it is, we shall find nothing simple in it regardless of our approach; everywhere and always there is the same complex equilibrium of terms that mutually condition each other. Putting it another way, *language is a form and not a substance*' (*CGL*-B: 122).

If I examine *signifiants* as purely linguistic units, then I can compare them only with entities of the same kind or the same level, which means I must compare them with other significants. Then they can only be defined as pure differential entities and they are, therefore, pure 'forms' (*CLG*: 166). If, however, I compare a sign's *signifiant* with its constituents (the phonemes), they turn out to be substances of a higher hierarchical unit. Once again, an apparent contradiction is resolved or can be reduced to two different points of view: the question whether a *signifiant* has to be considered as form or substance is not a question of principles but rather a question of perspective.

But let us now return to the anagram. The standard linguistic sign is pure form – anything that is not a form, is not considered an object of linguistics by Saussure. The anagram, however, is not a linguistic, but a poetic phenomenon – and this allows Saussure to include also substantial aspects into his anagram theory, namely phonemes and groups of phonemes. In a way, his theory plays with the formal and substantial aspects of the *signifiant*, using the higher or lower level of the hierarchy of constitutive units (*signifiants* – phonemes) as befits the case in point. The key word appears to be substance as long as it is regarded in its anagrammatised condition, i.e. as an aggregate of dispersed *diphones/polyphones*/phonemes. Before its anagrammatisation and after its restitution, however, it is a pure form.

As to the relation between form and substance, poetic freedom according to Saussure's anagram theory consists of the fact that the signs are not only used as forms but that their substantial aspect becomes relevant as well and plays a functional role. This does not contradict the comments made in the *Cours* but it represents a poetic epiphenomenon, which is superimposed on the standard language.

Whenever a divergence is found between the statements in the *Cours* and in Saussure's notes regarding the anagram, we are not dealing with a contradiction in the strict sense, but rather with different givens in the fields of standard and poetic language. Why his attempt nevertheless has to be considered a failure is shown by a comparison with some perspectives from poetry which are related to his approach, but are nevertheless structured in a completely different way.

As early as in the second half of the nineteenth century, one can detect reflections similar to Saussure's, when looking at Lautréamont and others. The most striking similarities are those found in Mallarmé, to whom I shall confine myself here. According to Mallarmé, a poetic text must appear trivial at first sight, for the essential part of the poetic message and the profound sense of the text under an apparently irrelevant surface are supposed to be revealed to the reader by committed and intensive reading: 'Au cours, seulement, du morceau, à travers des voiles feints, ceux encore quant à nous-mêmes, un sujet se dégage de leur successive stagnance amassée et dissoute avec art . . .' ('Only gradually from the fragment, through shrouded simulacra, especially those relating to us, a subject takes shape from the marasma, artfully garnered, amassed and dissolved . . .', Mallarmé, 1945: 384; see also p. 382 and passim).

This process of unveiling, of getting closer to the (poetic) meaning of the text step by step takes place on the basis of certain evocative and associative mechanisms. Mallarmé describes them as follows: 'L'air ou chant sous le texte, conduisant la divination d'ici là, y applique son motif en fleuron et cul-de-lampe invisibles' ('The melody or song under the text, leads the divination forward, weaving a pattern of invisible fleurons and ornamental endpieces', Mallarmé, 1945: 387).

The sense of a poetic message, therefore, results from a 'chant sous le texte', a 'song under the text'. But what is this, really? He regards the *chant*, or its genesis, as a sort of repetition of a motive, a repetitive structure: 'Cette visée, je la dis Transposition – structure une autre' ('This design – which I call Transposition – produces another structure', Mallarmé, 1945: 366). For Mallarmé, too, these structures are repetitions, equivalents, *couplaisons*, echoes within a text. This conception corresponds in broad outlines with Saussure's theory regarding the appearance of phonemes and *diphones* in pairs. In both, the essence of the poetic text is not to be seen right away, rather it has to be discovered and uncovered by the reader in the course of his reading. This, however, is the sum total of their common ground. For Saussure, the element which is to be discovered, is a key word or a name; for Mallarmé, in contrast, it is all about the discovery of the poetic meaning as such. In the case of Saussure, we are dealing with anagrams whereas with Mallarmé, we have to do with sense-evoking echoes and with structural equivalents, not to mention the fact that there is no strict rule and no given space for the formation of pairs. It must also be emphasised that in Mallarmé's eyes, syntagmatic relations are not sufficient in order to produce the meaning of the text; the elements, which form the basis of the relations (words, *monemes*, and so on), rather serve as centres of association for paradigmatic associations, which in their virtuality – independent of their contextual ties – cause the scope of meaning, which is completely determined by the linguistic system (Mallarmé, 1945: 368) which itself therefore participates in the meaning of the text:

Les mots d'eux-mêmes, s'exaltent à mainte facette reconnue la plus rare ou valant pour l'esprit, centre de suspens vibratoire; qui les perçoit indépendamment de la suite ordinaire, projetés, en parole de grotte, tant que dure leur mobilité ou principe, étant ce qui ne se dit pas du discours: prompts tous, avant extinction, à une réciprocité de feux distante ou présentée de biais comme contingence. (Mallarmé, 1945: 386)

(Words are displayed with their myriad facets, the most unusual and the most apt for the spirit, our centre of resonance; the spirit which perceives them outside the normal order of things, like an echo in a cavern, for as long as their mobility and unspoken effect lasts; words ever ready for a reciprocal kindling of lights in the distance or at a chance slanting angle, until they fade.)

One can find similar parallels between Saussure and Francis Ponge – at least considering the late period of Ponge's work, when he gave up his original *conception chosiste* of art. That is why, for him, for example, the text in *Le savon* (Ponge, 1967) became a 'concert de vocables, de sons significatifs' ('a concert of words, of meaningful sounds', Ponge/Sollers, 1970: 156)[4]. This does not mean anything other than that Ponge regards the order, the structure of elements as decisive. In this relational structure, the individual meaning of singular discursive elements is absolutely pushed into the background for the time being. The meaning of the poetic message is generated based on the structures in the field of the *signifiant*, on the basis of echoes, harmonies and contrasts. That is why Ponge, referring to Malherbe and himself, is able to say:

Il ne connaît qu'un seul thème, la parole comme telle, sonnant à la louange de la beauté comme telle. Il réalise à chaque instant la transmutation de la raison en réson. C'est la résonance, dans le vide conceptuel de la lyre elle-même comme instrument de la raison au plus haut prix. Il réalise un concert varié de vocables. (Ponge/Sollers, 1970: 164)

(He only knows one theme, the spoken word itself, ringing the praises of beauty itself. He achieves at every moment the transformation of reason into resonance. This is resonance in the conceptual void of the lyre as the instrument of reason at the highest possible level. He achieves a chorus of words rich in variations.)

The poetic text, therefore, does not have a real object, it becomes autonomous, impersonal and self-sufficient (Ponge/Sollers, 1970: 26, 40). It becomes a sort of formula, in which every reader can and must replace the variables by positive quantities of his or her choice. Based on the inclusion of the reader, one comes to an infinite quantity of meanings of the text (Ponge/Sollers, 1970: 113, 114, 170). When constituting or discovering the meaning of a text, syntagmatic relations based on individual *monemes* as well as paradigmatic relations play a decisive role, because they finally guide the constitution of the meaning. Consequently, Ponge does not hesitate to speak about an anagrammatisation with regard to sense-constituting structures of a text (Ponge/Sollers, 1970: 71f).

Despite all the similarities with Saussure, there are also decisive differences between the two opinions. These differences, however, are to a large extent congruent with those relating to Mallarmé. Ponge is far from demanding a perfect repetition of phonemes and *polyphones* in the scope of a limited text segment. He is much more liberal in dealing with the phonetic equivalents. His aim is not the discovery of a given name or key word, but rather revealing the sense of a text as such, which results from the more or less complete activation of the possible syntagmatic and paradigmatic relations. In Saussure's eyes, there is only the anagram, which is intended by the author, whereas in Ponge's eyes, a variety of meanings exist, which differ depending on the reader and which can be located at different levels of the interrelational structure.

A mutual influence between Saussure on the one hand, and Ponge and Mallarmé on the other hand, seems highly unlikely. If the linguist and the poets nevertheless come to similar conclusions, it only serves to show that Saussure's anagram studies were not as absurd as some have claimed (Déguy, 1969), as on this subject he is in very good company. Things are different if we consider the authors of the *Tel Quel* group; they never tired of citing the Genevan linguist, and it is evident that they owe him much. Julia Kristéva, for example, explains the following, although not without slightly modifying Saussure's opinion:

We accept the principles set out by Ferdinand de Saussure in his 'Anagrams', namely:
a) Poetic language adds a second, contrived, dimension to the original word
b) There is a correspondence between elements, in both metre and rime
c) Binary poetic laws transgress the rules of grammar
d) The element of the key word (or even letter) 'may be spread over the whole length of the text or may be concentrated in a small space, such as one or two words'. (Trans. of Kristéva, 1969a: 175)

The main objective of the semiology represented by the *Tel Quel* group is to eliminate the subjectivity and the impressionistic quality of literary analysis as far as possible by granting them only a limited and controllable scope within a kind of programmatic framework. The purpose of literary semiology would be, 'de trouver un formalisme isomorphe à la productivité littéraire se pensant elle-même' ('to find a formalism that coincided exactly with self-reflexive literary production', Kristéva, 1969a: 174), and this formalism is to have mathematical features (1969a: 176). Here too, the text becomes a kind of formula and its meaning presents itself as an actualisation of this formula through the reader: 'Meaning is not only what words want to say, it also indicates a direction . . . Translated into linguistic terminology, meaning is identified with the semiotic process, being presupposed by – and presupposing – a system and a programme, whether virtual or realised' (trans. of Greimas, 1970: 15ff.).

The semiotic processes, on which the constitution of sense is based, presuppose the structures of the *langue* as well as those of the *parole* ('des discours'), they activate the paradigmatic as well as the syntagmatic dimension. The limits between virtual and current, between paradigmatic and syntagmatic dimensions become blurred and in this way the reader's activity, which produces the meaning, becomes a kind of 'collective work' based on the text.

However, even if the authors of the *Tel Quel* group like to refer to Saussure, one should not ignore that their conception differs in various respects from those of the 'father of structuralism'. In Saussure, there is always an underlying key word, the *diphones* of which in a way form the skeleton of one or more verses. The members of *Tel Quel* do not have any equivalent: they are only interested in structures as such and relations of all sorts of textual and intertextual kinds. For them, the text can be much more extensive than in Saussure's analyses: the restriction to one or several verses is opposed to an unrestricted corpus of literature. Moreover, for Saussure the text only (re)produces the anagram, whereas for *Tel Quel* it produces the meaning itself. And finally it has to be pointed out that for Saussure everything depends on the poet's will, on his intention, whereas for *Tel Quel* the author's creativity supplies only the basis for the individual activity of the recipient.

If, to conclude, one raises the question why Saussure's study on anagrams led to a dead end, the answer is quite obvious: the failure was caused by the fact that both the law concerning the repetition of phonemes and *polyphones* as well as the rules for the anagram are formulated in far too rigid a way. If one dispenses with exact equivalents and is content with the possibility of equivalents within the scope of syntagmatic relations on different hierarchical levels of the text or text corpus, and if one accepts the constitution of meaning as a product of the (individual) reader's activity on the basis of a given text, resorting to the paradigmatic circumstances, one reaches an acceptable conception, which essentially coincides with the views of Mallarmé, Ponge, the *Tel Quel* group, and so on. Saussure was definitely going too far when he assumed that every structure of a literary text was the consequence of an intended creative act on the part of the author. Nonetheless, Saussure was not simply mistaken, his studies on the anagram are no *folie*. He discovered that certain laws of everyday language were (at least partly) repealed in poetic language (linear nature of the *signifiant*, purely formal character of the sign, inseparability of the signifier and the signified), that the meaning of a discourse is the product of a reader's activity on the basis of the text, and that syntagmatic and paradigmatic aspects within the scope of this process interfere to such a high degree that their limits become blurred.

(This chapter was translated by Gudrun Milde, assisted by Magdalena Trytko.)

12 Saussure and Derrida

Geoffrey Bennington

Derrida's explicit discussion of Saussure is essentially to be found in the chapter 'Linguistics and grammatology' in his *De la grammatologie* (1967a)[1], with some of his findings summarised in the collection of interviews entitled *Positions* (1972a), and in the essay 'Le cercle linguistique de Genève' (an extended abstract of the whole of *De la grammatologie*) reprinted in the volume *Marges – de la philosophie* (1972b). A further discussion of Saussure, concentrating on the latter's remarks about onomatopoeia, is to be found in *Glas* (1974), and scattered remarks can be found in many other books and essays. Although this amounts to a relatively small portion of Derrida's vast published output, it would not be an exaggeration to say that the reading of Saussure (we shall here be following almost exclusively the chapter from *De la grammatologie*) allows for one of Derrida's most perspicuous presentations of his 'early' thinking, and one of the clearest derivations of such famous 'concepts' as *différance, trace* and *archi-écriture*. In characteristic 'deconstructive' fashion, Derrida appears at first to be concentrating on a secondary or marginal aspect of Saussure's theory (the discussion of writing in chapter 6 of part I of the *Cours*), but then draws from that discussion startlingly broad and general claims about Saussure's theory as a whole, and about language, linguistics and indeed philosophy and thinking more generally. It should be pointed out from the start that Derrida's reading of Saussure is not that of a professional linguist, nor that of a Saussure scholar: he is at pains to point out in the introduction to his chapter that Saussure figures in his essay as a 'privileged example', the particularity of which should not affect the generality of the issues raised (Derrida, 1967a: 44), or, a little later, as 'a very conspicuous index in a given situation' (Derrida, 1967a: 67) and aims to raise questions which go well beyond the confines of Saussure's explicit concerns. As we shall see, those questions are not even quite philosophical, insofar as part of what Derrida is seeking in Saussure is a way of thinking which goes beyond the grasp of philosophy as traditionally defined. Thus he has also suggested that linguistics, along with psychoanalysis, is a privileged place for the development of a thinking that could hope to go beyond what he calls 'metaphysical closure' (Derrida, 1967a: 35).

Derrida's interest in Saussure's chapter on writing is dictated by the overall interrogation of *De la grammatologie* as to the very possibility of a science of writing (a 'grammatology', precisely). This interrogation is itself motivated largely by Derrida's earlier work on Husserl, and his perplexity faced with a tension between the latter's wholly traditional determination of language as being essentially to do with speech or voice, and some later insights into the constitutive importance of writing in establishing the very possibility of science and history through its capacity for ensuring transmissibility and, thereby, traditionality. (On these later insights see especially the posthumous text on the 'Origin of geometry', translated by Derrida with a long introduction – Husserl, 1963. See also Derrida, 1967b, 1967c, 1972b and 1990.) Writing is not just a means of recording scientific findings, on this account, but a positive condition of science's achieving scientific status in the first place (this Husserlian discussion is recalled briefly here in Derrida, 1967a: 42–3 and 60). The apparently crucial importance of writing in this respect sits oddly with a philosophical tradition, since Plato at least. This has systematically treated writing hostilely or at least dismissively, as at best a secondary (and potentially dangerous) form of language, and leads Derrida, in the introduction to his chapter, to list a number of disparate and difficult questions as to what a 'science of writing' could mean, given (1) that the very idea of science was born at a certain moment *within* the history of writing; (2) that the idea of science was moreover formulated within a certain way of construing the relationship between speech and writing; (3) that it was linked to a *specific* model of writing ('phonetic' writing); (4) that the idea of a general science *of* writing was itself born at a specific moment of history (around the eighteenth century); (5) that writing is not only an auxiliary to science, nor even only a potential object of science, but a condition of possibility of scientific objectivity itself; (6) that writing is a condition of possibility of the historicity of history in general (Derrida, 1967a: 42–3). Derrida is struck by the fact that positive histories of writing can only tend to repress such questions of principle, and that, for all their empirical richness, they are rarely related to the modern *scientific* study of language. Could not a prospective grammatology, given the difficulty of the questions it must face, reasonably expect to find theoretical resources in such a linguistics? Derrida will try to show two different things. The *first* concerns linguistics established as 'scientific' by Saussure and in his wake – in particular at the time of Derrida's writing – providing a model of scientificity for the 'human sciences' in general. This linguistics, according to Derrida, continues to rely on a largely unthought ('metaphysical') view of the relations between speech and writing. This determines language as essentially vocal and indeed often draws its strongest claims to scientificity from phonology. *Secondly*, however, according to Derrida, linguistics as represented by Saussure also provides other conceptual resources which can 'liberate the future of a general grammatology of which linguistics-phonology would be merely a dependent and circumscribed region' (Derrida, 1967a: 45). In reading the *Cours*, and notably its chapter devoted to writing, Derrida calls the explicit, and essentially traditional, claims about the relation of speech and writing Saussure's 'declared intention' (*propos déclaré*), but calls these other conceptual resources 'another gesture' (*un autre geste*) (Derrida, 1967a: 45): this other gesture is not to be found in Saussure's explicit claims (but rather elsewhere in the *Cours*), and requires an effort of reading if it is to be brought out. This 'other gesture' is not exactly another *propos*, rather something that Saussure *does* without saying so, or writes without explicitly saying, and the kind of 'reading' involved in bringing this out is something we shall have to address in due course. After these general reflections, Derrida's chapter falls into three main parts, the first establishing the *propos déclaré* by glossing Saussure's explicit discussion of writing in part I, chapter 6, of the *Cours de linguistique générale* (Saussure, 1972, referred to hereinafter as *CLG*/D), the second drawing out the *autre geste* from other parts of the *Cours* (with some extensive parenthetical discussions of Peirce, Jakobson, Hjelmslev and others), and the third developing some of the more general philosophical implications of Derrida's findings.

The first part of this task is relatively straightforward. In common with philosophers from Plato and Aristotle to Rousseau, Hegel and beyond, Saussure assigns to writing a derivative status with respect to speech (in the general sense – see Bennington, 1995), which alone is supposed to be the proper (or at least primary) form of language, and thus to constitute the true object of linguistics. Derrida (1972a: 32) suggests that Saussure's 'phonocentrism' flows directly from his use of the inherited concept of the sign: 'The concept of sign (signifier/signified) carries within it the necessity of privileging the phonic substance . . . For the *phonè* is indeed the signifying substance that *gives itself to consciousness* as the most intimately linked to the thought of the signified concept . . .' (see too Derrida, 1967a: 22–3). The position of writing is secondary and derivative in this tradition because it is seen as the external *representation* or *image* of speech: in Saussure's terminology, the written signifier *represents* a spoken signifier which alone stands in an essential and intimate relation to the signified. As mere external representative of the 'internal system' of language, writing can then be excluded from the domain of linguistics proper.

Saussure nonetheless recognises the need for a discussion of writing, and it is unclear why this should be so if writing really were quite so clearly external to the essential object of linguistics (Derrida's subtitle for this section of his chapter is 'The outside and the inside'). He asserts, for instance, that 'writing is in itself foreign to the internal system . . . Language [*Langue*] and writing are two distinct sign-systems; the sole *raison d'être* of the latter is to represent the former; the object of linguistics is not defined by the combination of the written word and the spoken word: this latter alone (*à lui seul*) constitutes that object (*CLG*: 44–5). If writing were indeed merely the kind of external representation that Saussure claims (*CLG*: 44–7), how could it bring with it what Saussure calls 'dangers' (*CLG*: 44) which need to be pointed out and even denounced in a tone which is more one of moralistic indignation than of scientific description? Writing, external and instrumental *image* of speech, can, it seems, on occasion contaminate the notional purity of the internal (vocal) system, what Saussure calls the *natural* link of sound and sense. The sign may be intrinsically *arbitrary* (i.e. non-natural), but there remains nonetheless a supposed *naturality* in the link of sound and sense in general, with respect to which writing is merely artificial – but artificial in a way that always might, so it would seem, come to affect or even infect the supposedly natural 'inside'. Saussure's indignation in chapter 6 of the introduction about the possible effects of writing on speech is born of a desire to keep the outside on the outside and preserve the supposed natural purity of the 'internal system'. According to a common metaphysical schema the supposedly natural and original purity of an inside has, in fact but also in principle, always to be achieved, after the fact, as it were, by an act of expulsion of what supposedly *belongs on the outside* but somehow, unaccountably, has come to appear on the inside, where it should never have been. (Derrida provides some detailed parallels with Rousseau and Plato here, and discusses their explicit theories of writing at length elsewhere – Derrida, 1967a, and 1972c.) Writing, says Saussure in this august tradition, *has no right* to 'usurp' the place of speech, but as a potentially fascinating and seductive *image*, *always might* tempt speakers and linguists to invert the natural order of things, to fall pathologically (the word is Saussure's: *CLG*: 53) into the 'trap' (*CLG*: 46) set by writing. Derrida's point here is simply to suggest that for this 'usurpation' of speech by writing *even to be possible*, something about speech (about nature, then, insofar as speech is the natural place of language) must from the start *lend itself* to such a possibility: that speech become affected by writing in a way it never should have must therefore nonetheless be a possibility, what Derrida would later call a *necessary* or *structural* possibility, of the supposedly 'natural' speech from the start. Nature does not simply come first, only subsequently to be affected by culture or technology, but is, from the first, in part constituted by this very possibility. As Derrida puts it:

> Why does a project of *general* linguistics, concerning the *internal system in general of language in general*, draw the limits of its field by excluding, as *exteriority in general*, a *particular* system of writing (i.e. phonetic or alphabetic writing), however important it be, and even if it were *in fact* universal . . . However important, and even if it were in fact universal or destined to become universal, this particular model of phonetic writing *does not exist*: no practice is ever purely faithful to its principle . . . And finally, the 'usurpation' referred to by Saussure, the violence with which writing would thus substitute itself for its own origin, for what should not only have engendered it but to have engendered

itself – such an overturning of power cannot be an accidental aberration. The usurpation necessarily refers us to a deep essential possibility. This possibility is without doubt inscribed in speech itself and it should have been interrogated, and perhaps even have been the starting point. (Derrida, 1967a: 58–9)

Saussure has no account of this essential possibility, and no real conceptual means to explain it. He sees phonetic/alphabetic writing, quite traditionally, as writing *par excellence*, the ideal toward which writing systems should tend, the *telos* of the concept of writing just because it best espouses the essentially vocal sign. Derrida points out that Saussure, dealing with this phonetic/alphabetic writing, and noting the aberrations he notes, can only fall back on vague psychological explanations. Derrida also notes in passing that Saussure explicitly suggests that it is for psychology to determine the exact place of semiology (*CLG*: 33; quoted by Derrida, 1967a: 60). But no psychology (or at least no psychology of intuitive consciousness, such as that loosely invoked here by Saussure) can provide an adequate account of this essential possibility of 'usurpation'. This is because the problem raised by the question of writing in its apparently malevolent capacity for infecting the purity of speech just is the general problem of language's potential functioning in the *absence* of intuitive plenitude, be it on the side of the subject or on the side of the object, a potential most clearly in evidence in writing, but one that in fact defines language as such. As Derrida (1967a: 60) says: '[Psychology] can never encounter within its space that through which is constituted the absence of the signatory, not to mention the absence of the referent. Now writing is the name of these two absences'. (See also Derrida, 1967b.) Whence Saussure's tone of indignation that prevails in the chapter on writing. Indeed, his apparently best explanation (that the fixity of the written object gives it a false prestige) is in contradiction with his own claim elsewhere that the oral tradition is the more fixed and durable (*CLG*: 46). Saussure's manifest outrage faced with examples such as 'Lefébure', where the 'u' comes from the pedantic respelling of the 'natural' evolved form 'Lefèvre', and the 'b' from a pedantic reintroduction of an etymological memory of the Latin *faber*, is born of an inability to explain: as Derrida mildly points out, 'Lefébure, *ce n'est pas mal'*, and so Saussure's angry complaint that such examples do not result from the 'natural play' of language, but from 'external' factors, betrays a theoretical inadequacy in the general account of the relation between speech and writing, and more especially goes against Saussure's own earlier recognition that 'the essential character of language (*langue*) is foreign to the phonic character of the linguistic sign' (*CLG*: 21 – see too *CLG*: 164). By allowing the argument from necessary possibility (something about speech makes it *essentially* contaminable by its supposedly external 'representation'), Derrida suggests the conclusion that 'writing in general is not external to the system of language in general', and that this should inspire a rethink whereby writing will not only be reinstated as a worthy object of study *within* theoretical linguistics, but in which certain features traditionally confined to a writing conceived as essentially external to that system be in fact considered as *constitutive* of it, so that language in general might be better (more consistently) described in terms of just those features, and thereby as *in some sense* essentially a kind of 'writing'. The rest of Derrida's chapter will, then, be concerned to bring out those features, and he finds that Saussure himself provides good grounds for doing so, though precisely not in the chapter of the *Cours* where writing is explicitly discussed.

The opening part of this second manoeuvre (Derrida's disconcerting subtitle here is 'The outside is the inside', with the 'is' crossed out in a gesture we shall come on to explain) is straightforward and trenchant: namely that the basic thesis of the arbitrary nature of the sign ought simply to disallow any radical theoretical distinction between the vocal sign (as 'natural') and the written sign (as its mere external image or representation). Even if Saussure clearly *intends* his description of the sign as being essentially 'unmotivated' to hold only within the supposedly 'natural' space of the vocal sign as definitive of the internal language system, it looks to Derrida as though considering signs *in general* as unmotivated institutions should make it impossible to posit any 'natural' hierarchy among different orders of sign or their substance. Indeed, the description of the sign in general as an unmotivated but durable institution or inscription will give Derrida his first reason for the startling claim that the predicates traditionally attached to the concept of 'writing' *better* describe language in general than those traditionally attached to speech. And Saussure himself is in contradiction here, having first suggested that writing is indeed a 'system of signs' (and therefore 'arbitrary' in the sense of being unmotivated), only then to condemn it to the 'outer darkness' (Derrida, 1967a: 66) on the grounds of its being merely an *image* (and therefore motivated, and thus *not* a sign in Saussure's sense, but rather a symbol) of speech. If the thesis of the 'arbitrariness of the sign' is taken seriously, then Saussure should at the very least have produced a more neutral account of writing.

But Derrida has ambitions beyond showing that Saussure (in keeping with 'the non-critical tradition' from which he inherits) is not entirely consistent or 'scientific' in his treatment of writing. There *is* a certain recognisable logic and consistency in Saussure's contradictions, and Derrida takes this 'quasi-oneiric' (Derrida, 1967a: 67) coherence as evidence of a deep metaphysical desire at work, and not merely a local problem in Saussure's thinking: indeed he believes that pursuing the index provided by the treatment of writing will allow him to 'broach the de-construction of *the greatest totality* – the concept of *episteme* and logocentric metaphysics – in which, without the radical question of writing ever having been raised, all Western methods of analysis, explanation, reading or interpretation have been produced' (Derrida, 1967a: 68). By pursuing a little further Saussure's thinking about the arbitrariness of the sign, and more especially the famous and enigmatic thinking about language as a system of differences, Derrida will attempt to derive a description of language in terms of *trace*, *archi-writing* and *différance* which have implications well beyond Saussure's explicit concerns in the *Cours*, and indeed well beyond the purview of linguistics itself considered as a science.

If writing, as a 'system of signs', cannot be thought of merely as a representation of speech, how in fact are we to construe it? On the one hand as *more external* to speech than its image, representation or symbol, and on the other as *more internal* to a speech which Derrida will now argue is itself better thought of as a species of writing. The claim here runs as follows: the traditional concept of 'writing' fundamentally signifies the 'durable institution of a sign' (Derrida, 1967a: 65) or an 'instituted trace' (Derrida, 1967a: 68). Derrida is trying to find a term that will avoid the traditional connotations attaching to 'sign' or 'signifier'. (See Derrida, 1967a: 32, n. 9 and 1972a.) This difficult motif of the *trace* will now become the centre of Derrida's concern, and will guide the rest of this presentation. The trace is 'instituted' in the sense that it is not naturally given, that it has, as Saussure says, glossing the sense in which the sign is 'arbitrary', no 'natural link' with its signified (or referent). Saussure discounts the traditional conventionalist accounts of how such an institution is possible. This he does, despite some terminological hesitation, in his strong claim that language is a 'pure institution', an institution like no other that nonetheless shows up something of the institutionality of all institutions. (See especially *CLG*: 26, 107, 110 and the helpful notes 137 and 157 by de Mauro – *CLG*/D: 442–3 and 449.) Once these traditional accounts are discounted, the possibility of 'arbitrary' institution entails the definition in terms of difference, again as Saussure recognises. He writes: 'Since there is no vocal image that answers better than any other to what it is charged with saying, it is obvious, even *a priori*, that a fragment of language can never be grounded, in the last analysis, on anything other than its non-coincidence with the rest. *Arbitrary* and *differential* are two correlative categories' (*CLG*: 163; see Derrida, 1967a: 77, n. 18). Signs achieve their identity (i.e. their potential recognisability or repeatability as the signs that they are in distinction from others), not through any positive or substantial features, but just insofar as they are different from other signs, and therefore in some sense bear with them the trace of all the signs they are not. This trace is not a *thing* in any normal sense, but the general possibility that there be recognisable things at all – to this extent Saussure's insight about 'difference without positive terms' (*CLG*: 166) is, on Derrida's reading, absolutely generalisable as a condition of possibility of any identity or positivity whatsoever. What Derrida calls 'metaphysics' always starts with the idea of some founding or originary *presence*, but the generalisation of the account of identity that Saussure believes describes only the domain of what he calls 'arbitrary signs' suggests that such apparent 'presence' is always only a secondary *effect* of the trace: no presence could ever be foundational just because *any* 'presence' (or what Derrida, 1972a: 90, would more precisely now call an 'effect of presence') always only emerges from the logically prior, never simply present, trace-relation. Without quite realising it, then, Saussure's definition of what he believes can be circumscribed as the proper object of a particular science affects the foundational definitions of what *any* object or science at all could conceivably be.

Derrida's rather more technical and difficult description of this situation (Derrida, 1967a: 68–9; and 1972a: 37–41) derives, then, from a simple extension of Saussure's insight about arbitrariness and difference. Once any element in a system is identified by its differential relationality, as it must be once 'arbitrariness' is taken seriously and radically, then the structure is one in which any given 'present' element is always haunted by the other ('absent') elements which it is not (Derrida, 1993; see also Derrida, 1967a: 64 and 1967b). In more phenomenological language, Derrida describes this as a situation which 'requires a synthesis in which the wholly other announces itself as such – without any simplicity, any identity [except in the differential sense we are exploring – GB] any resemblance or continuity – in what is not it' (Derrida, 1967a: 69). He is also rapidly prepared to claim that this structure is that of entities *in general*. Metaphysics always thinks of entities as in some sense *present*: Derrida, deriving the argument from Saussure himself, is claiming that that apparent *presence* must in fact be subsequent to the trace-relation, in which 'presence' is affected by absence and alterity from the start, in an endless movement of becoming, so that,

> the general structure of the unmotivated trace has to communicate in the same possibility and without it being possible to separate them other than by abstraction, the structure of the relation to the other, the movement of temporalisation (because any given element is identifiable only with respect to its difference from both earlier and subsequent elements) and language as writing. (Derrida, 1967a : 69)

The trace does not supervene on a nature (an origin) already there, but must be always already at work prior to any construal of what nature might be, and therefore also its apparent others (institution, law, technology). This 'always already' Derrida will later in the chapter refer to an 'absolute past'; here it is described as always (already) becoming but never quite become.

Derrida makes a detour via Peirce, with an approving account of the latter's dictum that 'we think only in signs' (Derrida, 1967a: 72). From this Derrida draws the thought that 'the thing itself is a sign', and that the sign-structure as described by Peirce is therefore structurally interminable, never arriving at some ultimate referent or signified – what he calls a 'transcendental signified' (see Derrida, 1972a: 30). Derrida further suggests that this structure of becoming has to be thought of as more originary than Saussure's distinction between the synchronic and the diachronic. Given the irreducibility of the 'play' (Derrida, 1967a: 73) that identifies any and all elements of language at all times, the active movement of the trace is necessarily happening 'in' whatever moment one might choose to identify as 'synchronic', and happening as constitutive of the synchronic itself. The movement we are dealing with (and which the 'active' ending of the neologism 'différance' is designed to capture – see Derrida, 1972b and also 1972a: 16–19) is not merely that of the dimension Saussure calls diachronic, just because it *inhabits* the synchronic itself, and affects any 'state' of language with an intrinsic mobility. In a general way, the claim here is that the trace-structure logically precedes *all* of Saussure's distinctions (see too Derrida, 1972a: 40), and that the 'general linguistics' within which Derrida found the hints that allowed him to develop it has to be resituated within that prior and more general structure. Whence the only half-serious suggestion that 'grammatology' might reasonably enough replace 'semiology' in Saussure's descriptions of the most general science of which linguistics would be merely a part, and that this replacement would have the advantage of avoiding the domination of semiology in general by the specific model of the *linguistic* sign, Saussure famously claiming that language is the most 'characteristic' of sign-systems, and that linguistics can therefore aspire to become the 'general pattern' of all semiology (*CLG*: 33 and 101; Derrida, 1967a: 74–5).

Just as we saw that the possibility that writing has supposedly nefarious effects on pronunciation implied a necessary possibility (where Saussure was reduced to thinking – or precisely not thinking – in terms of monstrosity or catastrophe), so Saussure's regular tendency to *illustrate* fundamental features of the language-system and its differential functioning (*CLG*: 33 and 165) by *comparing* it to the writing-system implies a 'common root' of speech and writing (Derrida, 1967a: 75–6) rather than the merely external imaging that is suggested in the chapter explicitly devoted to writing. The point at which the language-system (and its supposed natural vocality) and writing are comparable is that both function differentially: but as difference by definition is never a 'sensory plenitude' (Derrida, 1967a: 77: many commercial slogans notwithstanding, one cannot in fact taste or feel difference as such), it cannot in principle be given a 'natural' place in *any* particular substance, spoken *or* written. Derrida spends several pages here defending Saussure's own explicit 'reduction' of the phonetic component of language (quoting now from the much later chapters of the *Cours* on identity and value (*CLG*: 164, 166: Derrida, 1967a: 77–8) against the reservations of such as Jakobson and Halle, and Martinet. Derrida's point here, often misunderstood in spite of his explicit statements, is not at all to 'rehabilitate' or promote writing in its standard sense (if philosophers and linguists have habitually assumed or asserted that speech is *superior* to writing, Derrida is not concerned to argue back symmetrically that on the contrary writing is *superior* to speech), but to bring out this 'common root'. Logically prior to the distinction between speech and writing is the differential system and the trace-structure. (I use the notion of 'logical priority' for clarity and convenience here, but Derrida is quite consistently suspicious of the value of the logical, not at all in that he prefers or promotes illogicality, but in that the concept of logic is itself derived from *logos*, and *logos* is part of the ('logocentric') philosophical tradition which has massively determined it in terms of speech – see Derrida, 1967a: 366). The possible (and indeed perhaps inevitable) confusion here (see Derrida, 1967a: 26) stems from Derrida's almost militant determination to use the term 'writing' (or 'archi-writing') to refer to this 'deeper' system. But if archi-writing is not writing in the traditional sense (any more than it is speech in the traditional sense), why not simply choose a different term (Derrida after all often uses the neologism *différance* here) to name this new concept? Here is part of Derrida's justification:

> The point here is not, then, to rehabilitate writing in the narrow sense, nor to overturn the order of dependency when it is obvious . . . We would like to suggest, rather, that the supposedly derivative nature of writing, however real and massive it is, was possible only on one condition: that the 'original', 'natural', etc. language never existed, that it was never intact, untouched by writing, that it always was itself a writing. An archi-writing the necessity of which we wish to show, and the new concept of which we wish to sketch; and which we continue to call writing only because it communicates essentially with the vulgar concept of writing. This concept was only able to impose itself historically by the dissimulation of archi-writing, by the desire for a speech chasing out its other and its double and working to reduce its difference. If we persist in naming this difference 'writing', this is because, in the work of historical repression, writing was, by its situation, destined to signify what was most fearsome about difference. It was what, at the closest quarters, threatened the desire for living speech, what from the inside and from the start *broached* it (Derrida, 1967a: 83). ('Broach' here translates the French verb *entamer*: Derrida is exploiting an ambiguity between the sense of starting something, getting something going, and the sense of cutting into and breaking open.)

This decision to retain the word 'writing', and to court the confusion of its 'new' sense ('archi-writing', a structure logically prior to the standard conceptual distinction of speech and writing), is a complex one. It is justified by the thought that something of this 'new' sense is legible in the traditional discussions (and to that extent the sense is not exactly new at all, which is why Derrida's thinking always takes place in the form of readings of other texts), and the place of that legibility is systematically where writing (in its current or 'vulgar' sense) is at issue. Something about writing in the usual sense shows up something of the structure of archi-writing, even if only symptomatically, signalling an effort of repression. Metaphysics *desires* language to be normalised on the basis of speech and the 'presence' it appears to offer: writing in the usual sense is then charged with the task of bearing all the negative predicates a thinking that valorises presence wishes to exclude, but can then be used, against metaphysics, as a means to demonstrate that those negative predicates cannot in fact be thus confined to writing in the usual sense, but affect language in general, including speech.

This does not quite mean that, reading Saussure's later arguments about difference and value against the explicit claims in the writing chapter, Derrida considers that Saussure provides the grounds for a 'positive science' of writing. The trace-structure, insofar as it brings out a priority of difference with respect to any presence whatsoever, *ipso facto* exceeds the traditional concept of science, which is wedded, according to Derrida, to just the structure of presence which he describes as metaphysical. He spends several pages here considering the possibility that Hjelmslev and his followers in the 'Copenhagen school' might, however, provide grounds for such a science. This current of linguistic theory has the advantage of a much greater lucidity with respect to the status of writing than was evident in Saussure's explicit discussion, of allowing the thought that speech and writing are two systems equally worthy of attention, and thus also allowing access to specifically *literary* aspects of writing (Derrida, 1967a: 83–9). But even if this 'glossematic' approach is more lucid and consistent in this respect than Saussure himself, in that it does not need to affirm the superiority or even priority of spoken over written language, it does not begin to bring out the 'deeper' sense of writing that Derrida is concerned to develop: Hjelmslev and his followers still work within entirely conventional definitions of speech and writing, and simply allow these two 'substances of expression' equal dignity under the general formal umbrella of glossematics. As we have seen, Derrida is more concerned to argue that 'writing', taken in the extended sense of the trace, or 'archi-writing', better describes a *general* structure of language (and of more than language), and cannot be confined to its traditional determination: 'archi-writing, movement of *différance*, irreducible archi-synthesis, opening at one and the same time, in one and the same possibility, temporalisation, the relation to the other and language, cannot, as a condition of any linguistic system, be part of the linguistic system itself, cannot be situated as an object in its field' (Derrida, 1967a: 88).

Hjelmslev, in this perhaps accurately reflecting or predicting the inevitable disciplinary reaction of *linguistics* to Derrida's concerns, would have rejected the latter's constant tendency to overrun the limits of linguistics considered as a science, and 'would not have understood why the name "writing" should remain for that X which becomes so different from what has always been called "writing"' (Derrida, 1967a: 89).

The further argument for retaining that term now goes as follows: Saussure's (inherited) concept of writing describes it as a (graphic) signifier standing for a (phonic) signifier, which alone correlates with a signified and constitutes a sign. But as the Saussure of the thinking of linguistic 'value' and 'difference' increasingly suggests, language in general in fact functions through the general referral of signifiers to other signifiers, the 'value' of a given signifier summarising its differential relationships with all other signifiers in the system. This version of Saussure's theory seems not to need the all-too familiar description of the sign at all: the 'value' account of language can reasonably be taken to dispense with anything as mysterious as a signified (see Harris, 1987: 120[2]) – rather the 'meaning' of a given signifier accrues as an effect of its differential relation to all the others, so that, as Derrida puts it, a 'signified' is only ever a signifier placed in a certain position by other signifiers: if, for example, I wish to give the meaning (signified) of a given signifier, all I can ever do is produce more signifiers, organised in such a way that one or more of them *count as* a signified. Signifiers in general refer on to other signifiers, and the appearance of 'meaning' in the form of a signified is only ever an 'effect' (almost in the sense of an illusion) of that referral. A signifier is never in fact the signifier of a correlated signified, but always the signifier of other signifiers. Now if it be accepted that 'signifier of signifier . . .' be the preferable description of the operation of language, and if, as we saw '[graphic] signifier of [phonic] signifier' is the traditional description of writing, then it would appear justified, on the basis of the tradition itself – which must after all provide the basic means for our thinking and understanding anything at all, as Saussure (*CLG* part I, chapter 2, especially p. 108) well knew and as Derrida fully accepts – to extend the reach of 'writing' to describe language in general (see Derrida, 1967a: 63).

In moving on to this type of claim, Derrida is clearly doing a little more than merely glossing Saussure's doctrine. Saussure himself (or at least the text of the *Cours* as constituted by his students) was much more cautious about the implications of the 'differences without positive terms' argument. It will be remembered that in the 'Linguistic value' chapter of the *Cours*, Saussure advances the 'differences without positive terms argument' as valid only when the level of signifier or signified is taken separately. When the sign is, as it were, reconstituted and taken as a whole, Saussure claims that we are dealing with a positive entity, namely the sign, and that signs relate to each other no longer in the mode of difference, but of *opposition* (*CLG*: 167). This is a somewhat obscure claim: Saussure clearly needs to maintain a certain view of the sign as at least potentially a concrete entity (as opposed to the abstraction involved in considering, for theoretical purposes, signifier and signified as separable components of the sign). But as signifier and signified are in fact inseparable in the sign (chemical compound, *CLG*: 145, or better still *recto* and *verso* of the same piece of paper, *CLG*: 157, in two of Saussure's famous analogies), then he is driven to the thought that the structure of differences without positive terms cannot be valid at the level of the sign, just because signs taken as wholes seem to have an indubitable reality or, as Saussure puts it, positivity. But this thought is vulnerable to the following dilemma. Either, as in the more classical doctrine of the sign, the signified is in principle detachable from any signifier and can ideally exist independently or 'transcendentally'. However, this is just what Saussure is trying to combat, for example in everything he says against the view of language as nomenclature, or in his explicit contestation of the traditional analogy of signifier and signified as body and soul (*CLG*: 145, see Derrida, 1972a: 28 and 1967a: 52). Or else the signified is indeed inseparable from the signifier. But if it is inseparable from the signifier, and if the signifier is indeed to be understood through the argument about difference, then we seem justified in seeing the retreat from the negative differential definition to the positive oppositional one as something of a loss of nerve on Saussure's part, and a falling back into just the model of the sign he was trying to avoid. It seems to follow either that the sign will remain the metaphysical entity it always had been, or else will dissolve in the face of the more powerful argument about difference. Derrida considers it justifiable to pursue this consequence on the basis of an assessment of where the strength of Saussure's thought lies, even if many of Saussure's explicit claims appear to resist just that consequence. The tension between *propos declaré* and the *autre geste* in Saussure, which we saw most clearly operating between the chapter on writing and the chapter on linguistic value, continues here within that latter chapter.

Derrida himself reflects on the type of reading he is doing immediately after the discussion of Hjelmslev and his followers, in a parenthetical reflection on the phenomenological concept of 'experience' which need not perhaps detain us here, except insofar as it illuminates the general strategy of what we cannot quite call Derrida's 'method' (see Derrida, 1967a: 226–34). Derrida wants to suggest that, whatever the many virtues of Hjelmslev's work in rigorously (scientifically) determining the proper limits of the system of language, it stops short of asking the transcendental question as to the condition of possibility of that system as such (what Derrida is striving to formulate as trace, *différance*, archi-writing and so on), and by not asking that question he remains vulnerable to the metaphysics of 'scientistic objectivism'. To avoid this, certain transcendental questions must be put, even if the effect of those questions is ultimately to unsettle the limits of the science about which they were put, and even to undermine the very transcendental position from which they were put. Hence Derrida later develops the thought of a 'quasi-transcendental' (see Bennington, 1991). The danger of that undermining is that, unless certain precautions be taken, its results always might look just as though the question had never been put in the first place, and, as Derrida puts it, 'the ultra-transcendental text', which he is trying to produce, will 'look just like the precritical text'. This danger (which must be run) can be avoided only by eschewing confidence in the value of *conclusions* (here, something like 'it's all writing') in the interests of marking the *path* leading to those conclusions, what Derrida calls the *sillage*, the track or wake that the reading must leave in the text read, and that his chapter is trying to leave in Saussure.[3] At the point we have reached, such a path has led us to the need to posit that the trace is the 'origin' of the language-system as a whole: but just what makes 'trace' a difficult concept to think through is that it undermines the value of presence on which the notion of origin itself rests. If the 'origin' is a trace, then it is in fact and in principle no origin at all: what Derrida here calls the 'archi-trace' or 'originary trace' marks this problem in that it is explicitly a contradictory concept:

> For example, the value of transcendental *arkhè* must make its necessity felt before letting itself be crossed through [*raturer*] itself. The concept of archi-trace must allow for both that necessity and that crossing-through. For it is in fact contradictory within the logic of identity. The trace is not only the disappearance of the origin, it here means . . . that the origin has not even disappeared, that it was only ever constituted in return by a non-origin, the trace, which thus becomes the origin of the origin. (Derrida, 1967a: 90)

And it is just this gesture of 'crossing-through' that we saw in Derrida's subtitle to this section.

After some dense reflections on *différance* as the 'formation of form' and the 'being-imprinted of the imprint', which give some further philosophical precision to the philosophical status of the trace, Derrida's final section, entitled *la brisure*, 'The hinge', develops some of these questions further. The argument about the trace, developed from the correlative notions of arbitrariness and difference in Saussure, has established a conceptual zone that makes possible the science of linguistics, while falling outside its purview, and has justified the retention of the word 'writing', in its modified or generalised sense, to describe that zone. Only the work of the trace as *différance* allows effects of meaning to emerge, and provides the common root of speech and writing in their usual senses: this common root (no less than the 'origin of the experience of space and time', Derrida, 1967a: 96) then allows for the possibility that written (spatial) sequences appear to map onto spoken (temporal) sequences of language, and more generally for language to be *articulated*. What Saussure's more radical insights are groping towards is this possibility of language as articulation (*CLG*: 26, quoted Derrida, 1967a: 96: see too *CLG*: 156). That possibility, as Saussure is aware, implies a fundamental *passivity* of the speaking subject with respect to the language s/he speaks, and a passivity that relates to a kind of radical *past* in the sense that language is *always* there before me, 'always already', that I speak the way I speak because that's how people spoke before me, that I receive the language the way I receive the law (*CLG*: 104, 108). This 'pastness' of language is moreover not the sort of past I can think of as a past *present*, in that at no point *was it present*: the very functioning of language as such entails that that pastness inform it *from the start*. This type of 'past' is to that extent 'absolute', but thereby, still following the logic of the *rature* we have just sketched out, not adequately nameable *as* past, insofar as the traditional concept of 'past' always implies 'past present'. What Derrida has developed from Saussure in terms of the trace, then, not only exceeds the conceptual resources of the traditional characterisation of the relations between speech and writing, nor even only the resources of the traditional conception of what a science is, but also those of the traditional conceptualisation of time itself. This leads Derrida to some broader reflections on a thinking of time that would no longer answer to phenomenological categories, centred on the present, and would have to engage with the temporal structure that Freud famously called *Nachträglichkeit* (see Derrida, 1967c), and that again engages with the 'methodological' strand of the chapter. For just as the development of Saussure's thinking led to the strategy of *rature* we have summarised, so the argument from difference affects the way we can think about Derrida's own discourse, and the status of the terms he proposes. We have already witnessed an apparently exuberant use of a variety of terms – trace (as variously 'instituted', 'unmotivated', 'originary', 'pure'), *différance*, (archi-)writing and, soon, *espacement* and *texte* – to name what it is tempting to think of as 'the same thing' (even if that 'thing' cannot quite be a thing, but something like the condition of thinghood in general). Now Derrida returns to the choice of the term 'trace', and reflects on its use within the logic he has laid out:

> What guided us in the choice of this word? . . . If words and concepts take their meaning only in linkings of differences, one can justify one's language, and the choice of terms, only within a topology and a historical strategy. Justification can therefore never be absolute and definitive. It responds to a state of the forces in play and translates a historical calculation. (Derrida, 1967a: 102)

In this case, that choice is motivated by references to other thinkers: 'trace' appears, with varying degrees of elaboration, in Levinas, Freud and Nietzsche, for example, as well as in contemporary science, and Derrida necessarily draws on the 'meaning-effects' that accrue to the term in those discourses. 'Trace' is not, and on the difference account of how language works, never could be absolutely the 'right word', whence the apparent freedom with which it can be substituted in various contexts by *différance* or, here, 'writing'. Via these inputs, Derrida's 'calculation' is that the term 'trace' is *already* working for him along the lines of a questioning of metaphysical categories, many of which he summarises again in these closing pages. The quasi-concept[4] 'trace' provided an easier (more 'economical') way of thinking the general condition of difference as, for example: 'The opening to the first exteriority in general, the enigmatic relation of the living being to its other and of an inside to an outside: spacing.' A little earlier, Derrida has pointed out that the term *espacement* gathers a temporal sense to a spatial one (Derrida, 1967a: 99).

What has Derrida done to Saussure? Clearly more than is captured by the usual models of commentary or interpretation, however much commentary and interpretation we can find in this chapter. We have already noted that Derrida's interest in Saussure is not that of a scholar, nor that of a professional linguist. In the long final footnote to his chapter, Derrida returns to this situation again, and also addresses the issue of the status of the text of the *Cours*, from which he works almost exclusively – although this note also refers to Godel's *Sources manuscrites du cours de linguistique générale* (1957). After stressing that the choice of Saussure as his object is motivated both by the prominence Saussure's thinking still had in contemporary linguistics and semiology, and by the fact that Saussure appears to be situated on a limit between a traditional, 'metaphysical' thinking of the sign and a 'beyond' of that metaphysics, he proceeds as follows:

> it is not to be ruled out that that the literality of the *Cours*, to which we have been obliged to refer, should one day appear to be very suspect, in the light of material yet to be published. We are thinking particularly of the *Anagrams*. To what extent is Saussure responsible for the *Cours* as it was written up and given out after his death? The question is not a new one. Is it necessary to make it clear that, *here at least*, we cannot allow it the slightest relevance? Unless one has profoundly mistaken the nature of our project, it will have been perceived that, caring very little about the thought *itself* of Ferdinand de Saussure *himself*, we have been interested in a *text* whose literality has played the well-known role it has played since 1915, functioning in a system of readings, influences, misrecognitions, borrowings, refutations, etc. What it was possible to read in it – and also what it was not possible to read in it – under the title of *Cours de linguistique générale* was what mattered to us, to the exclusion of any hidden and 'true' intention of Ferdinand de Saussure. If it were to be discovered that this text has hidden another text – and we'll only ever be dealing with texts –, and hidden it in a determinate way, our reading would not (or at least not for that reason alone) be invalidated. Quite the contrary. (Derrida, 1967a: 107, n. 38)

'Derrida's Saussure', then, is not exactly proposing a *truth* of Saussure or of Saussure's thought, nor even a 'semiological' rather than 'philological' reading. Derrida would, however, undoubtedly subscribe to many of the methodological remarks made by Harris (1987) in the Preface to *Reading Saussure*, especially on the limits of historiographical reading and the notion of the 'unread'. The point of the reading is rather to follow, *through* Saussure, a line of thought that Saussure cannot be said to have mastered, nor even to have completely articulated, but which opens onto questions that Saussure himself, and linguistics as a science or a discipline, certainly cannot *contain*. This is in fact a consequence of the attempt to generalise the 'difference' argument Derrida found in Saussure: Saussure 'himself', the supposed identity of his thinking, has now *itself* to be conceived along the lines of the differential identity described by the trace-structure. Saussure's mobile, textual, place in the tradition is precisely homologous with that of an element in a language-system. (See too the parallel reflexions on the identity of 'Rousseau' in Derrida, 1967a: 147–8 and 230–1.) The reading, then, involves a constant, and necessarily incomplete, attempt to separate out the relatively heterogeneous strands of Saussure's text, to appreciate with as much care as possible the tension between those strands which remain tightly bound up with metaphysical presuppositions, and those which can open onto some other possibility, even if that possibility is one to which Saussure himself might very well not have assented, and which is therefore *produced by* the reading itself. What Derrida here calls 'grammatology' would then, in the words which end the interview in *Positions*, be 'less another science, a new discipline charged with a new content, a new clearly defined domain, than the vigilant practice of this textual separation' (Derrida, 1972a: 50).

Part IV

New debates and directions

13 Saussure's unfinished semantics

Simon Bouquet

Saussure as pragmatician?

Saussure's position with respect to meaning cannot be discussed without an in-depth analysis of the original texts, that is the students' notes from the lectures on general linguistics and writings by Saussure himself on general linguistics. While it is impossible to take the *Cours* as a literal basis for a semantics structured around a maximal ('textual') theory of meaning, which I shall call a *semiotics of interpretation*, such a structure can be deduced by looking at the original texts. The (re)reading of Saussure presented in this chapter points up not only the way Saussure's approach to semantics has gone largely unnoticed (in its production), but also the importance for Saussure's thought of the 'action value' of language – in other words, the central importance of the interpretative point of view. Having said that, his lectures and writings do not contain a developed theory of articulation from a 'grammatical' and an interpretative viewpoint – in other words, if one adopts my definition of the word *meaning*, there is no theory of meaning. But there are extremely clear suggestions – censored, forgotten or ignored in the *Cours* – which point the way towards such a theory.

With regard to the 'action value' of language, the original texts unveil a host of terms and descriptions which suggest an interpretative approach, subordinating the value of the '*signe de parole*', or a semiological approach to speech, to a description one can call *pragmatic*, if this adjective is used in its established sense of 'appropriate to action'. Thus, the third course (1910–11) contains the expressions '*actes de langage*' ('acts of language'):

we have found in *langue* . . . a definable object, separable from acts of language as a whole (*CLG*/E 1.42.252.5)

jeu de langage (the interplay of language/language-game):

we still have . . . to deal with the individual . . . We must take a look at the working of language in the individual. This practice of a social product by the individual . . . reveals the individual inner workings which must ultimately, in one way or another, have an effect on the general product, but which must not be confused, in analysis, with that general product . . . (*CLG*/E 1.515.429.5)

A handwritten preparatory note for the second course (1908–9) also uses the notion of 'will' (*volonté*), in an assertion to which I shall return, that of the duality of the science of language:

From the Individual, or Parole:
a) everything to do with Production of Sounds, b) everything to do with combination – Everything to do with Will.
Duality:
Parole; individual will / *Langue*, social passivity
Here for the first time question of two Linguistics. (*CLG/E* 1.515.429.5)

The notion of 'discourse' is another misunderstood Saussurean concept which I will consider at length below. In a long manuscript note, the unresolved problem of the nature of discourse is summed up in the following question: 'What is necessary to give us the idea that someone *wishes* to signify something, using the countless terms which are available in *langue*?'

Thus, what 'separates' (to use Saussure's term) 'discourse' on one hand, and on the other the 'mental store of *langue*' concerns the speaker's intentionality, and, above all, the recognition of this intentionality by the addressee. This is a long way from the essentially mechanistic and 'abstract' conception of language which reading the *Cours* alone lends to Saussure. As a great comparative linguist of the neogrammarian school, he inevitably draws, via the positivist Auguste Comte, on the epistemology of physics by applying the duality of synchronic and diachronic viewpoints to linguistic study. However, this does not necessarily make him party to the mechanistic abstraction likely to follow from an uncritical view of comparative grammar. The following passage, taken from manuscripts discovered in 1996 in the conservatory of the Saussure family home in Geneva, is perfectly explicit:

> The misunderstanding which initially dogged the school founded by F. Bopp was to give languages a body, an imaginary existence outside speaking individuals. Abstraction, within *langue*, even when appropriately applied, is in practice only of limited use – is a *logical* process – especially an abstraction which has been given a body . . . The Bopp school would have said that *langage* is an application of *langue* . . . It is now clear that there is a permanent reciprocity and that the linguistic system has its sole application and sole origin in acts of language . . . while language (*langage*) is both the application and the constant generator of the language system (*langue*), the act of language is to *langue* both its application and its sole origin. (*ELG*: 129)

This way of thinking highlights Saussure's distance from the logical-grammatical paradigm in language science, just as his theory of a 'linguistics of *langue*' fits perfectly within this paradigm – and was to occupy, after his death, a founding, redefining place. This epistemological distance is counterbalanced by one of Saussure's most misunderstood propositions, the one that deals with the object of linguistics. For Saussure, linguistics in no way came down to a mere linguistics of *langue*, whatever Bally and Sechehaye may have said. '. . . *la linguistique a pour unique et véritable objet la langue envisagée en elle-même et pour elle-même*' ('*the true and unique object of linguistics is language studied in and for itself*', *CGL*-B: 232). The last sentence of the *Cours* is not only apocryphal, but it is also completely contradictory.

Linguistics of *langue* and linguistics of *parole*

As unfortunate as it is famous, this final sentence is nowhere to be found in the Geneva lecture which is the source of the last chapter of the *Cours*, nor elsewhere in Saussure's lectures or writings. Bally and Sechehaye chose to round off the 1916 volume with a phrase drawn from Bopp (1816), thus giving a last-minute logical–grammatical turn of the screw to the book they fashioned and wrote up from the lectures of their teacher and colleague. Saussure, in fact, as we shall see, held a quite opposite view. The regression towards the German scholar's viewpoint is even more striking for today's reader who has access to the critique of Bopp's idea of language in the writings discovered in 1996. Not only did Bally and Sechehaye falsify Saussure's thought, they did so using a phrase and an author to whom he was opposed.

Let us look at the texts. A handwritten preparatory note for the 1908–9 course, *Here for the first time question of two Linguistics*, has already shown that while Saussure's courses at this time covered only the linguistics of *langue*, the omission of a linguistics of *parole* was the result of a deliberate decision taken for didactic reasons. But the most interesting text is the plan drawn up by Saussure for his last course in general linguistics. This plan, which represents the final known synthesis of his thought and which has all the appearances of being an epistemological programme, was outlined to his students at the beginning of the second lecture of the 1910–11 session on 4 November 1910: '1. Languages. 2. *Langue*. 3. The ability and the practice of language in the individual' (*CLG/E* 1.24.122).

Before the end of his lecture, he returned to his plan, commenting on it as follows:

I. The language of humanity as a whole is manifested in an infinite variety of languages . . .The linguist has no choice but to begin by studying languages . . .
II. The linguist will retain from the study and observation of these languages all that appears essential and universal . . . The collection of abstractions which results will be *langue* . . .
III. The individual remains to be dealt with, because only the common effort of all individuals can create general phenomena. It is thus necessary to take a look at the working of language in the individual. This practice of a social product does not come under what we have defined [for section II]. This third chapter then reveals the individual inner workings which must ultimately, in one way or another, have

an effect on the general product, but which must not be confused, in analysis, with that general product which is separate from the product itself. (*CLG*/E 1.65.429.5)

As can be seen, this comment, expanding on the third part of the plan, faithfully reflects Saussure's criticism of Bopp. In May 1911 Saussure confirmed his plan, as he was busy working on its second part. This is the point where, having distinguished the two possible uses of '*parole*', on one hand the production of sound and on the other the 'individual combinations, and sentences, dependent on the individual's will and coming from individual thought' (*CLG*/E 1.57.356.5), he states that while *langue* and *parole* imply each other's existence, they each require a separate theory (*CLG*/E 1.56.342.5) and asserts:

Within [this] area of inquiry, then, [one] part covers the study of the individual aspect of language, of *parole* . . . ; this is *the study of parole* and a second part [the] aspect of language which is a social convention and situated beyond the individual's will, *the study of langue* . . . These two paths cannot be followed simultaneously, they must be followed separately or exclusively. As we said, it is the study of *langue* which we have chosen to pursue [in this section of the course]. The question is whether to retain the name linguistics for both things together or to limit it to the study of *langue*? We need a linguistics of *langue* and a linguistics of *parole*. (*CLG*/E 1.56.342.5)

The text of the *Cours* which corresponds to this passage once again falsifies Saussure's words, as it occurs in the middle of a chapter which confusingly merges the two notions of '*parole*', one referring to the phonatory aspect of the *factum loquendi* and the other referring to its semantic dimension. In the students' notebooks, these two notions are actually distinguished. Bally and Sechehaye write that the study of *parole* may *à la rigueur* be considered part of linguistics; *CLG*: 38 (*CLG*/E 1.56–8.340–67.AM2–5). This *à la rigueur* was an addition to the students' notes, fed into the text on the editors' own initiative, and makes the whole thing mean exactly the opposite of the original sentence. As an afterthought, to justify their modification and lend credence to their final sentence in the *Cours*, they immediately inserted another remark of their own, unattested in any source: 'It [*parole*] must not be confused with linguistics proper, which takes as its sole object the language system.'

Far from excluding a linguistics of *parole*, as the *Cours* suggests, what Saussure upheld throughout the 1910–11 lecture series was that a linguistics of *langue* must be developed based on new epistemological principles which should in turn become the cornerstone for other approaches to language:

The best way to judge [the *parole* part of *langage*] is to take up position in *langue* from the start. (*CLG*/E 1.55.339.5)

Giving priority to *langue* (by taking it as the centre and starting point) provides the best platform for approaching other elements of language, and situating them accurately. (*CLG*/E 1.515.328.1) we have found in *langue* . . . a definable object, separable from acts of language as a whole. (*CLG*/E 1.42.252.5)

The activity of the speaking subject should be studied within a collection of disciplines whose position in linguistics depends on their relationship with *langue*. (*CLG*/E 1.42.252.5)

The coexistence of two complementary fields which are central to language science is once again explicitly attested to in Saussure's last manuscript text on general linguistics, dating from 1912. Ironically, it is the rough draft of a report on the creation of Bally's chair. It contains the same argument, still linked to a refusal of the 'misunderstanding which initially dogged the school founded by F. Bopp' (cf. *ELG*: 129):

The only problem, if I may say so, is the vast extent of linguistics. And the fact that it is made up of two parts: one which is closer to *langue*, a passive deposit, the other which is closer to *parole*, an active force and the true origin of the phenomena subsequently perceptible in the other half of *langage*. (*ELG*: 273)

If any doubts remained about the ultimate accommodation of objects drawn from two fields requiring differing methodological approaches, an equation found in the new manuscripts discovered in 1996 ('Semiology = morphology, grammar, syntax, synonymy, rhetoric, stylistics, lexicology etc., all of which are inseparable' (*ELG*: 45; see also *ELG*: 175–6) shows both how the 'meaning' part of language requires a multiplicity of *inseparable* descriptive approaches and how the science named *semiology*, a term here synonymous with *linguistic semiology* or *linguistics*, is, for Saussure, capable of encompassing this multiplicity of approaches, as long as these approaches fall within the two fields defined as the study of *langue* and the study of *parole*. Moreover, the equation cited above appears to link the dyad linguistics of *langue* / linguistics of *parole* to the age-old dyad of language science described by François Rastier, with logic and grammar on one side (i.e non-contextual, non-compositional theories and descriptions of meaning), and rhetoric and hermeneutics on the other (i.e. contextual and non-exclusive compositional theories and descriptions of meaning).

Given the distorting effect of the published *Cours* and the fact that the Geneva lectures, in which the third part of the 1910–11 series might have been developed, were cut short by Saussure's death, it was highly unlikely that his project for a linguistics of *parole* would be recognised, and of course in the *CLG* it was not. The *Cours*, particularly in the area of semantics, was read as purely logical–grammatical treaty which excluded the interpretative field.

The Saussurean concept of *langue* has been and continues to be adopted and championed by many linguists. The concept of *parole* has had less success.

Indeed, the word 'discourse' seems to have replaced Saussure's 'parole', though this has not led to the founding of a 'discourse linguistics' on epistemological grounds as solid as the Saussurean dyad might have suggested. What is striking is the way the term *discours* (discourse), which occurs repeatedly in the original texts with a meaning close to that of *parole*, was, with a few rare exceptions, censored out by Bally and Sechehaye. This excision helped the 'editors' to bury a *linguistique de la parole* once and for all. And the term *discours* was not the only victim; the editors' tampering made the structured relationship between *langue* and discourse, i.e. *langue* and *parole*, practically unrecognisable. We shall now look at these neglected occurrences of 'discourse', and the question Saussure repeatedly poses concerning them, in much more detail than is suggested by the 1916 volume.

'Discourse' as an object in Saussure's general linguistics

Here we are taking into account only references to *discours* in the sense of utterances in use, whether simple noun (*le discours*), adjective (*discursif*), or nominalised adjective (*le discursif*). Not only are these terms, which occur in the lectures on general linguistics as well in as Saussure's writings, generally ignored by the editors of the *Cours*, but so too are whole passages in which they occur. (Just two occurrences of *discours* can be found – *CLG*: 170–1.) The following brief presentation of these occurrences and passages, classified according to the theoretical arguments in which they feature, reveals a little-known facet of Saussurean thought and terminology. (We shall see that Saussure uses the terms *discours*, *discursif*, *langue discursive*, *langage discursif* in a similar way, and that all these expressions refer to *parole*.)

Firstly, the concept of 'discourse' is characterised by its exclusion, which is motivated by the need to qualify certain theoretical implications of taking *langue* as the object of study. In other words, the concept of 'discourse' as a clear synonym for 'parole' makes its appearance as one of the terms of the well-known opposition between *langue* and *parole*, the specific intention of which is to characterise *langue*.

A. The concept of 'discourse' is used with the intention of providing a general qualification of *langue* as a 'mental treasure'. This is the case in the *Notes Item*:

> the sentence exists only in *parole*, in discursive *langue*, whereas the word is a living unit independent of any discourse in the mental store. (*CLG*/E 2.40.3323.1)
>
> (The word) can be considered as having existed 'before' the sentence . . . Moreover, *even in discourse*, there are countless instances where one must say a *word*, and not a sentence (all the vocatives, for one). (*CLG*/E 2.41.3323.3)

B. The concept of 'discourse' is used *to qualify abstract units of langue*. For example, in the second course in general linguistics:

> *horse* and *horses* are also the same word, but to afford them unity, one must take neither *horse* nor *horses*, but a 'middle' encompassing both, an abstraction; one must take as a unit something which is not directly given but which results from a mental operation. But there is an alternative. By taking continuity of discourse as a basis, the word is seen as one section in a chain of discourse and not in signification as a whole (these are in fact the two possible ways of approaching the word). However, an immediate objection to this is the impossibility of so dividing up a foreign language. This implies that these units are not inherent in the acoustic matter, but must correspond to an idea. So, does taking the word as a piece of discourse give us concrete units? Let us go back to *horses* or even *month*, and consider *the month of December* phonologically, as if produced by a phonograph, without interruption (as in a Greek inscription, a true 'photograph' of discourse). (*CLG*/E 1.238–9.1730–1.2)

Or again in the course on Greek and Latin etymology of 1911–12:

> *Word* can have two meanings: (a) *concrete word* = word as it figures in discourse, therefore free of variation: ρητορσι, λεγετε; (b) *abstract word* = abstract unit formed by a collection of inflected, changing forms . . . (*CLG*/E 1.424.2800.3)

C. The concept of 'discourse' is used to qualify an associative link in *langue*. In the second course in general linguistics, for instance, to contrast the syntagmatic and associative fields, Saussure describes association as 'everything that we do not bring, but that we could bring, to discourse' (*CLG*/E 1.296.2087.2). In this same course the associative links are again repeatedly defined by opposition to syntagmatic production in discourse:

> In this mass of elements which we have a virtual, but effective access to, in this store, we make associations: each element evokes another; all that is similar and dissimilar in whatever way gathers around each word, otherwise the working of *langue* would be ruled out. A declension table is therefore a group of associations. This group may assert its unity, but this unity is absent from discourse. In such unity one thing varies and another does not vary; this is common to any associative group. In the name of what does not vary, *dominus* is associated with *domino*, and what does vary makes for differing units in this group:
> désireux} one common element [the suffix -*eux*]
> soucieux} one different element. [the root of each word]
> malheureux}
> These associative groups, then, are purely mental, and have no simultaneous existence in discourse. (*CLG*/E 1.289.2038–9.2)

> We speak only in syntagms, and the probable mechanism is that we have these types of syntagms in our head, and when we wish to use them, we call on the associative group. When we use the *lego-metha* group for instance, the fact that we use the exact

form *lego-metha* implies our possessing various associative groups containing *lego-* and *metha*, bracketed above and below in a sort of bubble. The continual opposition between members of the group, which insures the choice of an element at the moment of discourse, is merely change due to partial variation. (*CLG*/E 1.294.2070–1.2)

D. The concept of 'discourse' is used to qualify the way *langue* evolves, and is evoked in the chapter on analogy. In the first lecture course:

One cannot understand an analogical creation without a clear idea of the act of *parole*. The new form *I find* is not created in a meeting of learned lexicographers. If this form is to enter *langue*,
1. someone must have improvised it, and
2. improvised it in *parole*, in discourse, and the same goes for anyone coming across it subsequently. (*CLG*/E 1.384.2561–2.2)

On this occasion a definition of *parole* is given through *discours*: 'Anything brought to the lips by the needs of discourse and by a specific operation is *parole*' (*CLG*/E 1.383.2560.2). And the *Nouvelles Notes Item* contains the following reference to the concept of 'discourse' in the chapter on analogy and other linguistic change:

All changes, be they phonetic, or grammatical (analogical) occur in discourse alone. At no time does the individual go through the inner mental store of *langue,* and detachedly create new forms intended for 'insertion' into a coming discourse. All innovation comes in improvisation, in the act of speaking (and thence enters either the listener's, or the speaker's, personal store), but its production therefore concerns discursive language. (*ELG*: 95)

Only occurrences of *discours* and its derivatives, in passages not reproduced in the *Cours*, have been dealt with here. Occurrences of *parole*, whether taken up in the *Cours* or not, which confirm the synonymy of *discours* and *parole*, have not been considered. The other concept of 'discourse' is given a definition, although it is always a joint definition of *langue* and *discours*. Such a definition is to be found in the two first courses in general linguistics. In the first course:

there are two orders of things, corresponding to two types of relationship. On one side there is a discursive order, which must be the order of each unit within the sentence or the word: *signi-fer*. The other is the intuitive order, that of association (like *signifer*, *fero*, etc.), which is not in the linear system, but which may be readily understood by the mind. (*CLG*/E 1.278.1985.2)

And in the second:

by using a little leeway, we can bring together the words *discursive* and *intuitive*. [These terms] are, like *syntagmatic* and *associative*, opposed, if *intuitive* = *intuieri*, to contemplate platonically [*var*: abstractly], without being used in discourse. (*CLG*/E 1.292.2061.AM2/3)

Two functions concerning language . . . are also active within us. On one side an inner store which is the equivalent of the structured space (*casier*) of memory. Here we find the so-called storehouse which is one of the two places. Everything which may become active in the second place is arranged in this store.

And the second place is discourse, the chain of *parole*. Our perspective may be that of one or other of these places where words are found. In each case we will be faced with groups, but groups of a completely different type:

Store (storehouse): *associative* units; groups in the sense of *families*. Discourse (chain): discursive units (i.e. which are produced in discourse); groups in the sense of *syntagms*. (*CLG*/E 1.281.1998.2)

As can be seen, these bipolar definitions respectively incorporate *langue* into an associative order (posed elsewhere as that of having *in absentia* value) and discourse into a syntagmatic order (that of *in praesentia* value). We will come back to this.

Finally, in a handwritten text, discourse receives a more specific assessment, although its relationship to *langue* is still prioritised:

Langue is only created with a view to discourse, but what separates discourse from *langue*, or what determines the moment when *langue comes into action as discourse*? (*ELG*: 277)

Langue provides a range of ready-made concepts (i.e. equipped with a linguistic form) such as *ox*, *lake*, *sky*, *strong*, *red*, *sad*, *five*, *split*, *see*. At what moment, drawing on what operation, on what *interaction*, on what conditions, will these concepts form DISCOURSE?

The ideas evoked by a series of words, however rich they may be, will never indicate to a human individual that another individual, by saying them, wishes to communicate a meaning. What is necessary to convey the idea that someone wishes to communicate a meaning to us, using the countless terms at their disposal in *langue*? This is the same question as 'What is *discourse*?', and at first sight the answer is simple: discourse consists, even basically and in ways we do not understand, of asserting a link between two concepts which are provided with a linguistic form, whereas *langue* merely brings into being isolated concepts, which must be brought into association with one another so that the meaning of thought may be expressed. (Trans. of *ELG*: 277)

These fragments lead to the following conclusion: the omission of the term *discourse*, and of the passages on the ideas relating to this term, combined to obscure an important aspect of Saussure's conception of language. Clearly, this omission and that of the plan for a linguistics of *parole* are mutually strengthened. But it does not mean that because his theory has been deprived of one of its constituent parts that Saussure sees this part as comprising a fully developed theory in its own right. Quite the opposite: he confesses that the definition of 'discourse', though 'simple at first sight', is that of an element of language which creates relationships 'in ways of which we are unaware'. What then can be the status, in terms of linguistic value for example, of this idea of 'discourse' or 'parole', contrasted as it is with the 'mental store' of langue, and based on the premise of syntagmatic relationships? To try to answer these questions, we shall examine another aspect of Saussurean thought whose transposition into the *CLG* and subsequent reception were also highly problematic, that is the question of these same *rapports syntagmatiques* (syntagmatic relationships) themselves. (See also *ELG*: 258 where the properties of discourse are discussed.)

Between *langue* and *parole*: *in praesentia* relationships and syntax

The *Cours*, then, misrepresents Saussure's position on questions of discourse or a linguistics of *parole* by omission and by distortion. Its presentation of the theory of value also covers up an important problem that, as Saussure recognised, the same theory leaves partially unresolved: the problem of the semiological representation of syntax, linked to the more general problem of *in praesentia* relationships. We know that Saussure saw the incorporation of *parole* (or discourse) into the syntagmatic dimension as being within the framework of a theory of value. Yet a comparison of the *Cours* and the last lectures of June 1911 shows that his editors played down the crucial importance of syntagmatic relationships for the notion of value, just as they covered up Saussure's crystal clear admissions of the problematic nature of this aspect of his theory. For instance, Bally and Sechehaye's *Cours* faithfully reproduces a question from the lecture given on 27 June: 'The sentence is the best example of the syntagm. But it belongs to *parole*, not *langue*; does it not follow that the syntagm [belongs to] is part of *parole*?' (*CLG*: 172), and then inserts a reply of their own devising that the reader naturally attributes to Saussure: 'We do not think so' ('Nous ne le pensons pas'; *CLG*: 172). Yet all the students' notes indicate that the lecturer, in point of fact, indicated that this question was not easy to resolve, and perhaps because of a failure to define the notion of 'sentence' refused to answer this question in the negative (*CLG*/E 1.284.2013.5).

On the next page, the editors of the *Cours* now seem to reflect the linguist's doubts by rounding off the paragraph on syntagmatic relations with the words 'It has to be recognised that in the area of syntax, there is no clear distinction between linguistic phenomena, which bear the stamp of collective usage, and speech phenomena, which depend on individual freedom.' Yet what Saussure says, in the passage they are transposing, is formulated quite differently – with much greater accuracy and more radically:

Individual use of the code of *langue* throws up a question. Only in syntax, essentially, do we find a certain haziness between what is given [*var.* fixed] in *langue* and what is left to individual initiative. The limits are difficult to make out. It has to be said that in the field of syntax, a social fact and an individual fact, a putting into practice and a fixed association, get blended rather, end up more or less mixed up. Admittedly, on this one boundary a separation between *langue* and *parole* can be questioned. (*CLG*/E 1.285/286.2022.AM4/5)

The phrasing is more accurate: here only *syntax* is considered a difficult area, with respect to the previously established equivalence of *discourse* (or *parole*) = *syntagmatic relationships*. The phrasing is more radical, sticking unswervingly to the *langue/parole* opposition laid out so far – in other words incorporated into the opposition associative relationships/syntagmatic relationships, which are thrown into question by syntax. It follows from Saussure's admission that 'a separation between langue and parole can be questioned' that the equivalence he established previously, *discourse* = *syntagmatic relationships* could be replaced by *langue* = *(associative relationships)* + *(syntax)*, which implies *discourse* = *(syntagmatic relationships)* – *(syntax)*; or even, in equivalent terms: *langue* = *(in absentia value)* + *(syntax)*, which implies *discourse* = *(in praesentia value)* – *(syntax)*. Such an amendment to the theory of value would mean that syntax could be taken as presenting *in praesentia* relationships of a special type, '*in praesentia* relationships in *langue*' (or, as belonging to a system of logical–grammatical rules governing *in praesentia* places and positions). These relationships would be describable in a synchronic linguistics of *langue*, designed in fact as a 'general grammar', in a scheme Saussure repeatedly asserts and defends.

This problem with the semiological status of syntax in fact forms part of a larger question concerning *in praesentia* relationships in general, with which the theory of value is confronted. This is highlighted by the final Geneva lectures on general linguistics, which are largely given over to the internal dyad of linguistic value, and in which it is reasserted that value is the product of '*in absentia* relationships' and '*in praesentia* relationships' – in other words that, as far as value is concerned, 'these two types of relationships cannot be merged, they are both active' (*CLG*/E 1.283.2005.2). This position is argued at greater length than previously in the 1910–11 course, but it was nonetheless clearly stated in the teaching of 1908–9:

The two groupings, in space and in the mind (by family), are both active . . . This is true as far as one likes and in both directions; value will always be a result of family grouping and syntagmatic grouping . . . These two perpetual oppositions, of syntagms and of all that differs (what we do not bring to discourse, but could) – it is on these two oppositions, ways of being similar to, or different from something else, that the working of a state of *langue* depends. (*CLG*/E 1.295–7.2080/2087.2)

As far back as 1907 what Saussure calls these 'two types of value', the dyad they form and the way they interact, lead him to conclude his analysis of value in *in absentia* relationships with the words: 'Note that we took the unit of the word as our starting point quite arbitrarily; we could just as easily have chosen the unit of the sentence' (*CLG*/E 1.295.2081.2).

The principle of 'two types of value' does figure in the *Cours*, although it is seriously undermined by the organisation and the approach adopted in the last five chapters of part 2. Paying little heed to the 1910–11 lecture plan, Bally and Sechehaye reinterpret it in a way that gives a quite different slant to the original; their presentation of *in praesentia* relationships manages only to leave the reader in a state of uncertainty. Without a long and detailed analysis of how the original material was reorganised for the *Cours*, it can be noted that part 2, chapter 4, entitled 'Linguistic value', the chapter to which one quite naturally refers for a definition of 'value', deals only with *in absentia* value. The 'editors' moreover skewed the reception of Saussure's thought on this point by making up and inserting texts of their own, in this and the following chapter (which deals with *in praesentia* relationships), texts which indiscriminately lump together syntagmatic production and *parole*. These apocryphal passages are inserted at the expense of Saussure's original ones, which raised doubts about the distinction between *langue* and *parole* with respect to *in praesentia* value, doubts which, as we have seen, tend to bring the question of *in praesentia* value into the ambit of *langue*.

Even in his last lectures, Saussure gave no clear position on this theoretical point, as the students' notes of 27 and 30 June 1911 amply show. But why did Bally and Sechehaye choose to erase his doubts? Or, worse, not to transcribe faithfully assertions such as these:

> In any case, even in the phenomena of *langue*, there are syntagms. (*CLG*/E 1.284.2016.5)

> [On the categories *langue* and *parole*] . . . The second type of relationship [*in praesentia* relationships] seems to be a phenomenon of *parole*. Our reply is this: up to a certain point, *langue* itself has such relationships. (*CLG*/E 1.284.2011.2)

By answering in Saussure's place questions which he himself left unresolved, the editors of the *Cours* prepared the ground for a rejection of Saussurean thought by numerous researchers many decades later, whereas a more faithful presentation would have allowed them to find, in the presumed incompleteness of Saussure's speculative theories, a heuristic basis for carrying forward their enquiries into the philosophy and science of meaning. It is to be hoped that the editing of new material will still provide this opportunity and will draw people's attention back to the original texts. I shall therefore conclude by trying to set out just how Saussurean 'semiology', if it is to contribute to a science of meaning in language, needs to be completed, and how this might be done by pursuing the lines of inquiry that in its unfinished state it has left open.

A doubly incomplete semantics

The Saussurean principles that this chapter has tried to reconstruct were, as we have said, partially obscured by the 1916 'vulgate'. Its editors must have found them too unwieldy, or even, who knows, too heterodox in the light of the scientific climate of the early twentieth century for them to be reflected in the *Cours*. These relatively little-known principles, then, correspond to a definition of 'meaning' in the widest possible sense, and to a definition of science which can facilitate the study of this object 'meaning' – a science one can call *semantics*, regardless of the way the term was defined before Saussure or has been subsequently. My hypothesis here is this: the position taken by Saussure, which is not based on firm, established conceptions, but rather preliminary thoughts, hedged about with expressions of uncertainty, follows on from the doubly incomplete nature of the epistemological programme of what Saussure called *semiology* or *linguistic semiology*, or in other words, from the doubly incomplete nature of his conception of meaning. Furthermore, the two elements which constitute this incompleteness should be kept carefully apart.

The first way in which it is incomplete, of which the doubts about questions of syntax and *in praesentia* relationships are symptomatic, concerns the field of the linguistics of *langue*; to put it simply, Saussure's semiotic theory of *langue* is incomplete. While the nature of the linguistic sign in *in absentia* relationships is dwelt on at length, with Saussure asserting that some *in praesentia* relationships are also phenomena belonging to *langue*, he gives no properly semiotic theory of these *in praesentia* relationships. Neither their workings (i.e. the nature of the *in praesentia* semiotic phenomenon), nor the various types to which they might belong, nor their interaction with *in absentia* relationships, are appropriately theorised. Their description, in the chapter of the third course, which in the *Cours* is entitled 'Place de la langue dans les faits de langage', is particularly short and vague, taking up one sentence, and coming in the wake of a lengthy theoretical discussion of *in absentia* relationships: 'Another type will be needed, an act of co-ordination [*var.* an ability to co-ordinate] which occurs whenever several verbal images are received' (*CLG*/E 1.39.212.2/5).

It would appear that as a result of this glaring absence of a theoretical foundation, with a *philosophical* or *semiotic* grounding, on an undeniably major point of his thought, a definition apparently as crucial and essential as that of the nature of syntax (a phenomenon of *langue* or of *parole*?), remains unresolved for Saussure. Yet if his notion of 'syntagmatics', designed to incorporate 'syntax', is taken at the appropriate level of abstraction, it is capable both of bringing into one category the various components of linguistic meaning produced by a linear chain of signifiers, and of being applied to other systems of signs, thus providing the beginnings of a semiotic theory. The same is true of the notion of 'value', which is associated with two types of relationship. Saussure gives every impression that despite having the will to produce a semiotic framework, he had not investigated the purely philosophical aspect of linguistic enquiry into language in *in praesentia* relationships, an aspect which he specifically stated to be necessary and which he studied in depth in the context of *in absentia* relationships. It therefore seems that it is through philosophy that Saussure's incomplete semiotics of *langue* may be completed. I would add that Saussure's thought can usefully draw here on the work of Charles Sanders Peirce, along with the advantages that certain advances in twentieth-century linguistics may bring to Peirce's work.

The second way in which Saussure's epistemological programme is incomplete is connected with another 'semiotics' (presuming that this name can be applied, within language, outside the field of a linguistics of *langue*): Saussurean theory does not indicate to which 'semiotics' a linguistics of *parole* (which we can call a semiotics of *parole*) belongs, having established that it may be incorporated into 'semiotics' by virtue of the fact that it is strictly complementary to a semiotics of *langue*. This theory, which complements Saussure's theory of *langue*, was probably held back by the very incompleteness of Saussure's theory of *langue* itself; it follows that Saussure's theory of *parole* remains at the level of a pious wish with practically no theoretical underpinning. To be sure, this requires a very different conception of semiotic phenomena, which would necessarily take on a 'pragmatic' value (in the philosophical sense of the word). In this analysis of meaning, semiotic phenomena can no longer rest wholly on the logical–grammatical tradition of language science, but instead have to incorporate its rhetorical and hermeneutic traditions. Showing the way to such a 'semiotics of *parole*' will of course require much more than Saussure's theory of the *in absentia* sign, but neither is Peirce's wider-ranging semiotics sufficient, remaining as it does in the purely logical–grammatical tradition. What is above all necessary here is to break with the building block approach of the logical–grammatical tradition, to dispose of the idea that linguistic analysis has to be underpinned by traditional logic, and replace it with a different sort of 'logic' which can take account of an assessment of pragmatic value, observe the interaction between this and a semiotics of *langue*, and finally give shape to a semiotics of interpretation. This deconstruction of the traditional view of logic, when it is forced to deal with ordinary language and forge a 'new logic' based on that language, is a project whose main proponent would be the 'later' Wittgenstein, in his *Philosophical Investigations*.

(This chapter was translated by Matthew Pires and Carol Sanders. References to *CLG*/E are given as follows: volume, page, segment, column; e.g. 1.42.252.5 = vol. 1, p. 42, segment 252, col. 5.)

14 Saussure, linguistic theory and philosophy of science

Christopher Norris

This chapter will look at various aspects of the relationship between Saussurean linguistics and debates within twentieth-century philosophy of science. After all it was Saussure's chief aim to see linguistics placed on a properly 'scientific' footing, that is, to reconfigure the field in accordance with certain well-defined principles that would constitute an adequate, rigorously theorised account of language and signifying systems in general. The first task was to elaborate those various distinctions that would henceforth provide its working methodology, among them the cardinal oppositions between *langue* and *parole*, synchrony and diachrony, the paradigmatic and the syntagmatic, and the orders of signifier and signified. This would open the way to a structuralist account that left no room for naive (pre-scientific) ideas about the one-to-one 'correspondence' between words and ideas or words and objects. Rather it would show how the systematic character of language – its differential structures of sound and sense – can only be described by means of a theory which itself breaks free of such delusive 'commonsense' beliefs and acquires the full range of conceptual resources whereby to articulate its own grasp of those same signifying structures.

Implicit here is something very like the doctrine of 'semantic ascent' from material to formal or from linguistic to metalinguistic levels of description that characterised much philosophy of language, logic and science in the largely anglophone tradition of logical empiricism. Thus for any given first-order (e.g. natural) language one can devise a corresponding second-order (formal) language that translates it into more perspicuous or logically regimented terms (Carnap, 1959 and 1967; Tarski, 1956; also Ayer, 1959). What these philosophers sought to achieve was a precise notation for the physical sciences that would be subject to none of the inherent liabilities – the vagueness, ambiguity, or lack of referential precision – that were thought to vitiate natural language. I should not wish to press too hard on this comparison between Saussurean linguistics and the logical empiricist programme (very much in the tradition of Frege and Russell) for reforming language so as to meet the requirements of science and philosophy of science. (See especially Frege, 1952 and Russell, 1956.) No doubt Saussure had very different priorities – those of a linguist rather than a formal logician – in proposing a structural–synchronic theory that would grant linguistics its rightful place among the exact sciences through a process of conceptual abstraction from the otherwise inchoate mass of data produced by earlier methods. Still the comparison is useful up to a point since it brings out one salient feature of Saussurean linguistics, namely the idea that any discipline which aspires to scientific status must establish a certain formal distance between itself and its object of study, or – more precisely – between that object as construed on the linguist's theoretical terms and that object in its 'natural', spontaneous, or everyday-occurrent condition.

Such was indeed the paradigm of 'scientific' method that found voice in a number of representative texts from that period (see Ungar in this volume). Hence also Louis Althusser's claim for a 'symptomatic' reading of the Marxian text that would sharply distinguish the elements of immature (i.e. humanist or Hegelian) thought from the Marxist science whose advent required a decisive epistemological break, both in Marx's own thinking at a certain stage of development and in that of his critical exegetes (Althusser, 1969; Althusser and Balibar, 1970). This structuralist 'moment' has been much discussed by the commentators – whether in a spirit of nostalgic reminiscence or self-distancing irony – so no more will be said about it here (see Benton, 1984; Elliott, 1987). Sufficient to remark that it soon gave rise to a reactive post-structuralist trend which emphatically rejected any notion that theory could achieve such a standpoint of conceptual mastery outside and above the various first-order languages, discourses, or signifying practices that formed its objects of enquiry. (See for instance – from a range of viewpoints – Attridge, Bennington and Young, 1987; Barthes, 1975; Belsey, 1980; Harari, 1980; Harland, 1987; Young, 1981.)

This reaction is clearly visible in Barthes's later essays where he looks back on that moment as a passing dream – an illusion of scientific method – that had once (not so long ago) captured his mind (Barthes, 1977b). It is likewise evident in the switch of allegiance undergone by many theorists on the cultural left with the waning of Althusserian Marxism after the events of 1968 and the shift toward a more sceptical stance whose chief inspiration was Foucault's Nietzschean 'genealogy' of power-knowledge (Foucault, 1977a). For if one thing characterised this turn against theory in the high structuralist mode it was surely the insistence that all such ideas of methodological rigour, conceptual grasp, 'scientific' warrant, and so forth, were merely a product of the will-to-power disguised behind a rhetoric of pure, disinterested seeking-after-truth.

Of course there was much debate at the time as to whether the prefix 'post' in 'post-structuralism' should be taken as marking a radical break with those same concepts and categories or whether, on a somewhat more conservative construal, it should be taken to signify a further stage in the working-out of their implications for a new way of thinking about language, subjectivity, and the human sciences in general. This ambivalence was especially pronounced in the psychoanalytic writings of Jacques Lacan whose literalist approach to the texts of Freud and Saussure went along with a fondness for mathematical, topological and other 'scientific' analogies but whose treatment of them was – to say the least – characterised by a certain degree of associative whimsy. Thus Lacan's notoriously obscure style can be seen as resulting in part from a certain (albeit highly idiosyncratic) idea of scientific method, and in part from his determination to escape the Cartesian 'tyranny of lucidity' (Lacan, 1977; Roudinesco, 1990). Indeed, this is just the kind of ambivalence one might expect in a thinker much drawn to the structuralist distinction between language and metalanguage (here: the first-order discourse of the analysand and the second-order discourse of the analyst), yet one whose reading of the Freudian text brought him out implacably opposed to any notion of the talking cure – like that of the despised (mostly US) ego psychologists – as aimed toward restoring the subject to a state of lucid self-knowledge or psychic equilibrium (Horney, 1967; also Hale, 1995; Hughes, 1975; Kurzweil, 1989).[1] Moreover, as post-structuralists often remark, this dichotomy finds a curious parallel in Saussure's devotion to the project of establishing theoretical linguistics on a properly scientific basis while at the same time pursuing his strange, obsessive and (by most standards) very unscientific researches into the cryptograms or patterns of occult significance which he believed to constitute the subtext of much Greek and Latin poetry (Starobinski, 1971). Whence the idea – attractive to some – that structuralism was itself just a dream of method whose commitment to the Apollinian ideals of science, clarity and conceptual rigour was always threatened by this Dionysiac (Nietzschean–Freudian) return of the repressed.

What interests me here is the extent to which Saussurean linguistics likewise lay open to the kinds of charge brought against it – or 'abusive extrapolations' from it, in Perry Anderson's mordant phrase – by post-structuralists, Foucauldians and others with an ideological axe to grind (Anderson, 1983). In both cases a certain conception of scientific method proved susceptible to readings of a radically contextualist, holistic, or paradigm-relativist character which were strongly at odds with its original aims and ambitions. Thus Quine's assault on the two last 'dogmas' of empiricism was expressly intended as a ground-clearing exercise which would rid philosophy of its grandiose pretensions (like that of formulating logical ground-rules for the conduct of scientific thought) and restore it to a decently scaled-down conception of its role *vis-à-vis* the physical sciences. Such was the programme of 'naturalised epistemology' – the attempt to explain how such a 'meager input' of sensory stimuli could somehow give rise to such a 'torrential output' of statements, hypotheses, theories, etc. – which Quine saw as the sole legitimate task for philosophy of science. This could be achieved by restricting itself to the kinds of empirical observation that avoided any recourse to 'mentalist' talk about concepts, ideas, or 'laws of thought', and which instead made do with a behaviourist account of what subjects (whether scientists or 'native informants') were prompted to say in some given situation or when exposed to some given range of incoming physical stimuli. In short, Quine considered that the natural sciences were our best source of guidance in such matters and that his was an approach that respected the priority of scientific method over anything that philosophers had yet come up with in the way of formalised (metalinguistic) rules or methodical constraints (Quine, 1969).

Nevertheless it was largely on the basis of Quine's radical-empiricist programme that Thomas Kuhn went on to propose his more wholesale version of the paradigm-relativist case, that is, his idea that scientists living before and after some drastic paradigm change must be thought of as somehow quite literally 'living in different worlds' (Kuhn, 1970). Thus where Aristotle 'saw' a swinging stone as an instance of matter seeking out its proper place in the order of the elements, Galileo 'saw' a case of gravitationally induced pendular motion. In which case, according to Kuhn, it is only in the dubious wisdom of retrospect that we can take Galileo to have got things right and treat Aristotle's theories as false on account of their referring to non-existent substances or properties. Rather we should make every effort to suspend this old-fashioned Whiggish view of things and acknowledge that such theories are strictly 'incommensurable' in so far as they involve a whole different range of object-terms, predicates and putative 'laws of nature'. Like Foucault in his early 'archaeological' period Kuhn takes it that the process of theory change is one that comes about through such deep-laid and radical shifts of overall perspective that any talk of progress in our scientific knowledge of the world can only be a product of selective hindsight or naively 'presentist' bias.

On the face of it there is little in common between Quine's hard-headed empiricist outlook and Kuhn's often rather nebulous treatment of these issues, in particular – as critics have pointed out – his equivocal usage of the term 'paradigm' in various contexts of argument. (See Horwich, 1993.) Yet it is clear from Kuhn's methodological postscript to the second edition of his book that he takes Quine's radical empiricist approach as providing a source and justification for his own line of approach. Thus it allows him to answer his realist critics by acknowledging that scientists on either side of a major paradigm shift can properly be said to see 'the same thing' at least to the extent that their retinas are subject to an identical range of physical stimuli when confronted with a swinging stone. However this yields no ground to the realist when it comes to explaining why one such theory – Galileo on gravity – might actually possess a superior claim to have *got things right* in descriptive, theoretical, or causal-explanatory terms. For radical empiricism of the Quine–Kuhn variety starts so far back or at such an early stage in the process of sensory cognition that it places no effective (rational) constraint on the range of interpretations or physical theories that can lay equal claim to empirical warrant.

This is why Kuhn's Postscript (Kuhn, 1970) makes a cardinal point of endorsing the Quinean distinction between bare, uninterpreted physical 'stimuli' on the one hand and 'perceptions' (even the most basic, commonsense, or pre-scientific perceptions) on the other. Thus, according to Kuhn, one can plausibly maintain that the stimuli hold firm across variant paradigms or theoretical frameworks while nonetheless arguing that what scientists *perceive* – and thereafter work up into observation-statements, theories, or explanatory conjectures – will vary according to the aspect (or paradigm) under which those stimuli have to be brought before they can achieve any kind of articulate expression. And from here it is no great distance to Richard Rorty's claim that when 'Galileo saw the moons of Jupiter through his telescope . . . the impact on his retina was "hard" in the relevant sense', even though – when it came to interpreting the data – his idea of them as 'shattering the crystalline spheres once and for all' has to be treated (epistemologically speaking) as strictly on a par with that of his orthodox opponents, i.e. that they were 'merely one more anomaly which had somehow to be worked into a more or less Aristotelian cosmology' (Rorty, 1991: 81). To suppose otherwise – that Galileo got it right – is just the kind of error that realists typically make when they ignore the cardinal point that 'causation is not under a description, but explanation is'. Or again, as Rorty more picturesquely puts it: 'To say that we must have respect for unmediated causal forces is pointless. It is like saying that the blank must have respect for the impressed die. The blank has no choice, neither do we' (Rorty, 1991: 81).

The contrast could scarcely be greater – or so it might seem – between this chapter of developments in the wake of 'old-style' logical empiricism and the kinds of thinking about science and philosophy of science that emerged as a consequence of Saussure's revolution in theoretical linguistics. After all, his proposals were squarely based on a rationalist conception of method which invoked the precedent of Descartes and the Port Royal grammarians, and whose chief philosophical premise was its claim that the study of language could be rendered truly 'scientific' only through a sharp conceptual break with the loosely empirical or fact-gathering procedures of earlier (i.e. nineteenth-century) philological enquiry.[2] Such a break was precisely that which occurred – in Saussure's estimation and that of his disciples – at the point where his own thinking underwent the decisive transformation from a diachronic (historically oriented) approach concerned with reconstructing the development of various languages to a structural–synchronic approach that acknowledged the need to reconstitute its object of study (*la langue*) in properly scientific terms. Hence Saussure's insistence (in chapter 3 of the *Cours de linguistique générale*) that a true science of language can come into being only by observing this rigorous distinction between diachrony and synchrony, along with the various other distinctions – chiefly that between *parole* and *langue* – that follow from this cardinal precept.

Moreover, this approach is prerequisite for a science of linguistics that achieves the break with naive (empirically based) conceptions of what constitutes a 'fact' about language. That is to say, it makes possible the moment of conceptual abstraction whereby notions of the sign as a 'positive' correlation between discrete units of sound and sense give way to a grasp of linguistic 'values' as nowhere embodied in particular (phonetic or semantic) features of language, but rather as consisting in the structural economy of differences 'without positive terms'. The Port Royal grammarians may have gone wrong in all sorts of ways, but on this point at least they were on the right track and conceptually more in command of their subject than those later comparative grammarians who lapsed into vaguely diachronic and naively positivist or empiricist ways of thinking. Thus the Port Royal grammar 'attempts to describe the state of the French language under Louis XIV and to set out the relevant system of values'. In so doing, furthermore, 'it has no need to make reference to the French of the Middle Ages; it keeps strictly to the horizontal axis and never departs from it'. To this extent, Saussure maintains, 'its basis is less objectionable and its object of study better defined than is the case for the kind of linguistics inaugurated by Bopp' (*CGL*-H: 82). Where the latter falls short of scientific rigour and method is in attempting 'to cover an inadequately defined area, never knowing exactly where it is going. It has a foot in each camp, having failed to distinguish clearly between states and sequences.'

These passages have been cited at length since they bring out very clearly the extent of Saussure's allegiance to a rationalist conception of scientific method which stresses the need for linguistics to conceptualise its 'object of study' in such a way as to establish its own credentials as a discipline uniquely equipped to establish what counts as a relevant 'fact' within its own (properly specified) object-domain. It might well be argued that Saussure and Quine are representatives of two radically opposed traditions – French rationalism and anglophone empiricism – whose origins may be traced to a decisive parting-of-the-ways during the seventeenth century and whose differences have lately re-emerged with particular sharpness in such fields as linguistics, philosophy of language and epistemology of science. From which it follows, on the orthodox account, that any comparison between developments after Quine and Saussure – for instance, between the Kuhnian–Rortian idea of radical paradigm-relativism and the Foucauldian/post-structuralist conception of knowledge as a product of various historically shifting 'discourses' – is one that blithely ignores their provenance in two quite distinct (indeed antagonistic) lines of intellectual descent. And this despite the plain assertions of some, Rorty included, that their 'post-philosophical' view of these matters has its source and inspiration at least as much in the kinds of (mainly French) thinking that emerged in response to the claims of classic high structuralism as in developments nearer home, among them Quine's deconstruction of the two last dogmas of old-style logical empiricism (Rorty, 1991). Still the view persists that such promiscuous claims are merely the result of a failure (or a mischievous refusal) to respect the salient differences of background history and standards of competent debate.

It is not the intention here – far from it – to advocate a Rortian view of those standards as so many irksome and pointless constraints on the freedom of philosophers to devise new language-games or inventive modes of self-description that will show them (at last) to have broken the hold of such antiquated ways of thinking. What is more to the point, in this context, is the fact that Rorty can plausibly exploit a major blind-spot in the standard (doxographic) account of the 'two traditions', namely the idea of empiricism and rationalism as involving such radically divergent theories of language, truth and logic that any comparison between them – other than for purely contrastive purposes – must be historically and philosophically off the track. However this grossly simplified conception is one that has been challenged by recent scholars and which hardly stands up to close examination on either side of the supposed great rift. (See for instance Norris, 2000.) One result has been the growing awareness – due to the researches of Hans Aarsleff and others – that certain of Saussure's most 'distinctive' doctrines, such as that of the arbitrary (i.e. non-natural) relationship between signifier and signified, were in fact just as crucial to the thinking of seventeenth-century British empiricists like Locke, quite apart from their common source in the debate first broached in Plato's *Cratylus* (Aarsleff, 1967). Another is the recognition that Saussure's much-vaunted 'break' with the historically based methods of nineteenth-century philology was less complete than some commentators (not to mention Saussure himself) are on occasion disposed to maintain. Thus the *Cours* contains a great mass of philological evidence – grounded in his own earlier work and that of the comparative grammarians – concerning such 'strictly' diachronic or evolutionary aspects of language as phonetic shifts, semantic change, the disappearance of inflections, dialectal variation, interlingual exchange, geographical diffusion, the issue of linguistic identity across time, and so forth. Maybe it is the case, as Saussure constantly stresses, that 'the need to take account of the passage of time gives rise to special problems in linguistics and forces us to choose between two radically different approaches' (*CGL*-H: 79). All the same it is far from clear – even making due allowance for the well-known problems that confronted his earliest and subsequent editors – that Saussure ever managed to respect this rigorously formulated axiom of choice.

That is to say, the above-mentioned passages of philological interest are by no means so sharply or hermetically sealed off from his reflections on language in its structural–synchronic aspect as one might otherwise be led to believe by Saussure's more programmatic statements. Rather they often tend to crop up at just the point where he is making some vigorous claim about the need to keep these approaches firmly apart – and to respect the priority of a synchronic over a diachronic perspective – but where diachrony proves a vital source of evidence and thereby places a certain theoretical strain on this whole line of approach. Thus, for instance:

> Sound change . . . is a source of linguistic disturbance. Wherever it does not give rise to alternations, it contributes towards loosening the grammatical connexions which link words together. It increases the sum total of linguistic forms to no purpose. The linguistic mechanism becomes obscure and complicated inasmuch as linguistic irregularities produced by sound change take precedence over forms grouped under general types; in other words, inasmuch as what is absolutely arbitrary takes precedence over what is only relatively arbitrary. (*CGL*-H: 160)

Now of course Saussure is here talking about sound change as a 'disturbance' or a 'complicating' factor in so far as it affects the communicative power and efficiency of language as a social phenomenon, or an ideally economical means of conveying information between speaker and listener. Still it is hard to ignore the further suggestion that it complicates his own theoretical programme by introducing an element of 'absolute arbitrariness' – the irruption of sheerly random or unmotivated diachronic change – into the otherwise smooth functioning of a model (*la langue*) that can find no room for such chaotic phenomena.

Hence Saussure's quickness to insist that any threat this may pose is more than adequately counterbalanced by the workings of linguistic 'analogy', that is to say, by the 'regular imitation of a model' which acts as a brake upon phonetic drift or other such internal disturbances, and is best viewed as 'responsible for all the normal modifications of the external aspect of words which are not due to sound change' (*CGL*-H: 160). Hence also – a point routinely ignored by post-structuralist exponents of Saussure – his insistence on the strictly 'limited' or 'relative' degree of arbitrariness that can be seen to characterise language as soon as one moves from the paradigmatic to the syntagmatic axis, or from the purely differential (unmotivated) order of relationship that obtains between discrete signifying elements and the order of rational motivation which obtains when those elements enter into forms of successive or linear combination. Thus there is no reason why the terms *dix* and *neuf* should signify those particular numerical values but there is every reason – arithmetically speaking – why the expression *dix-neuf* should take that particular syntagmatic form (*CGL*-H: 131). What acts as a restriction on the 'arbitrary' character of language is precisely the requirement (again harking back to the Port Royal grammarians and the legacy of Cartesian rationalism) that linguistic structure should articulate the structures of logical thought. For if 'the entire linguistic system is founded upon the irrational principle that the sign is arbitrary', nevertheless applied 'without restriction, this principle would lead to utter chaos' (*CGL*-H: 131). However, Saussure continues, 'the mind succeeds in introducing a principle of order and regularity into certain areas of the mass of signs', such that – through the presence of 'relative motivation' – the linguist is able to 'study this mechanism as a way of imposing a limitation upon what is arbitrary' (*CGL*-H: 131). In which case the most basic precept of structural–synchronic linguistics is one that has to be given up – or at any rate subject to drastic restrictions – as soon as the focus of attention switches from language conceived *in abstracto* as a system of differential values (phonetic and semantic) 'without positive terms' to language as a means of communication between rationally motivated subjects.

This is why, as Saussure also remarks, the concept of 'difference' must likewise be kept within strict methodological limits, since 'it is suitable only for comparisons between sound patterns (e.g. *père* vs. *mère*), or between ideas (e.g. "father" vs. "mother")' (*CGL*-H: 119). Where it doesn't apply – although (again) post-structuralists are prone to ignore this point – is where the sign is considered as a whole, that is, as a motivated (non-arbitrary) conjunction of *signifiant* and *signifié* which alone makes it possible for language-users to communicate on a basis of shared understanding. Thus: 'The moment we consider the sign as a whole, we encounter something which is positive in its own domain' (*CGL*-H: 119). And again: although signifier and signified 'are each, in isolation, purely differential and negative', nevertheless 'their combination is a fact of a positive nature'. Otherwise – lacking such resources – language would indeed be a 'chaos' and not so much a *system* of differences 'without positive terms' as an undifferentiated flux devoid of intelligible structure or meaning. Yet this clearly raises problems for Saussure's claim – hammered home in numerous passages of the *Cours* – that if linguistics is ever to achieve the status of a genuine science then it must start out from the cardinal distinction between synchrony and diachrony. And it is then hard to see what room there is for compromise on those other related distinctions (*langue* vs. *parole*, the paradigmatic vs. the syntagmatic, language as a system of negative differential values vs. language as a chain of 'positive', 'rational' or 'motivated' signifying elements) where in each case methodological priority attaches to the antecedent term.

My point in all this – to recapitulate – is that Saussure's conception of linguistic science is one that encounters certain problems on its own theoretical terrain, problems that find their mirror-image in the aftermath of logical empiricism from Quine to Kuhn. With Saussure this difficulty arises chiefly from the conflict in his thinking between a realist conviction that linguistic science has to do with a well-defined object of study that should somehow – ideally – be set apart from all 'external' considerations like those of history, cultural influence, political events, conquest, colonisation, etc., and on the other hand his equally firm insistence that such an object is constituted *in and by* the very act of theoretical abstraction that brings it into being. Indeed it is precisely the principled exclusion of all those extraneous factors which leads Saussure to define *la langue* in terms that would make it a product of conceptual definition rather than a 'real' (independently existing) object of empirical study in anything like the sense envisaged by the neogrammarians and other positivistically inclined students of language. As Roy Harris succinctly puts it:

> A science of language, as far as Saussure was concerned, had to deal with linguistic *realia*, not metalinguistic fictions. And yet, as he was forced to admit, linguistics – unlike other sciences – had no object of study 'given in advance': in linguistics 'it is the viewpoint adopted which creates the object'. It is the tension between this admission and the claim to scientific status which is felt throughout the *Cours*. (Harris, 1988b: 126)

That is to say, Saussure's rationalist conception of scientific method could be seen as fixing an insuperable gulf between language (*langue*) as an object-in-thought 'created' through an act of theoretical abstraction and whatever 'reality' language might have as a set of 'positive facts' grounded in the actual process of linguistic communication. In the case of logical empiricism the problem was that most strikingly diagnosed by Quine when he showed how a more radically empiricist approach could be seen to undermine the analytic/synthetic dualism and, along with it, the 'metalinguistic' approach that presupposed the possibility of sharply distinguishing first-order empirical or observation-statements from higher-level theories, 'truths of reason', or self-evident logical axioms (Quine, 1961). Thus despite their deriving from two very different traditions of thought these programmes can be seen as each falling prey to internal conflicts of aim and method which neither was effectively able to resolve.

Moreover, as I have argued, both gave rise to a series of reactive developments which might seem worlds apart in philosophical terms but whose underlying kinship is not hard to discern. Thus – to take perhaps the most dramatic example – the 'eclipse' of Althusserian Marxism came about (most commentators agree) through its failed attempt to transpose the concepts and categories of Saussurean structural linguistics to the domain of political theory, and hence to articulate a Marxist 'science' whose claim to such status rested on its notion of a rigorous (theoretically elaborated) break between the 'real object' and the 'object-in-thought' (Benton, 1984; Elliott, 1987; Thompson, 1978). As the problems with this theory came into view – not least its commitment to what looked very like a full-blown idealist epistemology – so there emerged a post-structuralist and Foucault-inspired movement of thought which rejected the idea of 'scientific' method as anything more than a transient product of the various, historically shifting 'discourses' that defined its objects of enquiry from one period to the next. This Foucauldian approach to the 'archaeology' of scientific knowledge was one that also took its bearings from Saussurean linguistics, despite Foucault's well-known protestation that he had never been a 'structuralist' in any – to him – recognisable sense of the term (Foucault, 1970, 1972). That is to say, it is an approach which takes for granted Saussure's claim that linguistics has no object of study 'given in advance', since in this field of investigation 'it is the viewpoint adopted which creates the object'. Where Foucault most decidedly departs from Saussure is in extending the doctrine beyond linguistics – which Saussure considered unique in this respect – and applying it to a wide range of other sciences whose objects are likewise thought of as constituted in and by their various modes of discursive representation.

I shall not here pursue the many problems that result from this extreme version of the paradigm-relativist or linguistic-constructivist view, among them its total inability to account for our knowledge of the growth of scientific knowledge, or – what amounts to the same thing – its failure to provide any rational account of scientific theory change. (See Norris, 1994, 1996, 1997a.) My two chief points in this context are first the extent to which Foucault's ultra-sceptical approach derives from certain problems and unresolved tensions in Saussure's linguistic theory, and second the marked kinship it bears to the Kuhnian account of paradigm change as a process that likewise eludes explanation in progressive or rational-reconstructive terms (Kuhn, 1970).

Of course there are differences that need to be noted, among them Kuhn's allowance that 'normal' science typically proceeds through various kinds of problem-solving activity on the part of scientists working within some well-established paradigm, and that it is only during periods of pre-revolutionary 'crisis' that the problems (or conflicting solutions) pile up to the point of creating a major upheaval. But this difference will appear less crucial when set against Kuhn's treatment of such problems, even those of the 'normal' variety, as themselves taking rise only within some particular paradigm and as finding (or failing to find) a 'solution' only in paradigm-relative terms. And again, the very distinction – as Kuhn draws it – between 'normal' and 'revolutionary' science is one that must appear highly problematic when taken in conjunction with his Quinean (radical-empiricist) claim for the holistic character of scientific knowledge and the lack of any ultimate, i.e. other than pragmatic, grounds for holding a particular statement true given the range of possible variant construals.

Saussure himself was very firm in maintaining that most other sciences differed crucially in this respect, i.e. that they required no such rigorous conceptual break between their real objects of enquiry (or the order of 'positive facts' concerning them) and those objects as defined or specified through an act of theoretical abstraction which rendered them amenable to systematic study in the structural–synchronic mode. The relevant passage is worth citing at length since it brings out very clearly the extent of Saussure's disagreement with those later thinkers (like Foucault) who chose to disregard his cautionary statements on this point. What sets linguistics apart from 'most other sciences' is their *not* being faced with the need to opt decisively for one or the other (diachronic or synchronic) approach. Thus:

> In astronomy, it is observed that in the course of time heavenly bodies undergo considerable changes. But astronomy has not on that account been obliged to split into two separate disciplines. Geology is constantly concerned with the reconstruction of chronological sequences. But when it concentrates on examining fixed states of the earth's crust, that is not considered to be a quite separate object of study. There is a descriptive science of law and a history of law: but no one contrasts the one with the other. The political history of nations is intrinsically concerned with successions of events in time. None the less, when a historian describes the society of a particular period, one does not feel that this ceases to be history. The science of political institutions, on the other hand, is essentially descriptive: but occasionally it may deal with historical questions, and that in no way compromises its unity as a science. (*CGL*-H: 79)

With regard to each of these disciplines it would be forcing the issue – a misconceived theoretical issue – to require, as a criterion of 'scientific' rigour, that they adopt *either* a structural–synchronic *or* a diachronic (historical–developmental) perspective on their object-domain. Rather they can get along perfectly well by respecting that distinction – as practising astronomers or geologists do when they also take an interest in the history of their subject – but not raising it into a high point of methodological precept. For the result of transposing this precept from the science of structural linguistics (where it properly applies) to 'most other sciences' (where it has no legitimate place) is to set up a false and misleading idea of scientific method, one which effectively blocks the way to any adequate, historically informed grasp of present-day developments and what led up to them. The most striking exception, Saussure argues, is the study of economics where the theorist is 'forced to recognise this duality' since 'political economy and economic history constitute two clearly distinguishable disciplines belonging to one and the same science'.

Saussure's firm insistence on this point stands in marked contrast to Foucault's approach in *Les mots et les choses* where the sheer historical sweep and interdisciplinary breadth of coverage results from his failing – or programmatically refusing – to acknowledge any such distinction. Thus Foucault sets out to provide a kind of historical-comparative purview of various fields of knowledge – ranging from philosophy, linguistics and economics (or the earlier 'analysis of wealth') to natural history, geology, botany and the emergent life-sciences – which treats them diachronically as characterised by periods of long-term relative stability that on occasion give way to sudden ruptures or 'epistemological breaks'. (See Gutting, 1989.) However he also adopts a structural–synchronic perspective in so far as those breaks are conceived as occurring through a drastic reconfiguration of knowledge, one whose effects are registered in every field, and whose advent is no more explainable in terms of the history and development of these sciences than the state of *la langue* at some given point in time can be explained by 'extraneous' (diachronic) facts about the influence of geographical, cultural, or socio-political factors.

Indeed there are several striking features of Foucault's 'archaeological' approach that are perhaps best seen as resulting from his large-scale transposition of Saussure's structural–synchronic paradigm to the comparative analysis of episodes and developments in the history of thought. One, as noted above, is its holistic tendency to level the distinction between the various formal, natural, or social and human sciences, treating them all pretty much on a par as products of an overarching order of discourse (or 'episteme') which manifests its own internal economy of signifying contrasts and relationships. Thus – unlike Saussure – Foucault pays no regard to those salient differences of method and procedure that mark off (say) geology, chemistry and the life-sciences on the one hand from anthropology, philology and historiography on the other. Still less is he inclined to make the kind of sharp distinction that Saussure draws between economic history and political economy, since on Foucault's account any such distinction is itself just a transient product of some period-specific 'discourse' or *episteme* wherein it happens to play a significant role. Hence his well-known dismissive reference to Marxist economic theory as belonging to the same discourse as that of earlier political economists like Smith and Ricardo, whatever the apparent (merely surface) indications of a Marxist 'revolution' in thought (Foucault, 1970). Another, closely related consequence is Foucault's doctrine of paradigm-incommensurability, that is to say, his ultra-Kuhnian idea that whenever there *is* a such a radical theory change or 'epistemological break' then it will surely bring about so massive an upheaval across the entire field of knowledge as to rule out any possibility of meaningful comparison between paradigms. Along with this goes the clear implication that such changes occur for no assignable reason – least of all any reason having to do with scientific progress or the advancement of knowledge – since their occurrence is a matter of seismic shifts at a level of discourse beyond the scope of rational accountability.

What is involved here is a twofold extrapolation from Saussure's model of language (*langue*) as an object of structural–synchronic analysis. Firstly it involves treating entire 'discourses' (whether in the natural or the human sciences) as likewise subject to the 'arbitrary' link between signifier and signified, and hence as providing no possible basis for comparative judgements of truth or falsehood with regard to their various object-terms and predicates. In which case – reverting to Kuhn's well-known example – we can have no reason for thinking that Galileo's perception of gravitationally induced pendular movement was based on a sounder grasp of the scientific principles concerned than Aristotle's perception of matter seeking out its rightful place in the cosmic order of the elements. Rather we should see that such terms acquire their sense *and* their reference through the function they perform in some particular 'discourse' (or Quinean 'fabric' of beliefs-held-true at any given time), with the result that inter-paradigm translation or comparison becomes altogether impossible.

Whence the second of Foucault's extrapolations from Saussure, namely the idea that paradigm-change must be treated as wholly 'unmotivated', i.e. as permitting no rational account of those drastic changes in the structural economy of knowledge which mark an 'epistemological break' whose effects extend across the entire field of discursive representation.

We have seen already that Saussure is adamant in restricting the precept of non-motivation to language considered under its structural–synchronic aspect, or as a system of purely differential relationships and contrasts 'without positive terms'. No doubt it is the case, he writes, that 'the sign always to some extent eludes control by the will, whether of the individual or of society: that is its essential nature, even though it may be by no means obvious at first sight' (*CGL*-H: 16). However, once analysis proceeds beyond that level – once it takes account of morphological, grammatical, or larger-scale units of discourse – then this principle has to be abandoned or any rate qualified in various degrees. Thus:

> The fundamental principle of the arbitrary nature of the linguistic sign does not prevent us from distinguishing in any language between what is intrinsically arbitrary – that is, unmotivated – and what is only relatively arbitrary. Not all signs are absolutely arbitrary. In some cases, there are factors which allow us to recognise different degrees of arbitrariness, although never to discard the notion completely. *The sign may be motivated to a certain extent*. (*CGL*-H: 130)

This restriction on the claims of arbitrariness and non-motivation would presumably apply all the more when it comes to assessing scientific theories, that is to say, instances where the 'discourse' in question (more precisely: its object-terms, predicates, inferential procedures, and so forth) has been subject to intensive critical scrutiny and testing against the evidence. Thus Donald Davidson has pointed out that the argument for radical paradigm-incommensurability advanced by thinkers like Quine, Kuhn, Whorf and Foucault is one that collapses into manifest self-contradiction as soon as they purport to *describe* or to *specify* the particular differences concerned (Davidson, 1984; also Whorf, 1956). Indeed, it is a case that looks plausible only if one focuses on lexical or semantic issues (such as the famous non-translatability of certain colour-terms across languages) and ignores the whole range of other linguistic functions – among them various logico-syntactic devices for conjunction, disjunction, anaphora, pronominal reference, and so forth – in the absence of which no language could communicate effectively. Hence Davidson's proposal that philosophers should take more account of these invariant or trans-paradigm structures and thereby provide a more adequate basis for grasping the conditions of success (or failure) in translation.

Yet this is not to say that some version of paradigm-incommensurability is sure to result if one adopts a primarily semantic or a lexical approach to the topic of scientific theory change. Hartry Field has offered convincing evidence to the contrary by examining usages of 'mass' in Newtonian and Einsteinian physics and showing that this term can be held to exhibit a sufficient (albeit partial) continuity of reference just so long as one distinguishes various specific senses ('absolute mass', 'inertial mass', and 'rest-mass') in various, likewise specifiable contexts (Field, 1973, 1974, 1975). His main target here is the Quine–Kuhn doctrine of semantic holism and its presumptive consequence, i.e. the claim that such radically different scientific theories cannot be subject to comparative evaluation since we cannot be sure that any given term will have carried across with any part of its meaning unaffected by the intervening paradigm change. However his argument also applies to Foucault's quasi-Saussurean conception of knowledge as a shifting field of discursive representations which allows for no stability of sense or reference beyond the appeal to some favoured paradigm, discourse, or conceptual scheme by which to impose order on the otherwise inchoate signifying flux.

It is important to stress how remote this is from anything sanctioned by Saussure since his concepts of 'arbitrariness' and the 'non-motivated' character of the linguistic sign have enjoyed (or suffered) such widespread exposure in the work of theorists who pay little heed to his precise formulations of what constitutes linguistics as a genuine science and what sets it apart from other sciences. Here it is worth noting the affinity that exists between Saussure's project and certain developments in French philosophy of science during the early-to-mid twentieth century which likewise emphasised the notion of a break – a *coupure epistemologique* – with hitherto dominant methods, procedures, or 'commonsense' modes of thought. Gaston Bachelard and his student Georges Canguilhem were the two chief advocates of this approach, the one having devoted himself chiefly to issues in the history and philosophy of physics, the other to biology and the life-sciences. (See especially Bachelard, 1938, 1949, 1953, 1968, 1984; Canguilhem, 1968, 1969, 1978, 1988; also Lafrance, 1987; Lecourt, 1975; Tiles, 1984.) Its distinctive character – described by Bachelard in qualified Cartesian terms as a kind of *rationalisme appliqué* – is one that bears detailed comparison with Saussure's linguistic theory even though it first emerged some two decades after Saussure delivered his landmark series of lecture courses in Geneva (1907–11). So if indeed there is any 'influence' here it is one that runs from Saussure to Bachelard rather than Saussure's having drawn his conception of an adequate linguistic theory from Bachelard's epistemo-critical researches into the history of science. More likely both projects took rise from the conjuncture of a lingering Cartesian tradition – the idea of truths self-evident to reason through an exercise of disciplined investigative thought – with a strong countervailing tendency (most explicit in Bachelard) to deny the existence of such *a priori* truths and conceptualise science as a constant process of revising, challenging, or radically transforming our received habits of belief.

Thus Bachelard envisaged the process of theory change as one that began with an intuitive (often metaphorical) moment of insight but which then continued through stages of 'rectification and critique' to the point where science achieved the break with such 'naively' analogical, image-based, or anthropomorphic residues. Among his examples was that of the tetrahedral structure of the carbon atom, an image whose usefulness or heuristic yield Bachelard was far from denying, but which marked (as he saw it) a transitional phase in the progress toward more adequate conceptions of subatomic structure. That is to say, such advances might take rise from a state of intuitive 'reverie' which enabled thinking to perceive some resemblance – some metaphorical point of comparison – between disparate realms of knowledge or experience (Bachelard, 1971). However this moment had to be left behind since, in Bachelard's words, the 'danger of immediate metaphors in the formation of the scientific spirit is that they are not always passing images; they push toward an autonomous kind of thought; they tend to completion and fulfilment in the domain of the image' (Bachelard, 1938: 81).[3]

Hence Bachelard's distinction between *histoire sanctionée* and *histoire perimée*, the first having to do with currently accepted theories or those that have played some contributory role in the development of scientific knowledge to date, the second with theories that have proved invalid but which might be of interest from a merely historical or socio-cultural viewpoint. Thus, for instance, Black's 'caloric' theory of heat is one that no longer enjoys scientific credence but which none the less can be seen to have marked a crucial stage in the development of a theory (that of specific heat) which does have a place in our current-best scientific thinking. (See also Psillos, 1999.) Bachelard's insistence on maintaining this distinction is a clear sign that he opposes any paradigm-relativist approach – such as those of Foucault or Kuhn – that would level the difference between these two kinds of history by removing any grounds for rational comparison across major episodes of theory change. It is likewise sharply at odds with the 'principle of parity' advanced by strong sociologists of knowledge and by practitioners of science-studies as a sub-branch of cultural criticism. This principle holds that one should treat *every* theory – whatever its credentials in current scientific estimation – on exactly the same terms, i.e. with a view to its motivating interests, ideological values, or socio-cultural conditions of emergence (Barnes, 1985; Bloor, 1976; Collins, 1985). In other words it rejects the distinction between 'context of discovery' and 'context of justification' which formed a main plank in the logical-empiricist programme and which most philosophers of science (Bachelard included) have endorsed – albeit from differing theoretical perspectives – as the only way to make rational sense of scientific progress to date (Reichenbach, 1938). That Saussure considered this a vital distinction in the context of linguistic methodology is evident from passages throughout the *Cours*. Thus it figures crucially in his comparison between language and games like chess where the operative rules (or 'internal' structure of the game) must be treated as 'a system which admits no other order than its own' and where one has to distinguish clearly 'between what is external and what is internal' (*CGL*-H: 23). To this extent Saussure's conception of linguistic science falls square with Bachelard's critical-rationalist approach and comes out firmly opposed to any theory – such as Foucault's archaeology of knowledge – which treats the currency of 'truth' at any given time as a product of those shifting discourses or paradigms that belong to the domain of socio-historical enquiry. From his (Saussure's) point of view this could only amount to a gross confusion of realms, one that misapplies certain strictly synchronic principles (the arbitrary relation between signifier and signified and the unmotivated character of the sign) to a diachronic field of study and which moreover extrapolates wildly on this basis to a whole range of sciences where the linguistic model is of dubious relevance or value. Of course Saussure himself made some large claims for the extension of his theory to a semiological project that would study 'the role of signs as a part of social life', and would thus 'form part of social psychology, and hence of general psychology' (*CLG*-H: 15). Since such a science 'does not yet exist', he concedes, 'one cannot say for certain that it will exist'. All the same, 'it has a right to exist, a place ready for it in advance', in so far as the structural–synchronic approach as applied to issues in theoretical linguistics has been able to specify its operative terms and concepts (*CGL*-H: 15–16). This well-known passage from the *Cours* – much cited by theorists in various disciplines during the heyday of 'classic' high structuralism – is of particular interest for suggesting an analogy between the distribution of signifying values in *la langue* and the configuration of scientific fields according to their various distinctive interests and concerns. Thus in the former case 'each of a set of synonyms like *redouter* ["to dread"], *craindre* ["to fear"], *avoir peur* ["to be afraid"] has its particular value only because they stand in contrast with one another' (*CGL*-H: 114). And in the latter case, correspondingly, the scope that exists for some new theoretical endeavour (such as Saussure's projected general semiology) can be thought of as opened up 'in advance' by its potential yield in relation to other (existing) scientific disciplines. After all, 'if *redouter* did not exist, its content would be shared out among its competitors', just as (it is implied) the object-domain of this semiology-to-come has up to now been shared out – and prevented from attaining scientific autonomy – by the lack of adequate conceptual resources whereby to define and delimit that domain. All of which might be taken to suggest the idea of 'knowledge' at any given time as consisting – very much as Foucault conceives it – in those various transient configurations of 'discourse' that happen to prevail from one *episteme* to the next.

However it is sufficiently clear from Saussure's remarks elsewhere in the *Cours* that he rejects any such paradigm-relativist conception of scientific knowledge and regards it as a wholly unjustified conflation of the 'internal' (i.e. structural–synchronic) and 'external' (diachronic or historico-cultural) modes of enquiry. Thus to the question 'Why is it that semiology is not yet recognised as an autonomous science with its own object of study?' Saussure somewhat testily responds that 'here we go round in a circle', trapped by inadequate notions of 'language' and a fuzzy grasp of what constitutes the object of semiological enquiry. 'On the one hand', he writes, 'nothing is more appropriate than the study of languages to bring out the nature of the semiological problem. But to formulate the problem suitably, it would be necessary to study what a language is in itself; whereas hitherto a language has usually been considered as a function of something else, from other points of view' (*CGL*-H: 16). Here again there is a close affinity with Bachelard's stress on the normative distinction between history of science as a discipline that studies the conditions of emergence for scientific theories and philosophy of science as an epistemo-critical discipline concerned with establishing the point of transition from inadequate (metaphorical, image-based, or anthropomorphic) thinking to adequately theorised scientific knowledge. This distinction works out as closely equivalent to that proposed by the logical empiricists when they required that issues regarding the socio-historical 'context of discovery' not be confused with issues regarding the properly scientific 'context of justification'.

On the other hand it is equally important to note that Bachelard, like Saussure, is very far from dismissing diachronic approaches as 'unscientific' or irrelevant to the purposes of an adequately conceptualised philosophy of science. In Saussure's case the point is best made with respect to his early *Mémoire sur le système primitif des voyelles dans les langues indo-européennes* (published at the age of twenty-one) where, as Harris remarks, 'the word *système* already appears in the title' (Harris, 1988b: 39). The main problem that Saussure addressed here – one that had long preoccupied comparative philologists – was how to reconstruct the vowel system of a pre-literate ancestor language for which no records survived on the basis of later (recorded) languages presumed to have descended from it. (See Morpurgo Davies, this volume.) More specifically, the problem concerned the vowel *a* and the claim that this 'single' vowel must in fact have had two quite distinct pronunciations or phonetic roles in primitive Indo-European since only thus could one explain those later developments. 'Saussure's contribution', Harris writes,

> was to establish the fact that even postulating two different varieties of *a* still did not provide a satisfactory solution to the problem; and he postulated that in addition the language must have had a third sound, a mystery sound which was in certain respects like a vowel, but in certain respects like a consonant. Saussure could not say exactly what this mystery sound sounded like, because he thought that none of the modern European languages had a sound like it. But he claimed that it was possible to describe

the mystery sound in a purely abstract way, by specifying its formal properties. These included its distinctiveness from other vowels and consonants, its capacity to stand alone as a syllable, and its capacity to combine syllabically with vowels. This made it, in Indo-European terms, neither a consonant nor a vowel, and Saussure decided to call it a 'sonant coefficient'. (Harris, 1988b: 39–40)

As Harris further notes, this mode of inference to the best (most rational) explanation on hypothetico-deductive grounds is one that has also characterised various signal episodes in the history of the physical sciences. Thus, for instance, it comes into play when astronomers predict the existence of a 'new' (as-yet unobserved) planet from perturbations in the orbit of neighbouring bodies, or when subatomic physicists postulate some 'new' particle from its effect on other particles in a cloud-chamber or cyclotron (Harman, 1965; Lipton, 1993; Salmon, 1967). That is to say, Saussure's argument here is a striking example of scientific method not only in so far as it prefigures his later emphasis on the need to treat language in a 'formal', 'systematic', or 'purely abstract' way, but also in so far as it adopts the kind of reasoning that had long been applied – often with conspicuous success – in the natural sciences. As concerns Saussure's conjecture, its truth was borne out a half-century later 'with the decipherment of cuneiform Hittite, an Indo-European language which was found to have a phoneme with exactly the properties Saussure had specified for the mystery sound of primitive Indo-European' (Harris, 1988b: 40).

Harris sees this – justifiably enough – as a vindication fully on a par with what astronomers produce when they gain access to more powerful radio-telescopes, or what physicists obtain with the advent of electron microscopes with ever-greater powers of resolution. At the same time it cautions us against too readily accepting the idea that Saussure's thought underwent a 'radical' transformation between the early period of the *Mémoire* and the period of his lectures at Geneva. What emerges very clearly, in Harris's words, 'is Saussure's early insistence that the correct solution, however counterintuitive it might seem and however unprecedented, was to be found by treating the "sound" as defined in relation to a system' (Harris, 1988b: 40). But of course that 'correct solution' was applied to a problem in comparative philology, that is, a problem which arose from the field of historical–developmental research and which could only be resolved in terms appropriate to that field. So it is not so much the case that a truly 'scientific' study of language requires a clean break between the kinds of issue that preoccupied the nineteenth-century philologists and the kinds of issue that Saussure opened up through his structural–synchronic 'revolution'. Rather, it is the case – here as with Bachelard's philosophy of science – that the two approaches can indeed be combined to the benefit of both just so long as one maintains a firm sense of their distinctive methods, priorities and conceptual resources.

So there is reason to conclude that Saussure and Bachelard are united in offering an account of scientific theory change which insists on a careful separation of realms and which thus comes out sharply opposed to wholesale contextualist doctrines like those advanced by Foucault, Kuhn, Rorty and the 'strong' sociologists of knowledge. Where such thinking goes wrong – in Saussure's oft-stated view – is through the twofold error of illicitly importing synchronic concepts and categories into the diachronic study of language, and illicitly transposing diachronic data, methods or assumptions into the domain of structural linguistics. With Bachelard the emphasis typically falls on those confusions that result from eliding the distinction between pre- (or proto-) scientific stages of thought and the advent of a scientific theory, properly so called, which has reached the point of adequate conceptualisation. This is *not* of course to say – in his case any more than Saussure's – that historical concerns are relegated to a merely second-order or subsidiary status. Indeed one distinctive feature of Bachelard's work as compared with mainstream anglophone philosophy of science is the prominence it gives to episodes and developments in the 'context of discovery', even while insisting that interests of this sort, though perfectly legitimate on their own terms, not be allowed to obtrude upon issues in the 'context of justification'. For Saussure likewise, there is absolutely no question of diachronic studies being somehow rendered obsolete or 'pre-scientific' through the advent of a structural–synchronic approach whose claim is to place linguistics on a properly scientific footing. However, as in Bachelard's case, the overriding methodological imperative is to keep these concerns each within its own, theoretically specified domain and thereby prevent them from engendering all manner of hybrid or pseudo-scientific theories and conjectures.

I have suggested that this is just what happened – and with just such unfortunate results – when Saussure's proposal for a general semiology based on the principles of structural linguistics was taken up and applied to areas of study (like the natural sciences) far beyond its specific remit. That remit – to repeat – was conceived by Saussure as involving semiology's eventual assumption of its role as 'part of social psychology, and hence of general psychology'. At this stage of as-yet unachieved but preordained emergence the 'laws which semiology will discover will be laws applicable in linguistics, and linguistics will thus be assigned to a clearly defined place in the field of human knowledge' (*CGL*-H: 15–16). Yet just as linguistics can attain this role only on condition of accepting its place within a larger semiological science, so likewise that science must itself be subject to certain 'clearly defined' disciplinary limits, namely those which assign it a legitimate place within the social sciences and psychology. Thus Saussure is very far from envisaging a stage – that proclaimed by Foucault and by others with dubious Saussurean warrant – when its claims would extend (in principle at least) to every area of the natural as well as the social or human sciences. Much the same applies to Foucault's usage of the term 'epistemological break', a usage that clearly derives (*via* Canguilhem) from Bachelard's account of scientific theory change but which undergoes a notable loss of precision along with its massively extended scope as a covering term for all manner of deep-laid yet ill-defined shifts in the historico-discursive 'order of things'. Saussure makes this point with maximal emphasis when he declares that any 'notion of bringing together facts of such disparate nature would be mere fantasy', since 'in the diachronic perspective one is dealing with phenomena which have no connection with linguistic systems, even though the systems are affected by them' (*CGL*-H: 85). If one catches a distant rumble here it is the sound of whole theories collapsing, among them the Foucauldian archaeology of scientific knowledge and – in a different though related context – those paradigm-relativist approaches (such as Kuhn's) which likewise involve a failure to observe that cardinal distinction. What results in both cases is a radically holistic or contextualist theory wherein the truth-value of any given statement is somehow (impossibly) decided by the relationship it bears to the entire existing body of beliefs-held-true during this or that period of scientific thought. Michael Devitt – writing from a realist viewpoint – has described this chapter of developments as one that places the linguistic cart very firmly before the scientific horse (Devitt, 1986; also Devitt and Sterelny, 1987). That is to say, it involves the strange idea that certain highly contestable theories of meaning or discursive representation should be taken as possessing stronger epistemic warrant than the kinds of causal-realist approach *via* inference to the best explanation which provide the only adequate (i.e. non-miraculist) account of how science has achieved its various advances to date (Boyd, 1984; Putnam, 1975).[4] It is among the great ironies of recent intellectual history that Saussure's meticulous specification of the scope and limits of his project should since have given way to a movement of thought so markedly at odds with his own clearly stated aims and priorities.

15 Saussure's legacy in semiotics

Paul Bouissac

While the abstract notion of 'sign' has been intensively discussed in western philosophy at least since Plato and the Stoics (e.g. Manetti, 1993), a special theoretical domain devoted to the general study of signs did not emerge until the beginning of the twentieth century. As it emancipated itself from its philosophical cradle, this new kind of inquiry became variously known as 'semeiotic', 'semiotic', 'significs' (Peirce, 1977), 'semiology', 'signology' (Saussure, 1916) and 'semiotics' (Sebeok, 1976). What all these terms have in common is that they are coined from the ancient Greek word for 'sign': *sēmeion* and its Latin equivalent *signum*. Their etymology and terminological history is well documented (e.g. Sebeok, 1976; Moeller and Wulff, 1985; Bouissac, 1998).

During the second half of the twentieth century, 'semiotics' was increasingly accepted as referring to the branch of knowledge concerned with formal and empirical research on signs, signification, meaning and communication. It competed with the term 'semiology' (translated from the French *sémiologie*). Both semiotics and semiology are now used with more or less the same broad value, unless specified otherwise, and cover a great variety of schools each with its own theoretical and methodological approach. However, 'semiotics' tends to evoke the writings of American philosopher Charles Sanders Peirce (1839–1914) while 'semiology' sometimes exclusively refers to the traditions derived from the teaching of Swiss linguist Ferdinand de Saussure (1857–1913), principally in the Gallic context. Peirce and Saussure are indeed generally considered as the two initiators of the modern 'science of signs' for which they independently sketched tentative definitions and research blueprints. However, while Peirce was a prolific writer who produced many versions of his theoretical vision, Saussure did not publish any work on this topic in his lifetime and he communicated his ideas exclusively through his teaching and correspondence. These ideas were summarised and edited by two of his colleagues posthumously.

The purpose of this chapter is to review and assess Saussure's legacy in semiotics, the domain of enquiry he helped define under the names of 'sémiologie' or 'signologie' (Saussure, 1974: 48). This task requires a clear understanding of the process by which a thinker's statements eventually are considered by the following generations to have been seminal rather than merely historical. The fact that, after a century, there is still enough interest in Saussure's ideas to justify a book like this one bears witness to his continuing influence. In spite of some efforts made by American writers (e.g. Sebeok, 1989; Deely, 2001) opportunistically to downgrade the Saussurean semiotic stream to the status of a so-called 'minor tradition', as opposed to the supposedly 'major tradition' of semiotics heralded by Peirce, Saussure remains one of the most often mentioned authors in the semiotic literature. Although his ideas remained largely programmatic, they are still perceived today by some as being intellectually engaging, even provocative and controversial (e.g. Gandon 2001). His theoretical speculations on language, and more generally on signs (since he considered languages to be particular subsets of sign systems obeying the laws of all semiological systems), have over the years come to the attention of a sizable constituency of influential researchers in an indirect and staggered manner.

An epistemological vision

It is important to underline at the outset that the status of Saussure as a major fountainhead of semiotics is based on a short paragraph in the *Course in General Linguistics* and on a few remarks scattered throughout the book. This text has been quoted, paraphrased or alluded to countless times. It reads:

> It is therefore possible to conceive of a science *which studies the role of signs as part of social life*. It would form part of social psychology, and hence of general psychology. We shall call it *semiology* (from the Greek *sêmeîon*, 'sign'). It would investigate the nature of signs and the laws governing them. Since it does not yet exist, one cannot say for certain that it will exist. But it has a right to exist, a place ready for it in advance. Linguistics is only one branch of this general science. The laws which semiology will discover will be laws applicable in linguistics, and linguistics will thus be assigned to a clearly defined place in the field of human knowledge. (*CGL*-H: 15–16)

Saussure's efforts, however, were focused on the theoretical status of linguistic signs and did not deal at any significant length with any other semiological systems. While numerous and detailed linguistic examples were provided in his teaching, there is very little both in the course and in the manuscripts concerning this new science beyond some mentions of possible domains of enquiry: 'A language is a system of signs expressing ideas, and hence comparable to writing, the deaf-and-dumb alphabet, symbolic rites, forms of politeness, military signals, and so on. It is simply the most important of such systems' (*CGL*-H: 15).

The epistemological status of this virtual science of signs remains equally vague as Saussure, restricting his own competence to linguistics, leaves it to general psychology to determine the place of semiology in the mapping of future human knowledge: 'It is for the psychologist to determine the exact place of semiology. The linguist's task is to define what makes language a special type of system within the totality of semiological facts' (*CGL*-H: 16).

With respect to the method, Saussure does not attempt to provide any explicit guidelines concerning the analysis of any of the other sign systems listed as potential objects of study for semiology. However, given the fact that he aimed at reaching semiological definitions of 'linguistic facts', his elaborations of the theoretical notion of linguistic signs appeared general enough to provide a basis for extrapolations and generalisations beyond the realm of language. The semiotic legacy of Saussure is thus a series of attempts at meeting his epistemological challenge through applying his linguistic approach to other cultural institutions and productions. The abstractness of the principles proved to be both fertile and perilous. They are still the object of debates and controversies (e.g. Thibault, 1997; Harris, 2000).

Saussure did not have direct disciples who would have undertaken to implement their master's semiological vision. Charles Bally and Albert Sechehaye, the editors of the course, had their own linguistic and semantic agenda. However, special mention should be made of Russian linguist Serjei Karcevski who, in 1907, had emigrated to Switzerland where he attended some of Saussure's courses, and later lectured on Saussurean linguistics, albeit not uncritically, at the Russian Academy of Sciences after his return to Moscow in 1917–19. He is considered to be the main link which conveyed Saussure's oral tradition to Slavic linguists, such as Roman Jakobson, who were to become some of the most active proponents of semiotic research. But those who sought inspiration in Saussure's insights had to figure them out first from students' notes and recollections as well as from their interpretation and reconstruction by the editors of the *Course in General Linguistics*. To make things even worse, most of those who have repeatedly quoted Saussure in the form of aphorisms and diagrams purporting to capture the nature of the (linguistic) sign, principally since the 1960s, have consistently ignored the intellectual and historical context in which Saussure's views took shape, notably during the decade he spent in Paris before he was appointed in 1891 to the University of Geneva, first to teach Comparative Philology, then to take over the chair of General Linguistics only a few years before his death in 1913. Saussure's problematic theoretical positions, which he rather provocatively expressed in three courses between 1907 and 1911 (Saussure, 1993, 1996, 1997) were conceived in the wake of intense philosophical debates focused on the nature of signs, language and meaning (e.g. Schleicher, 1863, Whitney, 1875; Bréal, 1897) toward which Saussure occasionally expressed more or less critical judgements.

In spite of serious attempts at elucidating this intellectual tangle through scholarly historiography (e.g. Aarsleff, 1982; Koerner, 1972, 1973, 1988; Normand, 1978b), the epistemological context in which Saussure elaborated his semiological vision is far from being fully documented and understood, notably with respect to the influence on his thought of late eighteenth-century French philosophy, Husserl's phenomenology, Durkheim and Tarde's sociology, and Darwinism. Later, compared to the published works of his immediate contemporaries, Saussure's aphorisms appeared radically different. The relative novelty of his more abstract and more comprehensive approach was foregrounded by the epigones of the 1960s who construed his pronouncements into the absolute beginning of a new era, a 'rupture épistémologique' that marked the birth of 'sémiologie'. This making of a semiotic hero tended to take Saussure's insights out of their historical context and to frame them in the wider perspective of an eclectic discourse in which several epistemological streams had merged, mainly during the second half of the twentieth century, as we will see below.

New disciplines often tend to seek illustrious predecessors in order to establish their historical legitimacy. Semiotics is no exception. But we must not forget that Saussure himself did not consider that his semiological speculations were yet worthy of being published. His high epistemological standards prevented him from considering that, at the time when he was giving his last lectures, his tentative efforts amounted to a founding treatise on general linguistics, still less on semiology. Rather, he was aware that he was still struggling with the complexity and implications of the linguistic and semantic controversies of the late nineteenth century.

Saussurism at work

Saussure's most definite impact on the development of semiotics is usually traced along three paths: (1) the Slavic stream which first led, in the 1920s and 1930s, to the Prague school of linguistic functionalism and its extra-linguistic applications (e.g. Roman Jakobson), then, in the 1950s, to the Moscow-Tartu school, mostly devoted to the semiotic study of cultures (e.g. Juri Lotman); (2) the Danish school of theoretical linguistics which, in the 1940s, became known as *glossematics* (coined on the model of *mathematics* with the Greek work *glotta* or *glossa* meaning 'tongue') and whose theses were sufficiently abstract to be applicable beyond the realm of language proper (e.g. Louis Hjelmslev); (3) French structuralism, which rediscovered Saussure in the 1950s through the mediation of the first two streams and reconstituted an intellectual genealogy for the semiotic movement of the 1960s and beyond (e.g. Claude Lévi-Strauss, Roland Barthes, Algirdas Julien Greimas).

Naturally, this is a somewhat simplified vision of the way in which Saussure's semiotic legacy can be mapped, because other, more discreet, often critical streams could be identified (e.g. Buyssens, 1943; Prieto, 1966; Malmberg, 1977; Mounin, 1970), and because these various paths diverged, intersected and formed loops in the constraining geopolitical context of the Soviet revolution, the Second World War and the ensuing Cold War. It must be pointed out, however, that explicit references to Saussure as the prime mover are found in the writings of all the main exponents of the schools listed above, although they often endeavoured at the same time to establish the originality of their own approaches with respect to Saussure's assumed lack of theoretical consideration for the social and temporal dimensions of signs, the limits of his seemingly excessive notion of the arbitrariness of the relation between *signifiant* and *signifié*, or his neglect of the speaking subject. These various streams of Saussurean influence have been well documented, although perhaps not enough attention has been paid to the way in which they were selectively transformed through their interaction with other emerging epistemological movements such as Russian Formalism, Functional Structuralism, Cybernetics, Chomskyan linguistics, and Lacanian Freudism.

Russian Formalism is the name given to a group of literary scholars who, at the beginning of the twentieth century, in collaboration with linguists, started to question the historical approach to literature and art, and to focus their attention upon the formal and structural characteristics of artistic works, more particularly poetry. Through the 1920s and 1930s, they produced general theories aimed at accounting for the characteristics of the poetic function of language and for the formal devices through which poems, narratives such as epics and folk tales, and by extension all aesthetic objects were generated. Their foregrounding of formal differences and systemic features was very compatible indeed with Saussurism which thus became associated with research on artistic productions, a domain which Saussure himself apparently did not include in his tentative lists of the systems which should come under the purview of semiology, although his manuscripts on Latin poetics (Starobinski, 1964, 1979 [1971]) and on ancient myths (Avalle, 1973a) betray a deep, almost obsessive interest in the formal properties of literary texts.

Functional Structuralism, also known as the Prague school, which is one of the main sources of twentieth-century semiotics, originated in the late 1920s in Prague where some of the early Russian 'formalists' had emigrated. The influential linguistic theory they formulated was in part inspired by Saussure's ideas, but not uncritically. In particular, they conceptualised phonological systems as being ruled not only by intrinsic laws, but also by the constraints of social communication as well as by psychological considerations under the notable influence of German psychologist Karl Bühler (1879–1963). Formal differences were viewed as functionally motivated by communicative conditions. They also pursued the Russian formalists' agenda by bringing into focus semiotic analyses of literature, the arts and other symbolic artifacts. Their detailed expositions of phonological systems and their systematic use of Saussure's complementary notions such as paradigm/syntagm, *langue/parole* and diachrony/synchrony served to build a commonsensical approach for their more comprehensive semiotic method, thus somewhat trivialising the counterintuitive character of Saussure's insights. This is patent in the model constructed by Jakobson (1960) after an earlier schema of Bühler and with some notions borrowed from information theory, which purports to represent in a diagram the six functions that are necessary for completing all successful acts of linguistic communication. Each function corresponds to a distinct pole or factor of the process through which information is conveyed from an *addresser* (emotive function) to an *addressee* (conative function) by means of a *message* (poetic function) providing that the sender and receiver are in *contact* through a particular channel (phatic function), that they share the same *code* (metalinguistic function) and that they have access to the same *context*, at least in part (referential function).

This pragmatic model obviously concerns acts of speech (*parole*) rather than the linguistic system itself (*langue*). According to it, the relative weight of each function determines the dominant features of particular messages. This model has been widely applied to semiotic descriptions of non-linguistic cultural domains with appropriate adjustments, but can hardly qualify as a Saussurean model in spite of the fact that its promoters implied that '*langue*' and 'code' were equivalent notions as 'message' corresponded to '*parole*'. Such semiotic generalisations, or transmogrifications, of Saussure's linguistic concepts were achieved not only under the influence of functionalism but also by loosely borrowing terms from the vocabulary of cybernetics and the theory of information.

Cybernetics was indeed another epistemological movement which had emerged during the twentieth century in parallel with the developments of formalism and functionalism, and had created a set of conceptual tools which seemed appropriate to refer to both linguistic and non-linguistic semiotic systems. For those who were familiar with Saussure's ideas, the cybernetic notions of system states and system dynamics, state transitions and control, modelling of interacting components and interacting systems, provided an attractive metalanguage. Difference and information could be easily construed as kin concepts, as well as the notions of '*langue*', 'system' and 'code'. The works of Norbert Wiener (e.g.1961 [1948]), Gregory Bateson (e.g. 1967), Ross Ashby (e.g. 1956) and Abraham Moles (e.g. 1958) contributed to the diffusion of cybernetic models among the various schools which then mapped the incipient semiotic movements in Europe and North America while a parallel development was taking place in the Soviet Union. There, Saussure, structuralism and semiotics had indeed become unpalatable for the reigning ideology but the sort of research they inspired was tolerated under the name of cybernetics. These are the roots of the Moscow-Tartu school of semiotics which came to prominence under the leadership of Vjaceslav Ivanov and Juri Lotman who established the concept of cultural 'text' on formal grounds and developed the notions of primary and secondary modelling systems, blending Saussurism and cybernetics in their analysis of various cultural productions (e.g. Lotman 1990).

Chomskyan linguistics captured the epistemological imagination of some semioticians as soon as *Syntactic Structures* (Chomsky, 1957) appeared. Chomsky was adamant that language, more exactly grammatical knowledge, was a universal specific competence defined by an abstract representation of the sentence, that was totally independent from the whole range of communicative behaviour in which semioticians were showing interest. Nevertheless, the metaphor of normative 'deep structures' generating 'surface' phenomena and accounting for their regulated transformations was appealing for a generation which was struggling with Saussure's unfinished agenda. Chomsky's tree diagrams were adapted to whatever domains could be accounted for in terms of assumed rules, such as music and poetry (e.g. Ruwet, 1972), architecture (e.g. Boudon, 1973) or gestures (e.g. Bouissac, 1973). In spite of the misgivings of the promoter of linguistic generativism towards semiotics, some semioticians considered Chomsky – who himself endorsed the idea for a while – as a follower of Saussure in as much as he had provided formal analytical tools to operationally relate abstract structures to concrete manifestations of semiotic phenomena. Their assumption, which was not shared by Chomsky, was the Saussurean idea that linguistics should be considered a part of semiology.

Lacanian Freudism, which impressed a host of minds at about the same time, explicitly endeavoured to reformulate Freud's theory of the unconscious in terms of Saussurean concepts. Claiming that the unconscious was structured as a language, French psychiatrist Jacques Lacan (1901–81), under the influence of Roman Jakobson and Claude Lévi-Strauss, undertook an unwieldy synthesis of Saussure and Freud (Lacan, 1957), creatively translating Freud's theory into Saussure's conceptual idiom as it was perceived through the lenses of the Prague school and French structuralism. In the process, Lacan redefined the notions he was borrowing, coined new terms, and developed a theory aimed at transcending Saussurean semiology through his conceptually retooled psychoanalysis, a direction that was fully exploited by Julia Kristéva (e.g. 1981).

This cursory review shows that Saussure's insights were put to work in a great variety of intellectual contexts. At the same time, Saussurism underwent some kind of hybridising and creolisation. This is most apparent in works that have been dubiously considered to be examples of semiological 'applications' of Saussure's programmatic ideas, and which contributed to launch French structuralism as an intellectual fashion through anthropology and psychoanalysis rather than linguistics.

The semiotic generation of the 1960s

For the semiotic generation of the 1960s, the interface with Saussure's ideas was not in the form of textual erudition and exegesis. It was rather in the context of an overarching epistemological framework in which Saussure occupied the unquestioned position of the founding father to whom regular homage was rendered (Mounin, 1968). The Saussurean doxa, derived from the *Course in General Linguistics*, provided a stock of notions which were taken for granted, with the qualifications introduced by otherwise sympathetic linguists such as Emile Benveniste (1939, 1969) and Roman Jakobson (1966, 1980 [1959]) concerning respectively the role of the subject and the limits of the principle of arbitrariness. While philosopher Maurice Merleau-Ponty (1945) had focused attention on Saussure's views of language, albeit within the horizon of his own phenomenological perspective, anthropologist Claude Lévi-Strauss (1945, 1963 [1958]) was relying more precisely on the structural phonology of Nikolai Trubetzkoy (1939), to which he had been introduced by Jakobson in the 1940s. Later, the folk-tale narratology of Vladimir Propp, first published in Russian in 1928, which had been translated into English (1958), was to be influential for the constructing of structuralist models of myth interpretation (Lévi-Strauss, 1960). As to literary scholar Roland Barthes and lexicologist A. J. Greimas, their direct inspiration was admittedly coming from the writings of the Danish linguist Louis Hjelmslev (1899–1965) whose complex theory had developed during the 1930s in the wake of Saussure's ideas and was offering a more formal and better-articulated system than whatever could be surmised from the *Course in General Linguistics*.

In the first chapter of his *Prolegomena to a Theory of Language* (1961 [1943]), Hjelmslev had acknowledged Saussure as his sole linguistic precursor. Greimas and Barthes, then in Alexandria, became acquainted with Hjelmslev's text when it was first translated into English in 1953 (Greimas, 1986: 42). In his introductory essay to the French translation of Hjelmslev's *Sproget* (1963) [*Le langage* (1966)], Greimas introduces the author as 'the true, perhaps even the sole continuator of Saussure who succeeded in making explicit his insights and giving them a definitive form' (1966: 12). Hjelmslev's concepts and methods, which he had shown to be applicable beyond the linguistic domain to cultural artifacts such as traffic lights or telephone dials (1968 [1943]), became the focus of attention of this new wave of semioticians. By comparison, Saussure's notional dichotomies such as *langue/parole* or *diachronie/synchronie* were then considered to be mere 'heuristic concepts', as Greimas stated a few years later in an interview with Herman Parret (1974: 57).

Barthes's earlier attempt to present a comprehensive view of Saussurism and its Hjelmslevian developments in *Eléments de sémiologie* (1964) had initiated a critical debate by questioning one of the basic tenets of the *Course in General*

Linguistics which contended that linguistics should be a part of semiology. By inverting the relation Barthes started a process which not only – paradoxically – put Saussure in the 'glottocentric' camp, but also eventually was to lead to the undermining of the scientific ambitions of structuralist semiology itself. However, a somewhat cruder view prevailed in a larger population of students and researchers who were prone to assume that semiotics consisted of finding the equivalent of linguistic models in a vast array of cultural productions since Saussurean structuralist linguistics was assumed to be the 'pilot science'.

The semiotic praxis of the 1960s generation consisted of projecting onto any cultural institution and its productions a conceptual grid whose basic categories were derived from the principles of Saussurean linguistics but which also relied on a number of other sources, as was noted above. It was indeed considered that semiotic analysis required supplementary methodological tools, given the paucity of practical instructions found in the *Course in General Linguistics* as far as the construction of a general '*sémiologie*' was concerned. Cultural productions were construed as 'texts' and institutions as '*langues*'. In so doing, these notions were given more formal definitions than they had in poetics and linguistics proper. For instance, 'text' was heuristically construed as a finite set of mutually definable elements organised by a structure which was endowed with relative stability. These elements could be anything from words or objects to architectural or gestural components. The researchers first set for themselves the task of identifying the basic relevant units which corresponded to the 'phonemes' in the sense in which this term was understood in Trubetzkoy's theory of phonology (1936, 1939, 1964).

The researchers typically would endeavour to identify the minimal meaningless units whose absence or presence made a meaningful difference in 'textual' strings or sets of such units. Then, the next task was to take stock of the meaningful units themselves, the 'morphemes' which syntactically combined in larger sets corresponding to the sentences and discourses of language. The transformations taking place within the text itself were accounted for through the descriptive categories of narratology represented by a set of abstract functions. These analytical efforts generated a series of neologisms coined on the model of 'phonemes' and 'morphemes', the ending 'eme' indicating the functionality of the units or their relevance to the system, such as 'mythemes' (units of myths such as semantic relations and narrative or transformative functions arranged in paradigmatic tables), 'gustemes' (units of taste whose combinations actualised particular culinary systems), 'choremes' (units of space, such as centre and periphery, verticality and horizontality, conjunction and disjunction), 'kinemes' (units of movements, which served as a kernel for a host of neologisms which consisted often of simply rewriting all the analytical concepts of linguistics around the radical 'kine', meaning 'movement' in ancient Greek), 'graphemes' (units of writing whose variety was designated by terms borrowed from geometry and topology), 'vestemes' (units of clothing such as those which were used in the descriptive language of fashion and could be semiotically redefined), and the like. These were assumed to be the pertinent units whose various rule-governed combinations (or syntagms) produced respectively the particular meanings of myths, gastronomy, architecture, gesture, writing, fashion and so on.

This analytical process created a number of theoretical and methodological problems. For instance, it was not always clear whether the units which could be abstractly isolated were the equivalent of linguistic phonemes (meaningless units such as /a/, /b/, /l/, /s/) or morphemes (meaningful units such as /blue/, /go/, /-es/, /'s/). A typical debate of the time was bearing upon this issue of duality of patterning or double articulation, a notion expounded with great clarity by André Martinet in articles and books (e.g. 1949, 1967 [1960]). This latter work, *Elements of General Linguistics*, was then considered by many to be the bible of Saussurean linguistics in its updated functionalist version. Extrapolating analytical methods from natural languages to other semiotic systems was however rife with difficulties. How to functionally segment cultural productions is indeed rarely obvious. A historical building, a display window, a musical or acrobatic performance, a sports event and an advertisement are all meaningful cultural instances which involve multiple sensorial modalities and include already constituted signifying subsystems. If architecture, ballet, cinema, fashion, etc., are construed as languages, and monuments, performances, films, clothing, etc., as texts, it is necessary to create translinguistic concepts of paradigms, commutation, signification, code, grammar and rhetoric at the very least. The search for the building blocks and the rules of construction of these complex cultural productions was driven by the epistemological goal of reaching, beyond their spatial and temporal diversity, a vision of their structure, that is, a system of relations among abstract categories which could be expressed in the form of a table or an algorithm resembling those which were found in the metadiscourse of structural phonology.

The methodology consisted first of reducing the redundancies of the 'text' (that is, identifying and lumping together all the words or visual images referring to the same conceptual object or class of objects) in order to reach more general binary oppositions or systems of values: 'First, categorise!', as Greimas used to instruct his students. Then, the basic categories could be visually displayed and ordered through various schemata or algebraic representations. The particular tables thus elaborated purported to 'explain' cultural productions by providing conceptual access to their deep or true sense in the form of sets of relations (their *langue*) and to 'demonstrate' how they were generated, through successive stages of concretisation, as particular phenomenological experiences in time like the determinate and contextualised instances of language (their *parole*). These structures were given as the necessary general conditions for the very possibility of meaning production. This rewriting process was achieved with a mixture of self-assurance based on the principles spelled out by the linguistics masters, and great theoretical anxiety created by the scepticism with which these results were usually received beyond the small circles of semioticians who had started organising themselves in intellectual groups and scholarly associations such as the International Association for Semiotic Studies, which was incorporated in Paris in 1969.

Saussurism and its discontents

By the time of the association's first congress in 1974 in Milan, the theories of the other 'founder' of semiotics, C. S. Peirce, were already being promoted, by Roman Jakobson among others, as an American antidote to the perceived static quality and 'glottocentrism' of European Saussurism. Peirce's 'semeiotic' had been popularised by Charles Morris in the 1930s in the context of behaviourism and logical positivism. Peirce, who had been a prolific writer in many scientific and philosophical fields, was known mainly in philosophy as the founder of Pragmatism, but his speculations on signs were progressively foregrounded on the international semiotic scene. Like Saussure's, his thoughts on semiotics were accessible to the 1960s generation only in a fragmentary and indirect manner, through second-hand introductions (e.g. Morris, 1938; Ogden and Richards, 1923; Burks, 1949) or through extensively edited philosophical anthologies of his articles, e.g. Buchler, 1940). Peirce's contribution to semiotics was then mostly perceived, in a summary manner, first, as the classification of signs into three categories: *index, icon* and *symbol*, then, as the introduction of a dynamic dimension, *semiosis* (the action of signs) into the general conceptual framework of a science of signs. Although some philosophers such as Gilles-Gaston Granger (1968), Max Bense (1967) and Gérard Deledalle (1971, 1974) were showing a more sophisticated interest in Peirce's system, Barthes's *Eléments de sémiologie* made only a brief allusion to his categorisation of signs which he compares to other classifications. However, Peirce and Saussure, whose approaches were critically compared as early as 1923 by Charles K. Ogden and Ivor A. Richards, would progressively become narrowly associated in the semiotic *épistémé* of the second half of the century. Some would construe them as theoretical antagonists, pitching the assumed static nature of binary structures against the dynamism of triadic relations; others would attempt to work out some comprehensive or synthetic views of these two most influential systems of thought which had been elaborated almost simultaneously but in vastly different conceptual contexts and with mostly incompatible epistemological agendas (Deledalle, 1976; Broden, 2000). Saussurism, as it was packaged in the *Course in General Linguistics*, thus became entangled in defensive dialogues not only with Peirce supporters but also with Marxists in fields which were well beyond the domain of relevance that Saussure had claimed for his theoretical views. Benveniste and Jakobson consistently invoked Peirce in their criticisms of Saussure's theses. Jakobson (1980: 31–8) went as far as construing Peirce as a 'pathfinder in the science of language' in his efforts to bring the two into the same ring and act as the umpire. Saussure eventually was assigned the role of the straw man who embodied for many critics the linguistic and structuralist fallacies (e.g. Jameson, 1972; Reiss, 1988), thus ushering what, in their opinion, would be a Peircean or Marxist post-Saussurean, post-structuralist era more concerned with the subjective and dialogical dimensions of speech, and the social and historical processes of meaning-making than with the description of a-temporal systems of logical differences. This was indeed the view which prevailed from the other side of the fence, a perception which perhaps owed more to Saussurism than to Saussure himself. Interestingly, the perceptive chapter which Timothy Reiss entitled 'Semiology and its discontents: Saussure and Greimas' (1988: 56–97) is adorned with a quotation from Jakobson's *Essais de linguistique générale*: 'Those attempts made to construct a linguistic model without any connection to a speaker or a listener and which therefore hypostatize a code detached from actual communication, risk reducing language to a scholastic fiction.'

The purpose of this section in my chapter is not to engage in an explicit criticism of the Saussurean approach, but to document the theoretical difficulties encountered by the practitioners of semiotic analysis (for an application of structuralist methodology to an understanding of circus performances, see Bouissac, 1976). These difficulties arose from the ambiguities of the *Cours*, as well as from an attempt to blend different models. For instance, the related notions of code (a conventional system of equivalent values) and iconicity (the character of a sign which signifies through some similarity with its referent rather than through an arbitrary convention) fed a series of controversies which are still ongoing in some quarters. What is the extent of biological constraints on coding? What does happen to the principle of arbitrariness when one strays away from language proper? Which properties can, and which ones cannot, be transferred from a linguistic model to a general semiological model? Are all semiological processes necessarily mediated by linguistic ones? Can any meaning be articulated outside language? Various solutions were proposed to these questions. Roland Barthes's essay, 'Le mythe, aujourd'hui', published as a postscript to his *Mythologies* (1957), is symptomatic of the strategic importance of Saussure's semiological vision as it was then perceived on the basis of the *Course in General Linguistics*. At the same time, Barthes's essay struggles rather inconclusively with the ambiguities of what was construed as the 'problem of meaning' in a structuralist perspective and proposes eventually, after a perfunctory detour in the field of psychoanalysis, a Marxist interpretation of the few visual examples it discusses. Barthes's interpretative tactics are presented as a scientific enterprise which bears upon written texts as well as images, and will be replicated by many, using the same analytical notions ascribed to Saussure as a sort of conceptual machine geared to generate a discourse of 'semiotic enlightenment'.

In the same vein, Christian Metz (1931–94) undertook, in the wake of Barthes's earlier discussions of film from a 'semiological' point of view, to establish a semiotics of cinema based on Saussurean and Hjelmslevian notions (1968) before shifting in the 1970s to a purely psychoanalytical approach. During his semiological phase, Metz struggled with the difficulties involved in the direct application of the concepts and methods of Saussurean structural linguistics to a multimodal cultural object as complex and diverse as cinema. His own blend of semiotic optimism and epistemological anxiety is voiced in his landmark book *Langage et cinéma* (1971). In his *Essais sur la signification au cinéma* (1972), he credited Peirce for his leading role in the emergence of semiotics, thus signalling an epistemological shift among some prominent French thinkers.

The intense theoretical debate which ensued still maps the field of semiotic inquiry today. As we have seen above, Saussure's linguistics soon encountered the theoretical constructs coming from the Peircean and Marxist traditions. One may wonder to what extent this legacy actually represented the genuine continuation of Saussure's own thought and project, and to what extent it was a mere epistemological fantasy, mainly when Saussure came to be construed as an anti-Peirce in the sterile scholastic controversies of binarism versus triadism, or statism versus dynamism. Similarly, when Mikhail Bakhtin (1895–1975) and his proxies, who had mounted in the 1920s an anti-formalist attack against Saussure, became known in the West through translations, they added a new dimension to the debate and contributed to further reinforce the stereotype of a Saussurean doctrine which they contended had overlooked the social, processual, transformational and fundamentally temporal nature of languages and cultures. While many researchers drifted away from Saussurism under the pressure of these movements, others held on their course along directions which were more consistent with particular aspects of Saussurism such as the foregrounding of formal relations and the exclusive attention paid to differential values in the representation of semiological systems, although this approach also implies some selective use of the sources.

Extreme formalism

Given the peculiar circumstances of Saussure's scattered and fragmentary writings on the topic of a general science of signs, and their protracted and staggered appearance in print, it is impossible to relate the Saussurean legacy to a coherent textual body. Trying to reconstruct Saussure's assumed system from these bits and pieces has proved to be a frustrating enterprise, from the *Cours* on. John Joseph's chapter on the linguistic sign in this volume, and the entry on Saussure found in the monumental *Handbook on Sign-Theoretic Foundations of Nature and Culture* (Posner et al., 1997), again demonstrate the difficulty of the task even when it is limited to the linguistic domain. The most likely reason for this state of affairs is that such a system never existed in Saussure's mind. But the absence of a logically compelling theory upon which a science of language and, by implication, a science of signs could be created, does not mean that Saussure's approach was not insightful and valuable. His notes and fragments, which often point to problems rather than solutions, incited many minds to undertake the construction of a semiological system, and it is likely his legacy is not yet exhausted.

Saussure's axiom stating that in language there are no positive terms but only differential values and their relations first led to the application of systems of logical oppositions to the phonological descriptions of the Prague school. But it was clear that given the absolute homology that Saussure seemed to have asserted between the *signifiant* and the *signifié*, the same was necessarily true of the latter. It was just a matter of time before someone would pursue the task undertaken by Nicolai Trubetzkoy (1936, 1939) and apply the method of his *Principles of Phonology* to the domain that had previously come to be called 'semantic'. Lévi-Strauss's structuralism generalised the analogy from structural phonology to a macro-analysis of myths in a way that was only tenuously related to Saussurean linguistic principles but embodied for the early structuralists the spirit of Saussure's formal approach. This, however, left untouched the problem of a Saussurean semantics since anthropological structuralism was rather a metasemantic enterprise that took for granted the existence of the semantic systems which were a necessary part of the language spoken by the populations whose myths were scrutinised in the versions that had been recorded and translated by European explorers and colonists.

A. J. Greimas pushed further Lévy-Straussian formalism (Greimas, 1966b), as he had done a few years earlier with Georges Dumézil's comparative mythology (Greimas, 1963). Greimas was a lexicologist who had pursued an academic career at the University of Alexandria (Egypt) while obviously keeping abreast with the Paris intellectual scene. He had published ten years earlier an article entitled 'L'actualité du Saussurisme'(1956) in which he lamented the lack of influence of Saussure's ideas on French linguists, praised the recent development in France of structural anthropology in which he saw an application of the principles of the *Course in General Linguistics*, and outlined a programme of research consisting of trying to achieve for the *signifié* what the Prague and Copenhagen schools had done for the *signifiant* in the period between the two world wars. The article celebrated the dawn of structuralism as the long-overdue resumption of the Saussurean agenda, pointing out not only Lévi-Strauss's,

Barthes's and a few early structuralists' publications but also Merleau-Ponty's *Phénoménologie de la perception* (1945) which Greimas considered, perhaps opportunistically, to be a continuation of Saussure's approach to language. This article, at the same time, staked out a territory within the contemporary research in semantics, a move which was to produce a decade later the book that launched Greimas on the modern semiotic stage: *Sémantique structurale* (1966c). 'Structural' and 'structuralism' had then turned into buzz words, and Greimas later claimed that his publisher had insisted that '*structurale*' be included in his title for marketing purposes (personal communication), although the book's title echoes Hjelmslev's report to the VIIIth International Congress of Linguists: 'Pour une sémantique structurale' (1959 [1957]). Greimas's initial reluctance to sacrifice to what had become an intellectual fashion probably was caused by his conviction that the qualification would be redundant since Saussure's axioms regarding general linguistics were indubitable and that, consequently, there were not to be several kinds of semantics but simply a 'true' theory of the *signifié*, which was necessarily structural, as there already existed with Trubetzkoy's *Principes de Phonologie* (1964) a 'true' theory of the *signifiant.*

But for Greimas, as for Barthes in his semiological endeavours, implementing Saussure's programme required more than relying on Saussure's 'heuristic' notions. Greimas stood clear of Marxism and Freudianism which were from his point of view discourses to be semiotically analysed rather than sources of inspiration toward interpretive models of cultural productions. Instead, he undertook to derive his method from other sources, notably the formalisms he found in the Danish linguists Louis Hjelmslev (1953) and Viggo Brøndal (1943) as well as in logicians such as Hans Reichenbach (1947) and Robert Blanché (1966). The goal was to uncover the basic algorithms that account for the articulation of meaning at the most abstract level. In a manner that evokes Immanuel Kant's *a priori* forms of perception, Greimas contends that the human mind does not have direct access to meaning in itself but only in as much as it is articulated through fundamental categories of oppositions, namely contradiction and contrariness, hence the notion of elementary structures of signification through which any meaningful instance is generated and can be described. This extreme formalism, whose origin is explicitly ascribed to Saussure's thought, is expressed in the form of algebraic algorithms and geometric diagrams which purport to represent the necessary conditions for the very possibility of all discursive productions of meaning, thus giving some measure of operationality to the most radical Saussurean aphorisms. An early exposé of this systematic vision is found in an article published in the *Yale French Review* by Greimas in collaboration with François Rastier, 'The interaction of semiotic constraints' (1968).

Naturally, this approach encountered the opposition of those who considered it to be a mere avatar of philosophical idealism since all processes appeared to be ultimately referred to an abstract a-chronic basic structure, a sort of ontologism of Saussure's synchrony. The standard 'semiolinguistic' theory, as it came to be called by Greimas himself who at times echoed the rhetoric of Noam Chomsky through the use of expressions such as deep and surface structures, was said to be immune to empirically based criticism since its claim to scientific status was founded on its logical consistency with respect to its initial axioms. This, however, involved some degree of epistemological anxiety as well as in-group debates, typical of all attempts at establishing an ultimate theory. For instance, in the foreword to *Du sens* (On Meaning), a book that collected some of his most significant articles (Greimas, 1970), Greimas went as far as suggesting that since meaning can be apprehended only in as much as it is articulated through *a priori* semio-linguistic categories, the human mind has no direct access to meaning in itself. This prompted him to ironically undermine his own enterprise by paradoxically hinting that talking meaningfully about meaning would actually require a nonsensical discourse. Interestingly, this lucid remark, which confronted in jest the most haunting *aporia* of all extreme formalism, was truncated and downgraded to the status of a 'cursory remark' by the translator of the book into English. The reason for this treatment is not clear: either Greimas recoiled or the translator, who was keen on launching in North America Greimas's semiolinguistics as a credible, teachable theory, decided that such intellectual candour was inappropriate and would puzzle or discourage naive readers.

Perhaps it is this very epistemological difficulty, inherent in the semiological enterprise, which prevented Saussure from confidently expounding in writing the complete principles of the systematic science of signs he adumbrated in his remarks and fragments. In 1926, Nikolai Trubetzkoy wondered why Saussure 'did not dare draw a logical conclusion from his own thesis that language is a system' and he suggested that 'the cause must be sought in the fact that such a conclusion would have been at cross-purposes with the universally recognized notion of language history and of history in general' (Trubetzkoy, 2001:183). The extreme formalists like Greimas who, in the second half of the century, would lay the most vocal claim to the Saussurean heritage had liberated themselves from such hesitations to the point of construing history itself as a meaning-producing discourse subject, as all discourses, to universal semiotic constraints. This bold move, however, carried the cost of infinite regress which not even a metaphysical loop (in the form of still another meaningful discourse) could stop.

However, Saussure's advocating of a radical formalism, an algebraic or mathematical approach to semiology, which prompted him to assert, for example, that 'for linguistic facts, *element* and *character* are eternally the same thing [and that] language [*langue*], like all other semiological systems, makes no difference between what distinguishes a sign and what constitutes it' (*CLG*/E 2: 47), was rooted in a somewhat esoteric philosophical tradition going back at least to the *characteristica universalis* of Leibniz (1646–1716), whose fascination for combinatory systems had led him to study the hexagrams of the ancient Chinese *Yi jing* which he saw as a harbinger of his own binary calculus (Leibniz, 1987). The intellectual tendency to foreground and systematise formal differences for their own sake, which is usually credited for having ushered in contemporary information theory, has been pursued with renewed force beyond the immediate legacy of Saussure. George Spencer Brown's *Laws of Form* (1969), for instance, bears witness to this dynamism in a way which is not alien to the Saussurean unfinished agenda. It is not infrequent to find explicit references to Saussure's aphorisms in contemporary efforts to develop formal treatments of meaning in the framework of information technology (e.g. Beust, 1998).

Does Saussure still matter to semiotics?

Does Saussure still matter? Obviously, from a purely historical point of view, it would be difficult to fully understand the emergence of the semiotic movement in Europe and its promises and discontents without taking into consideration the impact of Saussure's ideas, however tentative they may have been. But beyond the anecdotal interest of retracing the various paths of his influence across the globe, or the philological fascination of reconstructing his virtual system of thought from tantalising fragments, is it still worth pondering his discontinuous insights as potential contributions to the advancement of today's linguistics and semiotics? Many have selectively gleaned from his manuscripts elements that appear to be compatible with their own theoretical views and thus have construed these glimpses as harbingers of their own endeavours, although this is done usually at the cost of glossing over some problematic statements. Others have simply discarded Saussure's pronouncements as only averagely interesting or even grossly overrated. Reference has been made earlier in this chapter to the downgrading by some American semioticians of the Saussurean 'school' to the status of a 'minor intellectual tradition' in semiotics. As early as the 1930s, Trubetzkoy himself had voiced such misgivings: 'For inspiration I have reread de Saussure, but on a second reading he impresses me much less. There is comparatively little in the book that is of value; most of it is old rubbish. And what is valuable is awfully abstract, without details' (letter to Roman Jakobson, 17 May 1932, Trubetzkoy, 2001: 255).

This section will attempt to show that Saussure's ideas remain relevant in today's context in as much as they point to problems which are still to be solved and directions which are currently being explored. It is therefore as a mine of heuristic questions and uneasy tentative solutions that Saussure's contribution to a general science of signs will be considered in this final section.

A recurring problem in Saussurean linguistics is the notion of *langue*. Since for Saussure, languages constituted merely a subset, albeit an important one, of a more encompassing class of sign systems, the notion of *langue* needed to be given a semiological rather than purely linguistic definition.

Let us remember that the great nineteenth-century debate was whether languages were kinds of organisms which changed along the same patterns as other organisms' life cycles or whether they were social institutions based on conventions supported by human abilities. (See Sanders, this volume.) In one of his rare references to other linguists reported in the *Cours*, Saussure designates W. D. Whitney as a valuable exponent of the latter approach, while at the same time criticising those who hold crude Darwinist views. However, the reference to Whitney is accompanied by some reservations, and, further, his endorsement of the movement which then defined itself by opposition to the organic hypothesis is not expressed in a wholehearted manner. Again and again Saussure returns to the few indications that led him to grapple with a paradox: *langue* as a set of differential terms is founded on arbitrary conventions that totally escape the conscious intentions of the individuals who use its resources for expressing their thoughts and communicating among themselves. Paradoxically, it is a contract without contractants. A common misreading has construed *langue* as a static, achronic or synchronic system, but for Saussure, time is of the essence for understanding the notion of *langue* (Choi, 2002). 'On peut parler à la fois de l'immutabilité et de la mutabilité du signe' ('the sign can be said to be both immutable and mutable'; *CLG*/E 1: 165). This remark appears in the context of attempts at circumscribing the elusive object of general linguistics, and more generally semiology: 'Tout ce qui comprend des formes doit entrer dans la sémiologie' ('whatever involves forms must come under the purview of semiology'; *CLG*/E 1: 154) ; but contrary to the comtemplative rationality of geometry, *langue* is an irrational force which imposes itself on humans :'La langue est quelquechose que l'on subit' ('*langue* is something which imposes itself upon us'; *CLG*/E 1: 159) ; its very foundations are irrational and it is driven by blind forces ('fondée sur l'irraison même', 'des forces aveugles'; *CLG*/E 1: 162, 171).

Indeed, alterations occur in the system itself and these alterations are not functional in the sense that they would be the effects of deliberate changes made through consensus to a social contract in order to improve its efficiency. Instead, they are neither free nor rational. 'Quand intervient le *Temps* combiné avec le fait de la psychologie sociale, c'est alors que nous sentons que la langue n'est pas libre . . . parce que principe de continuité ou de solidarité indéfinie avec les âges précédents. La continuité enferme le fait d'altération qui est un déplacement de valeurs' ('When *Time* combines with the reality of social psychology, we come to realize that *langue* is not free . . . because of the principle of continuity and solidarity with previous states. Continuity includes alterations in the form of shifting of values'; *CLG*/E 1: 173-4).

This way of thinking could be seen as remarkably Darwinian and more specifically adumbrates contemporary speculations on evolutionary semiotics and memetics which construe semiotic systems, including language(s), as semi-autonomous algorithms endowed with an evolutionary dynamic of their own akin to parasitic modes of adaptation, survival and reproduction (e.g. Deacon, 1997; Aunger, 2000, 2002). Saussure's puzzling image of *langue* as somewhat like 'a duck hatched by a hen', whose essential character is to 'always escape to some extent individual or social will' and which 'exists perfectly only in the mass of brains' (*CLG*/E 1: 40–1, 51, 57), evokes some kind of yet unclassified organism (*CLG*/E 1: 169). 'On s'est fait scrupule d'employer le terme d'*organisme*, parce que la langue dépend des êtres vivants. On peut employer le mot, en se rappelant qu'il ne s'agit pas d'un être indépendant' ('The word organism is used here reluctantly because langue depends on living organisms. Let us use it any way, keeping in mind that this organism is not independent'; *CLG*/E 1: 59). It is interesting to note that this characterisation meets the definition of parasitic organism, a recurrent theme in contemporary memetic literature. Furthermore, Saussure's paradoxical insights do not apply only to the object of linguistics but to semiology as a whole: 'La continuité du signe dans le temps, liée à l'altération dans le temps, est un principe de la sémiologie générale' ('the continuity of sign in time, linked to its alteration, is a principle of general semiology'; *CLG*/E 1: 171). But this continuity depends on transmission 'selon des lois qui n'ont rien à faire avec les lois de création' ('according to laws which are totally different from the laws of creation'; *CLG*/E 1: 170). Saussure repeatedly emphasises that the social nature of semiological systems is 'internal' rather than 'external' to these systems (*CLG*/E 1: 173). Continuity and change belong to their very essence and unambiguously, albeit not explicitly, locate them within an evolutionary process whose description fits, *avant la lettre*, the neo-Darwinian models in their more contemporary forms. This vision is emphatically underlined in the first Geneva lectures of 1891 in which even pauses in the evolution of *langue* – what some contemporary evolutionists controversially term 'punctuations' – are denied (*CLG*/E 2: 3–14).

Such remarks, and many others of the same vein, have not been foregrounded by his followers and commentators, or they have been interpreted as mere metaphors. Similarly, Saussure's assertions regarding the place he envisioned for semiology as a part of general psychology has been glossed over. However, the latter is not less striking. Many written remarks by Saussure anticipate the tenets of modern cognitive neurosciences and evolutionary psychology. His occasional criticisms of Broca's approach bear upon the restrictive localisations of linguistic functions. 'Il y a une faculté plus générale, celle qui commande aux signes' ('there exists a more general faculty, one which governs signs'; *CLG*/E 1: 36). This faculty is conceived as a brain function which made language possible without being its origin since the law of continuity shows that any 'langue' must be transmitted. A bold evolutionary theory emerges from his concise, at times cryptic, assertions: 'L'essentiel de la langue est étranger au caractère phonique du signe linguistique' ('the essence of langue is alien to the phonic character of linguistic signs'; *CLG*/E 1: 22); 'La langue n'est pas moins que la parole un objet de nature concrète' ('*langue* is as much as *parole* a concrete object'; *CLG*/E 1: 44) and 'Tout est psychologique dans la langue' ('the whole of *langue* is psychological'; *CLG*/E 1: 21). But shifting the problem to general psychology is also a way to project its solution into an unknown future because Saussure's conception of psychology as it was then is a critical one. It is, like semiology, or signology as he preferred at times to call the science of signs (*ELG*: 266), an emergent science which would come to be different from the discipline known by this name at the turn of the century. The condition for the emergence of a psychology that would encompass semiology is that psychology take the temporal dimension into account and overcome its tendency to speculate on intemporal signs and ideas: 'sortir absolument de ses spéculations sur le signe momentané et l'idée momentanée' (*CLG*/E 2: 47). This approach, perhaps, echoes more closely than is suspected James Mark Baldwin's (1861–1934) evolutionary psychology and epistemology. The American psychologist, whose impact on Piaget and Vygotsky is generally acknowledged, was a contemporary of Saussure and was widely read and discussed in Europe and in France in particular, where he lived from 1908 until his death (Wozniak, 1998). Baldwin's use of Darwinism in the rethinking of the traditional disciplines of his time was very different from Schleicher's literal applications of evolutionism to the history of languages denounced by Whitney and Saussure. As editor of *The Psychological Review* and the four-volume *Dictionary of Philosophy and Psychology* (1904), to which Peirce had contributed the article on sign among others, Baldwin not only put his mark on psychology at the turn of the century but made also many forays into other disciplines, stating for instance that the law of natural selection expresses a principle 'which finds appropriate application in all the sciences of life and mind' (Baldwin, 1909: 89). Saussure, who was then inconclusively engaged in an uneasy rethinking of linguistics, was projecting toward an ill-defined future the emergence of new epistemological horizons.

Are his tentative ideas now coming of age? Can they provide a useful reference for today's researchers, a sort of reflexive temporal depth, a heuristic framework beyond the earlier fossilisation of some restrictive interpretations? Bringing all the problems he raised and all the insights he jotted on paper in a single purview remains one of the most stimulating and challenging tasks of today. After all, the emergence of the epistemological resource which Saussure called 'semiologie' is not necessarily to be found under the official label of semiotics.

For instance, George Spencer Brown's logic of distinctions expounded in *Law of Forms* (1969) and the use of his calculus of indications by Francisco Varela in *Principles of Biological Autonomy* (1979) pursue one of the tenets of Saussure's conviction that 'tout signe repose purement sur un co-status négatif' ('any sign is based purely upon a negative co-status') or that 'l'expression simple sera algébrique ou ne sera pas' ('simple expression will be algebraic or will not be at all'; *CLG*/E 2: 28–9). Such is the goal of today's algorithmic and computational semiotics. Contemporary efforts to rethink the social sciences in semiological terms bear witness to the continuing of Saussure's seminal ideas (e.g. Baecker, 1999; Luhmann, 1999).

One may wonder whether, once the complete manuscripts left by Saussure have been published in their chronological order and are no longer seen through the prism of the *Cours*, a novel, perhaps surprising conceptual landscape will emerge. This may indeed show that Saussure had anticipated theoretical directions, such as evolutionary semiotics and memetics, which he could not fully explore in his own time, given the state of scientific knowledge at the turn of the twentieth century, and the linguistic doxa which then prevailed, with respect to which Saussure's insights were counterintuitive to the point of being scandalous. This will put to test the various versions of Saussurism that have been constructed so far on the basis of limited information, and stimulate anew the semiotic, or semiological, project which Saussure envisioned as an open-ended process when he wrote 'Où s'arrêtera la sémiologie? C'est difficile à dire' ('How far will semiology go? It is difficult to predict'; *CLG*/E 1: 46). Saussure's questions remain valid and his elusive agenda still provides a challenge for today's spirit of scientific enquiry into the realm of signs and signification.

Notes

1 SAUSSURE AND INDO-EUROPEAN LINGUISTICS

1 The first chapter of the *Cours* as compiled by Bally and Sechehaye offers a more conventional view of the development of the subject as moving from comparison (Bopp) to history, while still ignoring the more general problems. The students' notes offer a more muted view. A very interesting note recently published (Saussure, 2002: 130ff.) reveals a much more hesitant author (see below).
2 Here and below we use square brackets to include phonetic symbols and angular brackets to indicate letters. Thus in English we contrast <sing>, the standard spelling, with [sɪŋ] a phonetic transcription of the word's pronunciation.
3 The so-called sound laws, which normally were indicated by formulae of the type Latin *s* > *r* between vowels (> stands for 'becomes'), were the object of endless disputes but these concerned their status, their justification, and the possibility of exceptions. The general point that sound change was – unexpectedly – regular was no longer contested by the end of the century and regular or semi-regular instances of sound change had been identified much earlier. For Saussure's (widely shared) objections to the term 'law' in his 1909–10 courses, see Reichler-Béguelin (1980: 25) who points out that similar views were expressed by Hermann Paul.
4 The whole *Mémoire* was reprinted in Saussure (1922: 1–268). We owe to G. C. Vincenzi an Italian translation with notes and a long introduction (Saussure, 1979).
5 Karl Brugmann published at first under the name of Brugman but after 1882 the family changed their name to Brugmann; this is the name regularly used.
6 Some recently discovered notes by Saussure provide a luminous account of the type of argument which we find in his work:

> La linguistique procède de fait par induction et divination, et elle doit procéder ainsi pour arriver à des résultats féconds. Seulement une fois l'hypothèse aperçue on part toujours de là, de ce qui est reconstruit, pour assigner en suite sans préjuger à chaque langue ce qui lui revient de cette hypothèse. L'exposition y gagne en clarté, certainement. Pour preuve on se fie à l'ensemble satisfaisant que produisent les faits ainsi expliqués pour quelqu'un qui a admis l'hypothèse. (Saussure, 2002: 132)

This statement could refer both to theoretical discussion and to comparative work but the example that follows, where Saussure pleads guilty of having listed irrelevant material, comes from the *Mémoire*.

3 THE MAKING OF THE *COURS DE LINGUISTIQUE GÉNÉRALE*

1 Marginal notes written out in full opposite underlined passages in shorthand led me to imagine there was some correspondence (not, naturally, of spelling, but of sounds). From this I was able to draw up a list of signs.

2 As Engler (*CLG/E*, 1: xii and 2: i) explains in the introductory notes to his critical edition of the *Cours*, text contained within single diamond-shaped brackets (< >) represents either corrections or marginal notes which he found in the source manuscripts themselves. Also, empty square brackets [ ] in the text from *CLG/E* indicate a gap in the manuscript, while a forward slash followed by a number in square brackets /[25] indicates the page number of the manuscript. Otherwise the number in square brackets [2522] refers to the number that Engler has given to the relevant segment of the originally published text of the *CLG*. The letter 'R' stands for Riedlinger, i.e. for the manuscript of Riedlinger's notes. In general, material within square brackets in text from *CLG/E* has been introduced by Engler. – Editor's note.

4 THE LINGUISTIC SIGN

1 Adolphe Pictet, a polymath with long-standing ties to the Saussure family, and to whom the adolescent Ferdinand addressed his first linguistic essay, devoted an 1856 book to 'the beautiful', in which certain aspects of Saussure's mature theory of signs are anticipated. Saussure's familiarity with the book is proven: he writes about it in the first of three articles on Pictet and his work that he penned for the *Journal de Genève* in 1878 (Saussure, 1922; see Joseph, 2003).

5 *LANGUE* AND *PAROLE*

1 In addition to the eight paired terms that structure the entire *CGL*, the first chapter speaks of the two principles that establish the linguistic sign: arbitrariness and linearity. Arbitrariness will later form part of the eighth and final pair of terms presented in the *CGL*, arbitrariness/motivation; linearity will not. There is, in this sense, a ninth pair: arbitrariness/linearity, distinct from the other eight, because linearity is a descriptive feature, a distinguishing feature of language, but not a functional feature in the manner of those described by Saussure's well-known pairs of analytical terms. (See Gordon, 1999b.)

2 Among the other Saussurean complementarities, only *signifiant/signifié* is related to a third overarching term *signe*.

3 In this respect, Saussure's terminology constitutes a case for construing the polysemy of a single sign as homonymy among signs, indeed requires that it be so construed in order for the definitions of *différence/opposition* to apply consistently to both Saussure's complementary terms and the polysemy of such terms as *objet*.

4 Monosystematicity, or the analysis of language as a single system, rather than as interacting subsystems, was Firth's chief complaint against Saussure's approach to linguistics, and, in fact, the only complaint not subverted by Firth's own adherence to principles and procedures marked by some degree of affinity to those that he criticised in the *Cours*. Firth identified the monosystemic approach with what is termed *paradigmatic analysis* in the *Cours* (Firth, 1948: 121); his own polysystemic

approach aligned with *syntagmatic analysis* (1948: 128). He called attention to the shortcomings of a monosystemic approach to linguistic analysis, charging that it had been pushed beyond the limits of its applicability (1948: 137). In this respect, Firth's criticism may be construed not so much as a wholesale condemnation of a feature of Saussure's programme for linguistics but rather as a condemnation of the failure to make full use of the syntagmatic and the paradigmatic as complementary modes of analysis (see Gordon, 1979).

5 Whether the fault lies with Spence himself or with a typesetter to whose slip Spence was inattentive in correcting the proofs of his article, the model is incorrectly represented, showing roman numerals on the left side of the equation, where arabic numerals appear in the original version in the *CGL*. The deviation is diacritical, but critical.

9 THE RUSSIAN CRITIQUE OF SAUSSURE

The author would like to thank the AHRB for the generous support provided under its Research Grant Scheme during the period in which work on this chapter was carried out.

1 Translations of this, and of subsequent quotes from Russian sources, are the author's.

2 It is Potebnia's influence which led to the early formalist emphasis on 'the principle of the [visual] palpableness (*oščscutimost'*) of form as the specific criterion of perception in art' (Eikhenbaum, 1978: 12). Much more recently, Iurii Lotman's Soviet version of semiotics acknowledges the fruitfulness of approaches recognising 'the creative function as a universal quality of language and poetic language . . . as the most typical manifestation of language as such' – a view he traces to 'Potebnya's idea that the entire sphere of language belongs to art' (Lotman, 1990: 17–18).

3 The dispute over authorship of the writings of the Bakhtin circle has never been fully resolved. It seems likely, however, that Voloshinov and Medvedev, its other prominent members, did technically write the works which bear their name, but under the close supervision of Bakhtin himself.

4 There seems to be little question that Bakhtin's critique of the uniformity and monologism of Saussurean *langue* was in part a carefully coded assault on the increasing conformity required by the Soviet regime under which he worked. For more on this, see Emerson and Morson, 1990.

10 SAUSSURE, BARTHES AND STRUCTURALISM

1 For the sake of clarity, I equate the reference by F. Dosse to Parisian structuralism with what I will designate throughout this chapter as structuralism in France. Paris was, of course, not at all the sole site of structural analysis in France during the period in question. Yet its role as a centre of educational institutions (Ecole Pratique des Hautes Etudes, Collège de France, Université de Paris campuses at Vincennes and Nanterre) and journals (*Critique*, *Les Temps Modernes*, *Annales*, *Diogène*, *Tel Quel*, *Communications*, *Poétique*, *Change*) warrants an understanding that tends to stand for similar institutions and journals in other parts of France. I have rejected the expression 'French structuralism' in order to avoid conveying an essential difference at the level of nation and/or language, as in comparisons that might be made between 'French'

and 'American' practices. Such differences are reductive. In addition, they are belied by historical circumstances such as those that brought major figures such as Lévi-Strauss and Jakobson together in New York City in the early 1940s. See J. Mehlman, 2000.

2 Whenever possible, I have cited English translations of texts first published in other languages.

11 SAUSSURE'S ANAGRAMS AND THE ANALYSIS OF LITERARY TEXTS

1 In prose, only the third component of this triptychon remains.

2 $u = v$, $i = j$ must be applied according to the antique and medieval tradition.

3 Both contents, the one of the ordinary linguistic sign, which *means*, as well as the one of the name, which *designates*, are supposed to be applied as *signifié*.

4 Mallarmé speaks of a symphony. So, similarly, does Lacan: 'il suffit d'écouter la poésie . . . pour que s'y fasse entendre une polyphonie et que tout discours s'avère s'aligner sur les plusieurs portées d'une partition' ('One only has to listen to poetry . . . to hear a polyphony of sounds and to realise that any stretch of speech is displayed over the several staves of a musical score', Lacan, 1966: 260f.).

12 SAUSSURE AND DERRIDA

1 In English: *Of Grammatology*, tr. G. C. Spivak, 1976. In this chapter all translations from Derrida and from Saussure's *Cours* are my own.

2 This is what justifies Harris' complaint that Saussure's chapter on value gives rise to a 'bleak metaphysical limbo' (Harris, 1987: 120). Derrida's reading, which Harris mentions only in passing (p. x), suggests a less metaphysical (though perhaps still quite 'bleak') perspective.

3 This suggests a relationship between text and commentary quite different from that of traditional academic norms, at least insofar as it cannot, given the view of language developed from Saussure, be attempting to recover and present any ultimate 'meaning' of the text read (whereby deconstruction is not a hermeneutics). It should perhaps be pointed out that the type of presentation of Derrida offered here *is* itself essentially still traditional: nothing in Derrida's thinking simply disallows this, of course, but it should perhaps be pointed out that nothing resembling a 'Derridean' reading of Derrida has yet been achieved by Derrida's commentators (except, arguably, by Derrida himself, whose work can persuasively be read as, in part, a series of inventive rereadings of his own earlier texts).

4 'Quasi-concept' because the traditional concept of what a concept is relies on the 'logocentric' assumption of the ideal separability of the signified from its signifier(s), an assumption that the whole drift of Derrida's reading contests.

14 SAUSSURE, LINGUISTIC THEORY AND PHILOSOPHY OF SCIENCE

1 Roger Smith provides a useful brief summary which captures precisely what it was about the ego-psychological approach that provoked Lacan to announce his 'return to

Freud' as an antidote to all such normalising conceptions of psychoanalytic practice. This was a theory 'that described the ego as an original mental structure with its own positive powers. They [the ego psychologists] argued . . . that the psychic core of personality is a power with the capacity in a mature individual to integrate innate drives and social pressures in a genuinely self-fulfilling way. In popular versions – incompatible with the spirit of Freud's work but in keeping with US ideals – psychoanalysis was equated with a search for personal growth and for the true self, a fantasy of personality independent of culture' (Smith, 1997: 732–4). Lacan, on the contrary, stressed the unattainability of any such unified ego ideal and the late-Freudian idea that psychoanalysis was a strictly 'interminable' process, aimed toward achieving a state of mind that would always and of its very nature elude the best efforts of integrative thought. Thus ego psychology was itself a symptom of the narcissistic or 'imaginary' drive to substitute a false notion of the integrated ego for the endless 'detours' of the signifier in quest of some sheerly impossible idealised conception of self-knowledge and fulfilment (Lacan, 1977). Had Freud only read Saussure – so Lacan implies – then he would have couched his descriptions of the 'talking cure' in such a way as to prevent these gross misreadings. That is to say, he would have laid yet more emphasis on the 'bar' between signifier and signified, or 'the agency of the letter' as that which precludes any notion of psychoanalysis as a means of achieving some wished-for harmony between ego ideals and the requirements of a balanced, well-adjusted social life. In so far as the unconscious is 'structured like a language' – subject to the constant effects of desire as a process of displacement along the chain of signifiers – it remains forever beyond reach of the specular ('imaginary') ego. To this extent structuralism, or Lacan's interpretation of it, came out in strong opposition to received, i.e. Cartesian, ideas of scientific knowledge, rationality and truth. At the same time – not least in Lacan's case – it looked to Saussurean linguistics as a source of organising concepts and distinctions (like that between *langue* and *parole*) which still bore witness to a lingering dream of properly 'scientific' method.

2 On the other hand, as David Holdcroft remarks, 'it is arguable that he [Saussure] went further and maintained that there are no language-independent concepts, thus turning the position of the *Port Royal Grammar* on its head' (Holdcroft, 1991: 166n). One way of describing the transition from structuralism to post-structuralism is in terms of this unresolved tension in Saussure's thought between a rationalist approach premised on the basically Cartesian appeal to 'clear and distinct ideas' and a full-scale semiological doctrine committed to the thesis that all our operative concepts and categories are dependent upon (or 'constructed by') particular languages or signifying systems. For further discussion see Ducrot (1968) and Harland (1987).

3 This passage is cited in Jacques Derrida's essay 'White mythology: metaphor in the text of philosophy' (Derrida, 1982: 224). This is by far the most detailed, philosophically astute and wide-ranging treatment to be found in recent discussions of the topic, whether those belonging to the broadly 'analytic' (Anglo-American) or the 'continental' (mainland-European) traditions of thought. Above all it is explicit in rejecting the Nietzschean idea – much canvassed by 'literary' deconstructionists and strong-descriptivists like Rorty (1982) – that scientific concepts are *nothing more* than a species of sublimated metaphor, or that science amounts to just a kind of 'white mythology', a discourse that has lost the courage of its own primordial intuitions or perceptions. Thus 'there is also a *concept of metaphor*: it too has a history,

yields knowledge, demands from the epistemologist construction, rectification, critical rules of importation and exportation' (Derrida, 1982: 224). No doubt one has to make allowance for Derrida's use of an oblique ('free indirect') means of presentation when citing a source-text – here that of Bachelard – whose arguments he wishes to deploy strategically without perhaps fully endorsing them. All the same it is wrong to assume that Derrida is rejecting Bachelard's distinction between the realm of intuitive or pre-scientific metaphorical 'reverie' and the realm of elaborated scientific concepts where values of truth and falsehood come into play (see Norris, 1997b). Indeed this distinction is everywhere presupposed in Derrida's account of the history of philosophy's dealings with the problematic topos of metaphor, from Aristotle to Nietzsche, Bachelard and Canguilhem. For it would otherwise be impossible to explain how scientific knowledge could ever advance 'from an inefficient tropic-concept that is poorly constructed, to an operative tropic-concept that is more refined and more powerful in a given field and at a determined phase of the scientific process' (Derrida, 1982: 264).

4 The following passage is representative of Putnam's early (causal-realist) approach to issues of meaning, reference and truth.

> As language develops, the causal and noncausal links between bits of language and aspects of the world become more complex and more various. To look for any one uniform link between word or thought and object of word or thought is to look for the occult; but to see our evolving and expanding notion of reference as just a proliferating family is to miss the essence of the relation between language and reality. The essence of the relation is that language and thought do asymptotically correspond to reality, to some extent at least. A theory of reference is a theory of the correspondence in question. (Putnam, 1975: 290)

In his later (post-1980) work Putnam has moved away from this position under pressure from a range of counter-arguments which he now regards as posing insuperable problems for any such 'metaphysical'-realist line of thought. His first stop was a theory of 'internal' (or framework-relative) realism which allowed statements to possess a determinate truth-value but only in so far as that value was assigned with reference to some particular range of accepted criteria, investigative interests, disciplinary standards, etc. (see especially Putnam, 1981). Since then he has put forward a number of compromise proposals for conserving some plausible notion of truth and thus avoiding the nemesis of cultural relativism while also acknowledging the impossibility (as he sees it) of maintaining any stronger, i.e. objectivist or framework-transcendent, realist conception (Putnam, 1987, 1990, 1992). What is chiefly of interest in the present context is the fact that Putnam's long-haul retreat from causal realism has been prompted in large part by the same kinds of argument – holistic, contextualist, paradigm-relativist – that can also be seen to have influenced the reception history of Saussurean linguistics. That is to say it has resulted (in my view at least) from an over-readiness to concede the force of objections which take for granted the idea that truth cannot possibly transcend the limits of some given language-game, discourse, paradigm or conceptual scheme. See Norris, 2002, for a full-length study of Putnam's work that argues this case in detail.

Works by Saussure and further reading

WORKS BY SAUSSURE

(1878). Essai d'une distinction des différents *a* indo-européens. *Mémoires de la Société de linguistique*, 3: 359–70.

(1879). *Mémoire sur le système primitif des voyelles dans les langues indo-européennes*. Leipzig: Teubner.

(1908). *Mélanges de linguistique offerts à M. Ferdinand de Saussure* (no eds.). Paris: Champion.

(1909). Interview with *A. Riedlinger*, 19 January 1909. In Godel, 1957/1969a.

(1916). *Cours de linguistique générale* (published by C. Bally and A. Sechehaye in collaboration with A. Riedlinger). Lausanne and Paris: Payot. (*CLG*)

(1922). *Recueil des publications scientifiques*. Geneva: Editions Sonor.

Godel, R. (1957). *Les sources manuscrites du Cours de linguistique générale de F. de Saussure* (Société de publications romanes et françaises, 61). Geneva: Droz; Paris: Minard.

(1957). Cours de linguistique générale Cours II 1908–1909: introduction (d'après des notes d'étudiants) (ed. R. Godel). *Cahiers Ferdinand de Saussure*, 15: 3–103.

Godel, R. (1958/9). Nouveaux documents saussuriens: les cahiers E. Constantin. *Cahiers Ferdinand de Saussure*, 16: 23, 32.

(1960). Souvenirs de F. de Saussure concernant sa jeunesse et ses études (ed. R. Godel). *Cahiers Ferdinand de Saussure*, 17: 12–26.

Benveniste, E. (1964). Lettres de Ferdinand de Saussure à Antoine Meillet. *Cahiers Ferdinand de Saussure*, 21: 91–130.

(1964/5). Notes et documents sur Ferdinand de Saussure (1880–1891) (présentées par Michel Fleury). *Annuaire de l'Ecole pratique des Hautes Etudes*, Paris, 35–67.

(1968). *Cours de linguistique générale* (critical edition by R. Engler, vol. 1). Wiesbaden: Harrassowitz. (*CLG*/ E 1).

(1972 [1916]). *Cours de linguistique générale* (ed. T. de Mauro). Paris: Payot. (*CLG*/D)

(1974). *Cours de linguistique générale* (Notes personnelles) (critical edition by R. Engler, vol. 2). Wiesbaden: Harrassowitz. (*CLG*/E 2)

(1978). Essai pour réduire les mots du grec, du latin et de l'allemand à un petit nombre de racines (ed. B. Davis). *Cahiers Ferdinand de Saussure*, 32: 73–101.

(1979). *Saggio sul vocalismo indoeuropeo* (Italian edition, introd., trans. and ed. G. C. Vincenzi). Bologna: Libreria Universitaria Editrice.

(1994). [Letter dated September 1912 to Bally]. *Cahiers Ferdinand de Saussure*, 48: 132.

(2002). *Ecrits de linguistique générale* (ed. S. Bouquet and R. Engler). Paris: Gallimard. (*ELG*)

WORKS BY SAUSSURE, ENGLISH TRANSLATIONS AND BILINGUAL EDITIONS

(1959). *Course in General Linguistics* (trans. W. Baskin). New York: Philosophical Library. (*CGL*-B)

(1974 [1959]). *Course in General Linguistics* (trans. W. Baskin, with an introduction by J. Culler). London: Peter Owen. (*CGL*-B)

(1983). *Course in General Linguistics* (trans. and annotated by R. Harris). London: Duckworth. (*CGL*-H)

(1993). *Troisième Cours de linguistique générale / Third Course in General Linguistics (1910–1911), d'après les cahiers d'Emile Constantin* (ed. and trans. E. Komatsu and R. Harris). Oxford: Pergamon.

(1996). *Premier Cours de linguistique générale / First Course in General Linguistics (1907), d'après les cahiers d'Albert Riedlinger* (ed. and trans. E. Komatsu and G. Wolf). Oxford: Pergamon.

(1997). *Deuxième Cours de linguistique générale / Second Course in General linguistics (1908–1909), d'après les cahiers d'Albert Riedlinger & Charles Patois* (ed. and trans. E. Komatsu and G. Wolf). Oxford: Pergamon.

A SELECTION OF WORKS RELEVANT TO SAUSSURE PUBLISHED IN ENGLISH SINCE 1980 (OTHER THAN THOSE FEATURING IN THE LIST OF REFERENCES)

Arrivé, M. (1992). *Linguistics and Psychoanalysis: Freud, Saussure, Hjelmslev, Lacan and Others* (trans. by J. Leader of *Linguistique et psychanalyse*, 1986). Amsterdam: Benjamins. 15 + 178 pages.

Eschbach, A. and Trabant, J. (eds.) (1983). *History of Semiotics*. Amsterdam, Philadelphia: Benjamins. 16 + 386 pages.

Harris, R. and Taylor, T. J. (1990). *Landmarks in Linguistic Thought: the Western Tradition from Socrates to Saussure*. London: Routledge. 240 pages.

Mauro, T. de and Sugeta, S. (eds.) (1995). *Saussure and Linguistics Today*. Rome: Bulzoni. 352 pages.

Miller, J. M. (1981). *French Structuralism: a Multidisciplinary Bibliography with a Checklist of Sources for Louis Althusser, Roland Barthes, Jacques Derrida, Michel Foucault, Lucien Goldmann, Jacques Lacan, and an Update of Works on Claude Lévi-Strauss*. New York, London: Garland. 13 + 553 pages.

Simone, R. (ed.) (1995). *Iconicity in Language*. Amsterdam, Philadelphia: Benjamins. 11 + 317 pages.

Tallis, R. (1988). *Not Saussure: a Critique of Post-Saussurean Literary Theory*. Houndmills, Basingstoke, and London: Macmillan. 9 + 273 pages.

SELECTION OF ARTICLES AND CHAPTERS

Atkins, G. D. (1981). The sign as a structure of difference: Derridean deconstruction and some of its implications. In R. T. De George (ed.), *Semiotic Themes*. Lawrence: University of Kansas, pp. 133–47.

Bailey, C.-J. N. (1981). What if Saussure had extended developmental comparative analysis to description instead of proposing synchronic analysis? *Indogermanische Forschungen*, 86: 137–45.

Becker, L. A. (1981). De Saussure's laws: the origin of distinctive intonations in Lithuanian. *International Journal of Slavic Linguistics and Poetics*, 24: 7–21.

Bell, A. (1986). The articulatory syllable: Saussure to Stetson. *Colorado Research in Linguistics*, 9: 9–18.

Bergman, B. (1983). The Saussurean sign and its algebraic properties. *Semiotica*, 46(1): 41–8.

Bezeczky, G. (1995). The course, of course. *Journal of Literary Semantics*, 24(1): 57–78.

Birnbaum, H. (1995). The linguistic sign reconsidered: arbitrariness, iconicity, motivation. *Elementa*, 2(2): 101–29.

Bollag, B. (1988). Words on the screen: the problem of the linguistic sign in the cinema. *Semiotica*, 72(1–2): 71–90.

Brockman, L. (1993). Hittite evidence for 'Saussure's Law'. PhD thesis, Harvard University, 133 pages.

Brown, D. D. (1997). Structuralism and semiotics: two key concepts in linguistic theory. *Toshokan Joho Daigaku kenkyu hokoku* (Japan), 16(2): 85–96.

Cermak, F. (1996a). Ferdinand de Saussure and the Prague School of Linguistics. In E. Hajicova et al. (eds.), *Prague Linguistic Circle Papers*, vol. 2. Amsterdam: Benjamins, pp. 59–72.

(1996b). Synchrony and diachrony revisited: was R. Jakobson and the Prague Circle right in their criticism of de Saussure? *Folia linguistica historica*, 17(1–2): 29–40.

Coseriu, E. (1995). My Saussure. In T. de Mauro and S. Sugeta (eds.), *Saussure and Linguistics Today*. Rome: Bulzoni, pp. 187–91.

Covington, F. McRee (1996). Semio-rhetoric: re-evaluating logos in the context of the Saussurean sign. *Issues in Writing*, 7(2): 155–63.

Darden, B. J. (1984). On de Saussure's law. *Folia slavica*, 7(1–2): 105–19.

Deist, F. E. (1995). On 'synchronic' and 'diachronic': wie es eigentlich gewesen. *Journal of Northwest Semitic Languages*, 21(1): 37–48.

Derrida, J. (1982). The Linguistic Circle of Geneva (trans. from French). *Critical Inquiry*, 8(4): 675–91.

Dinneen, F. P. (1990). Ferdinand de Saussure (1857–1913). *The Georgetown Journal of Languages and Linguistics* 1(1): 31–53.

Engler, R. (1995). Iconicity and/or arbitrariness. In R. Simone (ed.), *Iconicity in Language*. Amsterdam and Philadelphia: Benjamins, pp. 39–45.

Falck, C. (1986). Saussurean theory and the abolition of reality. *The Monist*, 69(1): 133–45.

Fawcett, R. P. (1982). Languages as a semiological system: a re-interpretation of Saussure. *Lacus Forum*, 9: 59–125.

Godel, R. (1984). F. de Saussure's theory of language. *Cahiers Ferdinand de Saussure*, 38: 83–97.

Hammarström, G. (1998). Two basic problems: static synchrony and causes for change. *Folia linguistica historica*, 19(1–2): 3–6.

Harris, R. (1985). Saussure and the dynamic paradigm. In C. J. N. Bailey and R. Harris (eds.), *Development Mechanisms of Language*. Oxford: Pergamon, pp. 167–83.

(1993). Saussure and linguistic geography. *Language Sciences*, 15(1): 1–14.

(1995). Saussure, generative grammar and integrational linguistics. In T. de Mauro and S. Sugeta (eds.), *Saussure and Linguistics Today*. Rome: Bulzoni, pp. 203–13.

Harris, R. and Taylor, T. J. (1993). Saussure, Wittgenstein and 'la règle du jeu'. In R. Harre and R. Harris (eds.), *Linguistics and Philosophy: a Controversial Interface*. Oxford, New York, Seoul and Tokyo: Pergamon Press, pp. 219–31.

Harris, W. V. (1983). On being sure of Saussure. *Journal of Aesthetics and Art Criticism*, 41(4): 387–97.

Helsloot, N. (2003). Divine Rock. Ferdinand de Saussure's Poetics. *Beiträge zur Geschichte der Sprachwissenschaft*, 13: 187–231.

Hewson, J. (1985). Saussure and the variationists. *Lacus Forum*, 12: 104–9.

Humphries, J. (1983). Seeing through Lear's blindness: Blanchot, Freud, Saussure and Derrida. *Mosaic*, 16(3): 29–43.

Hurford, J. R. (1989). Biological evolution of the Saussurean sign as a component of the language acquisition device. *Lingua*, 77(2): 187–222.

Hussy, C. (1998). Signifier and signified: between insignificance and operability. *Semiotica*, 122(3–4): 297–308.

Hutton, C. (1989). The arbitrary nature of the sign. *Semiotica*, 75(1–2): 63–78.

Ihara, T. (1992). The illusion of Communal language: Saussurean and Wittgensteinian arguments. *Sophia linguistica*, 31: 13–28.

Itkonen, E. (1988). A critique of the 'post-structuralist' conception of language. *Semiotica*, 71(3–4): 305–20.

Jacobini, C. (1995). Saussure and generative morphology. In: T. de Mauro and S. Sugeta (eds.), *Saussure and Linguistics Today*. Rome: Bulzoni, pp. 215–30.

Koerner, E. F. K. (1984a). Saussure's French connection. *Canadian Journal of Linguistics*, 29(1): 20–41.

(1984b). Karl Bühler's theory of language and Ferdinand de Saussure's 'Cours'. *Lingua*, 62: 3–24.

(1996). Notes on the history of the concept of language as a system 'où tout se tient'. *Linguistica atlantica*, 18–19: 1–20.

Komatsu, E. (1996). How was Saussure's Course in general linguistics written? *Fenestra*, 2: 41–50.

Lee, B. (1985). Peirce, Frege, Saussure and Whorf: the semiotic mediation of ontology. *Semiotic Mediation*, 99–128.

Lepschy, G. (1986). European linguistics in the twentieth century. In T. Bynon and F. R. Palmer (eds.), *Studies in the History of Western Linguistics: in Honour of R. H. Robins*. Cambridge: Cambridge University Press, pp. 189–201.

Leska, O., Nekvapil, J. and Soltys, O. (1987). Ferdinand de Saussure and the Prague Linguistic Circle. *Philologia Pragensia*, 30: 77–109.

Lobo, F. (1995). Amado Alonso: translator and critical interpreter of the CLG. In T. de Mauro and S. Sugeta (eds.), *Saussure and Linguistics Today*. Rome: Bulzoni, pp. 231ff.

Matejka, L. (1997). Jakobson's response to Saussure's *Cours*. *Cahiers de l'Institut de linguistique et sciences du langage*, Laussanne, 9: 177–84.

Mazor, M. (1989). Really relativism: dialectic interpretations of Saussure. *Language and Communication*, 9(1): 11–21.

Naito, M. (1995). The theory of Saussure in China. In T. de Mauro and S. Sugeta (eds.), *Saussure and Linguistics Today*. Rome: Bulzoni, pp. 243–52.

Nerlich, B. (1986). Saussurean linguistics and the problem of meaning: form dynamic statics to static dynamics. *Language and communication*, 6(4): 267–76.

Newmeyer, F. J. (1990). Competence vs. performance; theoretical vs. applied: the development and interplay of two dichotomies in modern linguistics. *Historiographia linguistica*, 17(1–2): 167–81.

Nussbaum, A. J. (1997). The 'Saussure effect' in Latin and Italic. In A. Lubotsky (ed.), *Sound Law and Analogy: Papers in Honor of Robert S. P. Beekes on the Occasion of his 60th Birthday*. Amsterdam: Rodopi, pp. 181–203.

Peng, F. C. C. (1995). On de Saussure's theoretical construction of 'Le signe': a neurolinguistic view. *Journal of Neurolinguistics*, 7(1–2): 1–9.

Percival, W. K. (1981). The Saussurean paradigm: fact or fantasy. *Semiotica*, 36(1–2): 33–49.

Polome, E. C. (1990). Language change and the Saussurean dichotomy: Diachrony versus Synchrony. In: *Research Guide on Language Change*. Berlin: Mouton de Gruyter, pp. 3–9.

Porter, J. I. (1986). Saussure and Derrida on the figure of the voice. *Modern Language Notes*, 101(4): 871–94.

Priestly, T. M. S. (1983). The first Russian translation of Saussure's *Cours*: a note. *Historiographia linguistica*, 10(3): 363–4.

Rée, J. (1997). Subjectivity in the twentieth century. *Critical Studies*, 8: 17–28.

Schalkwyk, D. (1995). Saussure, names and the gap between word and world. *Journal of Literary Semantics*, 24(2): 127–48.

Shepheard, D. (1982). Saussure's Vedic anagrams. *Modern Language Review*, 77: 513–23.

Simone, R. (1995). The language user in Saussure (and after). In L. Formigari and D. Gambarara (eds.), *Historical Roots of Linguistic Theories*. Amsterdam: John Benjamins, pp. 233–49.

Singh, P. (1992). Saussure and the Indic connection. In R. N. Srivastava (ed.), *Language and Text: Studies in Honour of R. Kalkar*. Delhi: Kalinga Publ. pp. 43–50.

Stankiewicz, E. (1995). Saussure's Law and the nominal accentuation of the Lithuanian acute stems. *Linguistica Baltica*, 4: 61–73.

Strozier, R. M. (1985). Saussure and the intellectual traditions of the twentieth century. *Semiotica*, 57(1–2): 33–49.

Tobin, Y. (1996). Review article: Will the real Professor de Saussure sign in, please? The three faces of Ferdinand. *Semiotica*, 112(3–4): 391–402.

Ungerer, F. (1991). What makes a linguistic sign successful? Towards a pragmatic interpretation of the linguistic sign. *Lingua*, 83(2–3): 155–81.

Vasiliu, E. (1980). 'Signifié': some remarks on its nature. *Revue roumaine de linguistique*, 25: 631–4.

(1986). From de Saussure to Cratylus and backwards. *Revue roumaine de linguistique*, 31(6): 491–502.

Vaughan, G. (1981). Saussure and Vygotsky via Marx. *Ars semeiotica*, 4(1): 57–83.

Yngve, V. H. (1991). Saussure and objects given in advance. *Communications of the Workshop for Scientific Linguistics* (Chicago), 5: 83ff.

SELECTION OF RECENT WORKS IN OTHER LANGUAGES

Amacker, R. and Engler, R. (eds.) (1990). *Présence de Saussure: Actes du Colloque international de Genève* (21–23 mars 1988) (Publications du Cercle Ferdinand de Saussure, 1). Geneva: Droz. 9 + 265 pages.

Arrivé, M. (2002). *Saussure*. Paris: Les Belles Lettres.

Arrivé, M. and Normand, C. (eds.) (1995). *Saussure aujourd'hui: Actes du Colloque de Cerisy la Salle* (12 août 1992) (special edition of *Linx*). Nanterre: CRL Université de Paris X. 500 pages.

Badir, S. (2001). *Saussure: La langue et sa représentation*. Paris: L'Harmattan.

Capt-Artaud, M.-C. (1994). Petit traité de rhétorique saussurienne (Publications du Cercle Ferdinand de Saussure, 2). Geneva: Droz. 166 pages.

Maruyama, K. (1981). *Saussure no shiso* [Saussurean Thought]. Tokyo: Iwanami Shoten. 311+ 25 pages.

(1983). [Reading Saussure]. Tokyo: Iwanami Shoten. 4,311 + 23 pages.

Malmberg, B. (1991). *Histoire de la linguistique de Sumer à Saussure*. Paris: Presses Universitaires de France. 496 pages.

Normand, C. (2000). Saussure. Paris: Les Belles lettres. 174 pages.

Parret, H. (1993[1994]). Les manuscripts saussuriens de Harvard. *Cahiers Ferdinand de Saussure*, 47: 179–234.

Polo, J. (1992a). Presencia de Saussure en el mundo hispánico (introdución). *Cuadernos de investigación filológica*, 18(1–2): 189–96.

(1992b). Traducciones al español del CLG de Saussure. *Cuadernos de investigación filológica*, 18(1–2): 183–96.

Prampolini, M. (1994). *Ferdinand de Saussure*. Teramo: Giunti Lisciani editori. 128 pages.

Scheerer, T. M. (1980). *Ferdinand de Saussure, Rezeption und Kritik*. Darmstadt: Wissenschaftliche Buchgesellschaft. 10 + 222 pages.

Simone, R. (1992). *Il sogno di Saussure*. Rome, Bari: Laterza. 18 + 218 pages.

Utaker, A. (2002). *La philosophie du langage: une archéologie saussurienne*. Paris: Presses Universitaires de France.

References

AA.VV. (1979). Anagrammi, enigrammi. *Lectures* 3, Dec. 1979.

Adam, J.-M. and Goldenstein, J.-P. (1976). *Linguistique et discours littéraire: théorie et pratique des textes*. Paris: Larousse.

Aarsleff, H. (1967). *The Study of Language in England, 1760–1860*. Princeton, NJ: Princeton University Press.

(1982). *From Locke to Saussure: Essays on the Study of Language and Intellectual History*. London: Athlone.

Althusser, L. (1969). *For Marx* (trans. B. Brewster). London: New Left Books.

Althusser, L. and Balibar, E. (1970). *Reading Capital* (trans. B. Brewster). London: New Left Books.

Amacker, R. (1975). *Linguistique saussurienne*. Geneva: Droz.

Amacker, R. with the collaboration of S. Bouquet (1989). Correspondance Bally–Meillet (1906–1932). *Cahiers Ferdinand de Saussure*, 43: 95–127.

Amsterdamska, O. (1987). *Schools of Thought: the Development of Linguistics from Bopp to Saussure*. Dordrecht: Reidel.

Anderson, P. (1983). *In the Tracks of Historical Materialism*. London: New Left Books.

Anderson, S. R. (1985). *Phonology in the Twentieth Century: Theories of Rules and Theories of Representations*. Chicago and London: University of Chicago Press.

(1988). Morphological theory. In F. J. Newmeyer (ed.), *Linguistics: the Cambridge Survey*, vol. I. Cambridge and New York: Cambridge University Press, pp. 146–91.

Andresen, J. T. (1990). *Linguistics in America 1769–1924: a Critical History*. London and New York: Routledge.

Andreev, N. D. and Zinder, L. R. (1964). On the notions of the speech act, speech, speech probability, and language. *Linguistics*, 4: 5–13.

Antal, L. (1990). Langue *and* parole or *only* parole? *Historiographia Linguistica*, 17(3): 357–67.

Ashby, R. (1956). *An Introduction to Cybernetics*. London: Chapman and Hall.

Attridge, D., Bennington, G. and Young, R. (eds.) (1987). *Post-Structuralism and the Question of History*. Cambridge: Cambridge University Press.

Aunger, R. (2000). *Darwinizing Culture: the Status of Memetics as a Science*. New York: Oxford University Press.

(2002). *The Electric Meme: a New Theory of How We Think*. New York: The Free Press.

Auroux, S. (1985). Deux hypothèses sur les sources de la conception saussurienne de la valeur linguistique. *Travaux de Linguistique et de Littérature* (Strasbourg B1).

(1988). La notion de linguistique générale. In A. Meillet et la linguistique de son temps. *Histoire, Epistémologie, Langage*, 10 (2): 37–56.
(ed.) (2000). *Histoire des idées linguistiques,* vol. 3. Brussels: Mardaga.
Auroux, S. and Delesalle, S. (1990). French semantics of the late nineteenth century. In H. Walter Schmitz (ed.), *Essays on Significs*. Amsterdam: John Benjamins, pp. 105–31.
Auroux, S., Koerner, E. F. K., Niederehe, H.-J. and Versteegh, K. (eds.) (2001). *History of the Language Sciences*, vol. 2. Berlin and New York: Mouton de Gruyter.
Avalle, d'A. S. (ed.) (1972a). *Ferdinand de Saussure: note sulle leggende germaniche.* Turin: Giappichelli.
(1972b). *Corso di semiologia dei testi letterari*. Turin: Giappichelli.
(1972c). Dai sistemi di segni alle nebulose di elementi. *Strumenti critici*, 6: 229–42.
(1973a). *L'ontologia del segno in Saussure.* Turin: Giappichelli.
(1973b). La sémiologie et la narrativité chez Saussure. In C. Bouazis, d'A. S. Avalle and A. Brandt (eds.), *Essais de la théorie du texte* (coll. à la lettre). Paris: Gallilée, pp. 17–49.
Ayer, A. J. (1959). *Logical Positivism.* New York: Free Press.
Bachelard, G. (1938). *La formation de l'esprit scientifique.* Paris: Corti.
(1949). *Le rationalisme appliqué.* Paris: Presses Universitaires de France.
(1953). *Le materialisme rationnel.* Paris: Presses Universitaires de France.
(1968). *The Philosophy of No: a Philosophy of the New Scientific Mind* (trans. G. C.Waterston). New York: Orion Press.
(1971). *The Poetics of Reverie* (trans. D. Russell). Boston: Beacon Press.
(1985). *The New Scientific Spirit* (trans. A. Goldhammer). Boston: Beacon Press.
Baecker, D. (ed.) (1999). *Problems of Forms.* Stanford, CA: Stanford University Press.
Baetens, J. (1986). Postérité littéraire des anagrammes. *Poétique*, 17(18): 217–33.
Bakhtin, M. (1986). *Estetika slovesnogo tvorchestva.* Moscow: Iskussto.
Baldwin, J. M. (1901–5). *Dictionary of Philosophy and Psychology*, vols. 1–3. New York: Macmillan.
(1909). *Darwin and the Humanities.* Baltimore: Review Publishing.
Bally, C. (1889). De Euripidis tragoediarum partibus lyricis quaestiunculae. Diss. inaug. Berlin.
(1899). *Les langues classiques sont-elles des langues mortes? Quelques réflexions sur l'enseignement du grec et du latin.* Basle and Geneva: Georg.
(1905). *Précis de stylistique: esquisse d'une méthode fondée sur l'étude du français moderne.* Geneva: Eggimann.
(1908). Maître et disciples. *Journal de Genève*, 18 (7).
(1909). *Traité de stylistique française.* Heidelberg: Winter, Paris: Klincksieck.
(1912). Stylistique et linguistique générale. *Archiv für das Studium der neueren Sprachen und Literaturen*, 128(n.s. 287): 97–126.
(1913a). *Le langage et la vie.* Geneva: Atar.
(1913b). *Ferdinand de Saussure et l'état actuel des études linguistiques* (leçon d'ouverture du cours de linguistique générale, lue le 27 octobre, à l'Aula de l'Université). Geneva: Atar.
(1932). *Linguistique générale et linguistique française.* Paris: Ernest Leroux.
(1944). *Linguistique générale et linguistique française*, 2nd edn (4th rev. edn 1965). Berne: Francke.

(1952). *Le langage et la vie*, 3rd edn. Geneva: Droz and Lille: Giard.
Bally, C. and Gautier, L. (eds.) (1922). *Recueil des publications scientifiques de F. de Saussure*. Geneva and Heidelberg.
Baratin, M. and Desbordes, F. (1981). *L'analyse linguistique dans l'antiquité classique, I: Les théories*. Paris: Klincksieck.
Barnes, B. (1985). *About Science*. Oxford: Blackwell.
Barthes, R. (1957). *Mythologies*. Paris: Seuil.
(1964). *Eléments de sémiologie*. Paris: Seuil.
(1966) Introduction à l'analyse structurale des récits. *Communcations*, 8: 1–27.
(1967). *Elements of Semiology* (trans. A. Lavers and C. Smith). New York: Hill and Wang.
(1968a [1953]). *Writing Degree Zero* (trans. A Lavers and C. Smith). New York: Hill and Wang.
(1968b). *Elements of Semiology* (trans. A Lavers and C. Smith). NewYork: Hill and Wang.
(1972a). *Mythologies* (trans. A. Lavers). New York: Hill and Wang.
(1972b). *Critical Essays* (trans. R. Howard). Evanston: Northwestern University Press.
(1973). *Mythologies* (trans. A. Lavers). London: Paladin.
(1975). *S/Z* (trans. R. Miller). London: Jonathan Cape.
(1977a [1975]). *Roland Barthes by Roland Barthes* (trans. R. Howard). New York: Hill and Wang.
(1977b). *Image-Music-Text* (trans. S. Heath). London: Fontana.
(1978 [1977]). *A Lover's Discourse: Fragments* (trans. R. Howard). New York: Hill and Wang.
(1982). *A Barthes Reader* (ed. S. Sontag). New York: Hill and Wang.
(1983a [1963]). *On Racine* (trans. R. Howard). New York: Hill and Wang.
(1983b [1967]). *The Fashion System* (trans. M. Ward and R. Howard). New York: Hill and Wang.
(1987a [1954]). *Michelet* (trans. R. Howard). New York: Hill and Wang.
(1987b [1985]). *The Semiotic Challenge* (trans. R. Howard). New York: Hill and Wang.
(1993a). *Oeuvres complètes*, vol. 1, *1942–1965*. Paris: Seuil.
(1993b). *Oeuvres complètes*, vol. 2, *1966–1973*. Paris: Seuil.
(1995). *Oeuvres complètes*, vol. 3, *1974–1980*. Paris: Seuil.
Bateson, G. (1967). Cybernetic explanation. *American Behavioral Scientist*, 10 (8): 29–32.
Bauche, H. (1929). *Le langage populaire*. Paris: Payot.
Belsey, C. (1980). *Critical Practice*. London: Methuen.
Bennington, G. (1991). Derridabase. In G. Bennington and J. Derrida, *Jacques Derrida*. Paris: Seuil, pp. 1–297.
(1995). *Legislations: the Politics of Deconstruction*. London: Verso.
Bense, M. (1967). *Semiotik: allgemeine Theorie der Zeichen*. Baden-Baden: Agis.
Benton, T. (1984). *The Rise and Fall of Structural Marxism*. London: New Left Books.
Benveniste, E. (1939). Nature du signe linguistique. *Acta Linguistica*, 1: 23–29.
(1956). La nature des pronoms. In Benveniste, 1966: 251–7.
(1963). Saussure après un demi-siècle. *Cahiers Ferdinand de Saussure*, 2: 7–21.

(1964). Lettres de Ferdinand de Saussure à Antoine Meillet. *Cahiers Ferdinand de Saussure*, 21: 91–130.

(1966). *Problèmes de linguistique générale*, vol. 1. Paris: Gallimard.

(1969). Sémiologie de la langue (2). *Semiotica*, 1(2): 127–35.

(1970). *Problèmes de linguistique générale*, vol. 2. Paris: Gallimard.

Benware, W. A. (1974). *The Study of Indo-European Vocalism in the 19th Century, from the beginnings to Whitney and Scherer*. Amsterdam: Benjamins.

Beust, P. (1998). Contribution à un modèle interactioniste du sens: amorce d'une compétence interprétative pour les machines. Thèse de doctorat de l'Université de Caen.

Bergounioux, G. (1984). La science du langage en France de 1870 à 1885: du marché civil au marché étatique. *Langue Française*, 63: 7–41.

(ed.) (1994). *Aux origines de la linguistique française*. Paris: Pocket.

Bigongiari, P. (1970). La poesia come funzione del linguaggio. In AA.VV. *Critica e storia letteraria* (Studi offerti a Mario Fubini, vol. 1). Padova, pp. 175–200.

Blanché, R. (1966). *Structures intellectuelles: essai sur l'organisation systématique des concepts*. Paris: J. Vrin.

Bloch, B. (1941). Phonemic overlapping. *American Speech*, 16: 278–84. (Reprinted in Joos, 1958: 93–6.)

Bloomfield, L. (1914). *An Introduction to the Study of Language*. New York: Henry Holt.

(1917). *Tagalog Texts with Grammatical Analysis* (University of Illinois Studies in Language and Literature, 3). Urbana: University of Illinois. (Preface reprinted in Bloomfield, 1970: 78–81.)

(1922). Review of E. Sapir, *Language: an Introduction to the Study of Speech*, New York: Harcourt, Brace, 1921. *The Classical Weekly*, 15: 142–3. (Reprinted in Bloomfield, 1970: 91–4.)

(1924). Review of F. de Saussure, *Cours de linguistique générale*, 2nd edn. Paris: Payot, 1922. *Modern Language Journal*, 8: 317–19. (Reprinted in Bloomfield, 1970: 106–8.)

(1926). A set of postulates for linguistic analysis. *Language*, 2: 153–64.

(1927). On recent work in general linguistics. *Modern Philology*, 25: 211–30. (Reprinted in Bloomfield, 1970: 173–90.)

(1933). *Language*. New York: Henry Holt.

(1970). *A Leonard Bloomfield Anthology* (ed. C. F. Hockett). Bloomington, IN and London: Indiana University Press.

Bloor, D. (1976). *Knowledge and Social Imagery*. London: Routledge & Kegan Paul.

Boas, F. (1911). Introduction. In F. Boas (ed.), *Handbook of American Indian Languages* (Bureau of American Ethnology, Bulletin 40, Part 1). Washington, DC: Government Printing Office, pp. 1–83.

Bopp, F. (1816). *Über das Konjugationssystem der Sanskritsprache in Vergleichung mit jenem der griechischen, lateinischen, persischen und germanischen Sprache* (*Sur le système de conjugaison du sanskrit, comparé à celui du grec, du latin, du perse et du germanique*). Frankfurt am Main: K. J. Windischmann.

Boudon, P. (1973). Recherches sémiotiques sur le lieu. *Semiotica*, 7(3): 189–225.

Bouissac, P. (1973). *La mesure des gestes*. The Hague: Mouton.

(1976). *Circus and Culture*. Bloomington: Indiana University Press.

(1998). Semiotic terminology. In P. Bouissac (ed.), *Encyclopedia of Semiotics*. New York: Oxford University Press, pp. 568–70.

Bouquet, S. (1997). *Introduction à la lecture de Saussure*. Paris: Payot.

(ed.) (2003). *Saussure*. Paris: Cahiers de l'Herne.

Boyd, R. (1984). The current status of scientific realism. In J. Leplin (ed.), *Scientific Realism*. Berkeley and Los Angeles: University of California Press, pp. 41–82.

Bréal, M. (1879). La science du langage. *Revue scientifique de la France et de l'étranger*, 43 (26 April): 1005–11.

(1881). Qu'appelle-t-on pureté de la langue? (First published in 1881, and included as an appendix in Bréal, 1897.)

(1889). La réforme de l'orthographe française. *Revue des deux mondes*, 59 (3): 592–616. (English translation in Bréal, 1991: 176–98.)

(1897). *Essai de sémantique: science des significations*. Paris: Hachette.

(1900 [1897]). *Semantics: Studies in the Science of Meaning* (trans. Mrs Henry [Nina] Cust). London: William Heinemann.

(1991). *The Beginnings of Semantics: Essays, Lectures and Reviews* (ed. and trans. G. Wolf). London: Duckworth.

Broden, T. (2000). Greimas between France and Peirce. *The American Journal of Semiotics*, 15–16: 1–4; 27–89.

Brøndal, V. (1943). *Essais de linguistique générale*. Copenhagen: Munksgaard.

Brugman, K. (1876a). Nasalis sonans in der indogermanischen Grundsprache. *Studien zur griechischen und lateinischen Grammatik (Curtius' Studien)*, 9: 285–338.

(1876b). Zur Geschichte der stammabstufenden Declinationen, Erste Abhandlung: Die Nomina auf *-ar* und *-tar*. *Studien zur griechischen und lateinischen Grammatik (Curtius' Studien)*, 9: 361–406.

Brunot, F. (1922). *La pensée et la langue*. Paris: Masson.

Brown, G. S. (1969). *Laws of Form*. London: G. Allen & Unwin.

Buchler, J. (ed.) (1940). *The Philosophy of Peirce: Selected Writings*. London: Routledge & Kegan Paul.

Burger, A. (1961). Significations et valeur du suffixe verbal français -e. *Cahiers Ferdinand de Saussure*, 18: 5–15.

Burks, A. (1949). Icon, index, symbol. *Philosophy and Phenomenological Research*, 9 (4): 673–89.

Buyssens, E. (1943). *Les langages et le discours*. Brussels: Office de la publicité.

Calvet, L.-J. (1995). *Roland Barthes: a Biography* (trans. S. Wykes). Bloomington: Indiana University Press.

Canguilhem, G. (1968). *Etudes d'histoire et de philosophie des sciences*. Paris: Vrin.

(1969). *La connaissance de la vie*, 2nd edn. Paris: Vrin.

(1978). *On the Normal and the Pathological*. Dordrecht: D. Reidel.

(1988). *Ideology and Rationality in the History of the Life Sciences* (trans. A. Goldhammer). Cambridge, MA: MIT Press.

Carnap, R. (1967). *The Logical Structure of the World and Pseudoproblems in Philosophy* (trans. R. George). Berkeley and Los Angeles: University of California Press.

(1959). *Meaning and Necessity*. Chicago: University of Chicago Press.

Cassirer, E. A. (1945). Structuralism in modern linguistics. *Word*, 1: 97–120.

Cervoni, J. (1987). *L'énonciation*. Paris: PUF.

Chao, Y.-R. (1934). The non-uniqueness of phonemic solutions of phonetic systems. *Bulletin of the Institute of History and Philology, Academia Sinica* 4, Part 4: 363–97. (Reprinted in Joos, 1958: 38–54.)

Charle, C. (1990). *Naissance des 'intellectuels' (1880–1900)*. Paris: Editions de Minuit.

Chervel, A. (1977). *Histoire de la grammaire scolaire*. Paris: Payot.

Chiss, J. L. and Puech, C. (1997). *Fondations de la linguistique*, 2nd edn. Louvain: Duculot.

(1999). *Le langage et ses disciplines*. Louvain: Duculot.

(2000). Structuralisme: structuralisme linguistique, structuralisme et philosophie. In *Dictionnaire des genres et notions littéraires (nouvelle édition augmentée)*, Encyclopaedia Universalis/Albin Michel, pp. 793–820.

Choi, Y.-H. (2002). *Le problème du temps chez Ferdinand de Saussure*. Paris: L'Harmattan.

Chomsky, N. (1957). *Syntactic Structures*. The Hague: Mouton.

(1963). Formal properties of grammars. In R. D. Luce, R. R. Bush and E. Galanter (eds.), *Handbook of Mathematical Psychology*, vol. 2. New York, London: John Wiley and Sons, pp. 323–418.

(1964a). Current issues in linguistic theory. In J. A. Fodor and J. J. Katz (eds.), *The Structure of Language: Readings in the Philosophy of Language*. Englewood Cliffs, NJ: Prentice-Hall, pp. 50–118. (Revised and expanded version of 1964b.)

(1964b). The logical basis of linguistic theory. In H. G. Lunt (ed.), *Proceedings of the Ninth International Congress of Linguists, Cambridge, Mass., August 27–31, 1962*. The Hague: Mouton, pp. 914–78. (An earlier version appeared in M. Halle (ed.), *Preprints of Papers from the Ninth International Congress of Linguists*, pp. 509–74. Cambridge, MA, 1962.)

(1966). *Cartesian Linguistics: a Chapter in the History of Rationalist Thought*. New York and London: Harper & Row.

(1975). Questions of form and interpretation. *Linguistic Analysis*, 1: 75–109.

(1980). *Rules and Representations*. New York: Columbia University Press.

(1986). *Knowledge of Language: Its Nature, Origin, and Use*. New York: Praeger.

Christmann, H. H. (1974). Saussures Anagrammstudien, *Romanische Forschungen*, 86: 229–38.

Collins, H. (1985). *Changing Order: Replication and Induction in Scientific Practice*. Chicago: University of Chicago Press.

Costello, J. R. (ed.) (1994). Papers in honor of the 50th anniversary of the Linguistic Circle of New York – International Linguistic Association. *Word*, 45 (1).

Cowan, J. M. (1987). The whimsical Bloomfield. In R. A. Hall Jr (ed.), *Leonard Bloomfield: Essays on his Life and Work*. Amsterdam, Philadelphia: John Benjamins, pp. 23–37.

Culioli, A. (1983). Théorie du langage et théorie des langues. In *Emile Benveniste aujourd'hui*, Bibliothèque de l'Information Grammaticale.

Culler, J. (1975). *Structuralist Poetics: Structuralism, Linguistics and the Study of Literature*. Ithaca, NY: Cornell University Press.

(1976). *Saussure*. Hassocks: Harvester Press.

(1977). *Ferdinand de Saussure*. New York: Penguin.

(1983). *Roland Barthes*. New York: Oxford University Press.

(1986). *Ferdinand de Saussure*, 2nd edn. Ithaca, NY: Cornell University Press.

Damourette, J. and Pichon, E. (1930–50). *Des mots à la pensée: essai de grammaire de la langue française.* Paris: D'Artrey.

Darmesteter, A. (1886) *La vie des mots.* Paris: Delagrave.

Davidson, D. (1984). *Inquiries into Truth and Interpretation.* Oxford: Clarendon Press, pp. 183–98.

Deacon, T. W. (1997). *The Symbolic Species: the Co-evolution of Language and the Brain.* New York: Norton.

Décimo, M. (1994). Saussure à Paris. *Cahiers Ferdinand de Saussure*, 48: 75–90.

Deely, J. (2001). *Four Ages of Understanding.* Toronto: University of Toronto Press.

Déguy, M. (1969). La folie de Saussure, *Critique* 25: 20–6.

Deledalle, G. (1971). *Le Pragmatisme.* Paris: Bordas.

(1974). Qu'est-ce-qu'un signe? *Semiotica* 10: 383–7.

(1976). Peirce ou Saussure. *Semiosis* 1: 7–13.

Delesalle, S. (1986). Introduction to L'histoire des théories de l'énonciation, *Histoire, Epistémologie, Langage*, 8 (2): 7–22.

Derrida, J. (1967a). *De la grammatologie.* Paris: Minuit.

(1967b). *La voix et le phenomène.* Paris: Presses Universitaires de France.

(1967c). *L'écriture et la différence.* Paris: Seuil.

(1972a). *Positions.* Paris: Minuit.

(1972b). *Marges–de la philosophie.* Paris: Minuit.

(1972c). *La dissémination.* Paris: Seuil.

(1974). *Glas.* Paris: Galilée. (English trans. by John P. Leavey and Richard Rand, Lincoln: University of Nebraska Press, 1978.)

(1982). White mythology: metaphor in the text of philosophy. In J. Derrida, *Margins of Philosophy* (trans. A. Bass). Chicago: University of Chicago Press, pp. 207–71.

(1990). *Le problème de la genèse dans la phénoménologie de Husserl.* Paris: Presses Universitaires de France.

(1993). *Spectres de Marx.* Paris: Galilée.

Desmet, P. (1994a). Victor Henry et la philosophie du langage. In J. De Clerq and P. Desmet (eds.), *Florilegium historiographiae linguisticae.* Louvain: Peeters, pp. 361–400.

(1994b). *La linguistique naturaliste en France (1867–1922).* Louvain: Peeters.

Desmet P. and Swiggers P. (1995). De la grammaire comparée à la sémantique: textes de M. Bréal publiés entre 1864 et 1898. *Orbis Supplementa*, 4. Louvain: Peeters.

Devitt, M. (1986). *Realism and Truth*, 2nd edn. Oxford: Blackwell.

Devitt, M. and Sterelny, K. (1987). *Language and Reality: an Introduction to the Philosophy of Language.* Oxford: Blackwell.

Dosse, F. (1997 [1993]). *History of Structuralism*, 2 vols. (trans. D. Glassman). Minneapolis: University of Minnesota Press.

Ducrot, O. (1968). *Le structuralisme en linguistique.* Paris: Seuil.

Eco, U. (1985). Producing signs. In M. Blonsky (ed.), *On Signs: a Semiotic Reader.* Oxford: Blackwell, pp. 176–84.

Egger, V. (1904 [1881]). *La parole intérieure: essai de psychologie descriptive.* Paris: Alcan.

Eikhenbaum, B. (1978). Theory of the Formal Method. In L. Matejka and K. Pomorska (eds.), *Readings in Russian Poetics: Formalist and Structuralist Views.* Ann Arbor: University of Michigan Press, pp. 3–38.

Einhauser, E. (1989). *Die Junggrammatiker: ein Problem für die Sprachwissenschaftgeschichtsschreibung*. Trier: Wissenschaftlicher Verlag Trier.

Elliott, G. (1987). *Althusser: the Detour of Theory*. London: Verso.

Emerson, C. and Morson, G. S. (1990). *Mikhail Bakhtin: the Creation of a Prosaics*. Stanford, CA: Stanford University Press.

Engler, R. (1959). CLG und SM: eine kritische Ausgabe des Cours de linguistique générale. *Kratylos*, 4 (2): 119–32.

(1962). Théorie et critique d'un principe saussurien: l'arbitraire du signe. *Cahiers Ferdinand de Saussure*, 19: 5–66. (Diss. Berne 1963.)

(1968a). *Lexique de la terminologie saussurienne*. Utrecht and Antwerp: Spectrum.

(1968b). Saussure e la scuola di Ginevra. *Ulisse* (Florence: Sansoni), 9 (63): 158–64.

(1974). La linéarité du signifiant. In R. Godel, *Studi saussuriani*. Bologna: Mulino, pp. 111–20.

(1974/75). Sémiologies saussuriennes, 1: De l'existence du signe (A propos d'Arco Silvio Avalle sur Saussure linguiste et mythographe). *Cahiers Ferdinand de Saussure*, 29: 45–73.

(1987a). Charles Bally, Kritiker Saussures? *Cahiers Ferdinand de Saussure*, 41: 55–63.

(1987b). Die Verfasser des CLG. In P. Schmitter (ed.), *Zur Theorie und Methode der Geschichtsschreibung der Linguistik: Analysen und Reflexionen* (Geschichte der Sprachtheorie, 1). Tübingen: Narr, pp. 141–61.

(1997). Ferdinand de Saussure (1857–1913). In *Les linguistiques suisses et la variation linguistique* (Actes d'un colloque organisé à l'occasion du centenaire du Séminaire des langues romanes de l'Université de Zurich, Berne und Tübingen). *Romanica Helvetica*, 116: 21–29.

(2000a). La langue, pierre d'achoppement. *Modèles linguistiques*, 21 (1): 9–18.

(2000b). Stalder und Saussure. In K. Stalder, *Sprache und Erkenntnis der Wirklichkeit Gottes, Texte zu einigen wissenschaftstheoretischen und systematischen Voraussetzungen für die exegetische und homiletische Arbeit* (ed. U. von Arx with K. Schori and R. Engler). *Ökumenische Beihefte*, 38: 122–47.

(2001). Entre Bally, Spitzer, . . . Saussure. *Cahiers Ferdinand de Saussure*, 54: 61–81.

(2002). Die Zeichentheorie F. de Saussures und die Semantik im 20. Jahrhundert. HSK *Geschichte der Sprachwissenschaft* 249. Berlin: De Gruyter.

Epstein, M. (1995). *After the Future: the Paradoxes of Postmodernism and Contemporary Russian Culture*. Amherst, MA: University of Massachusetts Press.

Falk, J. S. (1992). Otto Jespersen, Leonard Bloomfield, and American structural linguistics. *Language*, 68: 465–91.

(1995). Roman Jakobson and the history of Saussurean concepts in North American linguistics. *Historiographia Linguistica*, 22: 335–67.

Fehr, J. (2000). *Saussure entre linguistique et sémiologie*, Paris: Presses Universitaires de France.

Field, H. (1973). Theory change and the indeterminacy of reference. *Philosophy*, 70: 462–81.

(1974). Quine and the correspondence theory. *Philosophical Review*, 83: 200–28.

(1975). Conventionalism and instrumentalism in semantics. *Nous*, 9: 375–405.

Firth, J. R. (1935). The technique of semantics. *Transactions of the Philological Society*, pp. 36–72.

(1948). Sounds and prosodies. In Firth, J. R. (1957) *Papers in Linguistics 1934–51*. London: Oxford University Press (repr. from *Transactions of the Philological Society*, 1948).

(1951). *Modes of Meaning: Papers in Linguistics 1934–1951*. London: Oxford University Press.

(1968). Ethnographic analysis and language with reference to Malinowski's views [1957]. In F. R. Palmer (ed.), *Selected Papers of J. R. Firth 1952–1959*. Bloomington: Indiana University Press, pp. 137–67.

Florenskii, P. (1990). Stolp i utverzhdenie istiny. Moscow: Pravda.

Foucault, M. (1970). *The Order of Things* (trans. A. Sheridan-Smith). London: Tavistock.

(1972). *The Archaeology of Knowledge* (trans. A. Sheridan-Smith). London: Tavistock.

(1977a). *Language, Counter-Memory, Practice* (ed. D. F. Bouchard). Oxford: Blackwell.

(1977b). *Discipline and Punish* (trans. A. Sheridan). London: Allen Lane.

Frege, G. (1952). On sense and reference. In P. Geach and M. Black (eds.), *Translations from the Philosophical Writings of Gottlob Frege*. Oxford: Blackwell, pp. 56–78.

Frei, H. (1947). La linguistique saussurienne à Genève depuis 1939. *Word*, 3: 107–9.

Fromkin, V. A. (ed.) (2000). *Linguistics: an Introduction to Linguistic Theory*. Malden, MA, and Oxford: Blackwell Publishers.

Frýba-Reber, A.-M. (1994). *Albert Sechehaye et la syntaxe imaginative: contribution à l'histoire de la linguistique saussurienne* (Publications du Cercle Ferdinand de Saussure, III; avec bibliographie chronologique des publications d'A.S. 183–8). Geneva: Droz.

Gadet, F. (1989). *Saussure and Contemporary Culture* (trans. G. Elliott). London: Hutchinson Radius. (Originally published in French, 1986.)

Gallop, J. (1985). *Reading Lacan*. Ithaca: Cornell University Press.

Gandon, F. (2001). Le dernier Saussure: double articulation, anagrammes, brahmanisme. *Semiotica*, 133 (1–4): 69–78.

Gardiner, A. H. (1932). *The Theory of Speech and Language*. Oxford: Oxford University Press.

Gautier, L. (1916). Compte rendu du CLG. *Gazette de Lausanne et journal Suisse*, 13 Aug.

Gilliéron J. and Edmont, E. (1902–9). *Atlas linguistique de la France*. Paris: H. Champion.

Gleason, H. A. Jr (1961). *An Introduction to Descriptive Linguistics*, rev. edn. New York: Holt, Rinehart and Winston. (1st edn, 1955.)

Gmür, R. (1986). *Das Schicksal von F. de Saussures 'Mémoire': eine Rezeptionsgeschichte*. Bern: Institut für Sprachwissenschaft der Universität.

(1990). Saussures 'Mémoire'-Prinzipien in seinen späteren indogermanistischen Arbeiten. In R. Amacker and R. Engler (eds.), *Présence de Saussure: Actes du Colloque international de Genève* (21–23 mars 1988) (Publications du Cercle Ferdinand de Saussure, 1). Geneva: Droz, pp. 39–51.

Godel, R. (1957). *Les sources manuscrites du Cours de linguistique générale de F. de Saussure* (Société de publications romanes et françaises, 61). Geneva: Droz, Paris: Minard.

(1958/9). Nouveaux documents saussuriens: les cahiers E. Constantin. *Cahiers Ferdinand de Saussure*, 16: 23, 32.

(1966). F. de Saussure's theory of language. In T. A. Sebeok (ed.), *Current Trends in Linguistics,* vol. III: *Theoretical Foundations*. The Hague and Paris: Mouton, pp. 479–93.

(ed.) (1969a) [1957]. *Les sources manuscrites du Cours de linguistique générale de F. de Saussure*. Geneva: Librairie Droz.

(ed.) (1969b). *A Geneva School Reader in Linguistics*. Bloomington: Indiana University Press.

Gordon, W. T. (1979). Les Rapports associatifs. *Cahiers Ferdinand de Saussure*, 33: 31–40.

(1989). Language philosophy and linguistics in inter-bellum Britain. *Historiographia Linguistica*, 16 (3/4): 361–77.

(1992). Review of David Holdcroft, *Saussure: Signs, System and Arbitrariness*. *Historiographia Linguistica*, 19 (2/3): 369–73.

(1994a). Bridging Saussurean structuralism and British linguistic thought. *Historiographia Linguistica*, 21 (1/2): 123–36.

(1994b). 68 ans de géométrie sémantique. In Cathérine Phliponneau (ed.), *Sociolinguistique et aménagement des langues*. Moncton, NB: Centre de recherche en linguistique appliquée de l'Université de Moncton, pp. 333–47.

(1996). *Saussure for Beginners*. London and New York: Writers & Readers Publishing.

(1997). Saussure as terminologist. In Lise Lapierre, Irène Oore and Hans R. Runte (eds.), *Mélanges de linguistique offerts à Rostislav Kocourek*. Halifax: Les Presses d'ALFA, pp. 263–9.

(1999a). Review of Paul Thibault, *Re-reading Saussure: the Dynamics of Signs in Social Life*. *Historiographia Linguistica*, 26 (1/2), 209–14.

(1999b). Ferdinand de Saussure: the anagrams and the *Cours* (with Henry Gilius Schogt). In Sheila Embleton, John E. Joseph and Hans-Josef Niederehe (eds.), *The Emergence of the Modern Language Sciences: Studies in Honour of E. F. K. Koerner*. Amsterdam and Philadelphia: John Benjamins, pp. 139–50.

Graffi, G. (1988). Luoghi comuni su Hermann Paul e la scuola neogrammatica. *Lingua e Stile*, 23: 211–34.

Granger, G.-G. (1968). *Essai d'une philosophie du style*. Paris: A. Colin.

Gray, L. H. (1939). *Foundations of Language*. New York: Macmillan.

Greimas, A. J. (1956). L'actualité du saussurisme (à l'occasion du 40e anniversaire de la publication du Cours de linguistique générale). *Le Français Moderne*, 24 (3): 191–203.

(1963). La description de la signification et la mythologie comparée. *L'Homme*, Sept.–Dec.: 51–66.

(1966a). Préface à la traduction française. In L. Hjelmslev, *Le Langage*. Paris: Minuit, pp. 7–21.

(1966b). Eléments pour une théorie de l'interprétation du récit mythique. *Communication*, 8: 28–59.

(1966c). *Sémantique structurale*. Paris: Larousse.

(1970). *Du sens: Essais sémiotiques*. Paris: Seuil.

(1986). Conversation. *Versus*, 43: 42.

Greimas, A. J. and Rastier, F. (1968). The interaction of semiotic constraints. *Yale French Review*, 41: 86–105.
Grosz, E. (1990). Conclusion: a note on essentialism and difference. In S. Gunew (ed.), *Feminist Knowledge: Critique and Construct*. London and New York: Routledge, pp. 332–45.
Grzybek, P. (1998). Moskow-Tartu School. In P. Bouissac (ed.), *Encyclopedia of Semiotics*. New York: Oxford University Press, pp. 422–5.
Guérard, A. L. (1922). *A Short History of the International Language Movement*. London: T. Fisher Unwin.
Guillaume, G. (1919). *Le problème de l'article et sa solution dans la langue française*. Paris: Hachette.
(1929). *Temps et verbe: théorie des aspects, des modes et des temps*. Paris: Champion.
(1964). *Langage et science du langage*. Québec: Presses de l'Université de Laval.
Gutting, G. (1989). *Michel Foucault's Archaeology of Scientific Reason*. Cambridge: Cambridge University Press.
Guy, G. R. (1988). Language and social class. In F. J. Newmeyer (ed.), *Linguistics: the Cambridge Survey*, vol. IV. Cambridge and New York: Cambridge University Press, pp. 37–63.
Hale, N. G. (1995). *The Rise and Crisis of Psychoanalysis in the United States: Freud and the Americans, 1917–1985*. New York: Oxford University Press.
Hall, R. A. Jr (1951–2). American linguistics, 1925–1950. *Archivum Linguisticum*, 3 (1951): 101–25, 4 (1952): 1–16.
(1990). *A Life for Language: a Biographical Memoir of Leonard Bloomfield*. Amsterdam and Philadelphia: John Benjamins.
Harari, J. V. (ed.) (1980). *Textual Strategies: Perspectives in Post-Structuralist Criticism*. London: Methuen.
Harding, Sandra G. (1976). *Can Theories Be Refuted? Essays on the Duhem–Quine Thesis*. Dordrecht and Boston: Reidel.
Harland, R. (1987). *Superstructuralism: the Philosophy of Structuralism and Post-Structuralism*. London: Methuen.
Harman, G. (1965). Inference to the best explanation. *Philosophical Review*, 74: 88–95.
Harris, R. (1987). *Reading Saussure: a Critical Commentary on the Cours de linguistique générale*. London: Gerald Duckworth.
(1988a). *Linguistic Thought in England 1914–1945*. London, Duckworth.
(1988b). *Language, Saussure and Wittgenstein: How to Play Games with Words*. London: Routledge.
(2000). Saussure for all Seasons. *Semiotica*, 131 (3–4): 273–87.
(2001). *Saussure and his Interpreters*. Edinburgh: Edinburgh University Press.
Harris, Z. S. (1940). Review of L. H. Gray, *Foundations of Language*, New York: Macmillan, 1939. *Language*, 16: 216–23.
(1941). Review of N. S. Trubetzkoy, *Grundzüge der Phonologie* (Travaux du Cercle Linguistique de Prague, 7), Prague, 1939. *Language*, 17: 345–9.
(1942). Morpheme alternants in linguistic analysis. *Language*, 18: 169–80. (Reprinted in Joos, 1958: 109–15.)
(1946). From morpheme to utterance. *Language*, 22: 161–83. (Reprinted in Joos, 1958: 142–53.)
(1951). *Methods in Structural Linguistics*. Chicago: University of Chicago Press.

Haugen, E. (1951). Directions in modern linguistics. *Language*, 27: 211–22. (Reprinted in Joos, 1958: 357–63.)

Hellmann, W. (1988). *Charles Bally: Frühwerk-Rezeption-Bibliographie* (Abhandlungen zur Sprache und Literatur, 8). Bonn: Romanistischer Verlag.

Henry, V. (1896). *Antimonies linguistiques.* Paris: Félix Alcan.

(1901). *Le langage martien: étude analytique de la genèse d'une langue dans un cas de glossolalie somnambulique.* Paris: Maisonneuve.

(2001[1896]). *Antinomies linguistique.* Avec *Le langage martien.* Louvain: Peeters, Coll. L'information Grammaticale, preface by J. L. Chiss and C. Puech.

Herdan, G. (1956). On communication between linguists. *Linguistics*, 9: 71–6.

Herdan, G. (1964). *Language as Choice and Chance.* Groningen: Nordhoff.

Hewson, J. (1976). *Langue* and *parole* since Saussure. *Historiographia Linguistica*, 3 (3): 315–48.

Hill, A. A. (1955). Linguistics since Bloomfield. *Quarterly Journal of Speech*, 41: 253–60.

(1964). History of the Linguistic Institute. *ACLS Newsletter* 15 (3): 1–12.

Hjelmslev, L. (1953). *Prolegomena to a Theory of Language* (trans. F. J. Whitfield). Baltimore, MD: Waverly Press.

(1959). Pour une sémantique structurale. In *Essais linguistiques.* Travaux du cercle linguistique de Copenhague, 12, pp. 96–112.

(1963 [1943]). *Prolegomena to a Theory of Language* (trans. J. Whitfield). Madison: University of Wisconsin Press.

(1966 [1963]). *Le langage* (trans. M. Olsen). Paris: Minuit.

(1968 [1943]). *Prolégomènes à une théorie du langage*. Paris: Minuit.

(1968). La structure fondamentale du langage. In *Prolégomènes à une théorie du langage.* Paris: Minuit, pp. 175–227.

Hockett, C. F. (1942). A system of descriptive phonology. *Language*, 18: 3–21. (Reprinted in Joos, 1958: 97–107.)

(1947). Problems of morphemic analysis. *Language*, 23: 321–43. (Reprinted in Joos, 1958: 229–42.)

(1948). A note on 'structure'. *International Journal of American Linguistics*, 14: 269–71. (Reprinted in Joos, 1958: 279–80.)

(1982). The changing intellectual context of linguistic theory. In J. Morreall (ed.), *The Ninth LACUS Forum 1982*. Columbia, SC: Hornbeam Press, pp. 9–42.

(1987). *Refurbishing Our Foundations: Elementary Linguistics from an Advanced Point of View*. Amsterdam and Philadelphia: John Benjamins.

(1989). Leonard Bloomfield: after fifty years. *Yale Graduate Journal of Anthropology*, 2: 1–11.

Hoenigswald, H. (1978). The *annus mirabilis* 1876 and posterity. *Transactions of the Philological Society*, pp. 17–35.

(ed.) (1979). *The European Background of American Linguistics: Papers of the Third Golden Anniversary Symposium of the Linguistic Society of America*. Dordrecht: Foris.

Holdcroft, D. (1991). *Saussure: Signs, System and Arbitrariness*. Cambridge: Cambridge University Press.

Horney, K. (1967). *Feminine Psychology*. New York: W. W. Norton.

Horwich, P. (ed.) (1993). *The World Changes: Thomas Kuhn and the Nature of Science*. Cambridge, MA: MIT Press.

Householder, F. W. Jr (1952). Review of Z. S. Harris, *Methods in Structural Linguistics*, Chicago: University of Chicago Press, 1951. *International Journal of American Linguistics*, 18: 260–8.

Hovelacque, A.(1876). *La linguistique*. Paris: Reinwald.

Hübschmann, H. (1875). Über die Stellung des armenischen im Kreise der indogermanischen Sprachen, *Zeitschrift für vergleichende Sprachforschung*, 23: 5–49.

(1885). *Das indogermanische Vocalsystem*. Strassburg: Trübner.

Hughes, H. S. (1959). *Consciousness and Society*. London: MacGibbon & Kee.

(1975). *The Sea Change: the Migration of Social Thought, 1930–1965*. New York: Harper & Row.

Huot, H. (ed.) (1991). *La grammaire française entre comparatisme et structuralisme: 1870–1960*. Paris: Armand Colin.

Husserl, E. (1963). *L'origine de la géométrie* (trans. J. Derrida). Paris: PUF.

Hymes, D. (1983). Traditions and paradigms. In *Essays in the History of Linguistic Anthropology*. Amsterdam, Philadelphia: John Benjamins, pp. 345–83.

Hymes, D. and Fought, J. (1975). American Structuralism. In Thomas A. Sebeok (ed.), *Current Trends in Linguistics*, vol. 13. The Hague: Mouton, pp. 903–1176.

(1981). *American Structuralism*. The Hague: Mouton. (Main body of text originally published in *Current Trends in Linguistics*, vol. 13, part 2, 1975.)

Jakobson, R. (1928). O hláskoslovném zákonu a teleologickém hláskosloví. *Časopis pro moderní filologii*, 14: 183–4. (Published in English translation, 'The concept of the sound law and the teleological criterion', Jakobson, 1962: 1–2.)

(1932). 'Fonéma' & 'Fonologie'. *Ottuv slovnik naučný*, Supplement 2 (608): 611–12. (Published in English translation, 'Phoneme and phonology', Jakobson, 1962: 231–3.)

(1933). La scuola linguistica di Praga. *La Cultura*, 12: 633–41. (Reprinted in Jakobson, 1971a: 539–46.)

(1939). Signe zéro. In *Mélanges de linguistique offerts à Charles Bally*. Geneva: Librairie de l'Université, 143–52. (Reprinted in Jakobson, 1971a: 211–19.)

(1944). Franz Boas' approach to language. *International Journal of American Linguistics*, 10: 188–95. (Reprinted in Jakobson, 1971a: 477–88.)

(1960). Linguistics and poetics. In T. A. Sebeok (ed.), *Style in Language*. New York: Wiley, pp. 350–77.

(1962). *Selected Writings*, vol. I: *Phonological Studies*. The Hague: Mouton.

(1963). Efforts toward a means-ends model of language in interwar continental linguistics. In C. Mohrmann, F. Norman and A. Sommerfelt (eds.), *Trends in Modern Linguistics*. Utrecht and Antwerp: Spectrum, pp. 104–8. (Reprinted in Jakobson, 1971a: 522–6.)

(1963–70). *Essais de linguistique générale*, vols. 1 and 2. Paris: Minuit.

(1966). A la recherche de l'essence du langage. In R. Jakobson, *Problèmes du langage*. Collection Diogène. Paris: Gallimard, pp. 22–38.

(1971a). *Selected Writings*, vol. II: *Word and Language*. The Hague: Mouton.

(1971b). The world response to Whitney's principles of linguistic science. In M. Silverstein (ed.), *Whitney on Language: Selected Writings of William Dwight Whitney*. Cambridge, MA, and London: MIT Press, pp. xxv–xlv.

(1978). *Six Lectures on Sound and Meaning* (trans. J. Mepham). Hassocks: Harvester Press. (Lectures given in 1942 and first published as *Six leçons sur le son et le sens*, Paris: Minuit, 1976.)

(1980 [1959]). Sign and system of language: a reassessment of Saussure's doctrine. *Poetics Today*, 2 (1a): 33–8.

(1980). *The Framework of Language*. University of Michigan: Michigan Studies in the Humanities.

(1990). *On Language* (ed. L. R. Waugh and M. Monville-Burston). Cambridge, MA: Harvard University Press.

James, T. (1995). *Dream, Creativity and Madness in Nineteenth-Century France*. Oxford: Clarendon.

Jameson, F. (1972). *The Prison-House of Language: a Critical Account of Structuralism*. Princeton, NJ: Princeton University Press.

Jankowsky, K. R. (1972). *The Neogrammarians*. The Hague: Mouton.

Joos, M. (ed.) (1958). *Readings in Linguistics: the Development of Descriptive Linguistics in America since 1925*, 2nd edn. New York: American Council of Learned Societies.

Joos, M. (1966 [1957]). *Readings in Linguistics*, vol. 1. Chicago: Chicago University Press.

Joseph, J. E. (1988). Saussure's meeting with Whitney, Berlin, 1879. *Cahiers Ferdinand de Saussure*, 42: 205–14.

(1989a). Bloomfield's Saussureanism. *Cahiers Ferdinand de Saussure*, 43: 43–53.

(1989b). The genesis of Jakobson's *Six Lectures on Sound and Meaning*. *Historiographia Linguistica*, 16: 415–20.

(1990). Ideologizing Saussure: Bloomfield's and Chomsky's readings of the *Cours de linguistique générale*. In J. E. Joseph and T. J. Taylor (eds.), *Ideologies of Language*. London and New York: Routledge, pp. 51–78.

(1995). Saussurean tradition in linguistics. In E. F. K. Koerner and R. E. Asher (eds.), *Concise History of the Language Sciences*. Oxford: Pergamon/ Elsevier Science, pp. 233–9.

(2000a). The unconscious and the social in Saussure. *Historiographia Linguistica*, 27, 307–34.

(2000b). Language and 'psychological race': Léopold de Saussure on French in Indochina. *Language and Communication*, 20: 29–53.

(2001). The exportation of structuralist ideas from linguistics to other fields. In S. Auroux, E. F. K. Koerner, H-J. Niederehe and K. Versteegh (eds.), *History of the Language Sciences: an International Handbook on the Evolution of the Study of Language from the Beginnings to the Present*. Berlin and New York: Walter de Gruyter, pp. 1880–1908.

(2003). Pictet's *Du Beau* (1856) and the crystallisation of Saussurean linguistics. *Historiographia Linguistica*, 30: 365–88.

Joseph, J. E., Love, N. and Taylor, T. J. (2001). *Landmarks in Linguistic Thought*, vol. II: *The Western Tradition in the Twentieth Century*. London and New York: Routledge.

Katz, J. J., and Postal, P. M. (1964). *An Integrated Theory of Linguistic Descriptions*. Cambridge, MA: MIT Press.

Koerner, E. F. K. (1972). *Bibliographia Saussureana 1870–1970*. Metuchen, NJ: Scarecrow Press.

(1973). *Ferdinand de Saussure: Origin and Development of his Linguistic Thought in Western Studies of Language*. Braunschweig: Vieweg & Sohn.

(1988). *Saussurean Studies / Etudes saussuriennes*. Geneva: Slatkine.

(1989). Leonard Bloomfield and the *Cours de linguistique générale*. In *Practicing Linguistic Historiography: Selected Essays*. Amsterdam and Philadelphia: John Benjamins, pp. 435–43.

(1994). Chomsky's readings of the *Cours de linguistique générale*. *Lingua e stile*, 29: 267–84.

(1995). Chomsky's readings of the *Cours de linguistique générale*. In *Professing Linguistic Historiography*. Amsterdam and Philadelphia: John Benjamins, pp. 96–114.

Kravis, J. (1976). *The Prose of Mallarmé*. Cambridge: Cambridge University Press.

Kristéva, J. (1969a). *Sêmeiôtikê recherches pour une sémanalyse*. Paris: Seuil.

(1969b). L'engendrement de la formule. *Tel Quel*, 37: 34–73, 38: 55–81.

(1981). *Desire in Language: a Semiotic Approach to Literature and Art* (ed. L. S. Roudiez). Oxford: Blackwell.

Kronenfeld, D. (1996). *Plastic Glasses and Church Fathers: Semantic Extension from the Ethnoscience Tradition*. New York: Oxford University Press.

Kuhn, Thomas S. (1970). *The Structure of Scientific Revolutions*, 2nd edn. Chicago: University of Chicago Press.

Kuryłowicz, J. (1927). ə indo-européen et ḫ hittite. In *Symbolae grammaticae in honorem Iohannis Rozwadowski* I. Cracow: Gebethner & Wolff, pp. 95–104.

(1978). Lecture du Mémoire en 1978: un commentaire. *Cahiers Ferdinand de Saussure*, 32: 6–26.

Kurzweil, E. (1989). *The Freudians: a Comparative Perspective*. New Haven: Yale University Press.

Labov, W. (1972). *Sociolinguistic Patterns*. Philadelphia: University of Pennsylvania Press.

Lacan, J. (1957). L'instance de la lettre dans l'inconscient ou la raison depuis Freud. *La psychanalyse*, 3: 47–81.

(1966). *Ecrits 1*, Paris.

(1977 [1966]). *Ecrits: a Selection* (trans. A. Sheridan-Smith). New York: Norton.

Lafrance, G. (ed.) (1987). *Gaston Bachelard*. Ottawa: University of Ottawa Press.

Lamb, S. M. (1965). Kinship terminology and linguistic structure. *American Anthropologist*, 67(5), part 2: 37–64.

(1966). *Outline of Stratificational Grammar*. Washington, DC: Georgetown University Press.

Lecourt, D. (1975). *Marxism and Epistemology: Bachelard, Canguilhem, Foucault*. London: New Left Books.

Lee, A. and Poynton, C. (eds.) (2000). *Culture and Text: Discourse and Methodology in Social Research and Cultural Studies*. Lanham, MD: Rowman & Littlefield.

Leibniz, G. W. (1987). *Discours sur la théologie naturelle des chinois* (trans. C. Frémont). Paris: L'Herne.

Leskien, A. (1876). *Die Declination im Slawisch-Litauischen und Germanischen*. Leipzig: Hirzel.

Levin, S. R. (1965). *Langue* and *parole* in American linguistics. *Foundations of Language*, 1: 83–94.

Lévi-Strauss, C. (1945). L'analyse structurale en linguistique et en anthropologie. *Word, Journal of the Linguistic Circle of New York*, 1(1): 1–21.

(1960). L'analyse morphologique des contes russes. *Cahiers de l'Institut de science économique appliquée*, 9 (series M, 7): 3–36.

(1963 [1958]). *Structural Anthropology* (trans. C. Jacobson and B. Grundfest Schoepf). New York: Basic Books.

(1973) *Anthropologie structurale*, vol. 2. Paris: Plon.

(1985 [1983]). *The View from Afar* (trans. J. Neugroschel and P. Hoss). New York: Basic Books.

Linda, M. (1995). Zur Verstellung Ferdinand de Saussures im 'Cours de linguistique générale': ein Beitrag zur Rekonstruktionsgeschichte der Genese des CLG. MA thesis, University of Essen.

(2001). *Elemente einer Semiologie des Hörens und Sprechens: zum kommunikationstheoretischen Ansatz Ferdinand de Saussures* (Tübinger Beiträge zur Linguistik, 456). Tübingen: Narr.

Lipton, P. (1993). *Inference to the Best Explanation*. London: Routledge.

Lodge, D. (1977). *The Modes of Modern Writing: Metaphor, Metonymy and the Typology of Modern Literature*. London: Edward Arnold.

Lossky, V. (1985). *In the Image and Likeness of God*. Crestwood, NY: St Vladimir's Seminary Press.

Lotman, Y. (1990). *Universe of the Mind: a Semiotic Theory of Culture*. Bloomington and Indianapolis: Indiana University Press.

Lough, J. (1978). *An Introduction to Nineteenth Century France*. London: Longman.

Lounsbury, F. G. (1953). The method of descriptive morphology. *Oneida Verb Morphology*. (Yale University Publications in Anthropology, 48.) (Reprinted in Joos, 1958: 379–85.)

(1956). A semantic analysis of the Pawnee kinship usage. *Language*, 32: 158–94.

(1964). The structural analysis of kinship semantics. In H. G. Lunt (ed.), *Proceedings of the Ninth International Congress of Linguists, Cambridge, Mass., August 27–31, 1962*. The Hague: Mouton, pp. 1073–90.

Luhmann, N. (1999). Sign as form. In D. Baecker (ed.), *Problems of Forms*. Stanford, CA: Stanford University Press, pp. 46–63.

Lunt, H. G. (ed.) (1964). *Proceedings of the Ninth International Congress of Linguists, Cambridge, Mass., August 27–31, 1962*. The Hague: Mouton.

Mallarmé, S. (1945). *Œuvres complètes* (ed. H. Mondor and G. Jean-Aubry). Paris: Gallimard.

Malmberg, B. (1977). *Signes et symboles*. Paris: Picard.

Manczak, W. (1969). Les termes 'langue' et 'parole' désignent-ils quelque chose de réel? *Linguistics*, 55: 48–55.

Manetti, G. (1993). *Theories of the Sign in Classical Antiquity* (trans. C. Richardson). Bloomington: Indiana University Press.

Martinet, A. (1949). La double articulation linguistique. *Travaux du Cercle Linguistique de Copenhague*, 5: 30–37.

(1955). *Economie des changements phonétiques: traité de phonologie diachronique*. Berne: Francke.

(1960). *Eléments de linguistique générale*. Paris: A. Colin.

(1965). *La linguistique synchronique*. Paris: Presses Universitaires de France.

(1967 [1960]). *Elements of General Linguistics*. Chicago: University of Chicago Press.

Martinet, J. (1993). Biographie d'André Martinet. In A. Martinet, *Mémoires d'un linguiste: vivre les langues*. Paris: Quai Voltaire, pp. 359–64.

Marty, A. (1908). *Untersuchungen zur Grundlegung der allgemeinen Grammatik und Sprachphilosophie*. Halle: Niemeyer.

Mayrhofer, M. (1981). *Nach hundert Jahren. Ferdinand de Saussures Frühwerk und seine Rezeption durch die heutige Indogermanistik* (with a contribution by R. Zwanziger; Sitzber. d. Heidelberger Akademie der Wissenschaften. Phil.-hist. Kl. Jhg. 1981, Bericht 8). Heidelberg: Winter.

(1983). *Sanskrit und die Sprachen Alteuropas: zwei Jahrhunderte des Widerspiels von Entdeckungen und Irrtümern* (Nachrichten der Akademie der Wissenschaftler in Göttingen. 1. Phil.-hist. Klasse. 1983 Nr. 5).

Mehlman, J. (ed.) (1972). 'The floating signifier': from Lévi-Strauss to Lacan. *Yale French Studies*, no. 48.

(2000). *Emigré New York: French Intellectuals in Wartime Manhattan, 1940–1944*. Baltimore: Johns Hopkins University Press.

Meillet, A. (1913). *Bulletin de la Société linguistique de Paris 18*, 1912/13, CLXXIV.

(1916). *La linguistique*. In *La science française*. Paris: Larousse.

(1921–36). *Linguistique historique et linguistique générale*. Paris: Champion-Klincksieck.

(1938). *Linguistique historique et linguistique générale*, vol. II. Paris: Klincksieck.

(1965). *Linguistique historique et linguistique générale*, Paris: H. Champion.

Merleau-Ponty, M. (1945). *Phénoménologie de la perception*. Paris: Gallimard.

(1963 [1942]). *The Structure of Behavior* (trans. A. L. Fisher). Boston: Beacon Press.

(1964 [1960]). *Signs* (trans. R. McCleary). Evanston: Northwestern University Press.

Meschonnic, H. (1995). Seul comme Benveniste ou comment la critique manque de style. *Langages*, 118: 31–55.

Metz, C. (1968). *Essais sur la signification au cinéma*, vol. 1. Paris: Klincksieck.

(1971). *Langage et cinéma*. Paris: Larousse.

(1972). *Essais sur la signification au cinéma*, vol. 2. Paris: Klincksieck.

Meyendorff, J. (1983). *Byzantine Theology: Historical Trends and Doctrinal Themes*. New York: Fordham University Press.

Moeller, K. D. and Wulff, H. J. (1985). *Zeichen, Function und Kontext. Zur Terminologie der Semiotik*, I: 3. Münster: Papmaks.

Moles, A. (1968[1958]) *Information Theory and Esthetic Perception*. Urbana, IL: University of Illinois Press.

Morpurgo Davies, A. (1978). Analogy, segmentation and the early neogrammarians. *Transactions of the Philological Society*, pp. 36–60.

(1994). Early and late Indo-European from Bopp to Brugmann. In G. R. Dunkel et al. (eds.), *Früh-, Mittel-, Spätindogermanisch*. Wiesbaden: Reichert, pp. 245–65.

(1998). Nineteenth century linguistics. In G. Lepschy (ed.), *History of Linguistics*, vol. 4. London: Longman.

Morris, C. (1938). Foundations of the Theory of Signs. *International Encyclopedia of Unified Science*, vol. 1:2. Chicago: University of Chicago Press.

(1946). *Signs, Language and Behavior*. New York: Prentice-Hall.

(1955). *Signs, Language, and Behavior*. New York: George Braziller.

Mounin, G. (1968). *Ferdinand de Saussure ou le structuraliste sans le savoir*. Paris: Seghers.
(1970). *Introduction à la sémiologie*. Paris: Minuit.
Murray, S. O. (1994). *Theory Groups and the Study of Language in North America: a Social History*. Amsterdam and Philadelphia: John Benjamins.
Napoli, D. J. (1996). *Linguistics: an Introduction*. New York and Oxford: Oxford University Press.
Nava, G. (1968). Lettres de Ferdinand de Saussure à Giovanni Pascoli. *Cahiers Ferdinand de Saussure*, 24: 73–81.
Naville, A. (1901). *Nouvelle classification des sciences, étude philosophique*, 2nd edn. Paris: Alcan.
Nerlich, B. (1986). *La pragmatique: tradition ou révolution dans la linguistique française*. Frankfurt am Main: Peter Lang.
Newmeyer, F. J. (1980). *Linguistic Theory in America: the First Quarter-Century of Transformational Generative Grammar*. New York and London: Academic Press.
(ed.) (1988). *Linguistics: the Cambridge Survey*, 4 vols. Cambridge and New York: Cambridge University Press.
Nida, E. A. (1948). The identification of morphemes. *Language*, 24: 414–41. (Reprinted in Joos, 1958: 255–71.)
Nisard, C. (1872). *Etude sur le langage populaire*. Paris: Franck.
Normand, C. (ed.) (1970). L'arbitraire du signe comme déplacement, *Dialectiques*, 1.
(ed.) (1978a). *Avant Saussure: choix de textes*. Brussels: Editions Complexe.
(ed.) (1978b). Saussure et la linguistique pré-saussurienne. *Langages*, 49: 66–90.
(1985). Le sujet entre langue et parole, *Langages*, 77: 33–42.
(1989). Constitution de la sémiologie chez Benveniste. *Histoire, Epistémologie, Langage*, 11 (2): 141–69.
(2000). La question d' une science générale; Les thèmes de la linguistique générale; La généralité des principes. In S. Auroux (ed.), *Histoire des idées linguistiques*, vol 3. Brussels: Mardaga, pp. 441–71.
Norris, C. (1994). *Truth and the Ethics of Criticism*. Manchester: Manchester University Press.
(1996). *Reclaiming Truth: Contribution to a Critique of Cultural Relativism*. London: Lawrence & Wishart.
(1997a). *Against Relativism: Philosophy of Science, Deconstruction and Critical Theory*. Oxford: Blackwell.
(1997b). Deconstruction, ontology, and philosophy of science. In *New Idols of the Cave: On the Limits of Anti-Realism*. Manchester: Manchester University Press, pp. 78–116.
(2000). *Minding the Gap: Epistemology and Philosophy of Science in the Two Traditions*. Amherst, MA: University of Massachusetts Press.
(2002). *Hilary Putnam: Realism, Reason, and the Uses of Uncertainty*. Manchester: Manchester University Press.
Odier, H. (1905). Essai d'analyse psychologique du mécanisme du langage dans la compréhension. Thèse de doctorat, University of Berne.
Ogden, C. K. and Richards, I. A. (1923). *The Meaning of Meaning: a Study of the Influence of Language upon Thought and the Science of Symbolism*. London: Kegan, Trench and Trübner.

(1927). *The Meaning of Meaning: a Study of the Influence of Language upon Thought and of the Science of Symbolism*, 2nd rev. edn. London: Kegan Paul, Trench, Trübner; New York: Harcourt, Brace.

(1994 [1923]). *The Meaning of Meaning* (ed. W. T. Gordon). London: Routledge/Thoemmes.

Osthoff, H. and Brugman, K. (1878). Foreword, *Morphologische Untersuchungen* 1: iii–xx.

Ouspensky, L. (1982). The meaning and language of icons. In L. Ouspensky and V. Lossky (eds.), *The Meaning of Icons*. Crestwood, NY: St Vladimir's Seminary Press.

Parret, H. (1974). *Discussing Language* (Janua Linguarum. Series Maior, 93). The Hague: Mouton.

Paul, H. (1880). *Principien der Sprachgeschichte*. Halle: Niemeyer.

Paul, H. W. (1987). *From Knowledge to Power, the Rise of the Science Empire in France (1860–1939)*. Cambridge: Cambridge University Press.

Pavel, T. (1990). *The Feud of Language: a History of Structuralist Thought*. Oxford: Blackwell.

Pedersen, H. (1962 [1924]). *The Discovery of Language: Linguistic Science in the Nineteenth Century* (trans. J. W. Spargo). Bloomington: Indiana University Press. (Reprint of 1931 edition, Cambridge, MA: Harvard University Press.)

Peirce, C. S. (1931–5). *Collected Papers*, 6 vols. Cambridge, MA: Harvard University Press.

(1977). *Semiotic and Significs: the Correspondence between Charles S. Peirce and Victoria Lady Welby* (ed. C. S. Hardwick). Bloomington: Indiana University Press.

Pictet, A. (1856). *Du beau, dans la nature, l'art et la poésie: études esthétiques*. Paris and Geneva: J. Cherbuliez.

(1859–63). *Les origines indo-européennes ou les Aryas primitifs: essai de paléontologie linguistique*, 2 vols. Paris: Cherbuliez.

Pike, K. L. (1943). Taxemes and immediate constituents. *Language*, 19: 65–82.

(1947). Grammatical prerequisites to phonemic analysis. *Word*, 3: 155–72.

(1954). *Language in Relation to a Unified Theory of the Structure of Human Behavior* (part I, prelim. edn). Glendale, CA: Summer Institute of Linguistics.

(1960). *Language in Relation to a Unified Theory of the Structure of Human Behavior* (part III, prelim. edn). Glendale, CA: Summer Institute of Linguistics.

Ponge, F. (1967). *Le savon*. Paris: Gallimard.

Ponge, F. and Sollers, P. (1970). *Entretiens de Francis Ponge avec Philippe Sollers*. Paris: Gallimard.

Posner, R., Robering, K. and Sebeok, T. A. (eds.) (1997). *Semiotics: a Handbook on the Sign-theoretic Foundation of Nature and Culture*, vol. 1. Berlin: De Gruyter.

Preston, W. D. (1948). Review of C. H. de Goeje, *Etudes linguistiques caribes II*, Amsterdam: North-Holland Publishing, 1946. *International Journal of American Linguistics*, 14: 131–4.

Prieto, L. (1966). *Messages et signaux*. Paris: Presses Universitaires de France.

Propp, V. (1958 [1928]). *Morphology of the Folktale* (trans. L. Scott). Bloomington, IN: Publication 10 of the Indiana University Research Center in Anthropology, Folklore and Linguistics.

Psillos, S. (1999). *Scientific Realism: How Science Tracks Truth*. London: Routledge.

Puech, C. (2000). L'esprit de Saussure – Paris contre Genève: l'héritage saussurien. *Modèles linguistiques* (ed. S. Bouquet), 20 (1): 79–93.

(2003). L'émergence d'un paradigme sémiotico-structural en France à la fin des années cinquante. In G. Bettetini, S. Cigada, S. Raynaud and E. Rigotti (eds.) *SEMIOTICA II* (Pubblicazioni del Centro di Linguistica). Turin: La Scuola, l'Università Cattolica.

(ed.) (2004). *Linguistique et partages disciplinaires à la charnière des XIXe et XXe siècles: Victor Henry*. Louvain and Paris: Peeters.

Putnam, H. (1975). *Mind, Language and Reality* (Philosophical Papers, 2). Cambridge: Cambridge University Press.

(1981). *Reason, Truth and History*. Cambridge: Cambridge University Press.

(1987). *The Many Faces of Realism*. La Salle, IL: Open Court.

(1990). *Realism with a Human Face*. Cambridge, MA: Harvard University Press.

(1992). *Renewing Philosophy*. Cambridge, MA: Harvard University Press.

Quine, W. V. (1961). *From a Logical Point of View*, 2nd edn. Cambridge, MA: Harvard University Press.

(1969). *Ontological Relativity and Other Essays*. New York: Columbia University Press.

Redard, G. (1978a). Deux Saussure? *Cahiers Ferdinand de Saussure*, 32: 27–41.

(1978b). Louis Havet et le Mémoire. *Cahiers Ferdinand de Saussure*, 32: 103–22.

(1982a). Charles Bally disciple de Ferdinand de Saussure. *Cahiers Ferdinand de Saussure*, 36: 3–23.

(1982b). Bibliographie chronologique des publications de Charles Bally (2 février 1865 – 10 avril 1947). *Cahiers Ferdinand de Saussure*, 36: 25–41.

Regard, P.-F. (1919). *Contribution à l'étude des prépositions dans la langue du Nouveau Testament*. Paris: Leroux.

Reichard, G. A., Jakobson, R. and Werth, E. (1949). Language and synesthesia. *Word*, 5: 224–33.

Reichenbach, H. (1938). *Experience and Prediction*. Chicago: University of Chicago Press.

(1947). *Elements of Symbolic Logic*. New York: Macmillan.

Reichler-Béguelin, M.-J. (1980). Le consonantisme grec et latin selon F. de Saussure: le cours de phonétique professé en 1909–1910. *Cahiers Ferdinand de Saussure*, 34: 17–96.

(1990). Des formes observées aux formes sous-jacentes. In R. Amacker and R. Engler (eds.), *Présence de Saussure: Actes du Colloque international de Genève* (21–23 mars 1988) (Publications du Cercle Ferdinand de Saussure, 1). Geneva: Droz, pp. 21–37.

Reiss, T. (1988). *The Uncertainties of Analyses: Problems in Truth, Meaning and Culture*. Ithaca: Cornell University Press.

Renan, E. (1950 [1871]). *La réforme intellectuelle et morale* (reprint edited by P. E. Charvet). Cambridge: Cambridge University Press.

Rorty, R. (1982). *Consequences of Pragmatism*. Brighton: Harvester.

(1991). *Objectivity, Relativism, and Truth*. Cambridge: Cambridge University Press.

Rose, J. (1986). *Sexuality in the Field of Vision*. New York: Verso.

Rossi, A. (1968). Gli anagrammi di Saussure: Poliziano, Bach, Pascoli. *Paragone*, 218: 113–27.

Roudinesco, E. (1990 [1985]). *Jacques Lacan & Co.: a History of Psychoanalysis in France, 1925–1985* (trans. J. Mehlman). Chicago: University of Chicago Press.

Russell, B. (1956). *Logic and Knowledge* (ed. R. Marsh). London: Allen & Unwin.

Ruwet, N. (1972). *Langage, musique, poésie*. Paris: Seuil.

Salmon, W. C. (1967). *The Foundations of Scientific Inference*. Pittsburgh, PA: University of Pittsburgh Press.

Sanders, C. (1979). *Cours de linguistique générale de Saussure*. Paris: Hachette.

(2000a). Saussure: Paris – Geneva vu de Londres, *Modèles Linguistiques*, 20 (1): 94–107.

(2000b). Saussure translated. *Historiographia Linguistica*, 27: 345–58.

Sapir, E. (1921). *Language: an Introduction to the Study of Speech*. New York: Harcourt, Brace.

Saussure, L. de (1899). *Psychologie de la colonisation française*. Paris: F. Alcan.

Sebeok, T. A. (1974). Semiotics: a survey of the state of the art. In T. A. Sebeok (ed.), *Current Trends in Linguistics*, vol. 12. The Hague: Mouton, pp. 218–322.

(1976). *Contributions to the Doctrine of Signs*. Lisse: Peter de Ridder.

(1976). *Contributions to the Doctrine of Signs*. Bloomington: Indiana University Press.

(1979). *The Sign and its Masters*. Austin: University of Texas Press.

(1989). *The Sign and its Masters*. Lanham, MD: University Press of America.

(1991). *Semiotics in the United States*. Bloomington: Indiana University Press.

(1994). *Signs: an Introduction to Semiotics*. Toronto: University of Toronto Press.

Sebeok, T. A., Hayes, A. S. and Bateson, M. C. (eds.) (1964). *Approaches to Semiotics: Cultural Anthropology, Education, Linguistics, Psychiatry, Psychology*. The Hague: Mouton.

Sechehaye, A. (1902). Der Konjunktiv Imperfecti und seine Konkurrenten in den normalen hypothetischen Satzgefügen im Französischen. Introduction and part 3 of inaugural dissertation, University of Göttingen.

(1905). L'imparfait du subjonctif et ses concurrents dans les hypothétiques normales en français: esquisse de syntaxe historique. *Romanische Forschungen*, 19 (2): 321–406.

(1908a). *Programme et méthodes de la linguistique théorique: psychologie du langage*. Paris: Champion.

(1908b). La stylistique et la linguistique théorique. *Mélanges de linguistique offerts à M. Ferdinand de Saussure*. Paris: Champion, pp. 155–87.

(1916). La méthode constructive en syntaxe. *Revue des langues romanes*, 59 (1–2): 44–76.

(1926). *Essai sur la structure logique de la phrase* (Collection linguistique publiée par la Société linguistique de Paris, 20). Paris: Champion.

(1927). L'école genevoise de linguistique générale. *Indogermanische Forschungen*, 44: 217–41.

Schleicher, A. (1863). *Die Darwinische Theorie und die Sprachwissensschaft*. Weimar: H. Böhlau.

Shklovskii, V. (1965). Art as technique. In L. T. Lemon and M. J. Reis (eds.), *Russian Formalist Criticism*. Lincoln, NB: University of Nebraska Press, pp. 3–24.

Silverstein, M. (1971). Whitney on language. In M. Silverstein (ed.), *Whitney on Language: Selected Writings of William Dwight Whitney*. Cambridge, MA, and London: MIT Press, pp. x–xxiii.

Smith, R. (1997). *The Fontana History of the Human Sciences*. London: Fontana.

Spence, N. C. W. (1957). A hardy perennial: the problem of *la langue* and *la parole*. *Archivum Linguisticum*, 9: 1–27.

Starobinski, J. (1964). Les Anagrammes de Ferdinand de Saussure (textes inédits). *Mercure de France*, 350 (Feb.): 243–62.

(1969). Le texte dans le texte: extraits inédits des cahiers d'anagrammes de Ferdinand de Saussure. *Tel Quel*, 37: 3–33.

(1971). *Les mots sous les mots*. Paris: Gallimard.

(1979 [1971]). *Words upon Words: the Anagrams of Ferdinand de Saussure*. New Haven: Yale University Press.

Steiner, R. P. (1984). *Russian Formalism: a Metapoetics*. Ithaca, NY: Cornell University Press.

Stetter, C. (1992). *Ferdinand de Saussure (1857–1913)*. In M. Dascal, D. Gerhardus, K. Lorenz and G. Meggle (eds.), *Sprachphilosophie, Philosophy of Language, Philosophie du Langage: Manuel international des recherches contemporaines* (*Handbücher zur Sprach- und Kommunikationsforschung*, 7.1). Berlin and New York: De Gruyter, pp. 510–23.

Streitberg, W. (1915). Ferdinand de Saussure. *Indogermanisches Jahrbuch*, 2: 203–13.

Strozier, R. M. (1988). *Saussure, Derrida, and the Metaphysics of Subjectivity*. Berlin: Mouton de Gruyter.

Swadesh, M. (1934). The phonemic principle. *Language*, 10: 117–29. (Reprinted in Joos, 1958: 32–7.)

Swadesh, M. and Voegelin, C. F. (1939). A problem in phonological alternation. *Language*, 15: 1–10. (Reprinted in Joos, 1958: 88–92.)

Szemerényi, O. (1973). La théorie des laryngales de Saussure à Kurylowicz et à Benveniste. *Bulletin de la société de linguistique*, 68: 1–25.

Taine, H. (1870). *De l'intelligence*, 2 vols. Paris: Hachette. (References are to vol. 2.)

Tallis, R. (1995 [1988]). *Not Saussure*. London: Macmillan.

Tamba-Mecz, I. (1983). A propos de la distinction entre sémiotique et sémantique. In: *Emile Benveniste aujourd'hui*. Paris: Bibliothèque de L'Information grammaticale.

Tarski, A. (1956). The concept of truth in formalised languages. In *Logic, Semantics and Metamathematics* (trans. J. H. Woodger). Oxford: Oxford University Press.

Taylor, T. J. (1988). Gardiner's *The Theory of Speech and Language*: empiricist pragmatics. In R. Harris (ed.), *Linguistic Thought in England 1914–1945*. London, Duckworth, pp. 132–47.

Thibault, P. (1997). *Re-reading Saussure: the Dynamics of Signs in Social Life*. London: Routledge.

Thompson, E. P. (1978). *The Poverty of Theory and Other Essays*. London: Merlin.

Tiles, M. (1984). *Bachelard: Science and Objectivity*. Cambridge: Cambridge University Press.

Trabant, J. and Ward, S. (eds.) (2001). *New Essays on the Origin of Language* (Trends in Linguistics). Berlin: Mouton de Gruyter.

Trubetzkoy, N. (1936). Essai d'une théorie des oppositions phonologiques. *Journal de Psychologie*, 33: 5–18.

(1939). *Grundzüge der Phonologie*. Prague: Travaux du Cercle Linguistique de Prague, 7.

(1964). *Principes de phonologie* (trans. J. Cantineau). Paris: Klincksieck.

(2001). *Studies in General Linguistics and Language Structure* (ed. A. Liberman, intro. A. Liberman, trans. M. Taylor and A. Liberman). Durham, NC: Duke University Press.

Turpin, B. (1993[1994]). Modélisation, langage et langue chez Saussure. *Cahiers Ferdinand de Saussure*, 47: 159–75.

(1995–6). Discours, langue et parole dans les cours et les notes de linguistique générale de F. de Saussure. *Cahiers Ferdinand de Saussure*, 49: 251–66.

Twaddell, W. F. (1935). On defining the phoneme. *Language Monograph*, 16. (Reprinted in Joos, 1958: 55–79.)

Tynianov, Iu. (1929). Literaturnyi fakt. In *Arkhaisty i novatory*. Leningrad: Priboi, pp. 5–30.

(1978). On literary evolution. In L. Matejka and K. Pomorska (eds.), *Readings in Russian Poetics: Formalist and Structuralist Views*. Ann Arbor: University of Michigan Press, pp. 66–79.

Tynianov, Iu. and Jakobson, R. (1978). Problems in the study of literature and language. In L. Matejka and K. Pomorska (eds.), *Readings in Russian Poetics: Formalist and Structuralist Views*. Ann Arbor: University of Michigan Press, pp. 79–82.

Ungar, S. (1983). *Roland Barthes: the Professor of Desire*. Lincoln: University of Nebraska Press.

(1997). From event to memory site: thoughts on rereading mythologies. *Nottingham French Studies*, 36, 1: 24–33.

Valéry, P. (1898). Review of Bréal, 'Essai de sémantique', *Mercure de France*, 25 (Jan.–March): 254–60.

(1973–77). *Cahiers* (ed. J. Robinson). Paris: Gallimard.

Valin, R. (1954). *Petite introduction à la psychomécanique du langage*. Québec: Presses de l'Université Laval.

Vallini, C. (1969). Problemi di metodo in Ferdinand de Saussure indoeuropeista. *Studi e Saggi Linguistici*, 9: 1–85.

(1974). La linguistica della 'parola': coincidenza o divergenza fra A. Sechehaye e F. de Saussure. *Studi linguistici in onore di Tristano Bolelli*. Pisa: Pacini.

(1978). Ancora sul metodo di F. de Saussure: l'etimologia. *Studi e Saggi Linguistici*, 18: 75–128.

(1979). La costituzione del testo del 'Cours de linguistique générale'. In *Del testo* (Seminario interdisciplinare sulla costituzione del testo, 1977–78). Naples: Istituto universitario orientale, pp. 65–96.

(1990). Continuità del metodo di Saussure. In R. Amacker and R. Engler (eds.), *Présence de Saussure: Actes du Colloque international de Genève* (21–23 mars 1988) (Publications du Cercle Ferdinand de Saussure, 1). Geneva: Droz, pp. 5–19.

Varela, F. (1979). *Principles of Biological Autonomy*. Amsterdam: Elsevier/North-Holland.

Vendryès, J. (1968 [1921]). *Le langage*. Paris: Albin Michel.

Verner, K. (1875). Eine Ausnahme der ersten Lautverschiebung. *Zeitschrift für Vergleichende Sprachforschung*, 23: 97–130.

Villani, P. (1990). Documenti saussuriani conservati a Lipsia e a Berlino, *Cahiers Ferdinand de Saussure*, 44: 3–33.

Voegelin, C. F. (1948). A sample of technical terms in linguistics. *International Journal of American Linguistics*, 14: 115–30.

Vogüé, S. de (1997). La croisée des chemins: remarques sur la topologie des relations langue/discours chez Benveniste. In C. Normand and M. Arrivé (eds.), *Benveniste vingt ans après*, *Linx*, special issue, pp. 145–57.

Voloshinov, V. N. (1929). *Marksizm i filosofija jazyka*. Moscow.

(1973). *Marxism and the Philosophy of Language* (trans. L. Matejka and I. R. Titunik). Cambridge, MA: Harvard University Press.

Waterman, J. T. (1956). Ferdinand de Saussure – forerunner of modern structuralism. *Modern Language Journal*, 40: 307–9.

Watkins, C. (1978). Remarques sur la méthode de Ferdinand de Saussure comparatiste. *Cahiers Ferdinand de Saussure*, 32: 59–69.

Waugh, L. R. (1984). Introduction à Roman Jakobson: la théorie saussurienne. *Linguistics*, 22: 157–96.

Weisler, S. E., and Milekic, S. (2000). *Theory of Language*. Cambridge, MA, London: MIT Press.

Wells, R. S. (1947). De Saussure's system of linguistics. *Word*, 3 (1/2): 1–31. (Reprinted in Joos, 1958: 1–18.)

(1949). Review of B. Russell, *Human Knowledge: Its Scope and Limits*, New York: Simon and Schuster, 1948; P. A. Schilpp (ed.) *The Philosophy of Ernst Cassirer*, Evanston, IL: The Library of Living Philosophers, 1949. *Language*, 25: 322–5.

Whitney, W. D. (1867). *Language and the Study of Language: Twelve Lectures on the Principles of Linguistic Science*. New York: Charles Scribner. (Preface and copyright dated 1867, 1st edn title page dated 1868.)

(1874). *Phýsei* or *thései* – natural or conventional? *Transactions of the American Philological Association*, 5: 95–116.

(1875). *The Life and Growth of Language: an Outline of Linguistic Science* (The International Scientific Series, XVI). New York: D. Appleton.

Whorf, B. L. (1956). *Language, Thought and Reality: Selected Writings of Benjamin Lee Whorf* (ed. J. B. Carroll). Cambridge, MA: MIT Press.

Wiener, N. (1961 [1948]). *Cybernetics or Control and Communication in the Animal and the Machine*. Cambridge, MA: MIT Press.

Wilmet, M. (1991). G. Guillaume et la psychomécanique du langage. In H. Huot (ed.), *La grammaire française entre comparatisme et structuralisme: 1870–1960*. Paris: Armand Colin, pp. 201–25.

Wonderly, W. L. (1952). Semantic components in Kechua person morphemes. *Language*, 28: 366–76.

Wozniak, R. H. (1998). Thought and things: James Mark Baldwin and the biosocial origins of mind. In R. W. Rieber and K. D. Salzinger (eds.), *Psychology: Theoretical-Historical Perspectives*. Washington, DC: American Psychological Association, pp. 429–53.

Wunderli, P. (1972a). *Ferdinand de Saussure und die Anagramme: Linguistik und Literatur*. Tübingen: Niemeyer.

(1972b). Saussure et les anagrammes. *Travaux de linguistique et de littérature*, 10 (1): 35–53.

(1972c). Ferdinand de Saussure: *1er cahier à lire préliminairement* – ein Basistext seiner Anagrammstudien, *Zeitschrift für französische Sprache und Literatur*, 82: 193–216.

(1976a). Zu Saussures Anagrammen: Diskussionen und Mißverständnisse. *Revue romaine de linguistique,* 21: 571–82.

(1976b). Saussure als Schüler Sechehayes? Zum Abhängigkeitsverhältnis hinsichtlich der Kreativitätskonzeption in der Genfer Schule. In F.-J. Niederehe and H. Haarmann (eds.), *In Memoriam Friedrich Diez: Akten des Kolloquiums zur Wissenschaftsgeschichte der Romanistik* (Trier 2–4 Oct. 1975). Amsterdam: Benjamins, pp. 419–60. (Reprinted in Wunderli, 1981: 180–200.)

(1977). *Valéry saussurien*. Frankfurt am Main: Peter Lang.

(1981). *Saussure-Studien: exegetische und wissenschaftsgeschichtliche Untersuchungen zum Werk von F. de Saussure* (Tübinger Beiträge zur Linguistik, 148). Tübingen: Narr.

Young, R. (ed.) (1981). *Untying the Text: a Post-Structuralist Reader*. London: Routledge & Kegan Paul.

Yule, G. (1996). *The Study of Language*, 2nd edn. Cambridge and New York: Cambridge University Press.

Index